Victory in Europe 1945

VICTORY IN EUROPE 1945
From World War to Cold War

Edited by Arnold A. Offner
and Theodore A. Wilson

UNIVERSITY PRESS OF KANSAS

Published by the University Press of Kansas (Lawrence, Kansas 66049),
which was organized by the Kansas Board of Regents and is operated
and funded by Emporia State University, Fort Hays State University,
Kansas State University, Pittsburg State University, the University of
Kansas, and Wichita State University

Library of Congress Cataloging-in-Publication Data

Victory in Europe 1945 : from World War to cold war / edited by Arnold
A. Offner and Theodore A. Wilson.
    p. cm.—(Modern war studies)
  Includes index.
  ISBN 0-7006-1039-1 (cloth : alk. paper)
    1. United States—Foreign relations—Soviet Union. 2. Soviet
Union—Foreign relations—United States. 3. Cold war.
4. Europe—Politics and government—1945– 5. World politics,
1945–1989. 6. World War, 1939–1945—Peace. I. Offner, Arnold A.
II. Wilson, Theodore A., 1940– III. Series.

E183.8.S65 V53 2000
327.73047—dc21   00-039873

British Library Cataloguing in Publication Data is available.

Printed in the United States of America

10 9 8 7 6 5 4 3 2 1

TO ROBERT H. FERRELL—
Distinguished practitioner of historical narrative,
indefatigable investigator, peerless mentor,
and a truly kind and gentle man.

Contents

Acknowledgments

This volume, as with all such works, is the product of many minds and hands. The editors wish first to thank the contributors to *Victory in Europe 1945: From World War to Cold War*. Individually and as a group, the authors responded to the sometimes intrusive counsel of the editors with grace and—in some instances—amazing tolerance. Initial impetus for the symposium came from then Dean of International Programs George Woodyard and Associate Director Terry M. Weidner. Financial support and organizational assistance were provided by the Office of International Programs, the Hall Center for the Humanities, the College of Liberal Arts and Sciences, and the Department of History of the University of Kansas and by the Dwight D. Eisenhower Foundation and the KU Endowment Association. For help in converting eleven disparate pieces into an electronic unity, the editors are deeply appreciative of the wonders wrought by Paula Courtney and the staff of the CLAS Word Processing Center. As usual, Fred Woodward, Mike Briggs, Susan Schott, and their colleagues at the University Press of Kansas performed with professionalism and contagious enthusiasm.

Four other persons require special regard. Garry Clifford, a friend and sympathetic critic since a common experience of graduate study with Robert H. Ferrell more years ago than any of us cares to admit, contributed the wrap-up chapter to the volume and offered encouraging counsel and aid at critical junctures. Ellen Offner and Judith Wilson deserve public acknowledgment. They endured with grace and tolerance affection the accumulating stacks of paper, the blizzard of faxes, and the early-morning/late-night phone calls that defined this long-distance editorial collaboration. We hope that belated sojourns in France and Scotland have offered partial compensation. Last but hardly least, we are delighted to have an opportunity to proclaim yet again the debt of gratitude owed by the large contingent of American historians who studied with Robert H. Ferrell or received his ever-generous help and sage advice. The dedication to this volume attempts to convey our conviction that Bob Ferrell established a standard of responsible historical scholarship, devotion to telling fascinating stories, and mentoring of doctoral students without parallel within the subfield known as diplomatic history and perhaps more generally. Although Bob will, we realize, respond with a wry smile and gentle disavowal of the assertion that there exists a Ferrell school of international/political history, one does in fact exist, grounded in the commitment to multiarchival, multinational scholarship and analytical narrative history that he has espoused over the course of a long and distinguished career. This volume is intended as a tribute to that heritage and to its consummate practitioner.

Beginnings and Endings

On May 8, 1945, T/5 Glenn Kappelman, with Troop B, 121st Cavalry Reconnaisance Squadron, somewhere in Austria, jubilantly wrote his family in Lawrence, Kansas: "Just imagine—the war in Europe is over. It is all finished and the Germans are beaten and smashed forever." Convinced that civilization had been dealt a crushing blow, he vowed that "we must make up for those months lost in blood and fire and snow and misery." While he admitted that the war "didn't end as I thought it would," Kappelman concluded, "It has ended and that is all that counts now."[1] Almost fifty years later, on April 21 and 22, 1995, the University of Kansas sponsored a commemorative symposium on the end of the war in Europe. Bringing together historians of the World War II era, eyewitnesses to the last days of the European conflict, and scholars in international affairs, this event, bearing a predictably academic/scholarly title—"Victory in Europe: Endings, Beginnings, Implications"—asked the participants and an audience of faculty and students from KU and area colleges and universities, veterans of World War II, and interested citizens to consider how and why the war in Europe ended as it did. Also emphasized was the significance of actions taken and not taken during the final months of the war in Europe for the world that has evolved since May 8, 1945.

As conceived by its organizers, the coeditors of this anthology, this V-E Day symposium envisaged a confrontation with the question of war termination in the context of the epochal events in Europe in spring 1945. Did it matter (and if so to whom) that the struggle with Nazi Germany ended as it did? What connections existed between those circumstances and such immediate concerns as prosecuting the war against Japan, sorting out relations among major belligerents and liberated peoples and between victors and vanquished, and dealing with the war's devastation?

The participants grappled with two basic issues. Were the circumstances (a bitter military struggle that ended only in the rubble of Berlin, desperate economic problems and near-starvation conditions throughout Europe, the shock that attended discovery of the unfathomable horrors in the death camps, and a massive population exodus) that attended the end of the war in Europe in 1945 inevitable consequences of Axis and Allied policies? Or might alternative outcomes have been possible? Second, did the way that World War II culminated in Europe significantly influence those conditions—

1

the collapse of the wartime Allied coalition and the emergence of a cold war environment, widespread economic and social dislocation, America's cultural aggrandizement—that were to typify the decades following V-E Day? More than five decades after this central event in world history, we still do not possess satisfactory answers to these questions.

The symposium's opening session, "Endings: How and When V-E Day was Supposed to Happen," offered an opportunity to look at plans and underlying assumptions of Allied and neutral governments about the anticipated circumstances at war's end. Next came an exploration of various counterfactual scenarios to V-E Day occurring as it did and a debate about what circumstances ruled out during winter–spring 1944–1945 any serious consideration of alternatives to the Götterdämmerung that engulfed Hitler's Germany. The afternoon began with eyewitness accounts by individuals— soldiers, concentration camp survivors, POWS—who had been caught up in the chaos that was Europe during the final days of World War II. Later Friday afternoon, "Endings: How and Why V-E Day Occurred as It Did," featured presentations about the circumstances and decisions on both sides that defined the months and weeks before and immediately after V-E Day. The second day of the symposium offered the session, "Beginnings: Projects and Realities Following V-E Day," in which three historians described how and why war's end in Europe gave way to cold war between east and west. The symposium concluded with an open-ended discussion: "Implications: How the World Has Changed Since V-E Day."

All who attended agreed that attention to how World War II ended and to the experiences of survivors made possible acknowledging and examining yet again the diverse meanings—for individuals, groups, and nations— of this most all-encompassing and costly conflict in human history. Moreover, the symposium made clear that how wars and other national and interstate conflicts end, what sorts of constraints operate, and what relationships exist between immediate circumstances and broader causal factors are issues with obvious relevance to the difficult challenges besetting the global community today.

The process of transforming the proceedings of the V-E Day symposium into a book began shortly after the audience dispersed, some participants driving to their homes and others boarding flights for Boston, Little Rock, Hartford, Dublin, and Moscow. We immediately decided to construct the volume from the formal papers delivered at the symposium. Grappling with the broad issues related to how and why the European war ended as it did and whether and why V-E Day proved to be both the final act of one conflict and the opening scene of the cold war dictated a focus on military, diplomatic, and political problems—with the challenges and dilemmas that confronted the leaders and governments of belligerent and liberated nations as World War II in Europe ground to an end. Considered as discrete historical analyses, the chapters treat important and in many instances hitherto unexplored problems, offering insights both for specialists and fledgling students of this critical juncture in world history. The carefully drawn chapters by David Hogan, Hal Wert, Ronan Fanning, Anna Cienciala, and Vladimir Pozniakov bring into sharp relief the central and often tragic results of actions taken to deal with immediate political, bureaucratic, and ideological concerns. The chapters by Pozniakov, Warren Kimball, Mark Stoler, Randall Woods, and Arnold Offner provide judicious assessments of the roles of individuals, agencies, and political/national agendas during the transition from World War II to the cold war. Theodore A. Wilson, Hogan, Offner, and J. Garry Clifford explore the major explanatory schemes and methodological issues regarding the chaotic termination of World War II that have bemused scholars and policy makers since 1945. Taken together, the chapters constitute a unique, multidimensional representation of a time and place that brings to life a pivotal and still little-understood event in modern history. In particular, the emphasis on those unanticipated consequences, chance, and accident achieves a serendipitous unity.

Victory in Europe 1945: From World War to Cold War also gives priority to the imaginative telling of cohesive, historically significant stories. This collection is grounded in what has tended over the past several decades to be dismissed among academic specialists as "mere" narrative history. International history—more than any other category of historical inquiry—has been widely characterized as arid, stolid, obsessively concerned with the piling up of insignificant facts, and totally lacking in creative insights. Indeed, this collection rebuts any such conclusion. How that happens is explained not by stipulating, as positivists such as Leopold von Ranke have asserted, that historical scholarship comprised mere activity—the historian's persistent vacuuming of the historical carpet until an underlying pattern heretofore obscured by the dust of ages stood forth. Rather, each historian selects from the impedimenta dumped from the bulging vacuum bag a different hodge-podge of items, establishes unique linkages among them, and thereby fashions a story that could not otherwise be told.

The narrative was the only mode of historical discourse until very recent times. In his classic essay on the subject, "History as a Literary Art," one of the great modern practitioners of narrative history, Samuel Eliot Morison, argued for narrative as central to the "great tradition" in the writing of American history. Though this essay was written in the 1930s, Morison's claim that history is preeminently a literary art, his plea for the commitment of the historian to the craft of writing, and his bemoaning the low estate into which good writing had fallen have a contemporary flavor.[2]

Why had this art—historical narrative as practiced by the professional guild—fallen so low by Morison's day? He proffered two chief causes. First was the dominance of the positivist school of "academic history," general acceptance of the precept that the past tells its own story and the historian's task is to uncover what already is there. Thus, Morison asserted, Ranke's laudable emphasis on the means of "discovery" (archival research, a hierarchy of evidence, rules about citations) became the sole and unremitting end.

The second chief nemesis of narrative history was rather nebulous in "History as a Literary Art" but is fully described in a vitriolic review essay, "History Through a Beard," of Charles Austin Beard's *President Roosevelt and the Coming of the War, 1941* and in Morison's AHA presidential address, "Faith of an Historian." That adversary was the dreadful blight of historical relativism as espoused by Beard, Carl Becker, and their ilk. The relativists had propounded two evils. They had mocked the very idea of an objective history. "Hoping to find something without looking for it, expecting to obtain final answers to life's riddle by resolutely refusing to ask questions—it was surely the most romantic species of realism yet invented, the oddest attempt ever made to get something for nothing," Becker had observed.[3] In an approach equally repugnant to Morison, the relativists had also dismissed as unimportant and trivial elements of the historical process national/international institutions and leaders, whose actions in the spheres of dynastic politics and diplomacy had been the focus of Ranke's inquiries and of positivist history generally.[4]

Samuel Eliot Morison saw nothing wrong in giving emphasis to "drum and bugle history" since recounting tales of grand adventure, of battles won and empires lost made possible the portrayal of great themes, painting those vast historical canvases that the artists/historians whom Morison most admired found congenial. Above all, the focus on individual action in the context of national and international conflict opened the way to artistic expression, what Morison termed style. The language and prescriptive claims regarding the correlation of writing and an elitist notion of what is "good" and "tasteful" may strike discordant notes today, but Morison's essay, "History as a Literary Art," is still worth reading for its practical suggestions about how one goes about the task of producing superior historical writing.

Unfortunately, the violent hostility of Morison (and the vast majority of his peers during the 1930s and 1940s) to relativism overcame an innate distaste for positivism. It seemed, indeed, that an entire generation of political and diplomatic historians followed in their footsteps. This should not be taken to mean that no outstanding narrative history was written, but what Dominic DiCapra was subsequently to term "gradgrind monographs," the fashioning of individual bricks while choking on brick dust, held sway. Indeed, the emergence of the *Annales* school—with all that has implied for the way historians do history and for the self-confidence of those of us who inhabit the subfield of international history—began as a rebellion against the prevailing fixation on politics, war, and diplomacy among French historians of the 1950s and 1960s. Lucien Febvre's disparagement of *histoire evene-mentielle* was a direct attack on the narrow, documents-grounded study of French diplomatic and political history then holding sway.

By the 1980s historical scholarship in America had reached a point at which narrative history was acknowledged as a mode of presentation peculiarly congenial to practitioners of diplomatic and military history and, therefore, proof of their antiquarian bent and of its want of "analytical vigor."[5] In one sense, the historiographical preoccupation of the past two decades in the subfield of international history resulted from a determination to find out why the subfield evolved in the "peculiar" way it did and whether some radical change of direction, influsion of new ideas, or transcendental insight can reinvigorate those who are its practitioners. While the process of self-examination continues, the conclusion of many scholars was to forgo reliance on archaic, childish storytelling in favor of nonnarrational systems of description such as that holding sway in social history.[6]

This was certainly the proscription of Peter Novick. In his encyclopedic survey of the doing of history in the United States, *That Noble Dream: The 'Objectivity Question' and the American Historical Profession,* Novick castigated attempts to reintroduce narration as a central, organizing force as intellectually feeble and politically debauched. He acknowledged that "the idea of a revival of narrative had several obvious attractions for historians. As disciplinary identities became blurred, historians could define the distinctive essence of their craft, their autonomous realm, as 'telling stories.' In the fact of multiplying centrifugal forces within the historical discipline, a narrative focus could be integrative."[7] He admitted that numerous distinguished historians had enlisted in the crusade for writing what Bernard Bailyn termed "essential narratives . . . the great challenge of historical scholarship."[8] But Novick argued that the narrative vogue soon collapsed and for good reasons. Some critics worried that, blinded by the "litcrit fog," historians would tumble into the abyss of total relativism. Others objected that narratives, grounded in implicit rather than explicit ontological arguments, did not contribute to the pivotal debate about overarching interpretation and methodology. These critics focus on the presumed proclivity of narrative historians to tell small, inconsequential stories, to celebrate discrete parts of the historical experience as equivalent to (or greater than) the whole.[9]

Still more serious, Novick and other critics claimed, advocates of the "new narrative history" had an unspoken agenda: defense of the objectivity of historical inquiry. Narrative construction thus represented a counterattack on the assorted manifestations of relativism—from Beard to Foucault and Geertz—that had toppled historical objectivity from its pedestal. Critics pointed to the inherent contradictions in the neonarrativist argument. Scholars such as J. H. Hexter (notably, many of those pushing for emphasis on narrative were historians of early modern Britain) espoused the centrality of narrative (what Hexter called "the rhetoric of history . . . ordinarily deemed icing on the cake of history, but . . . mixed right into the batter, . . . [affecting] not merely the outward appearance of history . . . but its inward character, its essential function—its capacity to convey knowledge of the past as it actually was") as a way to have their cake and eat it too.[10] Louis O. Mink has pointed out that Hexter's argument was meaningless, for he was trapped in a logical dilemma.[11]

Even more devastating to the cause of a narrative revival was the change that its ideological valence was inherently skewed. Eric Monkkonen observed that the call for a return to narrative offered "an interesting parallel with Reaganism and the New Right: a demand for a return to simpler times and simpler tales, for a world no longer mired in complexity and opacity."[12] Peter Novick's judgment was blunt: "Many objected to the inherent political conservatism of narrative histories, in which structures were implicitly accepted as a given background against which individual actors shaped events, treating those structures as unproblematic. Narratives were thus conservatives in a sense which transcended the left-right continuum." Novick drove home the point by suggesting that, like narrative history as practiced in the west, those Stalinist accounts that emphasized the role of Stalin rather than structural determinants were "conservative" by "their tacit exculpation of the system."[13] If one accepts Novick's logic, heaven forfend that anyone embrace narrative history!

Surprisingly few scholars have asked whether the alleged inadequacies of narrative to support sustained analysis come from the fact that diplomatic historians have either not tried very hard or have not found it easy to tell ingenious, interesting, original stories. Indeed, recent perspectives drawn from literary theory, the philosophy of history, and that arcane mathematical conceptualization, chaos theory, support the claim that narrative history is not a peripheral or trivial undertaking but is central to the historian's endeavor to reconstruct a meaningful past. The narrative form, storytelling, is not merely an option. It is what we do. As well, the narrative form is not linked to a particular ideological orientation but serves the purposes of story-tellers across the spectrum of conviction about the wellsprings of human behavior and individual/group action. As Peter Gay wisely observes, "Historical narration without analysis is trivial; historical analysis without narration is incomplete."[14] The crafting of "meticulous narratives" poses the greatest challenge that a historian confronts.

Human beings are essentially "storytelling animals" because they are aware of time (their own prospective mortality), and environmental historian William Cronon has urged historians "to acknowledge storytelling as the necessary core even of *longue duree* histories that pay little attention to individual people."[15] But what are we to conclude about the forms of story-telling, why and how narrative mediates knowledge (a reconstructed past) and understanding? Even though Hayden White may take the case too far, his emphasis on the "artificiality" of the idea that "events speak for themselves" and may best be represented as "telling their own story" is helpful. He perceives narrative as the solution to the universal human problem of "how to translate *knowing* into *telling*"—how to convey and interpret meaning. Knowledge becomes meaningful only when the historian/narrator imposes a structure, an "order of meaning," on a series of events/actions/ideas that is not present when viewed merely as sequence.[16]

In sum, telling stories is, in one way or another, central to our existence as human beings. Second, whether the stories we tell have meaning in some absolute sense, they represent our best way to communicate knowledge. Third, however limited and provisional, the narratives we create and recount—insofar as they are received as authentic—do stand as representations of a reality. Thus, "truth" is perceived reality—i.e., the reconstructed past the reader is persuaded to accept is what "actually" happened. In H. W. Brands's formulation, "Historians, like other artists, struggle to explain what it means to be human."[17]

Is narrative history innately conservative, unable in that romantic formulation of the historian's mission to "speak conscience to power"? No. Is narrative history value-laden? Yes, insofar as any form of intellectual inquiry reflects the assumptions and beliefs of the human being who is conducting the investigation. Historians tell different stories, and the landscapes of those stories is shaped by governing values and beliefs as well as by the time and place in which the stories are created and recounted. Do those stories "speak conscience to power"? The historian's stance until recently has been that of Saul Bellow in *Humboldt's Gift*, whose protagonist desperately wished to believe that those who thought and wrote and those who acted could communicate.[18] That pretense of objectivity is now gone. In fact, a notable element in present-day literary theory is awareness of the political agenda associated with narrative. If fashioning a narrative is "empowering," then whoever tells the dominating stories possesses power.

What benefits are conferred by the union of narrative and analysis? First, reconceiving a period or problem—seeing unity at some levels and discrete, possibly random behavior at others—offers opportunities for fascinating and instructive narratives. Second, telling these stories demands a commitment both to the totality of historical experience and to the awareness that insight comes from imaginative recourse to example, anecdote, the telling detail. Third, stories have natural (or seemingly so) beginnings, middles, and ends; they are complete in themselves; and they engage the curiosity/need of the reader to discover how the tale turns out, thereby enlisting its recipients in an unfolding drama. Narrative is arguably the most appropriate way for historians to organize and confer meaning upon existence. Historians tell stories. The aim of the authors of this anthology is to recount plain stories, tales varnished only by a passion for the past and faith in its imaginative reconstruction as vital to understanding our world and ourselves.

The authors of these chapters happily embrace the label of narrative history. Indeed, the eleven chapters that follow are intended to tell significant stories illustrated with those little-known or forgotten details that ground robust narratives and to provide insights into a critical period in Europe's and the world's history. They manifest, we assert, the continuing validity of studying the concerns and actions of political groups, national leaders, and relations among sovereign states. They also demonstrate the creative ways in which the examination of "high politics" is being shaped by methodological constructs derived from other academic disciplines and other approaches to historical scholarship. They affirm that narrative history can be both critical and analytical.

NOTES

1. Glenn Kappelman to Mom, Dad, Vernie, Neal, and Peg, May 8, 1945, Glenn Kappelman Papers, Kansas Collection, Spencer Library, University of Kansas, Lawrence.

2. Samuel Eliot Morison, *By Land and by Sea: Essays and Addresses* (New York: Alfred A. Knopf, 1953), 289–98.

3. Carl Becker, "Everyman His Own Historian," *American Historical Review* 37 (1932): 250.

4. Charles A. Beard, "Written History," *American Historical Review* 39 (1934): 221.

5. See for example, the critique by Michael Hunt, "The Long Crisis in Diplomatic History: Coming to Closure," *Diplomatic History* 16 (winter 1992): 115–40.

6. Any reader who attended the summer 1995 meeting of SHAFR, which emphasized cultural studies, would readily appreciate this point.

7. Peter Novick, *That Noble Dream: The "Objectivity Question" and the American Historical Profession* (New York: Cambridge University Press, 1988).

8. Bernard Bailyn, "The Challenge of Modern Historiography," *American Historical Review* 87 (1982): 7.

9. See Novick, *That Noble Dream*, 625.

10. J. H. Hexter, "Rhetoric," in *Doing History* (Bloomington: Indiana University Press, 1971), 68.

11. Louis Mink, "The Theory of Practice," in *After the Reformation: Essays in Honor of J. H. Hexter*, ed. Barbara C. Malament (Philadelphia: University of Pennsylvania Press, 1980), 19–20.

12. Quoted in Novick, *That Noble Dream*, 623.

13. See ibid., 622.

14. Peter Gay, *Style in History* (New York: Columbia University Press, 1974), 189.

15. William Cronon, "A Place for Stories: Nature, History, and Narrative," *Journal of American History* 78, 4 (March 1992): 1372–73.

16. Robert Hodge has observed: "The discourse of historians constructs belief by a variety of means, appealing to a taken-for-granted reality of the past as an outline that needs only to be filled in here and there, drawing on a set of documents whose reliability must be essentially accepted for the discipline itself to be viable. . . . Narrative is an all-pervasive form, existing in countless texts at every level of every society. Etymologically the word comes from the Latin *narrare*, to tell a story, which in turn probably derives from *gnarus*, knowledgeable about. 'Narrative' retains this potent link between knowing and telling which is central to its ideological effectiveness, since it seems to guarantee a transparent form of telling in which the form of speech closely matches its object" (*Literature as Discourse: Textual Strategies in English and History* [Oxford, U.K.: Polity Press, 1990], 173).

17. H. W. Brands, "Fractal History, or Clio and the Chaotics," *Diplomatic History* 16 (fall 1992): 509–10.

18. Saul Bellow, *Humboldt's Gift* (New York: Knopf, 1975).

1. Endgames: V-E Day and War Termination

Theodore A. Wilson

In the early morning hours of December 1, 1944, a "personal and secret" message from Pres. Franklin D. Roosevelt to Prime Minister Winston S. Churchill was decoded and placed among the boxed files to be read by the PM when he awakened. That afternoon, Churchill read the message, a "birthday card," with mounting irritation. While Roosevelt offered greetings on Churchill's seventieth birthday, the president's blithely confident note, in comparison with earlier effusions of friendship, gave emphasis to the centrality of ties with the Soviet Union first affirmed at Tehran twelve months before. "Ever so many happy returns of the day," FDR wrote. "I shall never forget the party with you and UJ [Premier Joseph Stalin] a year ago and we must have more of them that are even better."

Churchill responded with a note of appreciation for the president's birthday greeting and for the framed quotation by Abraham Lincoln that had accompanied it. As usual, he seized the opportunity to remind the U.S. leader of Britain's continuing importance in the Grand Alliance. Determined to dispel the sense of false confidence about the imminent collapse of German resistance apparently held by President Roosevelt and the British and American peoples, he followed up by lecturing FDR on how difficult still was the path ahead to final victory. "I feel that the time has come for me to place before you the serious and disappointing war situation which faces us at the close of this year," Churchill observed on December 6. Although "many fine tactical victories have been gained on the western front and Metz and Strasbourg [taken by the U.S. First Army after heavy fighting] are trophies," the strategic objective of crossing the Rhine in strength had not been achieved. "We shall have to continue the great battle for many weeks before we can hope to reach the Rhine and establish our bridgeheads." Further, German military strength elsewhere was still impressive. In Italy, some twenty-six German divisions still opposed the Allied armies, and difficult terrain had negated the substantial superiority of the Fifteenth Army Group in infantry, armor, and air cover.

The situation in the east, Churchill admitted, offered happier prospects. In recent weeks Soviet forces had undertaken only small-scale operations, intended to consolidate the gains achieved in the great summer-fall offensives that had battered open the way into Poland and, in the Balkans, had knocked Romania and Bulgaria out of the war. Stalin had promised a winter campaign, however, presumably to begin in January, and the German position was so strained that any heavy penetration might have brought partial, perhaps total, collapse. But Hitler's generals were successfully extricating some twelve divisions from Greece and the Balkans for possible use against the Russians or in the west.

Churchill concluded his global review with the observation that these grim realities clashed sharply "with the rosy expectations of our peoples" and asked rhetorically, "What are we going to do about it?" His answer was an urgent plea for an immediate meeting with FDR and his advisers or, failing that, of the British and American Chiefs of Staff. Long-suffering British civilians, now dealing with rocket attacks, would have lynched Churchill had he voiced such sentiments in a dilapidated London pub. Though the V-2 threat was rapidly diminishing by year's end, V-1 and V-2 attacks in December 1944 brought over 700 deaths and 1,500 injuries.

Roosevelt declined to respond to Churchill's gambit, having decided that all future summit conferences must involve the three Allied leaders. FDR and nearly everyone else in Washington dismissed the British leader's gloomy assessment of the war situation as a visit by "Winnie's black dog," the bouts of depression to which Churchill succumbed periodically. After all, the war was all but won.

A casual glance at newspaper headlines in early December appeared to justify "rosy expectations." German forces, although resisting stubbornly, were in retreat everywhere. On December 1, the Germans evacuated Suda Bay, Canae, and Maleme, bases on Crete they had occupied for more than three years. The last Nazi forces in the eastern Mediterranean were now gone. That same day, U.S. troops, having overrun and bypassed portions of Hitler's "West Wall," the Siegfried Line, were grinding forward into Germany along a thirty-mile front. In Italy the British Eighth Army on December 6 crossed the Lamone, another of the river barriers to penetration of the broad plains leading to the valley of the Po River and anticipated final destruction of Field Marshal Albert Kesselring's German and Italian armies.

German morale, already weakened by the massive shocks of summer and fall 1944 in the east and west and by the constant battering by Allied bombers, now confronted the fact that the sacred soil of the German Reich was a battleground. Hitler raged at his generals, relieving the commander of the First Army, Gen. Otto von Knobelsdorf, for cowardly behavior in permitting the Americans to penetrate the defenses of the Siegfried Line, and even criticizing openly the performance of his beloved *Waffen SS Leibstandarte* troops. Though the eastern front was relatively quiet for the moment, signs pointed to a gigantic mustering of Red Army forces (225 divisions and 22 armored corps along a front from the Baltic to the Carpathians) and to a deluge of steel within days or weeks. The Reich's erstwhile allies continued to drop away. A new government claimed power in Romania on December 7 and promised to purge all Nazis and "fascist sympathizers." On December 9, the Red Army launched a drive to expel the German forces from Hungary and quickly encircled Budapest. Everywhere Nazi leaders looked, their positions were coming apart. Field Marshal Gerd von Rundstedt, commander in chief in the west, was so appalled by the führer's detachment from reality that he refused to attend a special military conference in Berlin on December 2.

Anticipation of the total collapse of Nazi Germany and the certainty of ultimate triumph in the Pacific war spread rapidly. This had some negative manifestations; veteran British and American troops fighting in the Low Countries and Alsace-Lorraine suddenly lacked aggressiveness. No one wanted to be the last casualty of the war in Europe. Nonetheless, over the next six months many more lives—soldiers and civilians on all sides—were lost before the war in Europe ground to its inevitable end.[1]

The circumstances of war's end in Europe in May 1945 have received far less attention than the end of the war in the Pacific in August 1945.[2] The primary reason for this disparity in historical assessments of V-E and V-J Days was the conviction that a military Götterdämmerung was inevitable and essential, given the unspeakable crimes committed by Adolf Hitler and his Nazi henchmen. This belief led to the long-held view that the struggle between the Allies and the Axis powers in Europe was a religious crusade, one that stood outside history. Such a judgment was ironic, given the Anglo-American demonization of the Japanese and the prevalence of racism in the Pacific war.[3]

The unchallenged consensus about how the European war ended also inhibited serious analysis of the process of wartime politics, the decisions taken and those avoided, opportunities seized and others possibly missed. Elevation of the circumstances attending the end of World War II in Europe and Asia to the status of a unique event may also have muddled consideration of the theory and practice of war termination during the past half century. One of the few scholars to have dealt with the topic, political scientist Leon Sigal, writing at the time America was struggling to end the war in Vietnam, expressed his amazement at how little attention the issue of war terminations has received in scholarly literature.[4] The presumption prevailed that World War II was foreordained to end in apocalyptic fashion, with Nazism's immolation in the führerbunker and mushroom clouds towering over Hiroshima and Nagasaki.

By focusing on the questions of how and why World War II in Europe ended as it did, I seek to grapple with two important concerns. First, were the conditions that attended the end of the war in Europe in 1945 inevitable consequences of Axis and Allied policies, or might there have been alternative resolutions to some or all of these tragic events? Second, did the way that World War II concluded in Europe significantly influence the ensuing collapse of the wartime Allied coalition, European social and economic dislocation, and emergence of a cold war between the USSR and the west?

Fifty years after V-E Day, there are no wholly satisfactory answers to these questions. Only belatedly are historians, political scientists, social psychologists, and other scholars, who previously had focused on how and why interstate conflicts begin, starting to focus on how and why such conflicts end as they tend to do. One example is Sigal's study, *Fighting to a Finish: The Politics of War Termination in the United States and Japan, 1945,* which emphasizes the massive cultural misunderstandings within and between Japanese and American political elites and governmental bureaucracies.[5] Notably, there has been no comparable study of the ending of the war in Europe.[6]

Searching for insights, the historian becomes almost a scavenger rummaging through heaps of theories produced and then discarded by other disciplines. With depressing frequency, the aphorisms of sages from bygone days—Sun Tzu, Machiavelli, Clausewitz—are summoned in lieu of penetrating inquiry. Modern scholarship on the topic of war termination yields some gold nuggets and a heap of iron pyrites. Sigal's wry observation, that "in place of analysis there is metaphor: wars wind down, war machines grind to a halt, war weariness sets in," captures the state of play.[7] To a significant degree, this results from lack of understanding about the phenomenon of "ending" in all its manifestations. As one recent study has noted, "Our understanding of the way in which a war ends, and our expectancies about the way it should end, are derived from the experience of transition and separations in everyday life."[8]

But this insight does not automatically resolve the issue. Stuart Albert and Edward C. Luck have observed that many reasons explain why scholars have ignored how social and cultural events end. First, endings are difficult to observe because "they are often high-speed events. One person will say to another, 'Well, so long Bill, see you next week. Say hello to the wife, right.' 'Aye, bye'—and before you know it, the process . . . has been completed. Second, the ending stage of human interaction appears to be almost completely constructed from insignificant cultural rituals . . . and therefore appears to be an unlikely site for the study of important human issues.[9] Albert and Luck further note that "the working of a system that is dissolving itself is particularly difficult to observe in detail. . . . Everyday endings are often believed to be simple events, so the scientific yield from their detailed study would be minimal." They conclude that the "apparent simplicity" of endings chiefly reflect's failure to record "the fine-grained detail" of the event being observed. Surprisingly little observational data exists regarding endings in general.[10]

A final obstacle to understanding arises from terms such as "the terminal phase of a conflict," not to mention "defeat"and "victory."[11] What is needed, Albert and Luck conclude, is "an archaeology of human endings constructed according to culture, and sensitive to the dimensions of time, place, relations and situations, so as to uncover the structure of human endings and grasp the origin of our feelings about them."[12] Failing that, impressions need suffice, and the subjective nature of testimony about those endings that involve human passions and humankind's bottomless capacity for self-deception seriously weaken impressionistic judgments.

When considering general theories of war termination, essentially only a body of observation and opinion is available, roughly grouped into four main categories:

- *Rational actor/cost-benefit:* Leaders fight until they have gained agreed objectives or conclude that the costs of continuing to fight are too great. Scholar Bruce B. G. Clarke has expressed the importance of achieving national objectives: "Victory is achieved when the political objectives are accomplished. The key is to be able to clearly define both the political conditions and the situation that one envisions existing when both the conflict and dispute are over."[13] This was the model in the warfare of the eighteenth century and still is presumed by many observers as the dominant form today. Termination of the Gulf War of 1991 is generally described as representing rational assessment by both sides of costs and benefits.[14]
- *Win/lose:* The actual military situation determines how and in what circumstances a war ends. A people will fight until unable to do so any longer physically or psychologically. The American Civil War is often cited as an example of winning/losing.
- *Change of leadership:* The individual or group that leads a nation into war is incapable of a rational assessment of costs/benefits and the military balance; thus, replacement by new leadership is a necessary condition of war termination. The replacement of the British Parliament "war" faction by a "peace" faction during the the American Revolutionary War and—arguably—Harry

Truman's replacement by Dwight D. Eisenhower in 1953 exemplify this approach. Adolf Hitler's fixation upon the revolutionary effect on the fortunes of Prussia of the Russian tsar's death in 1756 (and the presumed significance of Pres. Franklin D. Roosevelt's death) also belongs in this category.[15]

- *Overcome by a new paradigm:* Leaders are compelled—either by a changed outlook or new information—to view the situation from a new or different perspective and to acknowledge that continued resistance will sacrifice aims more important than those originally set forth when the war began.[16] The American decision to pull out of Vietnam would appear to fit into this category.

Does the end of the war in Europe, the surrender of Germany on May 7–8, 1945, fit comfortably within any of these groupings?[17] Most scholars have characterized the conclusion of this conflict as an example of WIN/LOSE. German resistance continued until Allied armies extinguished it and asserted total military domination over German territory. Albert and Luck have argued that World War II ended as all wars should, for that conflict was not only "the central experience of a generation, but its ending left a feeling of long-sought victory and of closure."[18] Nevertheless, a cursory look at the end of World War II in Europe suggests otherwise.

Until very recently, scholars have assumed that national states (defined as "unitary purposive actors") decide to begin and end wars because their interests, rationally assessed, dictate doing so. They accept the analogy of war as chess and perceive war termination as incorporating the same process as the endgame strategy in chess. As in chess, the decision to accept defeat resides with the loser. Mindful of the winding down of World War II, H. A. Calahan wrote in 1944 that "war is pressed by the victor, but peace is made by the vanquished." The most explicit statement of this theoretical stance was offered by Nicholas S. Timasheff two decades later. Timasheff considered war to be "a means of solving an inter-state conflict by measuring the relative strength of the parties." He argued that the relative strength of belligerents was not fully known at the outset of a war, but over its course the relative balance of power became a matter of "objective fact." At that point, no "reasonable purpose" was served by continuing to fight and the war ended.[19]

Paul Kecskemeti, in his groundbreaking study *Strategic Surrender,* asserted that a war's terminal stage manifested rational calculation of costs and benefits for offering and accepting surrender. "What the loser avoids by offering to surrender," Kecskemeti argued, "is a last chaotic round of fighting that would have the characteristics of a rout. Surrender is then the only rational decision for the loser since it means that the losses that would result from the last battle are not incurred. By the same token, accepting surrender is a rational decision for the winner: he can obtain his objective without paying the costs of the last battle."[20] Unfortunately, modern wars in general and World War II in particular offer little evidence of rational actors' assessments. Indeed, nations have tended "to fight long past the point at which rational choice, in theory, predicts that they should have stopped fighting."[21] Why is this so?

One reason is that states are not "unitary actors" espousing common values and perceptions but amalgams of individuals and interest groups likely to disagree about means and ends. The inevitable result, as Fred Ikle—an early critic of rational actor theory—has suggested, was the emergence of proponents of a hard-line approach to peace making, "hawks," and those who advocated compromise, "doves," within the governing elite on each side. Ikle remarked that ending a war was difficult because hawks possessed much more political power in wartime and were able, through an unspoken congruence with their hawkish counterparts in the enemy camp, to block peace initiatives by branding as appeasers if not outright traitors those who wished to end the conflict.[22]

A more recent critique of rational actor theory disputes its assumptions that policy makers espoused principled, inherently consistent systems of values and beliefs, that they pursued what they believed to be the nation's interest, and that they behaved rationally. This scholar has written that most World War II leaders "showed little consistency in their orientation toward international relations in general or toward war termination in particular. Neither hawks nor doves, they behaved like politicians and bureaucrats."[23] One might add that they behaved as fallible human beings tend to do. Leaders and followers in the nation verging on defeat rejected "objective" evidence in favor of claims of new, awesomely powerful weapons, rumors of divisions among their adversaries, and mystical fixations. Politicians and officials in the soon-to-be-victorious nations shelved concerns about ending the war, giving priority to maximizing personal and organizational positions in the forthcoming new era. In sum, the only useful test of existing theories dealing with war termination derives from careful scrutiny of what in fact happened in an actual situation: e.g., what produced World War II's end in Europe.

Political scientist Michael Handel notes that "most studies of war termination have either tacitly or explicitly assumed the decision to stop fighting and start negotiating is a rational, well-calculated, cost-benefit type of decision taken by the states involved. . . . This premise ignores the . . . often central role of individuals (rather than the state) in the war termination process."[24]

The final year of conflict in Europe affirms Handel's dictum regarding the centrality of individual action. A Russian scholar has concluded: "Soviet rulers, who had mismanaged the outbreak of war at a horrible cost to their people, changed little . . . during World War II and afterwards, during the transition to the postwar settlement in Europe. Stalin, Molotov, and a small group of insiders were the primary force behind this continuity. [The] personal and political qualities of these individuals . . . mattered a lot in the diplomatic game that culminated in 1945."[25] Reflecting similar personal and political agendas, the "end of the beginning" from the perspective of Anglo-American leaders was D Day, June 6, 1944. Operation OVERLORD achieved all and more that had been hoped for in the immediate sense and at a far lower cost than generally anticipated.[26] Hitler's supposedly invulnerable *Festung Europa* had been breached, and Allied ground forces were grinding forward toward the Nazi heartland. Casual assumptions regarding the timing and circumstances of war's end became holy writ, the inalterable basis for action.

Allied leaders, accepting the rational actor model of war termination without testing its applicability to the "real world" situation they confronted, convinced themselves that the end would come quickly. They assumed that German commanders and troops, once defeated in the field, would acknowledge that fact by surrendering. This had been Winston Churchill's conviction from 1941 onward, according to historian Tuvia Ben-Moshe.[27] Indeed, the timetable for V-E Day (developed in 1943 prior to the evidence of German resilience in dealing with Russian military advance and round-the-clock Allied bombing) presumed a total collapse of German resistance by D+90 or early September 1944.

This projection was grounded in three interrelated assumptions. First, the Allied forces that entered Germany proper would deal with an essentially intact administrative apparatus; though Hitler, his intimates, and top-level Nazi *gauleiters* quite probably would have been removed by coup or assassination, that circumstance would not change the situation in any material way. Plans initially drawn up in early 1943, before the Allied bombing offensive had begun to flatten large and medium-sized cities across Germany, envisaged asserting control over communities in which water, electricity, and other essential services functioned and the technicians to maintain them remained in place. Whoever might be in charge in Berlin, Anglo-American civil affairs planners anticipated a general surrender of forces in place, without conditions.[28]

A second guiding assumption in London, Moscow, and—in particular—Washington was that the Allied wartime coalition would hold together following war's end.[29] At the outset, assuming Nazi Germany's eventual defeat, some sort of hegemonic Anglo-American consortium appeared the most likely mechanism to emerge from World War II. Long before America became involved, President Roosevelt had noted that "if any good could come out of the Second World War, it would be the opportunity afforded the Americans and the British to bring order out of the resulting chaos and, in particular, to disarm all those powers who [in his belief] had been the primary cause of so many of the wars of the preceding century."[30]

These views mirrored the position of that internationalist, largely anglophilic, eastern-based elite that had come forward in 1940 and 1941 to champion American intervention to save Britain and to restore the prewar European balance of power. Legatees of that long-established internationalism espoused by Theodore Roosevelt and Elihu Root, men such as Robert Patterson, James Forrestal, W. Averell Harriman, and Lewis Douglas worked assiduously to save Britain and to reestablish some sort of political equilibrium in a Europe shorn of its militaristic trappings and colonial entanglements.[31] Achieving these goals was esssential to America's pursuit of its "natural" hemispheric and Pacific interests. Along with FDR, they believed that a working arrangement with Stalin's Russia was possible and, therefore, entered into a temporary alliance with such liberal proponents of close ties with the USSR as Roosevelt's vice president and wartime spokesman, Henry A. Wallace.[32]

In a series of interviews during and immediately after a six-week tour of Siberia and Central Asia in May–June 1944, Wallace offered rapturous descriptions of what he had found and of the potential economic benefits to be gained by an ambitious American role in the region's agricultural and industrial development. "I am convinced," he proclaimed on his return to the United States, "that the main area of new development after this war—new enterprise, new investment, new trade, new accomplishments—will be in the new world of the North Pacific and Eastern Asia."[33] Effusions about postwar cooperation with the USSR were not limited to "wooly-headed idealists" such as Wallace. Recent events had seemed to affirm the likelihood of continuing goodwill and cooperation between the United States and the USSR. In November 1943, Secretary of State Cordell Hull, an outspoken skeptic about Soviet motives, had returned from the first meeting of Allied foreign ministers in Moscow convinced that the USSR was prepared to cooperate fully to establish a new world order. "As the provisions of the Four Power declaration are carried into effect, there will no longer be the need for spheres of influence, for alliances, for balances of power, or any other of the special arrangements through which, in the unhappy past, nations strove to safeguard their security or to promote their interests," Hull proclaimed to Congress.[34] FDR's description of the summit meeting at Tehran was decidedly more restrained, but Vice President Wallace noted in his diary on

December 18, 1943: "Apparently the President and Stalin spoke each other's language and got along famously."[35] Such judgments seem absurdly naive in retrospect, but in the context of 1944–1945 they were widely accepted.

Indeed, during 1944–1945 instances of Allied military collaboration dealing with logistics, operational planning, and sharing of intelligence appeared to justify faith in ongoing cooperation.[36] Allied coordination proved among the most striking features of the cross-Channel assault on June 6, 1944. The list of successes started with the creation of an integrated multinational staff at Supreme Headquarters, Allied Expeditionary Forces (SHAEF)–London.[37] As casualties mounted and the expectations of an immediate German collapse were dashed, Anglo-American support for the coalition on pragmatic grounds remained unshaken.

At the Yalta Conference in February 1945, the Allies agreed to continue coordination of air and ground operations, to effect a zonal occupation of Germany that approximated the projected final positions of individual armies, and to implement a four-power (with France's participation) occupation of Germany and of Berlin. The Soviet reaffirmation at Yalta of their pledge to enter the war against Japan and to engage the substantial Japanese forces still in China reassured American military leaders. Subsequently, use of the atomic bomb on Hiroshima and Nagasaki made irrelevant the projected Soviet role in reducing American casualties and speeding the Pacific war to a victorious close.[38] Nevertheless, historians using newly available Russian sources have characterized as "sincere and profound" Soviet expectations about postwar cooperation with the west.[39]

A third dominant conviction dealt with the timing and outcome of what those individuals wrestling with grand logistics and war/postwar finance had termed Stage 1 (prosecution of total war against Germany and Japan), Stage 2 (war against Japan waged preeminently by the United States), and Stage 3 (the period of transition from war through military demobilization and economic reconstruction).[40] The timetable established by the civilian production experts and their counterparts in Operations Division (OPD) and Army Service Forces originally projected the culminating act of Stage 1, V-E Day, for D+90, assuming a swift collapse of German military resistance after successful landings in northwest France and a likely political meltdown. Thus, after FDR's and Churchill's decision at Casablanca to renege on the commitment to open the second front in 1943, the end of the European war, based on launching OVERLORD in May or June 1944, was to occur by mid-September or, Eisenhower himself stated, no later than Christmas.[41]

Pursuing that timetable, victory in the war against Japan was not to arrive before fall 1946. The culminating stage of the Pacific war would be almost totally an American show, with Britain and Russia using Lend-Lease to rebuild and rehabilitate their war-devastated economies. Stage 3, the period of postwar reconstruction beginning in 1947, would see the United Nations up and running, United Nations Relief and Rehabilitation Administration (UNRRA) meeting the immediate challenges of population dislocation and relief, former enemies and allies disarmed by an Anglo-American-Russian politico-military consortium, and international economic institutions such as the International Bank for Reconstruction and Development fully operational.

The actual timetable contrasted dramatically with the orderly scenario constructed by wartime planners. V-E Day came eight months later than projected; while V-J Day arrived a mere three months later instead of adhering to the eighteen- to twenty-four-month gap projected by American and British strategists. These miscalculations levied overwhelming burdens upon the exhausted peoples of Europe and Asia and further exacerbated tensions among the victorious nations.[42]

Although FDR and his advisers should not be faulted for failing to read every detail of postwar international conditions, the broad outlines of that future were probably more visible than would seem to have been the case, suggesting that the planners were depressingly shortsighted. Though admittedly they were not thinking exclusively about how the war would end, it is difficult to understand how American planners, in particular, ignored the portents of Soviet-western conflict, the disintegration of the British Empire, and Europe's political and economic breakdown.[43]

Addressing the slightly less ambitious question of how and why the European war ended as it did demands attention to the political climates in which the Nazi leadership and the heads of the Allied coalition functioned during 1943–1945. The guiding assumptions on both sides were shaped by an astonishing capacity for self-deception about each side's own aims and wishful thinking about the intentions and tenacity of the adversary. In his chronicle of the Peloponnesian War, Thucydides emphasized *pronoia,* the ability to anticipate the course of events, as the essence of statesmanship. Were he to have been transported forward some 2,400 years, Thucydides would have found *pronoia* in short supply among the principal leaders of the nations flailing at each other during the final months of the European war.

From the vantages of Moscow, London, and Washington, three options existed: to abandon the commitment to Allied solidarity and seek a separate peace with Hitler; to explore alternative ways of ending the war and the suffering of Hitler's victims without endorsing the continuation of Nazism or

Germany's hegemony in Europe; and to maintain the policy of unconditional surrender and pursue a coordinated military effort to crush every vestige of German resistance.

Roosevelt, Churchill, and Stalin viewed the perceived advantages of arranging a separate peace with Nazi Germany as minimal. After spring 1943, the goad of survival no longer pricked and, thus, the principal benefits of a negotiated settlement to any or all of the Allies would be humanitarian and economic. An early peace would avoid further expenditure of life and material resources on both sides and, coincidentally, save several million lives of Jewish and other victims of the Holocaust. Joseph Stalin gave no thought to humanitarian considerations. He was committed to the maintenance of his personal authority and the territorial and political aggrandizement of the Soviet state. Those in the west not inclined to romanticize the goals of their Soviet ally understood. At the September 1944 QUADRANT Conference, Britain's Lord Alanbrooke stated that he "did not believe there was any chance of the Germans achieving a negotiated peace with the Russians who had too much to wipe off the slate." Gen. George C. Marshall said he had "received reports of Russian antagonism and contempt for the West. He asked for British views on Russia and whether Germany would let the West in if the Soviets were advancing." Alanbrooke replied that he was convinced that Russia "will be terribly weakened after the war and will require a period of recovery—thus a peaceful Europe." If the Russians achieved territorial aims in eastern Europe, they would eagerly cooperate in maintaining peace in Europe.[44]

Similar motives infused American and British policies. Largely on political grounds, the prospect of long casualty lists worried FDR and Churchill, but they allowed themselves to be persuaded—with Russia making the major sacrifices in the ground war and British and American bombers pounding German cities—that the application of overwhelming firepower and armored forces at decisive points would yield a swift victory at a relatively low cost. Churchill never entirely renounced the mirage of a sudden German collapse. The western Allies excused failure to deliver on their commitments to accept comparable sacrifices in the struggle to defeat Nazi Germany by protesting that they faced difficult problems (the technological and logistical challenges of waging aerial and amphibious operations from centers of power distant from the enemy's shores) and that the battles of production and shipping first had to be won.

A second criticism of the forms of warfare adopted by the western Allies derived from the assumption that the west was soft; its leaders unwilling to make politically unpopular demands on the citizenry, and its soldiers lacking any strong ideological motivation and unprepared to deal with the rigors of warfare against a determined, highly trained enemy.[45] That claim does not survive close examination. U.S., British, and Soviet military leaders made use of strikingly similar calculations about anticipated casualties. Indeed, *actual* casualty/wastage rates of the three coalition partners were similar *for operations of like character conducted at approximately the same time;* the enormous disparity in numbers of casualties within the coalition was the product of circumstance (i.e., the Soviet Union's geographical position and British and U.S. separation and distance) and of inadvertence (miscalculations of timing and manpower constraints) rather than deliberate, coldly calculated actions by Anglo-American leaders. Clearly, domestic political pressures, the range of choice afforded by secure frontiers and overall control of the seas, and limited capacity to maintain a constant stream of reinforcements led American and British planners to peg at a rather lower point than their Soviet counterparts (at least prior to late 1944) what were "acceptable" losses in a given operation. On the other hand, Gen. Omar Bradley's offhand comment about the need "to blood green troops" as a justification of the carnage on Omaha Beach suggests that American generals were prepared to expend American lives as easily as shells and tanks.[46]

The shock to American and British confidence resulting from Hitler's December 1944 attack in the Ardennes affirmed how strong were the links between the Allies. Without hesitation, SHAEF commander Gen. Dwight D. Eisenhower placed U.S. forces north of the German breakthrough under Field Marshal Bernard Montgomery's command. Aided by improving weather for Anglo-American tactical air forces and the Soviet opening (Stalin's response to an impassioned plea from Churchill) of a gigantic offensive all along the central sector of the eastern front, the British from the north and Patton's Third Army from the south eliminated the Ardennes salient. Ignoring the clamor to permit Montgomery to dash for Berlin, Eisenhower returned to the strategy of a broad front advance in early March. The People's Commissariat for the Defense of the USSR worked to coordinate military operations on the eastern front with the advancing forces of the western Allies.

Especially important were the "bomb line" discussions to ensure that Allied strategic air forces flying missions in the Balkans and elsewhere in eastern Europe would not inadvertently attack advance columns of the Red Army. As the end neared, interaction at the operational level became extensive. From the west, elements of British and Canadian forces under Field Marshal Bernard Montgomery and of the U.S. First and Third Armies were approaching their designated "stop" lines. On the Soviet side, the drive into Germany was done by the First Belorussian, First Ukrainian, Second Belorussian, and Third and Fourth Ukrainian Fronts. The coming linkup led to bilateral exchanges between SHAEF commander Eisenhower and Montgomery with their Soviet counterpart, Marshal Georgi K. Zhukov. Crude but functional identification signals were agreed to among Soviet, U.S., and British forces.[47] These ad hoc arrangements sufficed until the historic linkup of American and Soviet forces at Torgau on the Elbe River.

Writing about the Napoleonic era but also, perhaps, with an eye toward the demise of the World War II coalition, Henry A. Kissinger once posited, "As long as the enemy is more powerful than any single member of the coalition, the need for unity outweighs all considerations of individual gain. Then the powers of repose can insist on the definition of war aims which, in all conditions, represent limitations. But when the enemy has been so weakened that each ally has the power to achieve its ends alone, a coalition is at the mercy of its most determined member."[48] The Axis "have always planned on a split of the Allies," General Marshall admitted after Yalta. "They never for one moment calculated that the Allies could continue to conduct combined operations with complete understanding and good faith."[49] Given the conflicting ideologies and starkly differing cultural outlooks of the nations constituting the Grand Alliance, its survival was remarkable.[50]

Given the limits on Allied freedom of action and assuming continuing Soviet adherence, the United States was to be the catalyst for any reconsideration of the unconditional surrender policy. The notion was not original with FDR. British propaganda chief, Lord Vansittart, had advocated victory without conditions as early as 1941.[51] Vice President Wallace, in a speech before the Free World Association in New York City, May 8, 1942, had argued that World War II was "a fight between a slave world and a free world. Just as the United States in 1862 could not remain half slave and half free, so in 1942 the world must make its decision for a complete victory one way or the other."[52] FDR had converted rhetoric into policy by sanctifying unconditional surrender at the famous "off-the-cuff" press conference at Casablanca in January 1943.[53] The circumstances in which Roosevelt and Churchill promulgated the doctrine of unconditional surrender supposedly derived from an urgent need, having reneged on their promise to open a second front in 1943, to reassure the Soviets about Anglo-American commitment to the alliance. However, Roosevelt's statement reflected strongly held views and anxieties about domestic politics far more than concern for Russian sensibilities.

As Warren F. Kimball and John Lamberton Harper have persuasively argued, FDR was motivated by a powerful antipathy to Germans and Germany and an unbending determination, grounded in his experience as a junior member of Pres. Woodrow Wilson's administration, not to repeat the political blunders of 1918.[54] The president espoused what historian Arnold Offner has termed "retributive justice." He advocated "absolute ruthlessness" toward Nazi Germany and spoke on occasion of castration as a way to deal with "those Prussians." FDR desired to ensure that no one could say after the fact that Allied leaders were not sufficiently tough-minded.

Memories of World War I dominated the thinking of both FDR and Churchill. The political fallout of 1919–1920 was deeply etched into Roosevelt's memory, and he embraced the notion that World War II resulted directly from failure to make clear to the Germans that they were once and for all beaten. Gerhard Weinberg has noted: "When seen as a whole, the plans the Allies were developing for Germany were quite harsh, but given German behavior hardly surprisingly so. Putting them in front of the Germans instead of simply calling for unconditional surrender was not likely to make ending the war on Allied terms particularly attractive."[55] Manifestly, however, constant reiteration of unconditional surrender as the sole basis on which the conflict could be ended converted what had been a public relations ploy to the status of inalterable doctrine.[56]

An intriguing footnote to this story derives from speculation as to the president's motives for steadfastly refusing to consider modification of the unconditional surrender policy during summer and early fall 1944. Was concern about the political repercussions of V-E Day in, say, September 1944, as set forth in the original OVERLORD timetable, an element in the Roosevelt administration's dismissive treatment of the July 20 bomb plot and, more generally, of all reports of an anti-Hitler German resistance? President Roosevelt's landslide victory over the Republican challenger, New York governor Thomas E. Dewey, in November 1944, causes any such speculation to appear nonsensical. Seen from the vantage of early summer 1944, however, postponing V-E Day until after the November elections made political sense. Democratic party insiders viewed FDR's reelection to a fourth term as in no way guaranteed, especially if the war were to end either by means of a Germany military collapse or the replacement of Hitler and his Nazi thugs by a government intent upon peace at any cost. Public opinion polls revealed that American voters perceived their president chiefly as war leader.[57] "War is too political a thing," FDR once told his son, Elliott. "Depending on how desperate are a country's straits, she is likely to wage war only in such a way as will benefit her politically in the long run, rather than fighting to end the war as swiftly as possible." FDR may have been alluding to his own circumstances and American political realities in 1944 when making that wry observation.[58]

All that has gone before strongly implies that the march toward Götterdämmerung had gathered inexorable momentum by the time it became clear that casually embraced assumptions about the timetable for victory were not going to be met. However, implied proof does not always yield truth. What transpired between October 1944 and April 1945 did present choices. There might have been a pause in the relentless bombardment of Germany. A different approach to targeting by the planners of the bombing campaign might have been explored. Options to the broad front strategy adhered to with such determination by Eisenhower might have yielded a different military outcome. Efforts to assess the strength and motives of resistance inside Nazi Germany could have been undertaken. The fact that such alternatives were not seriously explored raises questions about who was determining Anglo-American policies. By default, after the Battle of the Bulge, annihilation became the only option, and the projected timetable for apocalypse came to be fall/winter 1945.

American political and military leaders faithfully replicated the confusion and rigidity of outlook of the people they represented. Anecdotal evidence about American attitudes toward when and how the war would end is available from a range of sources. When recovering GIs at the Seventy-seventh Station Hospital, England, were asked in interviews conducted by a U.S. Army psychologist on October 2–3, 1944, how long the war in Europe would last, the unanimous response was that it would be over by the end of 1944 if not before. When questioned as to what would bring the war to an end, however, the soldiers expressed differing opinions. Some said that the German army would have to be smashed. "I originally thought that the civilians would fold, but now I feel that the Army must be defeated," stated one officer. Several agreed with the view of an infantry second lieutenant: "I thought there would be a general collapse, but now they will fight to the end and only give up in pieces. A successful attempt on Hitler's life might stop the war." Still others believed, as one said, "The breakdown will come in the Army. The civilians are too hamstrung and can't organize well enough to plan a revolt." Though some GIs believed that a period of military occupation terms should be imposed and a few supported "Morgenthau's Plan," the majority believed that "the terms shouldn't be so harsh that [the Germans] can't live up to them."[59]

Indeed, several respondents made clear their willingness to allow the Germans to govern themselves and to decide the form of government under which they would live, once the war ended. Notably, no one cited unconditional surrender as dictating a fight to the finish. The contradictory views of Americans were summed up by a Tenth Infantry rifleman: "It ain't the people it's the leaders. As far as the civilians are concerned I don't think they had anything to do with it. The same as the US. Roosevelt says we go to war— we go. Put somebody over them for a couple of years till they start a good government and let 'em go. You have to punish but as far as the army is concerned, up to the Generals they are doing their jobs. Just the Higher ups like Hitler and those should be punished."[60]

Enormously influential was the highly bureaucratized process by which strategic decisions were made. By midwar, the western Allies had constructed a sprawling, complex set of arrangements embracing strategy and logistics. That apparatus produced elaborate plans for disparate operations around the globe—air campaigns, sea campaigns, ground campaigns, combined warfare, special operations, "psywar," economic warfare—and, inevitably, the planners became advocates for their particular spheres and campaigns with little or no attention to larger political aims. The means by which the war's ultimate purpose were pursued became ends in themselves.

The Roosevelt administration's bitter and convoluted debate in the months before V-E Day over "hard" and "soft" options for postwar Germany offers another example of politics driving policy. One historian's judgment is harsh: "The political and ideological composition of the Roosevelt administration itself was fluid and complex. Its foreign policy apparatus was a kind of carnival of cliques whose internal balance shifted according to the preference of the president, the settling of personal scores, and the pressure of events."[61] Fear of an unexpected shift in the military balance was also important. Although a select few knew that the German atomic program was effectively defunct and senior military commanders had discounted by fall 1944 the war-winning potential of the V-weapons, jet aircraft, and schnorkel-equipped submarines, western political leaders still worried that protracted negotiations might give the Germans a breathing space and time to unleash a hitherto-unknown superweapon. The SHAEF intelligence debacle with regard to German planning for the Ardennes counteroffensive led to exaggerated worries about Nazi secret technology during January–March 1945.

These diverse viewpoints suggest that groups and organizations within the Allied coalition were waging multiple wars—against the enemy and against each other—and bringing all these conflicts to a close simultaneously proved impossible to accomplish. Leon Sigal emphasized this phenomenon in his analysis of the Pacific war: "Wars may end, but the work of government bureaus goes on. There are still programs to promote and roles to perform, budgets to parcel out, missions to conserve or expand, careers to advance. . . . As wars draw to a close, officials do battle on two fronts at once: on one, to bring the enemy state to terms, and on the other, to end the war in a way that best serves their organizational interests."[62] In practice, personal and organizational loyalties exert greater influence than allegiance to abstractions such as the national interest. The aphorism, "where you sit is where you stand," appears especially germane to the messy business of concluding an interstate conflict. "Even at such momentous times as war's end, and perhaps especially then," Sigal has observed, "the national interest may not be easy to discern. Its ambiguity permits officials to identify the national interest with the interests of their own organizations."[63]

Thus, the process by which policy choices are taken is not necessarily rational, and the assumption that a government leader presides over a principled debate on the "intellectual merits" of a course of action is not justified by the evidence. Politics, especially bureaucratic politics, "involves bargaining—threats and promises, deals and logrolling, tactics and maneuvers—to influence results."[64] Sigal has concluded that "states are not unitary actors, but congeries of separate organizations with different routines, or shifting coalitions of participants with conflicting interests. Inconsistence is the rule, not the exception, in state action. Second, the interaction among enemy states does not take the form of action-reaction. . . . To bureaucrats working at their desks in the nation's capital, even to military officers at field headquarters, the . . . enemy state is an abstraction, only dimly apprehended, onto which officials often project their own mundane concerns." When confronted with pleas to bomb the rail lines leading to Auschwitz or even, if necessary, the sprawling murder complex itself, British and American military bureaucrats perceived any diversion from the agreed strategy of attacking "military" targets as a challenge to their autonomy and to the rigid timetable that had been established for the bombing campaign. Intervening on behalf of Jews being systematically slaughtered in Auschwitz was, therefore, irrelevant and inconsequential in comparison with the need to maintain airpower's doctrinal purity.[65]

The politics that matters is domestic and intramural, not international. The hackneyed phrase "politics stops at the water's edge" acquires new meaning in this context. Even the circumstances surrounding Germany's surrender or, more precisely, surrenders reflected the failures of coordination and clashing political priorities within the Allied camp at war's end.

In retrospect, the reality of Germany's eventual defeat was evident to anyone who studied the shifting calculus of manpower and munitions production between the Axis and the Allies. However, despite Stalingrad, the weakening grip of the U-boats in the Battle of the Atlantic, and the omnipresent drone of British and American bombers over German cities, the antiseptic evidence of growing Allied military power was discounted both by the Nazi leadership and by the Wehrmacht high command.[66] A combination of factors stoked German confidence in their ability to hold off the Russians and to deny the Anglo-American forces a foothold in northwest

Europe, ultimately leading to some sort of armistice that would leave intact the Nazi regime and German domination of Europe.

Basic was a conviction that British and American forces—poorly led, soft, and inexperienced—were no match for veteran German troops. Such judgments were not exclusively found in Berlin. In October 1943, testifying before a committee of the U.S. Congress, Maj. Gen. George V. Strong, assistant chief of staff (G-2), stressed how powerful remained the Axis powers:

> For months, by means of communiques, newspaper reports, and highly optimistic publicity regarding relatively minor victories, our people have been led to believe that we are winning the war to the extent that the collapse of Hitler's Germany is just around the corner, and thereafter concentration of our strength in the Pacific will promptly overwhelm the Japanese Empire. This magnification of relatively minor victories has resulted in a picture which is totally out of perspective and which has given rise to a dangerous optimism which is not justified by the facts.[67]

Though he acknowledged that the Soviets had reconquered a large part of their territory, "more than half the area taken by Axis forces in their victorious advances still remains in their hands, and there is no evidence that German military power has materially decreased." Strong asserted that "great forces of well trained enemy troops, well led and well equipped," were still available. Germany alone fielded some 300 divisions. While Axis forces were on the defensive, they controlled "vast territories and are able, willing, and ready to counter-attack with great force." Most important, Germany dominated Europe and thus was able to exploit the labor of 325 million people and practically the whole of Europe's industries and economic resources.

Strong offered a stark conclusion: "Our optimism for the future is based almost entirely on the ability of our Russian Allies to keep nearly three quarters of the German Army occupied in the East, and the ability of American and British aviators to keep up their tremendous raids on Germany's European Fortress."[68] Although Kursk and the attritional battles of summer–fall 1943 compelled acknowledgment even in Hitler's headquarters that the Wehrmacht had lost the strategic initiative on the eastern front, the pervasive pessimism that thereafter gripped German senior commanders and many veteran soldiers only rarely led to defeatism. A number of recent studies have confirmed that the German public, as well, doggedly supported the regime.

Why was that so? Of greatest importance were two psychological or, more precisely, pseudoreligious qualities: faith and fatalism. Faith in Hitler and the supremacy in Social Darwinist terms of Germany and Germans proved difficult to defy. The great majority of Germans believed with religious zeal well into 1944 that the Wehrmacht would overcome its adversaries—stopping the Red Army and pushing Anglo-American forces into the sea. Even after the

Allies broke out from Normandy, most German civilians and many military figures were confident that the new weapons proclaimed by the führer—the V-1 and V-2 rockets, jet aircraft, new types of submarines—would stem the tide.[69] Gerhard Weinberg has observed: "The key question in the last months of war in Europe was not what the German air force and navy could do but whether the German home front would remain solidly behind the army as it fought in the west, east and south. In spite of the enormous casualties of the summer and fall and in spite of the increasingly heavy Allied bombing offensive, the home front held up."[70] For most Germans, their mystical faith in Hitler remained strong to the end. In early February 1945, Count Folke Bernadotte, a Swedish diplomat visiting Berlin, commented that "people gave the impression of being utterly sick of the war and completely dominated by the wish to see it end quickly." However, while Berliners made caustic jokes (e.g., that when the Russians came to Berlin it would take them one hour and two minutes to capture each defensive position—one hour for Homeric laughter, and the remaining two minutes to smash through the barricade), Folke Bernadotte concluded that renunciation of the führer was unthinkable. Germans "could not bear to lose their faith in him, who had appeared to them as a Redeemer, and in the Nazi system."[71] A recently discovered journal kept by a German naval engineer trapped in Lubeck during the Third Reich's final agonies reiterated the author's confidence that Hitler would work some sort of miracle. "Do we really have new secret land and air weapons, ready for action?" he agonized in early April but concluded, "There is only one thing to do: to hold on to hope and to have faith in our Fuhrer. This, after all, is the test of true faith: to believe when all seems hopeless."[72]

Many historians claim that a powerful if unanticipated effect of the unconditional surrender policy was to strengthen German resolve to fight on because the alternative was deemed even less appealing.[73] They echo Michael Howard's observation: "Political warfare specialists might have quoted Sun Tzu's advice about leaving one's enemy a golden bridge for retreat. . . . There was no opportunity for such counsels to be heard at Casablanca. Had it been otherwise, the Allied leaders might have reflected a little more deeply on the question, whether total victory is necessarily the surest foundation for a lasting peace."[74] Nazi propagandists exploited Allied rigidity on this issue, but they had other, even more powerful weapons, as Gerhard Weinberg has noted, in the threat of Bolshevism and "virulent anti-German rhetoric" broadcast daily from Britain and America.[75] Surrender terms, after all, are important only to those contemplating surrender, and that was not the case in Germany until well after the question was moot.

Not until the bitter end did ordinary Germans renounce their loyalty to the regime and to the person of Adolf Hitler. When that happened, Douglas

Botting has written, "There were few signs among average Germans of responsibility for Nazism, the war, or any awareness of what the Allied conquest was all about."[76] Of course, by Hitler's death, while some still prayed for an understanding with the western Allies, most Germans were too deeply engaged in trying to eat and stay alive to "take much notice of Hitler's departure from the world scene."[77]

The German people's blind allegiance stemmed as much from resignation as from fear or hope of some sort of miraculous deliverance. Recent investigations into the thorny problem of why German soldiers continued to fight against hopeless odds down to the last days of the war have concluded that fatalistic fanaticism was the final recourse of individuals and groups who privately acknowledged the inevitability of Germany's defeat. Especially on the eastern front, the war had degenerated into a nightmarish struggle, and the only choice appeared to kill or be killed.[78]

These dualities coerced both Hitler and the Germans who plotted to supplant the Nazis and end the war. After the tide's turn in 1943, Hitler's plans, while muddled, manifested unyielding determination to fight on at whatever sacrifice. He ordered in March 1944 that all war production be moved into caves and excavated spaces; he betrayed an obsession with suicide attacks (talking with Japanese envoys about kamikazes and ordering that a squadron of single-seat fighters be trained in the technique of ramming Allied heavy bombers); he issued the "no retreat" order and moved stockpiles and factories for producing nerve gas out of areas being overrun by the Allies for possible use in a last-ditch defense of the Reich.[79] Hitler threw away the Wehrmacht's last reserves in the Ardennes gamble. That reflected his conviction that the Americans, the weak link because of their "mongrel origins" and their softness, would crumble under sustained pressure and cause the disintegration of the Allied coalition.[80] Here Hitler lapsed into mysticism, repeatedly proclaiming that he was destined, as had been Frederick the Great in similar circumstances, to rescue Germany from the abyss.

Prior to the failed coup of July 20, 1944, the most prominent resisters were hardly more realistic. According to the authoritative study of the German resistance movement: "As the war went on, the Western Powers and the German resisters found themselves on completely different wavelengths."[81] Most anti-Nazi Germans, especially those in the army and the upper classes, "believed firmly that a lasting peace was most likely to have been achieved by terms which left their country in roughly the same position as it was in 1914 or 1937. They believed it to be in the general interest that Germany should dominate Central South-Eastern Europe, if not the Continent as a whole." Ironically, by fall 1944, those resisters who survived concluded that Germany's unconditional surrender was not only unavoidable but necessary.

Germany had to go through the humiliation of total, absolute defeat as "a necessary prelude" to basic social and political reforms, and they admitted that the German people could not be trusted, as happened after World War I, to implement themselves the measures required to prevent the rise of a Fourth Reich.[82]

However attractive in theory was the prospect of Hitler's being deposed, the western Allies proved unwilling to give credence in practice to any of the numerous attempts by German groups to undertake discussions. Why? Because of the presumed impossibility of meaningful opposition arising within a "totalitarian" state, because of London and Washington's desire—given the strongly anti-Bolshevik stance of the most prominent resisters—not to jeopardize relations with Moscow, because of muddled intelligence about the strength and aims of the resistance, and, preeminently, because even should by some miracle a coup have succeeded, the political and bureaucratic imperatives driving Allied policy had generated their own momentum.[83]

By early 1945 the situation could only be likened to the sort of surrealistic art that Hitler so despised. Perceptions were out of kilter. Hitler was inclined to seek a settlement with the Soviet Union, looking toward a joint campaign against Stalin's erstwhile allies. Ribbentrop encouraged that scheme while edging toward trying for a separate peace with the Anglo-Americans. Through peace feelers to Sweden, Switzerland, Spain, and the Vatican, Ribbentrop "urged the Western Allies to make peace with Hitler and join Germany in fighting the Soviet Union, lest Germany join the latter in fighting them—while simultaneously either making the opposite suggestion to the Soviet Union or trying to find a way to do so."[84]

Heinrich Himmler did undertake an eleventh-hour exploration of wresting power from Hitler and raising the white flag, but even Himmler, arguably the Third Reich's most sinister figure, could not bring himself to challenge his enfeebled führer.[85] Gerhard Weinberg has written that the complete lack of realism demonstrated in these episodes is comparable to von Ribbentrop's efforts in the 1920s, while a salesman for a German wine exporter, to peddle German champagne in France. The bottom line was that the likelihood of an anti-Nazi coup was infinitesimal by fall 1944 and that not even during Germany's protracted death throes in spring 1945 was anyone in Hitler's circle willing to displace him.

Given the evident disinterest of Allied leaders in any resolution other than military conquest and the impossibility of significant change in German policy while Hitler remained in control, does any value derive from tracing the "paths not taken" in the months before V-E Day? Historians have generally argued that discovering and explaining what did happen is so challenging that speculation about what might have happened if this or that were different amounts to mere time-wasting. Yet, as Francis R. Nicosia and Lawrence D. Stokes have observed, "How can we appreciate the importance of what did happen without occasionally speculating what the alternatives might have been?" They go on to ask what might have taken place if the anti-Nazi resistance "had been more skillful or more fortunate" and conclude: "The upshot of these speculations would seem to be that elimination of Hitler in November 1939 would not have obviated the need to fight the war; his elimination in July or August 1944 would not have made any significant difference in the result of war for Germany, except by providing a spurious explanation for the defeat, and his elimination in March 1943 would have led to war's ending with a compromise peace rather than unconditional surrender."[86] One reading of the evidence suggests that had Hitler been overthrown before attitudes hardened on both sides, some sort of negotiated settlement yielding both immediate and long-term benefits might have transpired. At the other end of the spectrum stands the harsh indictment of the German people, and not merely their Nazi masters, as bearing collective responsibility for the terrible crimes perpetrated during World War II. In this regard, works such as Daniel J. Goldhagen's controversial *Hitler's Willing Executioners: Ordinary Germans and the Holocaust* echo the contemporary testimony of the few pitiful survivors and the horrified liberators of the death camps.[87]

Were, therefore, the national and individual tragedies that attended the final months of the war in Europe inevitable, etched in stone by the blind fanaticism of Hitler and his followers, the inflexibility of Allied policies and politicians, the dogged adherence to plans and timetables of military leaders on both sides? The logic of the argument put forward here leads to a conclusion of yes and, just possibly, no. Yes, for all the reasons previously mentioned, perhaps reinforced by the perception of those who opposed Hitler and Nazism as the embodiment of evil. Today, we look back at the events of fifty years ago with clearer vision but, perhaps, having lost the intuition of what those turbulent years meant—emotionally and in moral terms—to the human beings caught up in them.[88]

That observation leads to a tentative argument about what would have happened had the bomb planted on Hitler's plane in spring 1943 worked or, alternatively, had Colonel von Stauffenberg placed the briefcase slightly closer or had the oak table been less sturdy under which the bomb exploded on July 20, 1944, and had the Allies responded positively to the news that the arch-Nazi had been removed from the game. The myth of Hitler's greatness was yet another by-product of the cold war, in which unreasoning anticommunism of the McCarthy/Ustaschi variety made possible a creative rendering of the füehrer's demise, whereby cowering in a bunker far below a Berlin pulverized by Allied bombs and Soviet shells was transmuted into a heroic act of self-immolation and acquired the symbolic attributes of sacrifice for the German Volk's phoenixlike renewal. It is difficult to credit such an act of mythmaking surviving the reality of a twitching, emotionally shattered Hitler being turned over to the Allies by Germans for trial.

Individuals and nations respond to changed circumstances in unpredictable ways. In a prefatory essay to his study of the phenomenon of coming to North America in the seventeenth and eighteenth centuries, Bernard Bailyn stressed that the migration process "comprised millions of individual actions taken for uncounted, often unknowable reasons."[89] Bailyn drives home this point by comparing the human movement from Europe to America with the recent experience of astronomers for whom the perception of Saturn's rings as unitary, impermeable bodies collapsed at that moment when *Voyager*'s stunning images reached Earth. Seen up close, Saturn's rings were shown to comprise millions of separate bits and pieces of rock, all whirling about each other and the giant planet in incredibly convoluted orbits. *Voyager*'s data affirmed that this gigantic construction of nature is not an immutable object but a precariously stable coalition of individual elements. One small intrusion from outside could affect its structure, much as one seemingly trivial event can affect the course of history.[90]

That insight is reinforced by Stephen Jay Gould's marvelous depiction of a paradigm shift in evolutionary theory resulting from the ordering of 500 million years of biological successes and failures into a historical narrative. In *Wonderful Life: The Burgess Shale and the Nature of History,* Gould moves contingency front and center on the historical stage. "A historical explanation does not rest on direct deductions from laws of nature, but on an unpredictable sequence of antecedent states, where any major change in any step of the sequence would have altered the final result. This final result is therefore dependent, or contingent, upon everything that came before—the unerasable and determining signature of history," Gould reminds us.[91] He continues: "We are especially moved by events that did not have to be, but that occurred for identifiable reasons subject to endless mulling and stewing. . . . We can argue, lament, or exult over each detail—because each holds the power of transformation. Contingency is the affirmation of control by immediate events over destiny, the kingdom lost for want of a horseshoe nail."[92] This is heady stuff. It makes possible the fusion of an approach to historical explanation perhaps best termed "accidentalism" (which, as Gerhard Weinberg reminds us, emphasizes "the uncertainties inherent in developments, . . . the role of chance, [and] . . . the impact of the unanticipated"), with renewed attention to the significance of the exceptional, unique elements of the sociopolitical milieu attending the end of war in Europe.[93]

It is worth considering how many elements, how many players, how many possible incongruities were involved in the European endgame of World War II. The final report of the U.S. Strategic Bombing Survey, released in 1946, succinctly stated an essential truth: "While defeat is a military event, the recognition of the defeat is a political act. The timing of the political recognition of the military realities is only partly determined by the actual situation on the fronts. The international situation, the domestic balance of power, the interest and antagonisms of relevant political groups—they all weigh heavily when the grim realities of the armed contest have to be translated into the blunt language of capitulation."[94] What this suggests is the contingent nature of the familiar story we associate with victory in Europe in May 1945. Were Hitler to have been removed from the equation even a few months earlier, perhaps by remaining in his East Prussia military headquarters as John Lukacs has suggested, his successors, however repellent and unrealistic about obtaining favorable conditions for Germany, would have surrendered unconditionally.[95] With Hitler gone but with the apparatus of government intact, the rigid stance adopted by Allied leaders might well have eased, allowing some sort of new paradigm to emerge.

What might have been gained thereby? Possibly the lives of the Jews and other death camp inmates murdered and starved to death during the nine months from August 1944 through April 1945, the Allied and German soldiers killed in action, the civilians in Germany and surrounding nations caught in the fighting and bombing campaign. Would the Europe and the world that emerged have evolved along different lines if the war in Europe had ended nine months earlier and without the ongoing horrors inflicted at Auschwitz and Dachau, without the Ardennes counteroffensive (and Malmedy), without Dresden, without the battle for Berlin? Probably not. But maybe. The alternative merits consideration if for no other reason than that we may gain insight thereby about why conflicts do not end as logic and humanity inform us they should.

NOTES

1. This reconstruction of events in early December 1944 is drawn from a variety of sources but, in particular, from the *New York Times* and Martin Gilbert's day-by-day depiction of Winston Churchill's war: *Road to Victory: Winston S. Churchill, 1941–1945* (London: William Heinemann, 1986).

2. Scholarly studies that give substantial attention to the end of the European

war—such as Paul Kecskemeti, *Strategic Surrender* (New York: Atheneum, 1964), Herman Kahn, *War Termination: Issues and Concepts* (Croton-on-Hudson, N.Y.: Hudson Institute, 1968), and Fred C. Ikle's still-influential *Every War Must End* (New York: Columbia University Press, 1971)—mostly date from the 1960s. In contrast, works on how and why the Pacific war ended continue to pour forth, as witness the special section, "Hiroshima in History and Memory: A Symposium," *Diplomatic History* 19, 2 (spring 1995): 197–367.

4. See, for example, John W. Dower, *War Without Mercy: Race and Power in the Pacific War* (New York: Pantheon, 1987), and that powerful autobiographical testimonial to war's ability to "objectify" the enemy; E. B. Sledge, *With the Old Breed: At Peleliu and Okinawa* (New York: Oxford University Press, 1981). Of course, the Soviet-German conflict was at times fought as savagely as the Pacific war.

5. Leon V. Sigal, *Fighting to a Finish: The Politics of War Termination in the United States and Japan, 1945* (Ithaca, N.Y.: Cornell University Press, 1988), ix–x.

5. This process is usually referred to in scholarly jargon as "cognitive dissonance"—i.e., speaking past each other, not assimilating what the other is saying. For a full discussion, see Sigal's comparative assessment of "rational choice" theories of state behavior and cognitive dissonance (*Fighting to a Finish*, 12–25).

6. Such recent works as Martin Gilbert, *The Day the War Ended: May 8, 1945—Victory in Europe* (New York: Holt, 1995), Anthony Read and David Fisher, *Berlin: The Biography of a City* (London: Pimlico, 1994), and Klaus P. Fischer, *Nazi Germany: A New History* (London: Constable, 1996), offer broad-brush narratives, with little sustained attention to the questions of how and why the war ended as it did. Gerhard Weinberg's massive history of World War II, *A World at War* (New York: Cambridge University Press, 1994), offers useful insights; see also Gerhard Weinberg, "D-Day: Analysis of Costs and Benefits," in *D-Day 1944*, ed. Theodore A. Wilson (Lawrence: University Press of Kansas, 1994), 318–38.

7. Sigal, *Fighting to a Finish*, 13. For recourse to the insights of philosophical classics, see H. A. Calahan, *What Makes a War End?* (New York: Vanguard, 1944), Stephen J. Cimbala, *Conflict Termination in Europe: Games Against War* (New York: Praeger, 1990), Ikle, *Every War Must End*, and Keith A. Dunn, "The Missing Link in Conflict Termination Thought: Strategy," in *Conflict Termination and Military Strategy: Coercion, Persuasion, and War*, ed. Stephen J. Cimbala and Keith A. Dunn (Boulder, Colo.: Westview Press, 1987).

8. Stuart Albert and Edward C. Luck, eds., *On the Endings of Wars* (Port Washington, N.Y.: Kennikat Press, 1980), 3.

9. Ibid., 11–13.

10. Ibid., 13. The currently "hot" explanatory scheme known as "chaos/complexity theory" offers insights into this problem. As H. W. Brands has observed, the mathematical system known as fractal geometry demonstrates that complexity exists at all levels; thus, "There is no way of describing that is inherently more valuable, legitimate, or praiseworthy" ("Fractal History, or Clio and the Chaotics," *Diplomatic History* [fall, 1992]: 500–502. The proponents of complexity theory, the social scientific construct derived from chaos theory, argue that it offers a basis for understanding

human interactions, such as conflict, at all levels and especially at the level of inter-state relations. What seems to be irrational behavior may be the result of complex systems operating between the extremes of stability and chaos, with systemic uncertainty as a—perhaps the only—constant. As M. Mitchell Waldrop has noted, the "nested character" of the international system makes determination of the ultimate effect of actions within subordinate entities (such as the Nazi party or FDR's White House) extremely difficult (*Complexity: The Emerging Science at the Edge of Order and Chaos* [New York: Touchstone, 1992], 146). Ultimately, intuition, what one scholar has termed "a feel for the moments when change from one pattern to another is possible," is the most assured guide (W. Brian Arthur, "Positive Feedbacks in the Economy," *Scientific American* 67, 2 [February, 1990]: 99). On the basis of the paleontological record, would Darwin have predicted that tiny mammals scurrying through the underbrush would have become Earth's dominant species? Was the U.S.–Soviet arms race foreseeable from the vantage of 1938 or 1944?

11. Albert and Luck note: "Victory and defeat are strikingly symbiotic conceptions. *Webster's International Dictionary* offers only one substantive meaning for victory: 'overcoming of an enemy in battle, or of an antagonist in any contest; assertion of superiority in any struggle; conquest, triumph; the opposite of "defeat." ' To conquer, we learn elsewhere, . . . once meant 'to procure by effort, acquire,' and it still has meanings independent of any antagonist, e.g., conquer difficulties or temptation, to overcome obstacles by mental or moral power. But the primary contemporary meaning of conquer requires a defeated opponent—still more, an opponent defeated by violent means: 'to gain or acquire by force of arms; to take possession of by violent means; to gain dominion over; to subjugate, . . . to vanquish.' . . . The ancient images of victory and defeat are highly personalized: the conqueror stands erect and triumphant on the field of battle, the defeated kneels helpless at his feet. The victor is welcomed home in triumph; . . . the defeated drag along in chains, touching their foreheads to the ground. In its extreme form, victorious force is, as Simone Weil argues, that which 'turns anybody who is subjected to it into a thing.' Thus Achilles, in the final battles described in *The Iliad* slaughters the Trojans like animals, indifferent alike to valor and pleading, reducing them all to steaming meat" (*On the Endings of Wars*, 49).

12. Ibid., 24.

13. Bruce C. G. Clarke, "Conflict Termination: A Rational Model," *Studies in Conflict and Terrorism* 16, 1 (1993): 34.

14. For positive and negative critiques, see Richard Hobbs, *The Myth of Victory: What Is Victory in War?* (Boulder, Colo.: Westview Press, 1979), and Michael Handel, *War Termination—A Critical Survey* (Jerusalem: Hebrew University Press, 1978).

15. Mirroring the Vietnam War–era struggle between supposed "hawks" and "doves," Fred Ikle argued that the pivotal leadership change reflects the displacement of warhawks, those committed to prosecuting the war at all costs, by a more moderate faction (*Every War Must End*, 69).

16. Joseph Engelbrecht has written that leaders forced to confront the necessity to end a conflict "undergo a psychological process which forces them to see the problem

from a higher or second order paradigm," ("War Termination: Why Does a State Decide to Stop Fighting?" [Ph.D. diss., Columbia University, 1992], 98).

17. For these categories, I gratefully acknowledge the extremely useful evaluation of the scholarly literature on war termination in Lt. Col. Russell Glenn's seminar paper, "The Cacophonous Symphony: War Termination and Decision Gaming" (University of Kansas, December 1994). See also Cimbala, *Conflict Termination in Europe;* Dunn, "The Missing Link in Conflict Termination Thought"; Michael Handel, "The Study of War Termination," *Journal of Strategic Studies* 1 (May 1978): 51–75; Donald Wittman, "How a War Ends: A Rational Model Approach," *Journal of Conflict Resolution* 23, 4 (December 1979): 70–90; and Morton H. Halperin, "War Termination as a Problem in Civil-Military Relations," *Annals of the American Academy of Political and Social Science* 392 (November 1970): 86–95, as well as works cited previously.

18. Albert and Luck, eds., *On the Endings of Wars,* 12. This analysis relies heavily on the seminal work by Ikle, *Every War Must End.*

19. Nicholas S. Timasheff, *War and Revolution* (New York: Praeger, 1965), quoted in Albert and Luck, eds. *On the Endings of Wars,* 51.

20. Kecskemeti, *Strategic Surrender,* 8–9.

21. Sigal, *Fighting to a Finish,* 16.

22. Ikle, *Every War Must End,* 93–94.

23. Sigal, *Fighting to a Finish,* 19.

24. Handel, *War Termination—A Critical Survey,* 15.

25. Vladislav M. Zubok, "Cooperation or 'Go Alone': Soviet Dilemmas at the Transition from World War II to the 'Cold Peace,' 1944–1945," paper presented at the Sixth International Symposium on the U.S./U.K./USSR Experience in World War II, June 12–14, 1995, Roosevelt Study Center, Middelburg, the Netherlands, 2.

26. A voluminous literature exists on this subject. See, for example, the essays by Maurice Matloff, Mark A. Stoler, Gerhard Weinberg, and, in particular, Alex Danchev in Wilson, ed., *D-Day 1944.*

27. Tuvia Ben-Moshe, "Winston Churchill and the 'Second Front': A Reappraisal," *Journal of Modern History* 62 (September 1990): 528. On this point see also Ben-Moshe, *Churchill: Strategy and Victory* (Boulder, Colo.: Westview Press, 1992), and Theodore A. Wilson, *The First Summit,* rev. ed. (Lawrence: University Press of Kansas, 1991). A contrary view is offered by Alex Danchev, "Biffing: The Saga of the Second Front," in Wilson, ed., *D-Day 1944,* 24–41.

28. These issues are documented in Harry L. Coles and Albert K. Weinberg, *Civil Affairs: Soldiers Become Governors* (Washington, D.C.: OCMH, 1964). See also Gerhard Weinberg, *A World at Arms: A Global History of World War II* (New York: Cambridge University Press, 1994), Earl F. Ziemke, *The U.S. Army in the Occupation of Germany* (Washington, D.C.: GPO, 1975), Warren F. Kimball, *Swords or Plowshares? The Morgenthau Plan for Defeated Nazi Germany, 1943–1946* (New York: Lippincott, 1976), and John Gimbel, *The American Occupation of Germany* (Palo Alto, Calif.: Stanford University Press, 1968).

29. Studies that focus on the collapse of Soviet-Western cooperation as a political

process include Melvyn P. Leffler, *A Preponderance of Power: National Security, the Truman Administration and the Cold War* (Stanford: Stanford University Press, 1992), and Lloyd C. Gardner, *Spheres of Influence: The Great Powers Partition Europe, from Munich to Yalta* (Chicago: Ivan Dee, 1993). A helpful review of recent Russian scholarship on the Soviet leadership's wartime assessment of postwar policies is Vladimir O. Pechatnov, "The Big Three After World War II: New Documents on Soviet Thinking about Postwar Relations with the United States and Great Britain," Working Paper no. 13 (June 1995), Cold War International History Project, Woodrow Wilson International Center, Washington, D.C.

30. Sumner Welles, *Seven Decisions That Shaped History* (New York: Harper, 1950), 178.

31. For an extended discussion of this definition of American national goals, see John Lamberton Harper, *American Visions of Europe: Franklin D. Roosevelt, George F. Kennan, Dean G. Acheson* (New York: Cambridge University Press, 1994), 79–82.

32. One of the stories most often linked with Wallace describes his alleged observation to the wife of the Soviet ambassador that the war was being fought to "make sure that everybody in the world has the privilege of drinking a quart of milk a day." Wallace made the statement about war aims and postwar economic development, using the example of making milk available to all, in a speech, "The Price of Free World Victory," to the Free World Association in May 1942. He stated that he had made the comment "half in fun and half seriously" in a talk with Madame Litvinov to emphasize the point that "modern science, which is a by-product and an essential part of the people's revolution, has made it technologically possible to see that all of the people of the world get enough to eat" (Russell Lord, ed., *Democracy Reborn: Selections from the Public Papers of Henry A. Wallace* [New York: Reynal and Hitchcock, 1944], 193).

33. *New York Times,* July 10, 1944.

34. Cordell Hull, *Memoirs,* 2 vols. (New York: Macmillan, 1948), 2: 1314–15. For the reaction to Moscow, see also Keith Sainsbury, *The Turning Point: Roosevelt, Stalin, Churchill, and Chiang Kai-Shek, 1943—The Moscow, Cairo, and Teheran Conferences* (New York: Oxford University Press, 1985), 111–17.

35. John M. Blum, ed., *The Price of Vision: The Diary of Henry A. Wallace, 1942–1946* (Boston: Houghton Mifflin, 1973), 285.

36. For example, the shuttle bombing campaign from Soviet bases, while ultimately a failure, evinced a powerful manifestation of collaboration. See Richard C. Lukas, *Eagles East: The Army Air Forces and the Soviet Union, 1941–1945* (Tallahassee: Florida State University Press, 1970), 192–201, and the focused study by Mark Conversino, *Fighting with the Soviets: The Failure of Operation FRANTIC, 1944–1945* (Lawrence: University Press of Kansas, 1996). For intelligence cooperation, see Bradley F. Smith, *Sharing Secrets with Stalin: How the Allies Traded Intelligence, 1941–1945* (Lawrence: University Press of Kansas, 1996).

37. Among recent studies detailing these issues are Stephen E. Ambrose, *Eisenhower, 1989–1952* (New York: Simon and Schuster, 1983), Nigel Hamilton, *Monty: Master of the Battlefield, 1942–1944* (London: Hamish Hamilton, 1983), Omar Bradley, *A General's Life* (New York: Simon and Schuster, 1983), Richard Lamb,

Montgomery in Europe, 1943–1945: Success of Failure? (London: Buchanan and Enright, 1983), and Carlo D'Este, *Decision in Normandy* (London: Collins, 1983).

38. See Louis Morton, "Soviet Intervention in the War with Japan," *Foreign Affairs* 40 (July 1962): 653–62, and Barton J. Bernstein, "Writing, Righting, and Wronging the Historical Record: President Truman's Letter on His Atomic Bomb Decision," *Diplomatic History* 16, 1 (winter 1992): 163–73; recent debates about Soviet participation in the Pacific war are ably presented in Sigal, *Fighting to a Finish.*

39. Zubok, "Cooperation or 'Go Alone,' " 4.

40. That the three-phase construct by which Allied policies were to be implemented during the final stages of the war and the immediate postwar period treated military, political, and economic matters as an indissoluble whole was a given for memoirists and historians at the time. See, for example, Maurice Matloff, *Strategic Planning for Coalition Warfare, 1943–1944* (Washington, D.C.: OCMH, 1959), Robert W. Coakley and Richard M. Leighton, *Global Logistics and Strategy, 1943–1945* (Washington, D.C.: OCMH, 1968), and E. F. Penrose, *Economic Planning for the Peace* (Princeton: Princeton University Press, 1953). Unfortunately, most recent historical accounts follow exclusively one or another strand of coalition politics and thereby misconstrue and oversimplify the policymaking process.

41. David Eisenhower, *Eisenhower at War, 1943–1945* (New York: Random House, 1986), 448–49.

42. Useful summaries of these issues are found in Theodore A. Wilson, *The Marshall Plan, 1947–1951,* Headline Series no. 236 (New York: Foreign Policy Association, 1977), John Lukacs, *1945: Year Zero, The Shaping of the Modern Age* (Garden City, N.Y.: Doubleday, 1978; and Weinberg, *A World at Arms.*

43. For helpful discussions of wartime myopia in the United States, see the chapters in this volume by Randall B. Woods and Mark A. Stoler.

44. Memorandum by Gen. Henry H. Arnold [n.d.], Box 182, Henry H. Arnold Papers, Library of Congress, Washington, D.C.

45. For these claims, see S. L. A. Marshall, *Men Against Fire: The Problem of Battle Command in Future War* (New York: William Morrow, 1947); F. D. G. Williams, *SLAM: The Influence of S. L. A. Marshall on the United States Army* (Fort Monroe, Va.: TRADOC, 1990); Fredric Smoler, "The Secret of the Soldiers Who Didn't Shoot," *American Heritage,* March 1989, 37–45; and Martin Van Creveld, *Fighting Power: German and U.S. Army Performance, 1939–1945* (Westport, Conn.: Greenwood Press, 1982).

46. Melvin Small and J. David Singer, *Resort to Arms: International and Civil Wars, 1816–1980* (Beverly Hills, Calif.: Sage Publications, 1982), 102, table 5.1; one compilation concludes that the average daily casualty rate in eighty-two engagements during 1943–1944 was 1.2 percent for United States and 1.8 percent for German divisions; in comparison, Soviet casualties for the three phases of the Kursk battle in July 1943 have been estimated at 3.0 percent per day of combat and for the entire war at approximately 2.0 percent. British wastage rates would appear to be slightly less than the U.S. average. In contrast, casualty rates for USAAF and RAF bomber crews during the months of the most intense action over German-occupied Europe

hovered near 4.0 percent per mission. A 1.0 percent differential in an engagement of the magnitude of Kursk represents many thousands of lives lost. However, the record suggests that U.S. and Soviet battle losses during the period of heaviest sustained involvement with the enemy (which for the United States was July 1944–February 1945) was similar, once such factors as the far more substantial numbers of noncombatants in U.S. line units are adjusted for. This argument is confirmed by a glance at the experience of one U.S. division, the Twenty-eighth Infantry, in fall 1944. One study of the Siegfried Line battles reveals that the Twenty-eighth Division suffered 972 casualties on 10 November—a loss rate of 7.2 percent—and that other divisions fared even worse during this period of heavy fighting (Leonard Weinstein, "Rates of Advance in Infantry Division Attacks in the Normandy–Northern France and Siegfried Line Campaigns," Institute for Defense Analysis, Washington, D.C., December 1973, 67); see Edward Drea, *Unit Reconstitution: A Historical Perspective* (Ft. Leavenworth, Kans: Combat Studies Institute, 1983), for a full treatment of the Twenty-eighth Division in the Schmidt battle.

47. See D. Eisenhower, *Eisenhower At War*, 754–59.

48. Henry A. Kissinger, *A World Restored* (New York: Harper and Row, 1964), 109.

49. Mark A. Stoler, *George C. Marshall: Soldier-Statesman of the American Century* (Boston: Twayne Publishers, 1989), 127.

50. The butcher's bill for maintaining the wartime alliance—Stalin's wholesale deportations and such crimes as the Katyn Forest massacre, British policies in India, U.S. treatment of Japanese-Americans, and racial segregation—was enormous. Little attention has been accorded human rights issues within the wartime Allied coalition. See Theodore A. Wilson, "Questions Not Asked or Answers Ignored? Issues of Human Rights Within the World War II Allied Coalition," Working Paper, International Studies Seminar, University of Kansas (April 1994), and also Kurt Glaser and Stefan T. Possony, *Victims of Politics: The State of Human Rights* (New York: Columbia University Press, 1979), Edward A. Laing, "The Contribution of the Atlantic Charter to Human Rights Law and Humanitarian Universalism," *Willamette Law Review* 26 (1989): 112–28, and Michael Walzer, *Just and Unjust Wars*, rev. ed. (New York: Basic Books, 1990).

51. Victor Gollancz, *Shall Our Children Live or Die: A Reply to Lord Vansittart on the German Problem* (London: Victor Gollancz, 1942), 8.

52. Henry A. Wallace, "The Price of Free World Victory," May 8, 1942, Speech File, Box 63, Henry A. Wallace Papers, University of Iowa Department of Special Collections, Iowa City.

53. Recent analyses of the origins of the "unconditional surrender" policy include Warren F. Kimball, *The Juggler: Franklin Roosevelt as Wartime Statesman* (Princeton: Princeton University Press, 1991), and A. E. Campbell, "Franklin D. Roosevelt and Unconditional Surrender," in *Diplomacy and Intelligence During the Second World War*, ed. Richard Langhorne (Cambridge: Cambridge University Press, 1985).

54. See Kimball, *The Juggler*, 74, 76–77, and Harper, *American Visions of Europe*, 86–90.

55. Weinberg, *A World at Arms*, 798. This was borne out by the convoluted struggle

within the Roosevelt administration during winter–spring 1945 between advocates of harsh treatment of Germany and those who urged a softer, more pragmatic approach.

56. For the process and its implications, see Harper, *American Visions of Europe,* Campbell, "Franklin D. Roosevelt and Unconditional Surrender," and two helpful discussions of American wartime propaganda: James Warburg, *The Long Road Home: The Autobiography of a Maverick* (New York: Doubleday, 1964), and Clayton D. Laurie, *The Propaganda Warriors: America's Crusade Against Nazi Germany* (Lawrence: University Press of Kansas, 1996).

57. Almost everyone believed that a Democratic ticket headed by FDR would win in 1944 against any conceivable Republican combination (even one that included Douglas MacArthur) should the war in Europe not have ended. In June 1944, an internal poll, done for Vice Pres. Henry A. Wallace, confirmed large popular and electoral majorities for a Roosevelt-Wallace ticket and the Democratic party but revealed difficulties for any combination of Democratic candidates and, in particular, for Roosevelt running with a liberal such as Wallace or Justice William Douglas, were the war in Europe to have ended (HAW to FDR, "Polling Analysis Prepared by Louis Bean," May 12, 1944, Box 1174, Democratic National Committee Files, FDR Library [FDRL]). See also the collection of polls in Box 175, PSF: Political, FDR Papers (FDRP), FDRL.

58. Elliott Roosevelt, *As He Saw It* (New York: Duell, Sloan and Pearce, 1946), 129.

59. T/3 Daniel Camp, ETOUSA Research Branch, Interview Notes, October 2–3, 1944, based on interviews with wounded combat veterans, in Seventy-seventh Station Hospital, England, ETO–B17 Postwar Interview Notes, Box 1018–Entry 94, assistant secretary of defense (Manpower, Personnel, and Resources), Research Division, attitude reports of overseas personnel, 1942–1943, RG 94, NARA. See also Gerald F. Linderman, *The World Within War: America's Combat Experience in World War II* (New York: Free Press, 1997), 136–42.

60. Camp, Interview Notes, attitude reports, 1942–1943.

61. Harper, *American Visions of Europe,* 49.

62. Sigal, *Fighting to a Finish,* 23.

63. Ibid., 20.

64. Ibid., 23.

65. See Martin Gilbert, *Auschwitz and the Allies* (New York: Holt, Rinehart, and Winston, 1981), Michael Sherry, *The Rise of American Air Power* (New Haven: Yale University Press, 1987), and the closely reasoned critique of the "technological fanaticism" argument by Conrad C. Crane, *Bombs, Cities, and Civilians: American Airpower Strategy in World War II* (Lawrence: University Press of Kansas, 1993).

66. This judgment is fully explicated in Weinberg, *A World at Arms;* for a useful summary of his argument, see Weinberg, "D-Day: Analysis of Costs and Benefits," 324–26.

67. Maj. Gen. George V. Strong's congressional testimony, Executive Session, "The Strength of the Axis," October 21, 1943, HRH 219, CMH Archives, Washington, D.C.

68. Ibid.; during summer 1943, historian Kent Roberts Greenfield noted, following a discussion with Army Ground Forces Chief of Staff Gen. James Christiansen,

"I remarked that it had seemed . . . when it was decided to freeze the Army at 7,700,000, with 3,200,000 and the cream of quality allocated to the Air Forces, a fateful decision had been made, on the assumption that an air war plus the Russians could produce a decisive victory, and that this was to stake the future of the nation on a gamble. General Christiansen said that he felt that this was exactly true" (interview with Brig. Gen. James G. Christiansen, May 12, 1944, Box 19, RG 319, Records of the General Staff, OCMH Files, NARA).

69. Weinberg, "D-Day: Costs and Benefits," 325.

70. Weinberg, *A World at Arms*, 785.

71. Count Folke Bernadotte, *The Fall of the Curtain: The Last Days of the Third Reich* (London: Cassell and Company, 1945), 14.

72. Trudy McVicker, ed. and trans., "The World War Two Diary of Hans Arnold Siepmann," ms. in author's possession, 3; an impressive number of diaries, journals, and retrospective accounts offering similar testimony have come to light in recent years. See, for example, Marlis G. Steinert, *Hitler's War and the Germans: Public Mood and Attitude During the Second World War*, ed. and trans. Thomas E. J. DeWitt (Athens: Ohio University Press, 1977); Douglas Botting, *In the Ruins of the Reich* (London: Allen and Unwin, 1985); Anthony Read and David Fisher, *Berlin: Biography of a City* (London: Collins, 1994); and Johannes Steinhoff et al., eds., *Voices from the Third Reich: An Oral History* (Washington, D.C.: Regnery Gateway Press, 1989).

73. Kimball, *The Juggler*, 76; early condemnatory studies include James L. Chase, "Unconditional Surrender Reconsidered," *Political Science Quarterly* 70 (June 1955): 258–79; Kecskemeti, *Strategic Surrender*, and Michael Howard, *Grand Strategy, August 1942–September 1943*, 7 vols. (London: HMSO, 1970). See Raymond G. O'Connor, *Diplomacy for Victory: FDR and Unconditional Surrender* (New York: Norton, 1971), for a spirited if unconvincing defense of the policy.

74. Howard, *Grand Strategy*, 6: 285.

75. Weinberg, *A World at Arms*, 783.

76. Botting, *In the Ruins of the Reich*, 14.

77. Steinert, *Hitler's War and the Germans*, 313; also, a report of the Ohlendorf Bureau at the end of March 1945 traced the evolving attitude of the German public: "1. No one wants to lose the war. Everyone most fervently wished that we could win it. 2. Nobody believes anymore that we will win. The hitherto reliable flicker of hope is going out. 3. According to general conviction, if we lose the war we have ourselves to blame, and by that is meant not the little man but the leadership. 4. The Volk no longer has any confidence in the leadership. It is sharply critical of the Party, of certain leaders, and of propaganda. 5. For millions, the Fuhrer is the last support and the only hope, but even the Fuhrer is included more and more every day in the question of confidence and in criticism" (309).

78. See, for example, the insightful work of Omer Bartov, *Hitler's Army: Soldiers, Nazis, and War in the Third Reich* (New York: Oxford University Press, 1991).

79. Gerhard Weinberg succinctly describes what happened in practice: "Hitler had issued strict orders that all industrial, transportation and other facilities inside Germany should be destroyed lest they fall into Allied hands. Such orders had automatically

accompanied all other retreats forced on the Germans, and in most cases German commanders had carried them out ruthlessly to the greatest extent possible, with no thought to the future survival of people who had already suffered enormously. . . . That attitude started to change once the fighting moved inside Germany. Speer began to sabotage the sabotage orders, and many German commanders filed rather than implemented the orders to destroy everything that might support life in territory occupied by the Allies. As Allied forces advanced rapidly, they even encountered cases where the local German population tried to discourage the military from defending a particular community in order to keep it from being destroyed. . . . Many Germans, now losing confidence in the possibility of victory or even stalemate, preferred to spare their communities. . . . The white—or more likely grey—sheets of surrender appeared more and more frequently" (*A World at Arms*, 792).

80. "The End of the War—How the Events of Fifty Years Ago Shaped the World of Today: A Conversation between Chairman Sheldon Hackney and Historian Gerhard Weinberg," *Humanities* (March/April 1995): 53.

81. Klemens von Klemperer, *German Resistance Against Hitler: The Search for Allies Abroad, 1938–1945* (Oxford: Clarendon Press, 1992), 436.

82. Francis R. Nicosia and Lawrence D. Stokes, *Germans Against Nazism: Nonconformity, Opposition, and Resistance in the Third Reich, Essays in Honour of Peter Hoffmann* (New York: Peter Berg, 1990), 396.

83. A full discussion of these issues is found in Klemperer, *German Resistance Against Hitler,* passim.

84. Weinberg, *A World at Arms,* 783.

85. See the fascinating memoir by Bernadotte, *The Fall of the Curtain.*

86. Nicosia and Stokes, *Germans Against Nazism,* xii, 396.

87. Daniel J. Goldhagen, *Hitler's Willing Executioners: Ordinary Germans and the Holocaust* (Boston: Little, Brown, 1996).

88. A personal anecdote may drive home this point. In June 1994, I was invited by Princess Cruise Lines to serve as historian-in-residence on a so-called "D-Day Cruise," an ingenious marketing ploy to attract World War II veterans aboard the SS *Island Princess* for a voyage through the Baltic that wrapped up with a stopover in Le Havre and a tour of the Normandy beaches. The first dinner after departure from Southampton produced a revealing encounter with table companions, Mr. and Mrs. —— of Milwaukee, Wisconsin. Mr. —— introduced himself as a retired engineer and volunteered the information that he was not a World War II veteran, that he came from a German background, and that his wife's parents had emigrated from Croatia—significant items of information as it proved. He expressed great delight about having a professional historian as a tablemate and between courses chronicled an impressive number of books he had read in recent years. Mr. —— 's reading list, notably, emphasized biographies of Nazi leaders. His monologue concluded with a query put to me as an "objective" historian. "Is it not interesting," mildly asked Mr. —— , that Napoleon, once characterized as evil incarnate, now is widely admired as a statesman who sought to unify Europe?" Did I not think that Adolf Hitler would someday be admired in much the same way that people in the late twentieth century regard Napoleon? My answer

was an adamant no. I stated that, history's addiction to moral relativism aside, the Nazi responsibility for the Holocaust forever invalidated any possibility that posterity will view Hitler as a statesman.

89. Bernard Bailyn, *The Peopling of North America: An Introduction* (Cambridge: Harvard University Press, 1984), and *Voyagers to the West: A Passage in the Peopling of America on the Eve of the Revolution* (New York: Knopf, 1986).

90. Theodore A. Wilson, *The First Summit: Roosevelt and Churchill at Placentia Bay, 1941,* rev. ed. (Lawrence: University Press of Kansas, 1991), xv–xvi.

91. Stephen Jay Gould, *Wonderful Life: The Burgess Shale and the Nature of History* (New York: W. W. Norton, 1989), 283.

92. Ibid., 284.

93. Gerhard Weinberg, *World in the Balance: Behind the Scenes in World War II* (Hanover, N.H.: Dartmouth University Press, 1981), xii.

94. U.S. Strategic Bombing Survey, *Effects of Strategic Bombing on Japan's War Economy,* Report no. 53 (Washington, D.C.: GPO, 1946), 57; quoted in Sigal, *Fighting to a Finish,* 4.

95. Lukacs, *1945: Year Zero,* 20.

2. The View from Poland

Anna M. Cienciala

V-E Day in the United States and Western Europe saw parades and rejoicing, but that day had little meaning in Eastern Europe, because most of the region had been liberated by the Red Army and not by the western Allies, as its peoples had hoped. Both the populations of Eastern Europe and their exiled leaders in the west knew that Soviet liberation would not mean independence. Of course, East Europeans were grateful to the Red Army for driving out the Germans. However, with the exception of Czechoslovakia and most of Yugoslavia, they did not welcome new governments that owed their existence largely, or solely, to Soviet support, nor the terror that accompanied them. Thus the victory celebrations in Eastern Europe, held on May 9—the day the Germans surrendered to Soviet commanders in Berlin—were organized affairs rather than spontaneous outpourings of joy by the people. This was especially true in Poland, where the Communist Lublin government—which had moved from Lublin to Warsaw in February 1945—organized a victory parade in the ruined capital. These ruins symbolized the end of Polish hopes for independence. To understand this situation, one must look at the policy of the western powers toward the USSR, at Soviet policy toward other East European states, and particularly at the evolution of the "Polish question" in the course of World War II.

Like other East Europeans, the Poles had expected western troops to liberate their country. Their political leaders assumed that the western powers would be driven to oppose Soviet domination of Eastern Europe because it would pose a threat to Western Europe as well. Therefore, they expected western armies to reach most countries in the region before the Red Army, either through the Balkans, or in case of a German collapse in the west, by driving through Germany. In late 1944 and early 1945, when it was clear that liberation would come with the Red Army, Polish leaders hoped that at least a western military or diplomatic mission or both would supervise any interim administration. The Yalta Conference decisions were a tremendous shock and were rejected by the Polish government-in-exile, which, though located in London, enjoyed the support of the vast majority of Poles at home and abroad. Still, some Polish politicians both in the west and in Poland believed that the western powers would enforce the provisions of the Atlantic Charter of 1941 and the Declaration on Liberated Europe agreed upon at Yalta by Pres. Franklin D. Roosevelt, Prime Minister Winston S. Churchill, and Premier Joseph V. Stalin. According to this declaration, the Allied governments would help establish representative, provisional governments, which would proceed to hold free elections. Whatever the thoughts of Roosevelt and Churchill, Stalin had his own interpretation of this agreement. Many years later, Vyacheslav M. Molotov—commissar for Foreign Affairs from 1939 to 1949 and 1953 to 1956—reminisced about the Yalta declaration: "The Americans submitted a draft. I brought it to Stalin and said: 'This is going too far.' 'Don't worry,' he said, 'work it out. We can deal with it in our own way later. The point is the correlation of forces."[1]

It is true that the correlation of forces at this time placed the USSR in a position to control most of Eastern Europe, but this was not due to military factors alone. Pres. Franklin D. Roosevelt and American military leaders, who were greatly preoccupied with the need for Moscow's aid against Japan after Germany's defeat in Europe, had accepted Soviet predominance in Poland and the whole region by fall 1943. British Prime Minister Winston S. Churchill did not desire such an outcome but failed to persuade his American partner to launch a secondary invasion of the Balkans instead of southern France in summer 1944. Therefore, he signed the famous percentage agreement with Stalin in October 1944, assigning Romania and Bulgaria to the Soviet Union, Greece to Great Britain, and splitting British and Soviet influence fifty–fifty in Hungary and Yugoslavia. Nonetheless, he still retained hopes for an Allied landing in Istria until spring 1945.[2]

Stalin, for his part, took care not to provoke his Western allies. It is true that he acted quickly to install a Communist government in Romania, but this was an Axis ally. Moreover, like the czars, he regarded it as belonging to Russia's sphere of influence. Indeed, Churchill had consigned Romania to Russia in October 1944, and the western powers did not oppose the establishment of a clearly Communist government in Bucharest.[3] It was the same with Bulgaria, which had sided with Germany, though it had not sent troops to fight the Russians.[4] The United States and Great Britain also recognized the new Yugoslav government, though the Communist partisan leader, Josip Broz Tito—who had received British military support—used terror to secure an election victory in his country in November 1945.[5] Thus, Churchill's agreement with Stalin for a fifty–fifty share of influence in Yugoslavia came to nought. Stalin proceeded very carefully in Hungary, even though it was also an ally of Nazi Germany. Here he allowed completely free elections in November 1945, but the Communists won only 17 percent of the vote. It seems most likely that he sanctioned this course because, given the great popularity of land reform with the peasants, the Hungarian Communists predicted a landslide victory. Stalin also seems to have assumed that a Communist victory in free elections would help him elsewhere. Thus sometime in 1945, he told Hungarian Communist leaders that they would have to wait ten to fifteen years before taking full power. He intimated this delay would be a trade-off for ongoing repression in Poland and thus the imposition of Communism on that country.[6]

In Soviet relations with East European states—both Allied and hostile— Stalin made an exception for Czechoslovakia, whose president, Edward Beneš, had clearly indicated he would not pursue any policy not approved by Moscow. The Czechoslovak president signed an alliance with the USSR in December 1943. Later, he negotiated in Moscow for a coalition government with Communists in key posts and a radical reform program. He assumed that this would preserve Czechoslovakia's prewar territory as well as its democratic system. He was, however, bitterly disappointed on the first count when the Red Army and the NKVD set up local government bodies in Subcarpathian Ruthenia, which "petitioned" for union with the Soviet Ukrainian Republic. It is true Beneš had hinted to Stalin that he would be willing to sacrifice the region, if necessary, to the USSR, but he viewed this as a gesture of friendship and did not expect its implementation. Indeed, Stalin had not shown any interest, but at war's end he moved to annex the region on the basis of self-determination, as demanded by duly coached local representatives.[7]

As the Red Army and the NKVD flowed into Slovakia and the Czech lands, they also helped Communists set up local government councils, which they controlled. As elsewhere, so too in Slovakia: Soviet troops indulged in violence, pillage, and rape. Furthermore, as in Poland, thousands of people were arrested; some five thousand were deported to the USSR, though mostly from Slovakia, which had been a Fascist, puppet state dependent on Nazi Germany.[8] Beneš was deeply worried by these developments but hoped all problems would be solved in the near future. He believed that democracy would survive in Czechoslovakia because of its native roots and because Stalin would not need to impose Communism on a friendly country. He was right, but only until February 1948. In fact, as in Hungary, so too in Czechoslovakia: Stalin at first decided to move slowly. It is likely the Soviet dictator allowed Czechoslovakia more democracy than elsewhere in Eastern Europe because Beneš was no threat; Communists held the key posts, and the Soviet dictator wished to avoid provoking the western powers. He could also use democratic Czechoslovakia, together with Hungary, as a contrast to Communist repression in Poland, which could be blamed on Polish reactionaries and overzealous Polish Communists. Some years later, Václav Kopecký, a leading Czechoslovak Communist, said that his party could have taken power in 1945 but did not do so for "international reasons" and because this did not fit Soviet policy at the time.[9]

Despite his alliance with the USSR, Beneš had very much hoped that Gen. George S. Patton's troops—which reached Pilsen—would liberate Prague, so he was greatly disappointed when they withdrew from Czechoslovakia.[10] In fact, Gen. Dwight D. Eisenhower refused Churchill's plea that Patton be allowed to march on Prague, just as he refused his pleas, and Patton's, that American troops take Berlin and not withdraw to the occupation zones in Germany and Austria, as agreed at Yalta.[11] For the next three years, a fragile democracy existed in Czechoslovakia until the Communists seized total power in the Soviet-supported coup of February 1948.[12]

Poland played a special role in western-Soviet relations for three reasons. First, Poland was an ally of Great Britain, which had gone to war with Nazi Germany when the latter attacked the country in early September 1939. Britain was Poland's wartime ally (based on the Mutual Assistance Treaty of August 25, 1939), and British opinion strongly supported the restoration of an independent Poland after the war, as did the Polish armed forces fighting alongside the British. Thus, Churchill had to tread very carefully on the Polish question. Second, Pres. Franklin D. Roosevelt viewed the support of Polish-American voters as vital for a Democratic victory and for his own reelection in November 1944, so he had to avoid alienating them by openly abandoning the goal of a restored, independent Poland, though his private views were a different matter. (As it turned out, Polish-Americans voted overwhelmingly for Roosevelt though their vote was not crucial to his victory.) Finally, Moscow viewed Soviet control of the country as a vital interest of the USSR. Stalin, like the rulers of Imperial Russia before him, saw Poland as a Russian-controlled buffer against invasion from the west, though it could serve just as well as a stepping stone to Germany. Indeed, this was how Lenin saw it in 1920, and Stalin most probably viewed it as such in 1944 and 1945. However, Stalin had to tread carefully so as not to strain relations with his western allies, whom he always suspected of angling for a separate peace with Hitler.

Thus, it is not surprising that Poland constituted a major problem in relations between the western powers and the USSR. Still, the British did not oppose Stalin's territorial acquisitions in Poland. Yet Britain was Poland's ally when Stalin seized the eastern part of the country in accordance with the then widely suspected but unconfirmed Secret Protocol attached to the Nazi-Soviet Nonaggression Pact of August 23, 1939.[13] The official British protest as voiced by Prime Minister Neville Chamberlain was rather formal. Churchill, then first lord of the admiralty, went further; he said the Russian advance into Poland was a safety measure against the Nazi menace and created an "eastern front" that Germany would not dare assail.[14] The British attitude stemmed not only from wishful thinking but also, and more important, from the fact that all British governments since 1920 had considered the Curzon Line—proposed as an armistice line between Polish and Soviet armies by Foreign Secretary Lord Curzon in July 1920—as the rightful Polish-Soviet frontier.[15] The British justified this view on the basis of Soviet security needs, or because the Poles were a minority east of the line, or on both factors. In fact, the Poles formed an overall minority of about 6 million of 14.5 million people, with local majorities in the cities and districts of Wilno (Vilnius) and Lwów (Lvov).[16] Many Britons believed, however, that there were hardly any Poles in eastern Poland and that the local Ukrainians and Belorussians wanted union with the USSR, although the attraction the Soviets had exerted on these peoples vanished with the beginning of forced collectivization in 1929 and 1930. Moreover, the Ukrainians of East Galicia (now western Ukraine) wanted to have their own state. But few people in Britain had much information on this question, and in any case the British government wanted to draw Stalin away from Hitler; therefore, Soviet possession of eastern Poland could not stand in the way. However, British efforts in this direction were unsuccessful until Hitler's attack on the USSR on June 22, 1941.

Meanwhile, the Polish government-in-exile, which had moved to London after the fall of France in June 1940, refused to recognize the Soviet annexation of former eastern Poland. They had good reason not to do so. The USSR was aligned with Nazi Germany, and Soviet terror reigned in the annexed territories. Between September 17, 1939, and June 22, 1941, Soviet authorities killed an estimated 400,000 Poles (the Germans killed an estimated 100,000); they also deported between 1.25 million and 1.5 million Polish citizens. Just over half of these deportees (52 percent) were ethnic Poles, followed by Ukrainians, Jews, and Belorussians. Most of these people were transported to Siberian labor camps in atrocious conditions, which caused many deaths along the way, especially among the very old and very young. An estimated one-third of the deported Poles who reached their destinations died of malnutrition and exhaustion by summer 1941. Furthermore, Soviet-style rigged elections to West Ukrainian and West Belorussian soviets (legislatures) took place in late October 1939. These soviets then petitioned the Supreme Soviet of the USSR requesting union with the respective Soviet republics, which the Supreme Council granted in early November 1939. At that time, all persons living in former eastern Poland automatically became Soviet citizens.[17]

Such policies could only strengthen traditional Polish distrust of Russia. Nevertheless, after Hitler's attack on the USSR, Polish-Soviet negotiations opened in London. Aided by British Foreign Secretary Anthony Eden, who played the role of mediator, the Polish premier and commander in chief, Gen. Władysław Sikorski, and Soviet ambassador Ivan M. Maisky signed an agreement to restore mutual relations on July 30, 1941. This was a compromise: the Soviet Union declared its 1939 treaties with Germany to be null and void but did not recognize the prewar Polish-Soviet frontier. The two countries agreed to cooperate fully in fighting Germany. All Poles in the USSR were to be "amnestied" (a term demanded by the Soviet side), and a Polish army was to be formed there. An army was raised, led by Gen. Władysław Anders, but lack of supplies, Soviet insistence that it be sent to the front piecemeal—which Sikorski and Anders opposed—British need for troops in the Middle East, and Stalin's willingness to get rid of it combined to make the army leave the Soviet Union for Iran in summer 1942. It became the Polish Second Corps, which fought in Italy as part of the British Eighth Army.[18]

Stalin broke off relations with the Polish government in London in late April 1943. He justified this drastic step on the grounds of the Poles' reaction to the German announcement on April 13 of the discovery in Katyn Forest (near Gnezdovo, just north of Smolensk) of the mass graves of several thousand Polish officers, who the Germans claimed had been killed by the Soviets. These were some of the officers who had been taken prisoner by the Soviets in 1939 but could not be found when the Polish army was being formed in the USSR in 1941 and 1942. Polish military and diplomatic authorities in the USSR had asked their Soviet counterparts in vain for the whereabouts of some fifteen thousand missing army officers, policemen, border guards, and officials, who were known to have been captured, or arrested, and were deported to camps in Russia and the Ukraine. Correspondence with their families had ceased in spring 1940. The Soviets had always replied that all Polish prisoners of war had been released. After the German announcement, the Polish government asked the International Red Cross to investigate the Katyn massacre; coincidentally, the German government made the same request. Stalin made this a pretext for accusing the Polish government of collaboration with the Germans and broke off relations with the London Poles. Soviet authorities accused the Germans of perpetrating the massacre. The Soviet cover-up of the Katyn affair lasted forty-seven years, when it was finally admitted that the prisoners had been killed by the NKVD in spring 1940.[19]

Having broken relations with the Polish government in London in late April 1943, Stalin conditioned their resumption on the Poles' condemnation of their decision to request an investigation of the Katyn massacre, on dropping allegedly "Fascist" ministers—i.e., those openly distrustful of the USSR—and on the formal recognition of the Curzon Line as the Polish-Soviet frontier. The Soviet government justified the last demand by claiming that the elections of October 1939 (to the soviets of western Ukraine and

Belorussia) expressed the will of the people to join the USSR. However, the Polish government's agreement to the first two demands would have made it appear to most Poles as a puppet of Moscow, and the third would have meant giving up 51 percent of Poland's prewar territory, with several million Poles, without the consent of the Polish people and without any guarantees of compensation or of future Polish independence. At this time, most Poles saw the restoration of prewar Poland as elementary justice. They also viewed the prewar Polish-Soviet frontier as a requirement for Polish security against the USSR. Finally, most Poles believed that if this prewar frontier could not be restored, then Poland should at least keep the preponderantly Polish cities and regions of Wilno in the northeast and Lwów, with the oil fields of Drohobycz and Borysów in the southeast. Indeed, even the Polish Communists, who supported this cession, avoided disavowing the prewar frontier for fear of losing the little support they had in Poland. Therefore, they spoke of settling the Polish-Soviet border after the war on the basis of self-determination, implying that the predominantly Polish regions would stay in Poland. In view of all this, the Polish government's agreement to Soviet demands would have resulted in a loss of credibility with the vast majority of Poles at home and abroad and above all with the Polish armed forces in the west (some 115,000 in 1943 and 200,000 by 1945) and the Home Army in Poland (about 300,000 in 1943 and 400,000 in 1944).[20] Therefore, it is not difficult to surmise that in making these demands Stalin aimed either at discrediting the Polish government in London or splitting it and drawing some of its members into a future Polish government under his control.

Indeed, the Soviet dictator had begun preparing new Polish cadres well before April 1943. Having killed off the prewar Polish Communist leaders in the purges of 1936–1938 and having dissolved the party in 1938, he selected a new, embryonic leadership. It was active in Paris as the Initiative Group in January 1939–spring 1940, after which its members were transferred to the USSR. They began political training there in fall 1940, at which time Stalin also recruited some Polish officers from those who had declared readiness to serve in the Red Army and had thus survived the massacre. They were instructed to draw up plans for a Polish division in the Red Army, which was to be ready for action in July 1941. After the Sikorski-Maisky agreement of July 30, 1941, however, these officers were ordered to join the Polish army being raised in the USSR under the command of General Anders and to act as informers for Moscow. Most of them, however, did not do so and chose to leave with him for Iran in summer 1942; only a few stayed behind, casting their lot with Stalin.

Thus, the Sikorski-Maisky agreement did not prevent Stalin from nurturing this alternative cadre of Polish Communist leaders. In fact, the leaders of the new Communist party, now called the *Polska Partia Robotnicza* (PPR, Polish Workers' Party) and formed under the watchful eyes of Stalin and Comintern leader Georgii M. Dimitriev, first tried to fly to Poland in September, but the plane crashed on takeoff at Vyazma with the loss of one life. In late December 1941, that is, after Sikorski's visit to Russia and the signature of a Polish-Soviet Friendship Treaty, they parachuted from a Soviet plane into the suburbs of Warsaw. Their immediate task was to supply military intelligence to Moscow, recruit supporters, and organize military units. Their ultimate goal was to split the underground movement and build up a force outnumbering those loyal to the Polish government in London. They failed to achieve this, however, until the last months of the war, when they took power with the massive aid of the Red Army and the NKVD.

In early February 1943, as the Germans were capitulating in Stalingrad and thus before the discovery of the Katyn graves, Stalin told Wanda Wasilewska, the key pro-Soviet Polish Communist leader in the USSR, that he expected a break with the London Poles. He said that a new Polish center must be established in the USSR, even proposing its name: *Związek Patriotów Polskich w ZSRR* (ZPP, Union of Polish Patriots in the USSR). The first issue of its flagship newspaper, *Wolna Polska* (Free Poland), appeared on March 1, 1943. Meanwhile, in February, the PPR leaders in German-occupied Warsaw proposed talks to the underground authorities on establishing a new Polish government; they even said General Sikorski (head of the London government) would not be excluded but demanded a share in the command of the Home Army.[21] Nothing came of these talks, but Stalin went on with his plans while carefully adjusting his moves to the susceptibilities of his western allies.

The Soviet dictator's Polish policy was greatly aided by the fact that American and British leaders had different approaches to solving the Polish problem. Churchill supported a Polish-Soviet frontier on the Curzon Line with large though unspecified territorial compensation for Poland at German expense in the West. His key assumption was that a voluntary agreement by the Polish government to cede formerly Polish eastern territories to the USSR would ensure Stalin's acceptance of an independent, postwar Poland, a goal warmly supported by British public opinion. Thus, Churchill's aim was to secure a wartime Polish-Soviet agreement that would accept the new frontier in principle but that would postpone negotiations until the peace conference and therefore accord with the principles of the Atlantic Charter. If the existing Polish government decided that it could not proceed in this way, Churchill favored establishing a new one headed by Stanisław Mikołajczyk. The latter was the number-two leader of the Polish Peasant party, the largest in Poland,[22] and he had succeeded Sikorski as premier after the general's death in an air crash off Gibraltar on July 4, 1943. Churchill believed that if Mikołajczyk, along with his Peasant party and some Socialist supporters, formed a new government and recognized the Curzon Line as the Polish-Soviet frontier in return for a promise of gaining German territory, then British and Polish opinion would accept this as a just solution and Stalin would accept an independent Poland. At the same time, the British prime minister feared that any forcible solution of the Polish-Soviet dispute to the advantage of the USSR would be decried in Britain as another Munich, and this he was determined to avoid. In the long term, he also wanted an independent Poland in order to maintain some British influence in Eastern Europe and prevent its total domination by the USSR. President Roosevelt had his own ideas on Poland but allowed Churchill to lay the groundwork.

As the Red Army approached the prewar Polish-Soviet border in late 1943, Churchill took the initiative. He proposed to Stalin at the Tehran Conference of November 28–December 2 that Poland "be moved West, like a soldier taking two steps left close," which he illustrated on a map with the aid of two matches. He said he was sure the London Poles would accept this and that Polish-Soviet relations would resume. Stalin agreed since he had suggested a similar though even grander proposal on Polish frontiers to Anthony Eden in Moscow in December 1941, i.e., the Curzon Line as Poland's border in the east, with East Prussia and the Oder Line in the West. However, at Tehran he expressed reservations on dealing with the existing Polish government. President Roosevelt told Stalin he supported Churchill's proposal but hoped the Soviet leader would understand that he could not do so publicly, for he needed Polish-American votes in the upcoming presidential election. Stalin said he understood. Roosevelt also said he did not intend to go to war with Russia over the Baltic states but thought "world opinion would want some expression of the will of the people." Stalin answered this could be done according to the Soviet constitution, but he could not agree to any form of international control. Thus, at Tehran, the three leaders basically reached the agreement that the Polish-Soviet frontier should follow the Curzon Line and that Poland should be compensated with German territory in the west. The British and Americans generally understood this to mean East Prussia, except for Königsberg, later Kaliningrad, which was to go to Russia, and restoration of the Polish part of Upper Silesia. Stalin also planned to give Poland German Pomerania up to and presumably including Stettin—though his thoughts on the latter are not clear—and all of Upper Silesia, but he did not push these demands at Tehran. Here it was assumed that some arrangement on Polish frontiers would be formalized by securing the Polish government's consent. Roosevelt also indicated his agreement to the Soviet annexation of the Baltic states.[23]

When Churchill put the Tehran proposal to Mikołajczyk in late January and early February 1944, the latter said that prior to the peace conference he could only accept a demarcation line between Polish and Soviet administrations that would leave the preponderantly Polish cities of Wilno and Lwów on the Polish side. The British prime minister then publicized the Tehran agreements, presenting them as his own in a speech in Parliament on February 22, 1944. However, he proposed the Mikołajczyk compromise in his correspondence with Stalin in spring 1944 and also warned against Soviet interference in Polish internal affairs. Stalin, for his part, insisted that the Polish government accept all his demands.[24]

In late June 1944, after his return from the United States, where he saw President Roosevelt, Mikołajczyk confidentially told Victor Lebedev, the Soviet ambassador to all the emigré governments in London, that he could not accept the Curzon Line. Instead, he offered a demarcation line based on it, intimating that it would become the postwar Polish-Soviet frontier. On that same day, June 22, Stalin recognized the Home National Council, i.e., the Communist-dominated surrogate parliament (*Krajowa Rada Narodowa*, or KRN, established in Warsaw on January 1, 1943) as the true representative of the Polish people. On June 23, Ambassador Lebedev put the Soviet demands to Mikołajczyk on a take-it-or-leave-it-basis, and the latter declined. A month later, on July 22, 1944, when the Red Army was entering what the Soviet government recognized as Poland, Stalin unveiled his own embryo Polish government, the *Polski Komitet Wyzwolenia Narodowego* (PKWN, or Polish Committee of National Liberation), made up of members of the Union of Polish Patriots (ZPP) and the Home National Council.[25]

Mikołajczyk learned of this event on his way to Moscow, where he traveled in late July after seeing Roosevelt in Washington in June. In fact, the president had advised him to make changes in his government and to go to Moscow to talk with Stalin and the Poles there. He told Mikołajczyk that he had *not* accepted the Curzon Line at Tehran and, at least according to a Polish account of the conversations, promised that he would try to get Lwów, Tarnopol, and Drohobycz for Poland. At the same time, however, he assured Stalin that he continued to consider all matters between them in the spirit of Tehran and inquired only about Lwów.[26]

The Polish premier, accompanied by his foreign minister Tadeusz Romer and National Council chairman Stanisław Grabski, was in Moscow from July 30 to August 10. The men spoke with Stalin and with members of the PKWN, but Mikołajczyk could not accept the demands he had rejected earlier, nor the PKWN demand, seconded by Stalin, that he agree to only three out of fifteen seats in a new Polish government and thus be a prime minister without power. Although Mikołajczyk rejected these proposals, he said he would put them before his cabinet. He also secured Stalin's vague promise of help for the Warsaw Uprising against the Germans, which broke out during his stay in Moscow on August 1, 1944.[27]

Stalin, however, not only refused to help the Warsaw insurgents but also refused permission for Allied planes to land behind Soviet lines after dropping supplies over Warsaw. (RAF planes with multinational crews, including Poles, had been flying from southern Italy to Warsaw and back without landing, suffering great losses). He finally agreed to this in mid-September as his troops were taking east-bank Warsaw. At this time, one flight of American fortresses from England, which was allowed to land, dropped supplies to the Warsaw insurgents on September 18, but this was too little, too late. Meanwhile, Marshal Konstantin K. Rokossovsky's First Ukrainian Front stood by as the Germans crushed the uprising and then destroyed 80 percent of the city. It is true that five German divisions had stemmed the advance of Rokossovsky's vanguard in early August, but they were soon defeated, and the general's War Council informed Stalin they could start operations to take the city at the end of August if they received support from Soviet forces to their south. However, Rokossovsky's army group received no such support or orders to advance, so it stopped after taking the eastern part of Warsaw, Praga. There was one attempt by a unit of Polish troops in the Rokossovsky army group to help the insurgents by landing on the west bank, but they had no Soviet artillery or air support, suffered great losses, and were forced to retreat. Rokossovsky's troops did not enter the ruined capital until mid-January 1945. Meanwhile, the Red Army advanced on all other sectors of the front.

The Polish leaders in London were strongly criticized, both then and later, for sanctioning the uprising in the absence of Polish-Soviet diplomatic and military relations and in view of the demonstrated Soviet hostility to the Home Army. By late July, however, while German troops were in full retreat, the German military authorities in Warsaw were clearly determined to make the city a fortress. Russian guns could be heard on the eastern outskirts, and Polish-language radio broadcasts from the Soviet lines, as well as from Moscow, called on the population to help the Red Army take the city, as did Gen. Michał Rola-Żymierski, commander of the First Polish Army in the Rokossovsky army group. Finally, Mikołajczyk was on his way to Moscow, and the Home Army leaders expected him to secure at least a local Polish-Soviet military agreement. This expectation was based on their belief, shared by Mikołajczyk, that Stalin wanted to press on as fast as possible to Berlin; therefore, he would help liberate Warsaw, the key road and railway center between Moscow and Berlin. In view of these factors, the Polish underground army commander, Gen. Tadeusz Bór-Komorowski, was given permission by the Polish government in late July to start the uprising when he believed the time was right. With the Red Army expected to take the city in a few days, the Home Army leaders felt they had to liberate Warsaw—or confirm Soviet and PKWN claims that they were not fighting the Germans. There was also a very important political aspect to the decision for an uprising at this time. The Home Army and underground political leaders aimed to defeat the Germans in the city and act as hosts to the Russian forces as they entered, thus forcing the latter either to recognize them as partners in negotiations on postwar Poland or to crush them in full view of world opinion. Instead of moving to take Warsaw, however, Rokossovsky's army group stopped in mid-September after taking the city's eastern suburb of Praga.

The Polish government in London and Polish communities in the west were horrified. British and American public opinion also expressed shock as the uprising dragged on without Soviet help. The London Poles begged the Allies to pressure Stalin to help the insurgents. Although the Soviet leader had promised Mikołajczyk to do everything possible to help, he does not seem to have had any intention of doing so—unless, perhaps, the Polish premier joined the PKWN. The result was that the uprising ended on October 2, and the Germans destroyed most of the west bank section of the city, with the loss of an estimated 250,000 lives out of a total prewar population of some 1.7 million.[28] The Red Army did not enter Warsaw until January 14, 1945.

This calamity portended another—the fate of democracy in Poland. Churchill wanted a new Polish government dominated by Mikołajczyk and his supporters. Roosevelt, however, was ready to accept one dominated by Stalin's nominees, as long as it was headed by Mikołajczyk, so as to make it acceptable to Polish Americans. In February 1944, without consulting Churchill, the president granted Stalin's request to allow two Polish Americans to travel as "private citizens" to Moscow. They flew to Russia in May 1944, on U.S. and Soviet military aircraft, via Alaska. One of these travelers was Oskar Lange, a freshly minted U.S. citizen (October 1943), and a professor of Economics at the University of Chicago. He had never concealed his radical Socialist views and had close ties with Polish-American Communists. Most important, he was a personal friend of Wanda Wasilewska from prewar days and thus an open supporter of the Union of Polish Patriots, the Kościuszko Division (the embryo of a new, Communist-led Polish army in the USSR), and the KRN. Lange had corresponded with Wasilewska through the Soviet consulate in New York at least since January 1944, always insisting that Mikołajczyk be part of any new Polish government, which was also Roosevelt's condition for recognizing such a government. There are indications that the president was kept informed: Lange's letters to Wasilewska were in English, though she did not know this language. And Lange was in constant touch with officials of the Foreign Nationalities Branch (FNB) of the Office of Strategic Services (OSS), who reported to the State Department. The second traveler to Russia in May 1944 was Father Stanisław Orlemański, a parish priest from Springfield, Massachusetts, whose naive populism led him to support the Communist-led Kościuszko League in the United States. (It propagandized the Kościuszko Division and thus the ideas of the Union of Polish Patriots.)[29]

During Lange's visit to Moscow, Stalin treated him as an unofficial envoy of President Roosevelt. Indeed, the professor's confirmation to Stalin that the American president would recognize a new Polish government if it included Mikołajczyk, and the positive attitudes displayed by Lange, U.S. Ambassador W. Averell Harriman, and British Ambassador Sir Archibald Clark-Kerr toward the delegates of the Communist-dominated Home Council, who arrived in Moscow during Lange's stay there, probably encouraged Stalin to form the PKWN in late July 1944. However, the anger of Polish Americans, first over the Lange-Orlemański trip, when it became known, and also Anglo-American anger over Stalin's treatment of the Warsaw Uprising delayed the establishment of a new Polish government dominated by Polish Communists and headed by Mikołajczyk. Nevertheless, the Lange-Orlemański venture demonstrated Roosevelt's readiness to accept such a solution. This is also revealed by his remark, noted by Harriman in May 1944, that "he didn't care whether the countries bordering on Russia became communized."[30] The president's thoughts were, however, unknown to all but a chosen few. In November 1944, he was reelected for the fourth time. Polish Americans voted for him on the strength of his promise to support the establishment of a strong, independent Poland and because most of them supported his New Deal policies.

Meanwhile, at Churchill's urging, Mikołajczyk traveled again with Tadeusz Romer and Stanisław Grabski to Moscow, where they stayed five days, from October 13 to 18, 1944. They held talks with Stalin as well as with Churchill and Eden, and Ambassador Harriman sat in as an observer. Mikołajczyk also talked briefly with Bolesław Bierut, a veteran Communist (alleged by some to have been an NKVD agent). Bierut was president of the Communist-dominated KRN, which acted as a surrogate parliament; and a radical Socialist, Edward Osóbka-Morawski, was head of the PKWN. Mikołajczyk now learned for the first time that the Curzon Line had been agreed on as the Polish-Soviet frontier by the Big Three at Tehran and that Stalin's demand that Königsberg, East Prussia, go to the USSR had not been granted. Still, Churchill at first supported Mikołajczyk's proposal that the Curzon Line be recognized as a demarcation line between the Polish and

Soviet administrations, though leaving Lwów on the Polish side. The British prime minister also tried to persuade Stalin to allow at least 50 percent of the cabinet seats in the new government to go to Mikołajczyk and his supporters. Stalin, however, insisted on the immediate acceptance of the Curzon Line, which he had already obtained from the PKWN in a secret treaty signed on July 26. He also insisted that only 25 percent of cabinet seats go to non-Lublin Poles. (The PKWN was located in Lublin, a city about one hundred miles southeast of Warsaw, until February 1945, when it moved to Warsaw).

Churchill pressed Mikołajczyk to accept these conditions in order to preserve his chances of playing a significant role in postwar Poland. Mikołajczyk, however, said he could not go beyond his cabinet's resolution of August 29, which agreed to the postwar settlement of the Polish-Soviet frontier by the Polish parliament on the basis of self-determination. This resolution implied that the preponderantly Ukrainian and Belorussian regions would go to the Ukrainian and Belorussian Soviet republics, while preponderantly Polish areas would stay with Poland. In early November, under great British pressure to give a final answer to Soviet demands, the Polish cabinet rejected them because there was no guarantee of Polish independence, nor of what Poland would obtain as compensation from Germany. (The British did not want to spell out future German losses for fear of strengthening German resistance and thus prolonging the war.) Churchill proposed an Anglo-Soviet guarantee of Polish independence, which the Polish government found insufficient; Roosevelt said he was constitutionally unable to offer such a guarantee. Mikołajczyk resigned at the end of November, as did the Peasant party ministers and a few other supporters, but he had hopes for the future. He believed that his party, the largest in Poland, would win free elections, though this would be possible only if he and his supporters joined a new Polish government acceptable to Stalin. Churchill promised his support, and Mikołajczyk decided to bide his time.[31]

By February 1945, the prospects for an independent Poland were dim. The Polish Committee of National Liberation had proclaimed itself the Provisional Government of Poland on December 31, 1944, and was recognized as such by Stalin four days later, despite appeals from Roosevelt and Churchill that he wait until the upcoming Big Three conference. Meanwhile, the situation in Poland was grim. The underground leaders treated the new government as a usurper; the Peasant party and the Polish Socialist party disowned their left-wing token parties as represented in the provisional government. The Red Army and the NKVD were arresting and deporting Home Army officers both east and west of the Curzon Line while pressuring rank-and-file soldiers to join the First Polish Army advancing alongside the Red

Army. The NKVD was also arresting all the civilian administrators loyal to the Polish government in London as they came out of the underground to assume their duties. Indeed, Gen. Nikolai A. Bulganin, a member of the Politburo in Moscow, and appointed as Soviet envoy to the PKWN in late summer 1944, was given full powers to use the Red Army and the NKVD to find and arrest all Polish military and civilian personnel loyal to the government in London. Home Army soldiers were to be conscripted into the First Polish Army, and officers were to be deported.[32]

When the Yalta Conference opened on February 4, Soviet troops had liberated all of Poland from the Germans, and some Red Army units stood within forty miles of Berlin. Poland's eastern frontier was settled without any difficulty. After a few half-hearted suggestions by Roosevelt that Lwów be awarded to Poland, which Stalin easily turned aside, the western leaders gave their final agreement to the Curzon Line as the Polish-Soviet frontier. They managed, however, to postpone the decision on Poland's western frontier, being loath to grant Stalin's Poles all the German territory they and Stalin demanded. The dispute centered on Poland's western frontier, i.e., whether the southern part of the new Polish-German frontier was to follow the western Neisse River, thus awarding all of Upper Silesia to Poland, as demanded by Stalin and his Poles, or the eastern Neisse, as proposed by the British, thus leaving western Silesia to Germany. (This issue was finally resolved in Poland's favor at the Potsdam Conference in July–August 1945, in return for the Warsaw government's promise to conduct free elections as soon as possible.)

The real issue at Yalta, however, was not frontiers but the makeup of the new Polish provisional government. Churchill in particular pressed hard for a representative body, including non-Lublin Poles from both Poland and London. On this key issue, the western leaders based their stance on a project submitted to them by Mikołajczyk. They even proposed that Poles from both sides be invited to Yalta to form a government then and there, but Stalin scotched this suggestion. He did not have much difficulty in getting his views accepted, for Roosevelt made only half-hearted efforts to ensure a democratic provisional government for the Poles. Indeed, he declared that Poland had been "a headache for five hundred years." He also said that he cared only for free elections, which would satisfy Polish Americans.[33] Many years later, Molotov indicated his and Stalin's opinion of the western proposals. He said the British and Americans had tried to encroach on Soviet interests by imposing "a bourgeois government on Poland that would certainly have been an agent of imperialism."[34]

Ultimately, the western leaders had to content themselves with Molotov's proposal to establish a Commission of Three to conduct consultations with eligible Poles. The commission was to be made up of Molotov, U.S. Ambassador Harriman, and the British ambassador in Moscow, Clark-Kerr. The language of the agreement, published in a special communique, strongly suggested that the core of the new provisional government was to be made up of the existing provisional government already recognized by Stalin, although this was questioned later by both Churchill and Roosevelt.[35] Having lost his fight for a representative Polish provisional government, Churchill pinned his hopes on the promised free elections, as did Roosevelt. On returning home, they presented Yalta as a great triumph of Allied diplomacy. Indeed, the agreements reached on the United Nations and on Soviet help against Japan seemed to augur well for the future. However, James F. Byrnes, who had attended some of the plenary sessions and was given the task of selling Yalta at home, misrepresented the Polish problem to the American public. He compared the differences between the Lublin and London Poles to those between the Democratic and Republican national committees.[36]

Given Stalin's goals regarding Poland, it was not surprising that in early spring 1945 Molotov blocked the attempts of the British and American members of the Commission of Three to bring in non-Lublin Poles for consultations. At the same time, Stalin made sure that Polish political leaders recognized and supported by most of their countrymen would not be invited for consultations. In late March 1945, NKVD general Ivan A. Serov, Laverenty P. Beria's deputy in Poland and acting on his instructions, set an elaborate trap for the Polish politicians who refused to recognize the existing provisional government. These leaders had, unlike the Polish government in London, accepted the Yalta decisions on Poland, though under protest. They did so because they expected to be called for consultations in Moscow on establishing the new interim government. Sixteen leaders, including Gen. Leopold Okulicki, the last commander of the Home Army (dissolved in January 1945), and fifteen politicians, including four proposed by the western powers as candidates for consultations, were lured to a meeting with a Russian general called Ivanov (Ivan A. Serov) to discuss emerging from the underground. They asked for and were promised a plane to fly to London for consultations with the Polish government there before going on to Moscow. Instead, they were flown to Moscow and, after a near crash, landed in the Soviet capital only to be lodged in the Lubianka prison. There, they were subjected to the usual NKVD methods: constant hunger and cold, lack of medication, and interrogations day and night for over two months to force the accused to confess to fabricated charges. These charges included their alleged orders to the Home Army to fight the Red Army; espionage; and planning Poland's participation in a British-organized anti-Soviet bloc, including Germany. (The last charge was based on a letter found on Okulicki at the time of his arrest, in which he wrote that he expected Great Britain to form such a bloc.) A few of the accused broke down and admitted to some of the charges, but most only admitted indirect responsibility for anti-Soviet actions and of having radio contact with the Polish government in London. (Possession of unlicensed radios was forbidden by Soviet law.)[37]

It was both ironic and tragic that Mikołajczyk negotiated in Moscow from June 16 to 21, 1945, for his access to the new Polish provisional government, while some of his colleagues were undergoing a rigged public trial in the Soviet capital. Indeed, the negotiations ran almost parallel to the trial, held in the Palace of Trade Unions where the purge trials had taken place from 1936 to 1938. The trial was directed by the Soviet Military attorney general, Vassily Ulrykh, who had also participated in the purge trials. It is likely that Mikołajczyk's agreement to participate in the new government, as well as the pleas of President Truman's emissary Harry Hopkins—who had visited Moscow in May to arrange a new summit meeting with Stalin—resulted in verdicts that were mild by Soviet standards, though three of the key leaders died later in prison. (In April 1990, the charges were declared as having no criminal character, and the accused were "rehabilitated," i.e., recognized as innocent.)[38]

The verdicts coincided with the agreement, reached on June 21, on the composition of the new Polish Provisional Government of National Unity, which was duly proclaimed a week later. Mikołajczyk accepted the post of second deputy premier and minister of agriculture. Edward Osóbka-Morawski, formerly premier of the PKWN, was also premier in the new government, and Władysław Gomułka, leader of the Communist Polish Workers' Party, was first deputy premier. The non-Lublin Poles obtained only four cabinet seats out of twenty-one. Thus Stalin showed he could do what he wanted with Poland. The new Polish government, which was committed to carrying out free elections as soon as possible, was immediately recognized by the western powers and China on July 5, 1945. It renewed its promise to hold free elections as soon as possible at the Potsdam Conference of July–August 1945. However, these elections were delayed until January 1947 and were then rigged to ensure a Communist victory.

Some Polish and western historians have contended over the years that timely consent to Stalin's demands by the Polish government in London could have preserved Polish independence, or at least saved the people from the repression and suffering visited on them in 1944 and 1945, especially the Warsaw Uprising of 1944. During the period of Communist power and Soviet domination—though both became much more tolerable after Mikhail S. Gorbachev's accession to power in the USSR in March 1985—the official verdict was that the Polish government not only could but should have agreed to Stalin's demands during the war; i.e., it should have recognized the Curzon Line as the Polish-Soviet frontier, condemned the request to the International Red Cross to conduct an inquiry into the Katyn massacre, and dropped allegedly Fascist ministers. Some western historians of Poland still believe that, at least in 1943, the Polish government should have viewed the USSR as its partner and ally, rather than looking to Great Britain and the United States.[39] Most western historians, if not going that far, have also condemned the Polish government for being "romantic," too tardy in responding to Soviet demands, and living in "cloud cuckoo land."[40]

There are two key problems with this point of view. First, most Poles, both in occupied Poland and in the west, were adamantly opposed to ceding half of prewar Poland with several million Poles to the USSR. Indeed, in July 1940, Polish émigré politicians tried to overthrow General Sikorski, the premier of the exiled government, when a memorandum was leaked proposing Polish recognition of the Soviet annexation of eastern Poland in exchange for raising a Polish army there to fight the Germans alongside the Red Army. A year later, three ministers resigned, and émigré opinion was split by Sikorski's signature on the Polish-Soviet agreement to restore normal relations without a Soviet recognition of the prewar Polish-Soviet frontier.[41] Most Poles also rejected the other Soviet demands as unwarranted interference in Polish internal affairs. These attitudes were consistently expressed in the Polish underground press in occupied Poland as well as in the Polish-language press published in Great Britain and the United States. They are also evidenced in the correspondence between Polish prime ministers and cabinet ministers on the one hand, and political and military leaders in the underground on the other.[42]

Warren F. Kimball is right in stating that the Polish government in London always took "an all-or-nothing approach to Soviet-Polish problems."[43] Yet it had to do so because of Polish public opinion, especially in the armed forces. Nevertheless, its leaders privately accepted the inevitability of territorial concessions to the USSR. Thus, General Sikorski accepted the need to give up most of eastern Poland to the Soviet Union, except for the then preponderantly Polish cities and regions of Wilno and Lwów. However, he knew this could not be admitted publicly and must be settled after the war, and he hoped for a large East European federation. Mikołajczyk shared these views and made an indirect proposal to Stalin along these lines as early as November 1943, though without demanding Wilno.[44] Indeed, in view of the opposition of Polish public opinion and the military, the most that any Polish government could officially propose was its resolution of August 29, 1944, that the Polish-Soviet border be settled on the basis of self-determination by the Polish parliament after the war.[45] Mikołajczyk went further by proposing a demarcation line, based on the Curzon Line, though leaving Lwów on the Polish side; but he failed to carry his cabinet with him and resigned when British and American guarantees were lacking. Furthermore, despite Stalin's insistence on Polish recognition of the Curzon Line as the Polish-Soviet frontier, even the Polish Communists and their sympathizers did not dare speak of giving up Lwów and Wilno, declaring instead that the future border would be settled on the basis of self-determination. Thus, the frontier treaty signed by the PKWN and Soviet leaders in late July 1945 remained a state secret for some time.

The second problem with the argument that the Polish government could have gained independence, or at least spared the people much suffering by accepting Stalin's demands in good time, is that no one knows whether this would have persuaded the Soviet dictator to refrain from repressing the pro-London Poles, who represented majority opinion in Poland, and if so for how long. In the absence of relevant Soviet documents on this subject, Stalin's preparation of his own Polish cadres and his track record of repressing any sign of dissent in his bailiwick indicate there was very little likelihood of his accepting a truly independent Poland, even if the Polish government in exile had agreed to his demands.

In reality, it was not what the Polish government did or did not do, but the combination of Soviet military might and positive western reactions to Soviet territorial and political demands that determined the outcome of the war for Poland, as for most of Eastern Europe. Great Britain and the United States rightly saw the military power of the USSR as vital to winning the war against Germany in Europe, and American leaders also believed they needed Soviet help to defeat Japan. The British and American leaders diverged, however, on the fate of postwar Eastern Europe. Roosevelt was ready to acknowledge Soviet predominance in the region, but Churchill was not. Contrary to some historians, the British prime minister was concerned not just with preserving British influence in Greece, Yugoslavia, and Hungary but also with preserving some kind of balance of power in Europe after American troops withdrew—hence his attempts to persuade Roosevelt to launch a secondary invasion of the Balkans, which fell through in August 1944 with the invasion of southern France, though he nursed this hope until spring 1945. To preserve British influence and some independent states in the region, he signed the "percentage agreement" with Stalin in October 1944. Above all, he worked hard to establish a really independent Polish government under Mikołajczyk as a possible check on Soviet power.[46] For the same reasons, he tried at the end of the war to convince President Truman and General Eisenhower to leave Allied troops where they stood, instead of withdrawing to the preagreed zones of occupation; and he begged Truman to delay the withdrawal of American armies from Europe. Churchill's policy may appear as mere posturing for the benefit of the British electorate, or to secure a favorable judgment from history.[47] In fact, however, Churchill was a British statesman with a profoundly European outlook; therefore, he wished to prevent the preponderance of one power on the Continent that would, by the same token, be a threat to Great Britain.

The British prime minister could not, however, prevail against the policy of Franklin D. Roosevelt. This policy was largely dictated by the need to secure Soviet help, first to defeat Germany and then Japan, with the latter looming ever larger as the war in Europe drew to a close. There is also something to be said for the theory that Roosevelt was a Jeffersonian president in his desire to prevent U.S. entanglement in postwar Europe and that this explains the broad agreement existing between his views and Stalin's.[48] But whatever interpretation of Roosevelt historians may favor, it is clear the president had made up his mind at least by May 1943 that the price of continued Soviet military participation in the war against Germany and then Japan, and Soviet postwar membership in the United Nations, was agreement to Stalin's territorial demands regarding Poland and the Baltic states.[49] It is also clear that by fall of that year he was envisaging Communist governments in Eastern and Central Europe and perhaps even a Popular Front government in France.[50] Although the president could not openly sanction Soviet territorial claims, he clearly intimated his agreement with Stalin as early as summer 1943, before confirming those claims personally at Tehran.[51] Thereafter, his main concern was the establishment of a new Polish government acceptable to Polish Americans, i.e., one headed by Mikołajczyk, even if most of the ministers were Stalin's appointees. By May 1944, if not earlier, he had accepted the possibility that the states bordering the USSR would be communized.[52] Thus, given Roosevelt's policy, American preponderance in the Anglo-American partnership, and Soviet military might, Moscow's domination over Poland and most of Eastern Europe was inevitable, regardless of the policies of the governments-in-exile, including the Polish government, and the wishes of all the peoples involved.

NOTES

1. For East European leaders' hopes and fears, see histories of these countries during the war: R. J. Crampton, *A Short History of Modern Bulgaria* (Cambridge: Cambridge University Press, 1987), 124–65; Victor S. Mamatey and Radomir Luza, *A History of the Czechoslovak Republic 1918–1948* (Princeton: Princeton University Press, 1973), part 2; Peter F. Sugar et al. eds., *A History of Hungary* (Bloomington: University of Indiana Press, 1990), chap. 28; Jan Karski, *The Great Powers and Poland*

1919–1945: From Versailles to Yalta (Lanham, MD: 1985), part 2; Keith Hitchins, *Rumania 1866–1947* (Oxford: Oxford University Press, 1994), chaps. 11,12; Robert J. Kerner, ed., *Yugoslavia* (Berkeley and London: University of California Press, 1949), chaps. 19 and 20. For an overview of the Balkans in World War II, see Barbara Jelavich, *History of the Balkans*, vol. 2, *Twentieth Century* (1983; Cambridge: Cambridge University Press, 1993), chap. 7. For Molotov on Stalin and the Declaration on Liberated Europe, see *Molotov Remembers: Inside Kremlin Politics, Conversations with Felix Chuev*, ed., intro. (Chicago: University Press of Chicago Press, 1993), p.51.

2. For the Churchill-Stalin deal over the Balkans, see Albert Resis, "The Churchill-Stalin Secret 'Percentages Agreement' on the Balkans, Moscow, October 1944," *American Historical Review* 83, 2 (April 1974): 368–87. For an American view accepting Russian domination of postwar Eastern Europe, and perhaps even most of Europe, because of the need for Soviet aid against Japan, see "Russia's Position," paper sent to Harry Hopkins in Quebec, August 1943, by Major-General James Burns, head of President's Protocol Committee, *Foreign Relations of the United States* [FRUS], *Conferences in Washington and Quebec* (Washington, D.C.: GPO, 1970), 625; see also Roosevelt's statements to Archbishop, later Cardinal, Francis J. Spellman of New York in early September 1943, on the probable Russian domination of part of Europe after the war, cited in Robert J. Gannon, *The Cardinal Spellman Story* (Garden City, NY: Doubleday, 1962), 22–24, 246; see also Mark Stoler, *The Politics of the Second Front: American Military Planning and Diplomacy in Coalition Warfare, 1941–1943*, Westport, Conn., London: Greenwood Press, 1977), chap. 8.

3. See Hitchins, *Rumania 1866–1947*, 501–34, and Cortlandt V. Schuyler, "The View from Romania," in *Witnesses to the Origins of the Cold War*, ed. Thomas T. Hammond (Seattle and London: University of Washington Press, 1982), 126–60. See also Ghita Ionescu, *Communism in Rumania 1944–1962* (Oxford: Oxford University Press, 1964), part 1, *The Establishment of Soviet Control over Rumania, 1944–1947*, 71–146, and Stephen Fischer-Galati, *20th Century Rumania* (New York, London: Columbia University Press, 1970), chap. 5, 91–109.

4. On the events in Bulgaria, see Cyril E. Black, "The View from Bulgaria," in Hammond, ed., *Witnesses*, 60–97; see also Michael M. Boll, *The American Military Mission in Bulgaria, 1944–1947. History and Transcripts*, East European Monographs no. 186 (Boulder, Colo., and New York: Columbia University Press, 1985).

5. On Yugoslavia, see Michael B. Petrovich, "The View from Yugoslavia," in Hammond, ed., *Witnesses*, 34–59. For works criticizing Churchill's switch from supporting the royalist, "chetnik" resistance leader, Draza Mihailovic, to the Communist partisan leader, Josip Broz Tito, see David Martin, *The Web of Disinformation: Churchill's Yugoslav Blunder* (San Diego, New York, London: Harcourt Brace Jovanovich, 1990), and Michael Lees, *The Rape of Serbia: The British Role in Tito's Grab for Power, 1943–1944* (New York: Harcourt Brace Jovanovich, 1990).

6. In Hungary, the Communists expected to win 70 percent of the vote; however, the Smallholders' party won 57 percent, and the Social Democrats and Communists won 17 percent each and the National Peasant party 7 percent; see Charles

Gati, "From Liberation to Revolution," chap. 20 in Sugar et al., eds., *A History of Hungary*, 371, and for Stalin's statements to Hungarian Communist leaders, see 370, and Michael Charlton, *The Eagle and the Small Birds: Crisis in the Soviet Empire, from Yalta to Solidarity* (Chicago: University of Chicago Press, 1984), 68–69.

7. On Beneš's negotiations for a new government with Czechoslovak Communists in Moscow, see Mamatey and Luza, *A History of the Czechoslovak Republic*, 390–92. On his offer of Subcarpathian Ruthenia to the USSR, his later suggestions on the region's links with Soviet Ukraine, and on its possible autonomy in Czechoslovakia, see Edward Taborsky, *President Edvard Beneš Between East and West, 1938–1948* (Stanford: Stanford University Press, 1981), 3, 136, 156, 182, 204.

8. On the Soviet promotion of a movement for union with the USSR in 1944 and Beneš's disillusionment, see Mamatey and Luza, *History*, chap. 7, 175–93. The Soviet-Czechoslovak treaty on the union of Subcarpathian Ruthenia with the USSR was signed in Moscow on June 29, 1945.

9. For Kopecký's statement, see Karel Kaplan, *The Short March: The Communist Takeover of Czechoslovakia, 1945–1948* (London: Hurst, 1987), 16.

10. See Josef Korbel, *The Communist Subversion of Czechoslovakia, 1938–1948: The Failure of Coexistence* (Princeton: Princeton University Press, 1959), 128.

11. For Churchill's pleas and appeals, see Winston S. Churchill, *The Second World War*, vol. 6, *Triumph and Tragedy* (Boston: Houghton Mifflin, 1954), and Martin Gilbert, *Winston S. Churchill*, vol. 7, *The Road to Victory 1914–1945* (Boston: Houghton Mifflin, 1986), 1322–24.

12. For the Communist coup of February 1948 in Czechoslovakia, see Kaplan, *Short March*, and Korbel, *Communist Subversion*.

13. For the Nazi-Soviet nonaggression pact and Secret Protocol of August 23, 1939, see *Documents on German Foreign Policy*, ser. D, vol. 7 (Washington and London: GPO, 1956), nos. 228, 229. In late December 1989, after five decades of denial, the Soviet authorities finally acknowledged finding the Russian copy of the Secret Protocol of August 23, 1939, with Molotov's signature in their archives, and the pact was condemned by the Supreme Soviet. For a Russian historical note on the subject, see *Dokumenty Vneshnei Politiki. 1939 god* (Documents on foreign policy. The year 1939), vol. 22, part 2, Moscow, 1992, n. 178, 590–92. The original Russian text was found in the Presidential Archive, in the Kremlin. The demarcation line between Soviet and German Poland ran along the Narew, Vistula, and San Rivers, thus dividing Warsaw between the two aggressors. This line, supplemented by the Pissa River in the north, was printed in *Pravda* on September 23, 1939, and reprinted in the London *Times*, and is rarely marked on historical maps because it was replaced by the Ribbentrop-Molotov Line of September 28, 1939, which approximated the Curzon Line of July 1920 (see 15).

14. For Prime Minister Neville Chamberlain's statement in the House of Commons, September 20, 1939, and the debate that followed, see *Parliamentary Debates, House of Commons*, 5th ser., vol. 351, cols. 975–1003, 1015–17, reprinted in Wacław Jędrzejewicz, ed., *Poland in the British Parliament, 1939–1945* (New York: n.p., 1946), 1: 269–85; see also *Documents on Polish-Soviet Relations 1939–1945*, vol. 1, *1939–1943*

(hereafter *DOPSR*), ed. Stanisław Bagiński et al. (London: General Sikorski, 1961), doc. nos. 47, 48. For Churchill's radio speech of October 1, 1939, see his memoirs: *The Second World War,* vol. 1, *The Gathering Storm* (Boston: Houghton Mifflin, 1954, 1976. 1983), 449.

15. The Curzon Line drawn up at Spa in early July 1920 was based on the demarcation line between Polish and White Russian administrations as proposed by the Allied powers in December 1919; it approximated the eastern frontier of Congress or Russian Poland, 1815–1915. Its final version, as amended in the Foreign Office, London, left East Galicia on the Soviet side. On the Curzon Line, see Piotr S. Wandycz, *Soviet-Polish Relations, 1917–1921* (Cambridge: Harvard University Press, 1969), chaps. 10–11; on the war, see Norman Davies, *White Eagle Red Star: The Polish-Soviet War, 1919–1920* (1972; London: Macdonald and Company, 1983); see also Adam Zamoyski, *The Battle for the Marchlands,* East European Monographs no. 88 (Boulder, Colo., and New York: Columbia University Press, 1981). The official reason for the Soviet rejection of the Curzon Line in July 1920 was Moscow's readiness to give Poland more territory in the east. Lenin, however, confidentially explained the rejection at the Ninth Party Conference in late September 1920, by the Soviet desire to help the Polish proletariat establish a Socialist Poland, to aid the expected revolutions in Germany and Italy, to ignite revolution in Hungary and Czechoslovakia, and to overthrow the whole Versailles settlement; see Russian archival documents cited in Richard Pipes, *Russia Under the Bolshevik Regime* (New York: Knopf, 1993) 177, 181–82.

16. Of the total population of eastern Poland, estimated at about 14.6 million in 1939, 6.17 million were ethnic Poles; see statistics provided in the article by Polish demographic expert Dr. Marek Tuszyński, ed. by Dale F. Denda: "Soviet War Crimes Against Poland During the Second World War and Its Aftermath: A Review of the Factual Record and Outstanding Questions," paper read at the Fifty-sixth Annual Conference and Meeting of the Polish Institute of Arts and Sciences of America, June 13, 1998, Georgetown University, Washington, D.C. (printed by the Federation of Polish Americans, 2000 L. Street NW, suite 200, Washington, D.C., 20036), 8.

17. On Soviet policies in former eastern Poland, 1939–1941, see Jan T. Gross, *Revolution from Abroad: The Soviet Conquest of Poland's Western Ukraine and Western Belorussia* (Princeton: Princeton University Press, 1988), and on the elections, see chap. 2; see also Keith Sword, ed., *The Soviet Takeover of the Polish Eastern Provinces, 1939–1941* (New York: St. Martin's Press, 1991), and *Deportation and Exile: Poles in the Soviet Union, 1939–1948* (Basingstoke, UK, and New York: St. Martin's Press, 1994), chaps. 1–4.

18. For the texts of the Polish-Soviet agreement of July 30, the military agreement of August 14, and the Declaration of Friendship and Mutual Assistance signed by Sikorski and Stalin in Moscow on December 4, 1941, see *DOPSR,* 2, London, 1967, nos. 106, 112, 161, reprinted in Antony Polonsky, *The Great Powers and the Polish Question, 1941–1945: A Documentary Study in Cold War Origins* (London: London School of Economics, 1975), nos. 17, 22, 29; see also Anna M. Cienciala, "General Sikorski and the Conclusion of the Polish-Soviet Agreement of July 30, 1941; A

Reassessment," *Polish Review* 41, 4 (1996): 404–34. On the Anders army—some 76,000 men accompanied by about 40,000 civilians, mostly families—see Władysław Anders, *An Army in Exile: The Story of the Polish Second Corps* (Macmillan, 1949); see also Sword, *Deportation and Exile*, chaps. 2, 3.

19. The Germans found some 4,700 bodies at Katyn, not 10,000 as they originally announced. These men, and one woman—a reconnaissance pilot—had been held in the Kozelsk camp, south of Smolensk; those held in Ostashkov, north of Smolensk, were shot and buried in NKVD grounds at Mednoye, near Tver (Kalinin); those from the Starobelsk camp, southeast of Kharkov, were shot in the NKVD cellars at Kharkov and buried in the woods outside the city. Of the 15,000 originally held in the three camps, 400 were spared, based on varying criteria unclear to this day, though at least one-third were informers. They were joined later by some 1,000 officers formerly interned in Lithuania. On April 13, 1990, Pres. Mikhail S. Gorbachev acknowledged Soviet responsibility by handing over NKVD lists with some 15,000 names to Gen. Wojciech Jaruzelski, then president of Poland. In October 1992, Russian president Boris N. Yeltsin gave the Polish government photocopies of Soviet documents on the massacre and the cover-up. According to a Russian document, the total number of Polish prisoners killed by the NKVD in spring 1940 was 21,857. For the most comprehensive study of the whole question, based on Russian documents, see Natalya Lebedeva, *Katyn': Prestuplenie protiv chelovechestva* (Katyn. A crime against humanity) (Moscow: Izd-Ka Gruppa "Progress," 1994). For Russian documents, mostly on the cover-up, with English translation, see *Katyn: Documents of Genocide: Documents and Materials from the Soviet Archives Turned over to Poland on October 14, 1992,* ed. Wojciech Materski, intro. Janusz K. Zawodny (Warsaw: Instytut Studión Politycznych Polskiej Academii Nauk, 1993); for the Politburo decision of March 5, 1940, to execute the prisoners and for the total of 21,857 dead, see ibid., documents nos. 1 and 10. A large selection of Russian documents covering the period from August 1939 to October 1940 was published as *Katyn: Plenniki neb'iavlennoi voiny* (Katyn. Prisoners of an undeclared war), ed. Natalya S. Lebedva, Wojciech.Materski et al. (Moscow: Mezhdunarodny Fond "Demokratiia," 1997); in Polish translation, with the same editors, *Katyń. Dokumenty Zbrodni. Tom 1. Jeńcy niewypowiedzianej wojny* (Katyn. Documents of a crime. Vol. 1. Prisoners of an undeclared war) (Warsaw: "Trio," 1995), and vol. 2. *Katyń . . . . . Zagłada* (Extermination) (Warsaw: "Trio," 1997). Russian and Polish volumes on the survivors and the cover-up are to follow, and an English language volume on Katyn and other massacres, edited by Anna M. Cienciala in cooperation with Natalya S. Lebedeva and Wojciech Materski, is to be published by Yale University Press in 1999 or 2000. Zawodny's book, *Death in the Forest: The Story of the Katyn Massacre* (Notre Dame: University of Notre Dame Press, 1962), and reprints, based on the documents collected and published by the Congressional Inquiry Commission, 1951–1952, can still be read as a useful complement to Lebedeva and Materski.

20. For English language material on official Polish attitudes as expressed in memorandum to the British and U.S. governments, and for attitudes in Poland as documented in correspondence with underground leaders, see *DOPSR,* vols. 1 and 2. For

an extensive selection of Polish language material, see *Armia Krajowa w Dokumentach* (The Home Army in documents), vols. 1–6 (London: Studium Polski Podziemne, 1970–1986). On the adamant attitude of the Polish émigré press on eastern Poland, see Stanisława Lewandowska, *Prasa polskiej emigracji wojennej 1939–1945* (Warsaw: Instytut Historii Polskiej Akademii Nauk, 1993), 329–38. For a study of the most important segment of the underground press loyal to the Polish government in London, see Grzegorz Mazur, *Biuro Informacji i Propagandy SZP-ZWZ-AK, 1939–1945* (The Information and Propaganda Office of the Service for Poland's victory—Association of armed struggle—Home Army) (Warsaw: Instytut Nyadawniczy Pax, 1987).

21. For studies on the Polish Communist party and Polish Communists in World War II, see M. K. Dziewanowski, *The Communist Party of Poland*, 2d ed. (Cambridge: Harvard Univerisity Press, 1976), and Jan B. de Weydenthal, *The Communists of Poland: An Historical Outline*, rev. ed. (Stanford: Stanford University Press, 1986). See also Anna M. Cienciala, "The Activities of Polish Communists as a Source for Stalin's Policy Toward Poland in the Second World War," *International History Review* 7, 1 (1985): 129–35, and her paper based on Russian archival documents, "Stalin's Changing Policies on Poland, 1939–1941," read at the Woodrow Wilson International Center for Scholars, Washington, D.C., March 22, 1995. On Polish Communists in the USSR, see also Sword, *Deportation and Exile*, chap. 5.

22. The number-one leader of the Peasant party was the old and ailing Wincenty Witos (b. 1874), who was living in German-occupied Poland. He died in 1945.

23. For Churchill's account of the talks on Poland in Tehran, see his *History of the Second World War*, vol. 5, *Closing the Ring* (1951; Boston: Houghton Mifflin, 1979, 1983), 361–62; see also *FRUS: The Conferences at Cairo and Tehran, 1943* (Washington, D.C.: GPO, 1961). For an account of the Polish question at Tehran, see Jan Karski, *The Great Powers and Poland, 1919–1945*, chap. 29. The Russian documents do not include Churchill's matchstick proposal on Poland, made after dinner on November 28, 1943, though they include the prime minister's later proposal on Polish borders in the notes on the roundtable meeting held on the afternoon of December 1; see *Tegeranskaia konferentsiia rukovoditelei trekh soiuznykh dzierzhav—SSSR, SShA i Velikobrytanii (28 noiabria–1 dekabria 1943 g)* (Moscow: Politizdat, 1978), no. 62, 167, and for the Stalin-Roosevelt meeting on the afternoon of December 1, 1943, see no. 63, American record in *FRUS 1944*, 3: 594–95. For the Eden-Stalin talks, Moscow, December 1941, see Lewellyn Woodward, *British Foreign Policy in the Second World War*, 2d ed. (London: HMSO, 1971), 2: 222 ff.; for Russian documents on the same, see Oleg. A. Rzheshevskii, ed., *War and Diplomacy: The Making of the Grand Alliance. Documents from Stalin's Archives* (Amsterdam: Harwood Academic Publishers, 1996), part 1.

24. For the Churchill-Mikołajczyk talks in January–February 1944, see *DOPSR* 2, nos. 83, 96, 105; for the Churchill-Stalin correspondence on Poland in February–April 1944, see Polonsky, *The Great Powers*, nos. 87–94. For Churchill's speech and the debate on the Tehran Conference, February 22–24, 1944, see *Parliamentary Debates: House of Commons*, 5th ser., vol. 397, 696 ff., reprinted in W. Jędrzejewicz,

Poland in the British Parliament (NewYork: n.p., 1959), 2: 311–407; for extracts from Churchill's speech of February 22, 1944, see *DOPSR* 2, no. 109.

25. For the Mikołajczyk-Lebedev talks in June, see British summary in Eden to Sir Archibald Clark-Kerr, Moscow, July 8, 1944, Polonsky, *The Great Powers*, no. 99. On these talks and the creation of the PKWN in Moscow, see Krystyna Kersten, *The Establishment of Communist Rule in Poland*, trans. John S. Micgiel and Michael Bernhard, foreword by Jan T. Gross (Berkeley: University of California Press, 1991), chap. 2.

26. For Mikołajczyk's talks in Washington, June 1944, see Richard C. Lukas, *The Strange Allies: The United States and Poland, 1941–1945* (Knoxville: University of Tennessee Press, 1978), 56–59. Roosevelt's promise to try to get the three cities for Poland—Drohobycz was the center of the East Galician oil region—is cited in Mikołajczyk's memorandum of his Washington conversations dated June 12, 1944, and submitted to the State Department (see *DOPSR* 2, doc. no. 141, 252); this promise is hinted at in the American record (Cordell Hull's summary to Harriman of June 17, 1944), and the State Department did not protest it in acknowledging the Polish memorandum. For the official American records of the conversations, see: *FRUS, 1944*, 3: 1272–78, 1280–82, and summary, 1285–89, with the hint of Roosevelt's promise on 1288, point 6, par. 2; on Roosevelt's assurances to Stalin and inquiry on Lwów, see Ambassador W. Averell Harriman's report of his conversation with Stalin, June 12, 1944, 1282.

27. For Mikołajczyk's Moscow talks, July 31–August 9, 1944, see Kersten, *The Establishment*, chap. 2, and Polonsky, *The Great Powers*, nos. 101–3; for Polish documents, see *DOPSR*, vol. 2, nos. 141–47, and 177–89. On August 3, Stalin told Mikołajczyk he would do "everything in his power" to help the Warsaw insurgents and confirmed this promise on August 9 (see ibid., pp. 311, 337); for the Russian document on the same, see *Voenno-Istoricheskii Zhurnal* 3 (Moscow, 1993): 23.

28. For the view that the uprising should never have taken place, see Jan Ciechanowski, *The Warsaw Uprising of 1944* (London: Cambridge University Press, 1974); for the view that it was unavoidable, see Janusz K. Zawodny, *Nothing but Honour: The Story of the Warsaw Rising, 1944* (Stanford: Stanford University Press, 1978). For recent evaluations, see Anna M. Cienciala, "The Diplomatic Background of the Warsaw Uprising of 1944; The Players and the Stakes," *Polish Review* 39, 4 (1994): 393–414, and Andrzej Chmielarz, "Warsaw Fought Alone: Reflections on Aid to and the Fall of the 1944 Uprising," *Polish Review* 39, 4 (1994): 415–34. For the consensus among Polish historians today that the uprising was doomed but that given the circumstances, it was unavoidable, see Andrzej Friszke, "Polscy historycy o powstaniu warszawskim," (Polish historians on the Warsaw Uprising), *Zeszyty Historyczne* 109 (Paris, 1994): 3–27.

29. For a study of Oskar Lange's activities in 1944, based on American archival sources, see Robert Szymczak, "Oskar Lange, American Polonia, and the Polish-Soviet Dilemma in World War II," part 1, "The Public Partisan as Private Emissary," *Polish Review* 40, 1 (1995): 3–27; and part 2, "Making a Case for People's Poland," *Polish Review* 40, 2 (1995): 131–58. For a study based mainly on Russian sources, see Anna

M. Cienciala, "New Light on Oskar Lange as an Intermediary Between Roosevelt and Stalin in Attempts to Create a New Polish Government (January–November 1944)," *Acta Poloniae Historica* 73 (1996): 89–134. For Roosevelt's agreement to Stalin's request to send some Polish-Americans to Moscow, see Ambassador Andrey Gromyko's telegram to the Soviet Commissariat of Foreign Affairs, February 21, 1944, "Sovetsko-Amerikanskie otnosheniia bo vremiia Velikoi Otechestvennoi Voiny, 1941–1945" (Soviet-American relations during the Great Fatherland War, 1941–1945), 2, 20 (1984), 43–44. Orlemański's trip, made without his bishop's permission, and his declarations on Stalin's religious toleration—and on his alleged desire to reach an agreement with the Vatican (!)—did not go down well with his superiors. He was suspended from his parish but allowed to return because of the pleas of his parishioners.

30. See William Larsh, "W. Averell Harriman and the Polish Question, December 1943–August 1944," *East European Politics and Societies (EEPS)* 7, 33 (fall 1993): 545; see also, Larsh, "Yalta and the American Approach to Free Elections in Poland," *Polish Review* 40, 3 (1995): 280.

31. For Mikołajczyk's Moscow talks in October 1944 and Churchill's pressure on the premier to accept Stalin's conditions, the Polish cabinet's rejection thereof and his resignation, see Kersten, *The Establishment*, 103–7, 110–11, and Karski, *The Great Powers and Poland*, chaps. 34, 50. For Polish documents on the Moscow talks, October 1944, and the Polish cabinet resolutions of August 29 and November 3, 1944, see *DOPSR* 2, nos. 237–46, and 214, 259. For the British side of the Moscow talks, see Polonsky, *The Great Powers*, no. 112. For the Harriman, Churchill, and Mikołajczyk reports to Roosevelt, see *FRUS: 1944*, 3: 1322–30.

32. For Soviet repression of the Home Army and pro-London civil administrators in Poland, 1944–1945, see Sword, *Deportation and Exile*, chap. 6; for Russian documents on the same, see *NKVD i pol'skoe podpol'e, 1944–1945. (Po 'osobym papkam' I. V. Stalina)* (The NKVD and the Polish Underground according to the "Private Files" of J. V. Stalin), ed. Albina F. Noskova et al. (Moscow: Institut Slavovedeniia i Balkanistikii, Russian Academy of Sciences, 1994), and also for excerpts from the instruction given to Bulganin, 12.

33. For an overview of the Polish question at Yalta, see Karski, *The Great Powers and Poland*, chap. 37. For relevant documents, see *FRUS: The Conferences of Malta and Yalta* (Washingon, D.C.: GPO, 1945); see also Polonsky, *The Great Powers*, nos. 123–30. For Roosevelt's comment on Poland as a headache for five hundred years, see "The Crimean Conference: Minutes of Meetings Prepared by James F. Byrnes," Naval Aide Files, Box 9, Notes for February 6, 5, Harry S. Truman Presidential Library, Independence, MO. According to Churchill, Roosevelt said Poland had been a source of trouble for five hundred years; see Churchill, *Triumph and Tragedy*, 6: 372. For Roosevelt on free elections and Polish-Americans, see the H. Freeman Matthews minutes for February 9, where the president is noted as saying, "I don't want the Poles to be able to question the Polish elections. The matter is not only one of principle but of practical politics" (*FRUS, Conferences*, 854). The Charles Bohlen notes speak not of Poles but of "the six million Poles in the United States," (848), and this is clearly what Roosevelt had in mind.

34. See Molotov, *Molotov Remembers,* 53.

35. For the communiqué see *FRUS: Conferences at Malta and Yalta,* 973–74; reprinted in Polonsky, *The Great Powers,* doc. no. 130.

36. James F. Byrnes cited in David Robertson, *Sly and Able: A Political Biography of James F. Byrnes* (New York, London: Norton, 1994), 458 (where Lublin is misspelled as Lubin). For Churchill's speech and the debates on the Yalta agreements in the House of Commons and House of Lords, February 27–28, March 1, 1945, see *Parliamentary Debates: House of Commons,* 5th ser., vol. 408, 1275 ff.; *House of Lords,* vol. 135, March 1, 1945, 233 ff.; reprinted in W. Jędrzejewicz, *Poland in the British Parliament* (New York: n.p., 1962), 3: 374–596. The House of Commons voted 396 to 26 in favor of the government.

37. For Serov's correspondence with Beria and some of the interrogation protocols of the Polish leaders, written up by their interrogators, see Noskova et al., eds., *NKVD i pol'skoe podpol'e,* nos. 25–28, 31–35, 37–38. Many more are available in Polish translation in Andrzej Chmielarz and Krzysztof Kunert, eds., *Proces Szesnastu. Dokumenty NKWD* (The Trial of the sixteen. NKVD documents) (Warsaw: Oficyna Wydawnicza Rytm, 1995). These documents, including the trial itself, were filed in thirty-six volumes of Investigation Case no. 7859 and kept in the Office of the Soviet Military Prosecutor General. Copies of part of the material were delivered to the Office of the Polish Prosecutor General in 1990 and published in the book just cited. See also articles by the senior Soviet military prosecutor, Stepan Radevich, "The Case of Sixteen," *International Affairs* (May 1991): 114–27, and (June 1991), 107–18.

38. Three of the sixteen were declared innocent and most of the others received short sentences. Three key leaders, Gen. Leopold Okulicki, last commander of the Home Army; Jan Stanisław Jankowski, government delegate for Poland and formally deputy premier of the Polish London government; and Stanisław Jasiukowicz, deputy government delegate and a government minister, received longer sentences and died in prison. For biographical sketches of the sixteen and an account of their arrest and trial, see Eugeniusz Duraczyński, *General Iwanov zaprasza. Przywódcy Podziemnego państwa polskiego przed sądem moskiewskim* (The Polish Underground leaders before the Moscow court) (Warsaw: "Alfa," 1989), and Artur Leinwand, *Przywódcy Polski Podziemnej przed sądem moskiewskim* (The leaders of Underground Poland before the Moscow court) (Warsaw: "Placet," 1989). Both authors cite the memoirs of those prisoners who managed to write them as well as oral interviews. The Soviet Supreme Court Plenum declared on April 19, 1990, that the activity of the accused had no criminal character and recognized the results of the special rehabilitation inquiry carried out at the request of the Polish prosecutor general. See also Radevich, "The Case of Sixteen," May and June 1991.

39. For a recent study along these lines by a historian of Poland working in England, see Anita J. Prażmowska, *Britain and Poland 1939–1948: The Betrayed Ally* (Cambridge: Cambridge University Press, 1995). The author claims that in 1943, the Polish government "had ended up in the wrong place and had committed all its resources to the wrong ally" (166). The implication is that the right place and the right ally was the USSR.

40. On Polish "romantic nationalism" and living in "cloud cuckoo land," see Robin Edmonds, *The Big Three: Churchill, Roosevelt and Stalin in Peace and War* (New York: Norton, 1991), 382. An eminent specialist on Roosevelt's foreign policy, Warren F. Kimball, agrees with Molotov that "the Poles had consistently been late" (Warren F. Kimball, *Churchill and Roosevelt: The Complete Correspondence*, vol. 3, *Alliance Declining* [Princeton: Princeton University Press, 1984], 259).

41. On the July 1940 crisis, see Anna M. Cienciala, "The Question of the Polish-Soviet Frontier in 1939–1940: The Litauer Memorandum and Sikorski's Proposals for Re-establishing Polish-Soviet Relations," *Polish Review* 33, 3 (1988): 295–323. On Polish-Soviet negotiations and the government crisis of July 1941, see John Coutovidis and Jaime Reynolds, *Poland, 1939–1947* (Leicester, UK: Leicester University Press, 1986), 59–77; see also Cienciala, "General Sikorski."

42. See for example, *DOPR*, vols. 1 and 2; *Arma Krajowa w Documentach;* and Mazur, *Biuro Informacji i Própagandy.*

43. "From the onset of the war, the Polish government had taken an all-or-nothing approach to Soviet-Polish problems" (Kimball, *Churchill and Roosevelt*, 3: 259).

44. On Sikorski's view that most of eastern Poland should be ceded to the USSR after the war while at the same time creating a Polish-Lithuanian federation, see the diary notes of Col. Leon Mitkiewicz for early March 1942, cited in Sarah Meiklejohn Terry, *General Sikorski and the Origin of the Oder-Neisse Line, 1939–1945* (Princeton: Princeton University Press, 1983), 129–30. According to a reliable Czech source, Mikołajczyk told Czechoslovak president Edvard Beneš in November 1943 to pass on to Stalin his view that if Lwów and a part of eastern Galicia could be saved for Poland, the Poles would become reconciled to losing the rest (see Taborsky, *President Edvard Beneš*, 101). Taborsky, Beneš's private secretary, was present at the conversation. Mikołajczyk omitted Wilno because the British government would not support him on this.

45. See Keisten, *The Establishment;* Kaiski, *The Great Powers and Poland;* and *DOPSR*, 2, for documentation.

46. On Churchill's policy toward Poland, see Anna M. Cienciala, "Great Britain and Poland Before and After Yalta (1943–1945): A Reassessment," *Polish Review* 40, 3 (1995): 281–313.

47. As suggested by Warren F. Kimball in *The Juggler: Franklin D. Roosevelt as Wartime Statesman* (Princeton: Princeton University Press, 1991), 175, 181.

48. "The fact is that Stalin's European aims—Soviet hegemony in Eastern Europe, a dismembered Germany, a weakened Western Europe, friendly relations with Britain—coincided with Roosevelt's" (see John Lamberton Harper, *American Visions of Europe: Franklin D. Roosevelt, George F. Kennan, and Dean Acheson* [Cambridge: Cambridge University Press, 1994], 124).

49. According to Edward Beneš, Roosevelt told him in May 1943 that he had no objections to the Soviet annexation of the Baltic states and eastern Poland and asked him to pass this on to Stalin; see Taborsky, *President Edward Beneš*, 121–22, and Edward Beneš, *Memoirs of Dr. Eduard Beneš* (London: Allend and Unwin, 1954), 195. In late June 1943, the Soviet ambassador in Washington, Maxim M. Litvinov,

reported that the United States was not concerned with Baltic and Polish frontier problems, though Roosevelt had to bear in mind voters who came from these regions. Therefore, the president could not support Soviet claims until he was faced with a fait accompli. In early July, Litvinov's successor, Andrey Gromyko, reported statements to the same effect made to him by Sol Blum, chairman of the House Foreign Affairs Commitee; see Amos Perlmutter, *FDR and Stalin: A Not So Grand Alliance, 1943–1945* (Columbia, MO, and London: University of Missouri Press, 1993), 243–51. The Russian text of the Gromyko report was first published in *Sovetsko-Amerikanskiie Otnosheniia* 1, 206 (1984), 338–39.

50. See Roosevelt to Spellman, in Gannon, *Spellman Story,* September 1943, 22–24, 246.

51. See Polonsky, *The Great Powers,* no. 99, and Kersten, *Establishment of Communist Rule in Poland.*

52. Larsh, "Harriman and the Polish Question," 545, and "Yalta and the American Approach," 280.

3. Berlin Revisited—and Revised: Eisenhower's Decision to Halt at the Elbe

David Hogan

On March 28, 1945, General of the Army Dwight D. Eisenhower directed that the main thrust of the final Allied advance east from the Rhine into the heart of Germany would be carried out by his center toward Leipzig and Dresden, not by his northern wing to Berlin. Two weeks later, the Ninth U.S. Army, poised on the Elbe River only fifty miles from the Nazi capital, received orders to stop there and not to drive on Berlin, which was left to the Soviet Red Army. Among Eisenhower's decisions in a distinguished career as soldier, supreme commander, and president, none has been more controversial. For fifty years, fierce debate has raged between those observers who see his decision as a naive miscalculation that abandoned Central Europe to Communism and those who defend it as judicious and realistic, given the circumstances. Because of repeated cold war crises centered on Berlin, the decision became an emotional focus for the generation that fought World War II only to face another confrontation. For students of war termination, the decision and the context in which it was made present a valuable case study of the interplay of strategy, national politics, and personalities at the close of one conflict and the beginning of another.

The events surrounding the decision can be briefly summarized. Before D day, June 6, 1944, long-range plans by Eisenhower's Supreme Headquarters, Allied Expeditionary Force (SHAEF) envisioned a main effort in the north German plain combined with a secondary drive near Frankfurt, with the two prongs encircling the key industrial area of the Ruhr. While pinpointing Berlin as the ultimate Allied objective, SHAEF planners at the time believed the Nazi capital to be beyond the reach of the western Allies. Following the rapid Anglo-American drive across France in July and August 1944, British Field Marshal Sir Bernard L. Montgomery repeatedly advocated a single, concentrated thrust by his Twenty-first Army Group across northern Germany toward Berlin, and, on March 27, 1945, having crossed the Rhine, he issued orders for a drive by his First Canadian Army, Second British Army, and Ninth U.S. Army to the Elbe and, possibly later, to Berlin. But the next day, Eisenhower, in a dispatch to Soviet leader Joseph Stalin, proposed that his forces, once they had finished the encirclement and mop-up of the Ruhr "in late April or even earlier," make their main effort on the Erfurt-Leipzig-Dresden axis to a junction with the Red Army. He would then follow with a secondary drive southeast to a linkup with the Soviets in the Regensburg-Linz area, thus preventing consolidation of German resistance in "a redoubt in southern Germany." That same day, while waiting for Stalin's response, he shifted the Ninth Army back to Gen. Omar N. Bradley's Twelfth Army Group in the center and directed Bradley to make the main effort to Leipzig.[1]

Eisenhower's unilateral action sparked a furor between his British and American superiors. The British Chiefs of Staff protested to their American colleagues about the sudden change of plan and the direct contact with Stalin. Once the British chiefs had made their case, Prime Minister Winston Churchill entered the fray, arguing that Berlin was strategically important and warning that capture of the city by the Soviets might cause them to believe that they had been the "overwhelming contributor" to victory. The U.S. Joint Chiefs of Staff, however, backed their general, and the British had to acquiesce. Eisenhower had a last opportunity to reconsider in mid-April, when the Ninth Army reached the Elbe and Lt. Gen. William H. Simpson asked for permission to advance on Berlin. Eisenhower said no, leaving Berlin to the Soviets. The Red Army finally began its offensive on April 16 and, after a bitter struggle, occupied the city on May 2.[2]

Although controversy over Eisenhower's decision was probably inevitable, given Berlin's status as the ultimate Allied objective in so many minds, the speed with which the dispute erupted appears to have caught the main actors off balance. Even before the end of the war in Europe, Drew Pearson, the controversial columnist for the *Washington Post* and an old nemesis of Eisenhower, announced that, on April 13, American advance patrols had reached Potsdam, "which is to Berlin what the Bronx is to New York City," but had withdrawn the next day to the Elbe, largely because of a prior understanding with Stalin in February at the Yalta Conference that the Red Army would occupy Berlin. Although President Roosevelt's confidant, Harry Hopkins, and others who had attended the Yalta Conference denied any secret agreement, and despite the fact that American units had never come near Potsdam, Pearson had planted a pernicious and all too durable seed. Thereafter, many Americans and Europeans believed that the late President Roosevelt, whether through illness or treason, had struck a secret deal with Stalin to leave Berlin to the Red Army.[3]

Initial debate over Eisenhower's decision, though vigorous, did not approach the vehemence that it would reach in later years. Harry C. Butcher, Eisenhower's former naval aide, mentioned in his published diary the general desire among soldiers and reporters for an advance on Berlin, and he quoted passages from press conferences in which Eisenhower and his chief of staff, Lt. Gen. Walter B. Smith, stated that the relative proximity of the Red Army to Berlin and the overriding goal of destroying the German army precluded a drive on the Nazi capital. Nevertheless, Butcher's duties with press relations at the time prevented him from giving the insider's view of decision making characteristic of the book's earlier sections. Smith himself, in a series of articles for the *Saturday Evening Post,* denied that any "political consideration" figured in the decision and contended that Berlin, although seen as the "political heart and ultimate goal" by Allied planners at the start of the campaign, had lost all meaning as a military objective by late March 1945. For its time, his account devoted an unusual amount of space to the Berlin decision, largely because Smith was responding to Ralph Ingersoll, former editor of *PM* magazine, member of Bradley's staff, and author of an anglophobic tome that argued that Bradley had outfoxed Eisenhower and the British to ensure the Americans their proper place in the final campaign. In contrast to Smith, John Deane, the American liaison in Moscow, gave scant space to the Berlin issue in his account, and Montgomery's 1947 memoir, intentionally bland to promote Anglo-American unity, provided only a basic outline of the subject.[4]

When Eisenhower wrote his memoirs a year later, however, deteriorating east-west relations clearly had an impact on his spirited response to the charges by Pearson and Ingersoll. Not surprisingly, his prior report to the Combined Chiefs of Staff, published in 1946, had emphasized the military benefits of the center thrust in terms of flexibility, division of enemy forces, and cutting off a possible last stand in an Alpine redoubt. The 1948 memoir, however, provided a more extended defense. The supreme commander pointed out that, in late March, the Red Army was 250 miles closer to the capital than the Anglo-Americans, who would have had to immobilize units on the rest of the front to sustain a drive on Berlin. Such a course of action he dismissed as "stupid." Eisenhower also argued that it was vital to occupy the whole of Germany as quickly as possible to preclude the formation of a guerrilla organization that might prolong the war. He claimed that the prior Allied agreement to split Germany into occupation zones did not affect his decision, but he did state in his final chapter that he believed the western Allies could have gained a better deal on zones with the Soviets than they did. Most of the last chapter consisted of a plea for conciliation with the Soviet Union, arguing that the Anglo-American experience at SHAEF showed that peoples of different outlooks and ways of life could work together.[5]

By the time *Crusade in Europe* appeared in November 1948, the cold war had intensified, as had the debate over the crucial decisions at the end of World War II. The Soviet blockade of Berlin in June 1948, and the Anglo-

American airlift during the summer and autumn, inevitably called attention to Eisenhower's decision among critics who questioned how the west could have reached such a predicament. In Britain, Sir James Grigg, Churchill's secretary of state for war, stated in his memoir that, had Eisenhower adopted Montgomery's single-thrust strategy, the Allies would have reached Berlin first and ended the war by Christmas 1944, thus moving the iron curtain to the east. J. F. C. Fuller, the noted British strategist and military critic, criticized the supreme commander's ultra caution, which, he argued, threw away the sole chance for salvaging Central Europe at war's end. American critics such as Hanson W. Baldwin saw the decision to halt at the Elbe as part of a larger failure by naive American policy makers to perceive the Soviet threat and to develop a realistic design for the postwar world. With the end of the American nuclear monopoly, the outbreak of war in Korea, and the growing suspicion of Communist influence in government as the 1950s began, some Americans were ready to believe Sen. Joseph R. McCarthy's charge that the Berlin decision was part of a plot by the former army chief of staff General of the Army George C. Marshall and other American leaders to leave Eastern Europe to the Soviets.[6]

In this atmosphere of fear and recrimination, Omar Bradley's *A Soldier's Story*, which appeared in 1951, provided ammunition to both sides. Interestingly, Bradley treated the decision to halt at the Elbe almost as an afterthought, within the context of the problem of avoiding accidental clashes with the onrushing Soviets. The general seemed to feel that the real strategic debate had been settled earlier in March 1945, when Eisenhower called Montgomery's bluff about the need for ten more American divisions to support his attack on the Ruhr from the north, deciding instead on a double envelopment of the Ruhr. When Bradley discussed the Berlin decision, he minimized his own role and downplayed the return of the Ninth Army from the Twenty-first Army Group to his Twelfth Army Group. Bradley viewed Eisenhower's decision as correct. He had told the supreme commander that the capture of Berlin would cost one hundred thousand casualties, "a pretty steep price to pay for a prestige objective, especially when we've got to fall back and let the other fellow take over." In this, he was referring to the prior agreement that had left Berlin in the proposed Soviet zone. Yet Bradley gave ammunition to critics of the decision by admitting his concurrence in the "great illusion" of peaceful Soviet postwar intentions. Implying that the British might have been right about the political advantages of capturing Berlin, he confessed, "As soldiers we looked naively on this British inclination to complicate the war with political foresight and nonmilitary objectives."[7]

The theme of American naïveté in the face of Soviet political ambition is echoed by Chester Wilmot's 1952 study, *The Struggle for Europe*, still an influential analysis of the campaign in northwest Europe. Wilmot, an Australian journalist, believed that, by late March 1945, the sinister trend in Soviet policy and behavior, including violation of the Yalta agreements wherever tested, should have been as obvious to the Americans as it was to Churchill, who wanted the Allies to take Berlin and advance further eastward to ensure a stronger bargaining position. Wilmot was certain that the Anglo-Americans would have won a race for Berlin, citing the lack of meaningful enemy defenses and resistance, but, he laments, the supreme commander would not even try. Wilmot pointed to the last chapter of Eisenhower's memoirs, with its warm portrait of the average Russian and his natural bond with Americans, as evidence of the supreme commander's credulity. He stated that Eisenhower made his decision only on the military basis of defeating Germany as soon as possible at minimum cost, without regard to recent Soviet behavior; and he implied that the real responsibility for the decision, given Roosevelt's ill health, lay with the Joint Chiefs, who could have acted but instead backed Eisenhower. The Berlin decision, Wilmot concluded, contributed to the western Allies winning the war but losing the peace.[8]

As influential as was Wilmot's argument, the final volume of Winston Churchill's memoirs of World War II, *Triumph and Tragedy*, elevated the Berlin controversy to its central place in the debate over Anglo-American wartime strategy. Written with Churchill's dramatic flair, the prime minister took as his central theme the tragic return of the triumphant democracies to "the follies which had so nearly cost them their life." Arguing the critical importance of politics as a coalition war draws to an end, Churchill contends that the "deadly hiatus" between Roosevelt's fading strength and Harry S. Truman's grasp of affairs left American policy rudderless and Churchill able only to "warn and plead . . . with an aching heart and a mind oppressed by forebodings."[9]

Churchill argued that, with the destruction of German power and the growing menace of Soviet imperialism by late March, the western democracies should have adjusted their strategic goals to include Berlin as their "prime and true objective." He endorsed the protest of Eisenhower's decision by his military chiefs but contends they were bringing in many tangential issues rather than focusing on the overdispersion of the Twenty-first Army Group and Berlin's political and psychological importance. Churchill's status as hero, elder statesman, and serving prime minister when the book appeared in 1953 ensured it a wide reading, although the ongoing east-west conflict clearly shaped his interpretation of events.[10]

By 1953, the year Eisenhower entered the White House, most analysts tended to agree with Churchill that the decision to forgo Berlin had been a mistake, but many questioned whether the supreme commander could have acted differently. With the publication in 1954 of SHAEF's official history, and an elaboration of its main points on the Berlin decision in a 1960 essay, Forrest C. Pogue emerged as Eisenhower's most effective advocate on the subject. Pogue emphasized the agreement on zones, the eagerness of American leaders to end the European war in order to focus on the Pacific, and Eisenhower's background in a military tradition in which commanders concentrated on military factors and left political considerations to civilians. Although in September 1944 the supreme commander declared Berlin to be the ultimate objective, he recognized that he might need to adjust his plans according to the progress of the Red Army. By late March 1945, Soviet proximity to Berlin, the difficult terrain between the Elbe and that city, and the prospect of heavy losses in taking it caused him to change his mind, just as the pressing need to coordinate movements with the Red Army led him to contact Stalin directly. As Pogue pointed out, Eisenhower never received political guidance from Washington on Berlin; it is hard to argue that he should have taken an action with so many political overtones on his own initiative. Thus, Pogue implicitly criticized not Eisenhower but his superiors for their lack of policy guidance.[11]

Other official histories, even by British authors, were almost as sympathetic. Published in 1959, Roland G. Ruppenthal's landmark study of American logistics in the European theater laid out the much greater ability of SHAEF to support a center drive, where communications existed to support fifty divisions, rather than a main effort in the north, where congested communications could support only thirty-six Allied divisions. Meanwhile, John Ehrman's well-respected British study of Allied grand strategy, published in 1956, implies that much of the fault for the Anglo-American dispute over SHAEF's change of strategy could be traced to chronic communication problems between Eisenhower's headquarters and the British chiefs, who underestimated the thought that went into SHAEF's decision.[12]

If Ehrman was conciliatory, Britain's two leading wartime soldiers were not. Two years after Ehrman's volume appeared, with east and west again confronting each other over Berlin and Anglo-American relations only beginning to recover from what the British viewed as betrayal in the Suez crisis, Montgomery and Alanbrooke criticized of Eisenhower's decision. Irritated by his unfavorable treatment at the hands of American authors, Montgomery composed a second memoir, in which he contended that the western Allies could have taken Berlin and ended the war quickly if they had followed the original, single-thrust strategy that he had proposed in August 1944. The field marshal stated that he had been careful to take into account political considerations, including the value of Berlin, Vienna, and Prague for the postwar era. But American strategists, he complained, focused too heavily on military factors, causing the west to lose the war politically.

Montgomery's criticism was matched by that of Sir Alanbrooke, his patron and predecessor as chief of the Imperial General Staff. In Alanbrooke's wartime diaries, edited by Sir Arthur Bryant and published in 1959, one finds disillusion and a certain bitterness over what Alanbrooke saw as the sacrifice of Britain's wartime aims—the early liberation of Holland, the occupation of the North German ports, and a free Denmark—to increase the prestige of American arms with a center drive. Yet Alanbrooke, ever the realist, recognized that the British could do little to change American minds, and he had quickly reconciled himself to Eisenhower's decision.[13]

Despite the swings in Anglo-American relations, Eisenhower retained in Great Britain several old friends and associates who sprang to his defense. Lord Ismay, Churchill's trusted wartime adviser, recalled the atmosphere of the times and pointed out the inability of the democracies to reverse policy, renege on prior zonal agreements, and race the Red Army to Berlin after years of pro-Soviet propaganda. Maj. Gen. Sir Francis W. De Guingand, Montgomery's chief of staff, had remained silent on the Berlin issue in his 1947 memoirs; but in 1964 he contended that, given existing agreements, the premise that the capture of Berlin by the western Allies would have made a difference in the postwar world was at best debatable. In 1966, Air Marshal Sir Arthur W. Tedder, Eisenhower's deputy at SHAEF, pointed out that he and the supreme commander had always viewed political considerations to be outside their sphere and that March 1945 was too late to revise their directive in order to capture points to the east. Maj. Gen. Kenneth W. D. Strong, SHAEF's intelligence chief, attacked Churchill's criticism of Eisenhower's direct contact with Stalin as unfair and stated that, if any chance existed of avoiding a cold war, it was better to have at least tried to avoid confrontation and leave the city to the Red Army. Even Lionel Ellis's official British history of the final campaign admitted that Eisenhower was pursuing the military objective he had received at the start, an objective that his superiors had never required him to change.[14]

Viewing the debate as commander of the North Atlantic Treaty Organization, president, and private citizen, Eisenhower ventured a long way from the good soldier who, in 1946 and 1948, had pushed conciliation and unity in the quest for world peace. As a candidate for president in 1952, running against alleged Democratic softness on Communism, he apparently told Republican advisers nervous about his Berlin decision that he had warned Roosevelt in January 1944 against the European Advisory Commission's (EAC) proposal for occupation zones, recommending instead a quadpartite governing body for Germany. He also recalled to the assembled that he had Smith recommend to Allied leaders at the Malta Conference in January 1945 that they press the Soviets for revisions in zonal boundaries. Eisenhower's account, to which he alluded in 1948, might be true, but his most diligent biographer has found nothing in his wartime papers to indicate any special prescience about the Soviets. As president, having to deal with a divided Berlin, Eisenhower supposedly told Mayor Willy Brandt in 1958 that if he had to make his decision again, he would act differently; and he complained he had received bad political advice. In retirement, he repeated the accounts of his meeting with Roosevelt and the Malta Conference, and he even stated in his 1967 memoirs that he had warned Alanbrooke in January 1943 that a Mediterranean-oriented strategy might leave the Soviets in control of Central and Western Europe. Finally, shortly before his death, he listed both the zonal agreements and military considerations as factors in his decision.[15]

Since Drew Pearson's observations, analysts of Eisenhower's decision had been well aware of the importance of the zonal agreements. The story of those agreements goes back to the Quebec Conference in August 1943, when SHAEF's predecessor, COSSAC (Chief of Staff, Supreme Allied Command), presented an occupation plan that assigned northwest Germany, including the Ruhr, to British forces and a southwest zone to the Americans. The plan left undefined the eastern boundaries of the two zones, since no one could be sure how far the Soviets would advance into Germany. In a November meeting en route to the Cairo Conference, President Roosevelt told his military advisers that he did not want the southwest zone, with its implied responsibility for French internal affairs; and he drew a zonal map that gave the United States control of a northwest zone extending east to, and including, Berlin. The British proposal at the first EAC meetings in January 1944, however, again placed the British in the northwest zone, with the boundary between the Soviet zone and the two western zones about 150 miles west of where Roosevelt had wanted it. In this proposal, Berlin lay well within the Soviet zone. The Soviet proposal in February was almost identical to that of the British. For a year, the three powers haggled over the zonal protocols, but Roosevelt soon acquiesced in leaving Berlin in the Soviet zone and concentrated his eventually unsuccessful efforts on securing the northwest zone for the United States. From the beginning, the Allies viewed Berlin as a separate jurisdiction, which they would rule through a joint occupation; but when inter-Allied agreements left Berlin in the Soviet zone, the western Allies did not press the issue of access, an omission they would later come to rue. Eisenhower's concept of an inter-Allied occupation headquarters that would govern without zones apparently never received serious consideration among the Allied leaders.[16]

As Earl Ziemke later noted, periodic rediscoveries of the Roosevelt map in subsequent years would inspire grumbling over American "giveaways," as if the United States could have disposed of Germany at its own discretion. Many of the "who-lost-the-zonal-agreements" postmortems blamed either the State or War Departments. Lucius D. Clay, commander of the American zone in postwar Germany, and Robert Murphy, Eisenhower's political adviser, castigated State Department negotiators—specifically Ambassador John G. Winant, the American representative on the EAC—for not pressing the access issue from a naive fear that it would upset the Soviets; and Herbert Feis and Philip E. Moseley, former State Department officials, censured the War Department for obstructing State's efforts on grounds that occupation issues were military matters. Other studies by William H. McNeill, Stephen E. Ambrose, and Forrest Pogue faulted the Roosevelt administration in general for uncoordinated policy making and a general aversion to postwar planning. Pogue absolved the War Department of any scheme to shelve Roosevelt's zonal plan; State's ignorance of the plan, he argued, resulted from Harry Hopkins's negligence in forwarding it to that agency. The most complete account of the agreements on Berlin, written by Daniel J. Nelson in the cooler atmosphere of the late 1970s, did not take sides but argued the fallacy of assuming the EAC could have reached a more favorable agreement than the one that worked, despite numerous obstacles, for three years after the war.[17]

By the mid-1960s, as the anticommunist consensus reigned supreme in the west and American troops deployed to Vietnam, World War II literature was beginning to shift in emphasis from memoirs to histories and biographies, as the leading participants, their versions written, passed from the scene. At this time, two popular American historians, known for their effective, large-scale use of interviews to reconstruct events, turned their attention to the Berlin decision. In a 1965 study, John Toland found Eisenhower to be politically naive, arguing that his desire to alleviate Soviet suspicions regarding the Italian surrender negotiations caused him to leave Berlin to the Red Army. Drawing on Samuel P. Huntington's classic analysis of American civil-military relations, Toland also censured the Joint Chiefs for losing professional impartiality and backing dubious administration policies favoring collaboration with the Soviets, despite the implications for American security. Cornelius Ryan alleged that Eisenhower could have taken Berlin but that he was not trained to take political factors into account in military strategy and was overly worried about the possibility of a redoubt in the Alps. Thus, he left the city to Stalin, who fought for political as well as military victory. Based heavily on interviews, including, in Ryan's case, conversations with Red Army leaders, both books drew large audiences and influenced the views of thousands on the Berlin decision.[18]

The popular historians, however, drew a harsh response from Stephen Ambrose, editor of Eisenhower's papers and later his most notable biographer. In a slashing review of Ryan's work, and later in his own book-length study of the Berlin decision, Ambrose portrayed Eisenhower as far more politically astute than his critics claimed, although he concedes that the supreme commander did try to base his decisions on military grounds. Eisenhower, Ambrose stated, knew that the United States sought the earliest possible defeat of the Axis and continued friendship with the Soviet Union; indeed, the general sensed that a decision to take Berlin involved such immense political implications that it should not be left to a general. Ambrose dismissed much British criticism of Eisenhower's action as scapegoating to rationalize British postwar weakness, and he chided Ryan for giving Stalin more credit for Machiavellian ingenuity than the Soviet dictator deserved. Bringing up the usual factors of comparative distance from Berlin, the advantages of a center drive, and anxiety about prolonged German resistance in a redoubt— a concern he saw as reasonable—Ambrose contended the Allies had reached their logistical limits at the Elbe; and he stated pointedly that Anglo-American capture of Berlin would have made no difference, since Roosevelt was not ready to risk World War III to scrap the zonal agreements. In the midst of the cold war, Ambrose was not ready to say definitively that Eisenhower made the right decision, but he found it to be a reasonable one.[19]

Other authors also defended Eisenhower against the charge of naïveté. In 1969, the year of the general's death, his son argued that Eisenhower made his decision only after having failed at Malta to induce Allied leaders to revise the zonal agreements. That same year, Ambrose's *The Supreme Commander* presented Eisenhower as a shrewd strategist who did not question limits on his policy making but believed that he had the right to try to influence decisions on such issues as occupation zones. After newly released records of the Combined Chiefs of Staff and the memoirs of Nikita Khrushchev seemed to show that Eisenhower had implicitly colluded with Stalin to permit the Red Army to take Berlin, some of the general's old Republican cohorts published a transcript from the July 1952 conference in which the presidential candidate informed them that he had opposed occupation zones for postwar Germany and had sent Smith to Malta to request revised zonal boundaries. The substance of the disclosure was hardly new to scholars, having been revealed by Eisenhower to some extent in *Crusade in Europe*, but the picture of a supreme commander suspicious of the Soviets and eager to bring Berlin into western hands had never been more clearly drawn. Other accounts by Charles B. MacDonald, Peter Lyon, Russell F. Weigley, Eric Larrabee, and Merle Miller likewise depicted Eisenhower as far more politically aware in his decision than his critics allowed.[20]

Another group of historians agreed on Eisenhower's political sagacity, but for different reasons. During the late 1960s and 1970s, as Americans increasingly questioned their institutions in the wake of an unpopular war abroad and social upheaval at home, the New Left historians used neo-Marxist concepts to challenge traditional assumptions about American foreign policy. Analyzing Eisenhower's decision to halt at the Elbe, Gabriel Kolko found the supreme commander's strategy hardly less political than that of the British. Kolko argued that Roosevelt and Hopkins very much wanted Berlin but that in February 1945 the strength of opposing forces on the western front was nearly equal, and the Germans had not yet stopped the Soviet drive in the east. Faced with the likelihood that the Soviets would reach Berlin first and realizing that they were already assured of a joint occupation, American policy makers looked toward other objectives, notably the Baltic port of Lubeck, whose capture would keep the Red Army from advancing into Denmark. Thus, Eisenhower shrewdly moved to ensure the occupation of as much of the British, French, and American zones as possible, allowing the Soviets to pay the heavy price for Berlin.[21]

In some quarters, even in the late 1970s and 1980s, suspicion of the Berlin decision had not entirely dissipated. For Gen. James M. Gavin, former commander of the Eighty-second Airborne Division, which had prepared to drop into the city in the event of a German collapse, Eisenhower's stated reasons for the decision did not ring true. His distrust led the former paratrooper to speculate, somewhat in the fashion of Senator McCarthy, that the supreme commander might have had a secret understanding with Marshall about Berlin. In his 1981 potboiler focusing on personalities and national rivalries in the Allied high command, British author David Irving ascribes the Berlin decision to Bradley, who, he claimed, persuaded Eisenhower over lunch on March 28, the night after, Irving alleges, a visit by the general and his British driver, Kay Summersby, to Paris's Raphael Hotel. Similarly, Piers Brendon, British author of a 1986 biography of Eisenhower, dismissed the general's claims that military factors and circumstances forced his decision. From Brendon's perspective, Eisenhower's loss of patience with Montgomery led the supreme commander to reward the loyal Bradley with the main effort. Indeed, Brendon stated, if the Twenty-first and Twelfth Army Groups had reversed positions, Eisenhower might well have raced the Soviets to Berlin.[22]

Most Eisenhower biographies of the 1980s, however, took a much more positive view of the supreme commander's motives regarding Berlin. Perhaps reacting to the widespread cynicism about American institutions in the late 1960s and 1970s, these studies suggested that Eisenhower, if hardly naive, was given to idealism. Blanche Wiesen Cook pointed out his readiness to use covert means to gain national ends, but she also contended that he

shared Roosevelt's enthusiasm for international organization and cooperation with the Soviets. Although such American policy makers as Secretary
of the Navy James Forrestal, Secretary of State Edward R. Stettinius Jr., and
Ambassador to the Soviet Union Averell Harriman saw the wartime alliance
as over and wanted a tougher stance toward the Soviets, Eisenhower sought
a quick, noncompetitive victory over the Nazis. In his 1983 biography,
Stephen Ambrose revised his portrait of the politically astute Eisenhower to
argue that his subject possessed a "Wilsonian idealism" about the prospect of
the Great Powers acting in concert to preserve world peace and prosperity.
Ambrose even stated that Eisenhower cherished dangerously inappropriate
ideas about the similarities between Anglo-American ties, such as those that
existed at SHAEF, and Soviet-American relations. Eisenhower's genuine
belief that conciliation with the Soviets was possible, Ambrose thought, was
the real reason he allowed the Red Army to have Berlin; and Ambrose found
the general's later attempts to revise the record on his feelings about the Soviets to be unconvincing.[23]

It was left to David Eisenhower to take up the cudgels in defense of his
grandfather. The younger Eisenhower used materials and contacts unavailable to other researchers, including an interview in which Bradley revealed
that he and Eisenhower had decided in mid-March that Berlin was attain-
able but not worth the risk or cost of a race. David Eisenhower found the
supreme commander's freedom of action restricted by his interpretation of
his original directive, which mandated German unconditional surrender and
cooperation with the Soviets as his objectives, and by the lack of guidance
from his superiors, due to the "deadly hiatus" in Washington. The younger
Eisenhower also presented the novel argument that British leaders did not
really want Berlin so much as a northern drive, which would secure historic
British interests along the North Sea coast and in Denmark. The supreme
commander, however, knew that Marshall would not tolerate leaving the
main role to the British, and he doubted Anglo-American leaders were as
ready to write off cooperation with the Soviets as the prime minister's statements indicated. Under the impetus of Marshall's March 27 dispatch, which
seemed to advocate a drive to the redoubt area and warned of the need to
coordinate with the Soviets, Eisenhower sent to Stalin a letter shrewdly calculated to draw out the latter's intentions. In the end, David Eisenhower
argued, his grandfather's carefully considered actions shortened the war
more quickly than a Berlin drive could have.[24]

As did others before him, David Eisenhower argued that the main responsibility for the decision rested with his grandfather's superiors. Numerous
evaluations of Roosevelt as wartime statesman have dwelled on his distaste

for postwar planning, haphazard administrative methods, and relish for play-ing off advisers and agencies against each other. Historians have been fasci-nated with the question of whether he was prepared for the kind of shift in American policy toward the Soviets that would have made a decision to go for Berlin worthwhile, with recent studies developing the picture of a crafty juggler moving toward a harder line but sensing that public opinion and the demands of the Pacific war would not stand a major policy change over Berlin.[25]

By March 1945, however, Roosevelt was a mere shadow of his former self, and he was leaving more strategic policy in the hands of his advisers. Judging from the existing literature, Army Chief of Staff Marshall was the only official in Washington substantially involved in the Berlin decision. Mar-shall never wrote his memoirs, but he did grant interviews, including one session in which he defended the Berlin decision of his protégé, Eisenhower, as fully in accord with the conciliatory American policy at the time; and he dismissed criticism of it as "Monday morning quarterbacking." According to Forrest Pogue's magisterial biography of Marshall, the chief of staff in the last months of the war was suspicious of British motives and unwilling to pick a fight with the Soviets, who he knew would be the leading power in Europe after the defeat of Nazi Germany. Thus, he fully backed Eisenhower in his desire to give Bradley the main effort in the final drive.[26]

Among the supreme commander's American subordinates, Bradley emerges as the one most involved in the decision, if not the main impetus for it. Normally, Bedell Smith would have exercised considerable influence, but by late March, as D. K. R. Crosswell's biography of Smith states, Eisen-hower increasingly relied on Bradley as his main confidant over his chief of staff, who was bedridden at the time. As Smith's memoirs showed, he loy-ally backed the decision, although he later speculated on how the postwar world might have been altered if Churchill's counsel had prevailed. In his pseudomemoir with Clay Blair, Bradley is quoted as stating that the Soviet advance and reports from ULTRA—British intelligence intercepts of Ger-man radio communications—that German governmental agencies and army headquarters were being moved toward a possible redoubt in the south determined Eisenhower's decision for a center drive. Once the Ninth Army reached the Elbe, it was tempting to let Simpson go on to Berlin; but, according to Bradley and Blair, military prudence and logistics dictated a halt. Even in this new memoir, Bradley remained coy about his role. Gen. George S. Patton Jr., the colorful commander of the Third Army, was not involved in the actual decision, but according to his papers as edited by Mar-tin Blumenson, he made no secret of his belief that the Anglo-Americans should "take Berlin and quick, and on to the Oder." Inevitably, some observers have speculated on what might have happened had the volatile Patton been in Simpson's place on the Elbe.[27]

One of the more intriguing aspects of the Berlin controversy has been debate over the centrality of the rumored Alpine redoubt as a factor in the decision. Evidence of its importance seems overwhelming in Eisenhower's report and memoirs as well as in many other accounts, but Pogue and Ambrose later downplay it as a consideration. As Rodney Minott pointed out in the most thorough treatment of the subject, the redoubt never existed except in the minds of a few Nazis and German generals; the Germans in late March simply lacked the morale, leadership, supplies, plans, or time to develop one. Yet many in Allied headquarters believed the reports. Responses to rumors of the redoubt ranged from British skepticism, according to John Ehrman's British official history, to the credulity of the Twelfth Army Group and Seventh U.S. Army. SHAEF intelligence chief Kenneth Strong, in his memoirs, portrayed a supreme commander and SHAEF staff skeptical of the confused and unconfirmed reports of the redoubt but leery of ignoring the possibility of its existence. As Ambrose stated, the idea of a Nazi last stand in a natural Alpine fortress had substantial plausibility. Minott blamed faulty American intelligence evaluation, including a tendency to stress evidence supporting preconceived conclusions and a possible subconscious effort to compensate for past intelligence failures. Although the Bradley-Blair memoir listed ULTRA as a factor, Ralph Bennett's authoritative study of ULTRA found little evidence of a redoubt in the intercepts until the very last days of the war.[28]

Analysts of the Berlin decision have also been interested in the motives behind Prime Minister Churchill's actions, especially his status as a latterday Cassandra. Beginning with Chester Wilmot, many authors, including both John and David Eisenhower, have praised Churchill's prophecy of the Soviet menace. Dwight Eisenhower, in his memoirs, was more guarded in assessing Churchill's motives, and Ralph Ingersoll perceived an outright play for the prestige of British arms. In his 1974 official history, based on the papers of the British War Cabinet, Roger Parkinson found that only on April 1, having protested the decision on military grounds, did Churchill belatedly recognize the diplomatic importance of reaching Berlin before the Soviets. Nevertheless, Martin Gilbert's biography has confirmed Churchill's longstanding suspicions of the Soviets. Why was the prime minister so slow to state his misgivings in the case of Berlin? Brian Gardner, in 1963, speculated that Churchill recognized Eisenhower's reluctance to consider political factors in his decisions; and Gilbert, Eric Larrabee, and Robin Edmonds pointed out Churchill's ambivalence in his dealings with the Soviets. Most recently, Tuvia Ben-Moshe depicted a prime minister who, like Roosevelt, doubted the value of postwar planning and oscillated in his views of the Soviets until late March 1945, when Stalin's accusations and the disintegration of German resistance finally opened his eyes to the Red menace.[29]

Scholars who have focused on Churchill's subordinates have perceived personalities, rather than issues, at the heart of the controversy. David Fraser confirmed Arthur Bryant's portrayal of Alanbrooke as a dour professional who believed in the balance of power and the need to guard against Soviet expansionism with the disintegration of German influence. Yet Fraser counters some interpretations, most notably David Eisenhower's, with his view that Alanbrooke's heart was not in the argument, put forward by the British Chiefs of Staff, that SHAEF should make its main effort in the north to secure the north German coast. He also points out, as does Bryant, Alanbrooke's distaste for the use of Berlin as a bargaining chip. Among the Montgomery biographies, Ronald Lewin had sympathy for Eisenhower's situation in a political vacuum and found Montgomery's judgment warped by personal ambition and a romantic belief that capitals still mattered. On the other hand, Richard Lamb criticized the decision on military grounds and blamed it on Eisenhower's desire for revenge against a Montgomery who treated his superior with condescension. In his landmark biography of the field marshal, Nigel Hamilton agreed that Montgomery's poor personal relations with Eisenhower influenced the Berlin decision. But Hamilton also blamed the vengeful Bradley and Alanbrooke's unwitting authorization for a decision that, in Hamilton's view, ignored the true strategic objective: northern Germany.[30]

Soviet views have been largely absent from the Berlin debate, due to the near impossibility of obtaining reliable accounts of high-level Soviet decision making during the cold war. Available Soviet versions have tended to view the controversy as either a British plot, the fruits of a German scheme to sow discord in Allied ranks, or an attempt by bourgeois historians to minimize the achievements of the Red Army. In the latter view, the western Allies turned away from Berlin not because they did not want it, but because they recognized they could not win a race to the city. Most available accounts of the Soviet high command and the Berlin decision have been written by British or American scholars. They almost all present a picture of a Stalin suspicious of Eisenhower's March 28 dispatch and rushing to finalize his own preparations for a drive on the Nazi capital while sending soothing messages to his allies that his final offensive would not start before mid-May.

Ironically, the Soviets have had their own Berlin controversy. In the mid-1960s, Vasili Chuikov, a former army commander, accused his superiors of missing an opportunity for an offensive that could have overrun the Nazi

capital in early February 1945. Earl Ziemke's official U.S. Army study generally agreed with Chuikov, but British Sovietologist John Erickson argued
that the Red Army by February had suffered heavy losses and lacked the
logistics and local superiority for a successful drive. A better picture of the
Soviet side of the debate awaits examination of the Soviet archives.[31]

In the six years since the collapse of the Berlin Wall, there seems to be
emerging consensus among historians that Eisenhower could not reasonably
have reached any other decision. H. P. Wilmott's recent survey argued convincingly that confirmation of the zonal agreements at Yalta sealed Berlin's
fate. After that point, the only justification the western Allies could have
claimed for a drive on Berlin would have been either that Berlin possessed
overwhelming strategic importance—a value that, in his view, it clearly did
not have—or that new reasons existed to renege on their agreements and
ensure exclusion of the Soviet Union from central Germany, a course, he
believed, that was never considered by any responsible western leader. Tuvia
Ben-Moshe added to the zonal agreements thesis another factor that made
any other decision by Eisenhower implausible: the Allied policy of unconditional surrender, which ensured that a line between western and Soviet
spheres of influence would exist in central Europe. Other scholars, such as
Gerhard Weinberg and John Ellis, have brought up the importance of political considerations in coalition warfare, specifically Eisenhower's desire to
give the main effort to the Americans; but Weinberg acknowledges the centrality of the zonal agreements in Eisenhower's decision.[32]

Despite the attention devoted to Eisenhower's decision, we will probably
never know with absolute certainty his reasons for stopping at the Elbe. His
original directive, which was never changed, called on him to work with the
other United Nations, including the Soviet Union, to "enter the heart of Germany" and destroy the German armed forces. The Red Army, in late March,
was much closer to the Nazi capital than were the western Allies. Even if
Eisenhower, as Bradley stated, still thought that he might win a race, his
directive and conciliatory outlook toward the Soviets, and his training on the
priority of enemy armed forces over mere geographic points as military
objectives, inclined him to conclude that the ravaged city was not worth the
cost or the risk. Eisenhower knew that, under prior agreements, he would
have to return Berlin to the Soviets; and he shared the view of most Americans of the time that cooperation with the Soviets would be necessary to
ensure a peaceful postwar world. He also found convincing the many military arguments for a center drive—division of the remaining German forces,
the logistical ability to concentrate more of his divisions, the lure of Germany's second largest remaining industrial area, and the capacity to overrun potential guerrilla bases, including a possible Alpine redoubt. At least

as compelling was the political necessity in a coalition war for the over-whelming American representation in his forces to have the main effort in the final drive. His growing rift with Montgomery and his desire for Bradley to have the major role must have had some impact. These two latter factors might explain his failure to consult the British and his later sensitivity on the subject.[33]

The Ninth Army having reached the Elbe, Eisenhower might have allowed it to continue to Berlin, despite its overextended state, if not for the British reaction to his decision. The dispatch to Stalin clearly surprised British leaders, although Gavin, Lamb, and David Eisenhower point out indications that should have alerted London to the coming change in strat-egy. The British Chiefs of Staff were especially irritated with SHAEF's approach to Stalin, even though they had discussed direct contacts at Yalta. Concerned about the impact of growing Soviet domination of Central Europe on the balance of power, Alanbrooke was taken aback by the re-pudiation of the main effort in the north, a strategy that he had long sought at least in part to secure historic British interests along the North Sea coast. Nonetheless, with victory at hand, he turned philosophic, dismissing the new strategy as minor changes for American prestige. As for Churchill, the record indicates that the prime minister, at least initially, was not as opposed to the decision on diplomatic grounds as he later argued in his memoirs. Although he had often warned of Soviet expansionism, he had also been conciliatory toward Stalin and solicitous of Soviet interests on several occasions. His ini-tial opposition was apparently motivated more by a desire for a major British role in the last offensive and for the capture of Berlin for its psychological value. Only belatedly did he point to the Soviet menace and the need to advance as far east as possible. Throughout the dispute, he always kept in mind his first priority: to maintain the western alliance.[34]

Churchill and others who thought the Allies should have taken Berlin assumed that the Anglo-Americans would have won a race, a presumption by no means certain. True, by late March, the western allies had built an im-pressive logistical structure to support an offensive east of the Rhine by a force that had shown its mobility during the pursuit across France. Still, they would have needed to advance ten times as far as the Red Army to reach Berlin. Although the Soviets did not launch their Berlin offensive until April 16, they probably would have hastened their preparations if they had sensed a race in prospect. By mid-April, the disparity in distances had greatly decreased, as the Ninth Army stood at the Elbe, only fifty miles from Berlin, twenty miles farther than the Soviets, with no meaningful defenses and only the enemy Twelfth Army—later dubbed by Charles MacDonald "an army of children"—in its path. The Ninth Army, however, could mass only fifty thousand troops for a Berlin drive, mostly armored spearheads that, though suited for pursuit, lacked the infantry and artillery needed for street fighting. They held only a small bridgehead over the Elbe, with their depots far behind them and several waterways in their path to Berlin. In contrast, the 1.25 million-man Soviet force, backed by twenty-two thousand artillery pieces and holding two solid bridgeheads, was about to start its drive across a dry, level plain to Berlin. Maj. Gen. Raymond L. McLain of the Ninth Army's Nineteenth Corps was probably right when he figured that, at best, he could push only a few patrols into Berlin's suburbs.[35]

Thus, after fifty years, Eisenhower's decision to halt at the Elbe still appears to have been correct. To win the war, his directive and inclination were to destroy the German armed forces, an objective that the capture of Berlin would do little to achieve. Even if his objective were broadened to encompass the much more nebulous goal of breaking the German will to resist, the fall of Berlin would not necessarily have achieved that goal, especially if Hitler had escaped to another location. Thus, Eisenhower could not be sure that the capture of Berlin would be so decisive as to justify concentrating his forces on that endeavor, especially with the Red Army on the verge of capturing the city.

As for the political goal of a more advantageous position vis-à-vis the Soviets for the postwar period, the western Allies, despite their disillusionment with Stalin after Yalta, had not—and indeed, given years of pro-Soviet propaganda and the constraints of diplomacy in a democracy, could not have—abandoned all hope of postwar cooperation with the Soviet Union. In evaluating the zonal agreements, one can lament the bureaucratic wrangling that hampered American policy making, the rush for a deal by a British government concerned about its declining power relative to its allies, and the omission of an access agreement; but the fact remains that the zonal accords represented a good bargain for the west at the time when they were reached. Furthermore, prior to the allocation of a sector to the French, the three zones were roughly equal in size, a good basis for future cooperation among the Great Powers. Repudiation of the agreement might well have caused the Soviets to seize valuable territory in return. In short, Eisenhower could not have attempted to keep Berlin from the Red Army without jeopardizing the existing policy of conciliation.

Eisenhower later liked to state that he made his decision solely on the basis of military factors, a somewhat artificial distinction. It became fashionable later to note the different approaches to wartime decision making of the two allies and to chide the Americans for naïveté by seeking to win the war militarily without considering politics. In fact, the president and a few civilian advisers did leave the conduct of military operations to the generals, whereas the British prime minister, who also served as the minister of war, interacted much more with field commanders regarding details of strategy. The difference in approaches certainly contributed to the irritation in London that Eisenhower had made his decision without consulting British leaders. Still, the two nations' approaches were not as different as first impressions would indicate. Both Roosevelt and Churchill reserved major decisions for themselves, preserving the principle of civilian supremacy, although in the president's last months, his poor health created a near paralysis of policy. Nevertheless, there is scant evidence that a healthy Roosevelt would have changed the Berlin decision. American generals, including Eisenhower, were involved in politics and policy decisions and kept political factors in mind in making decisions, which they knew would have political consequences. Eisenhower weighed political factors in his Berlin decision, which was in accord with the overall policy of collaboration that had guided the Allies to that point.[36]

Ultimately, the discord that arose over the decision stemmed from different visions of how to approach the postwar era. Both the Americans and British hoped for Great Power cooperation but were skeptical over the prospects for it. As they neared victory, differences in outlook and interests became more apparent. British leaders took what Eric Larrabee would call a "European" point of view, keenly aware of the balance of power and national rivalries in Europe. They were concerned about Soviet domination of a Europe in which Germany lay prostrate; and they sought continued Great Power status, which depended largely on continuation of the Anglo-American alliance. Though Roosevelt had expressed a fondness on several occasions for the "Four Policemen" concept, American policy makers were often suspicious of British designs and European balance-of-power politics. They wanted to rely on Great Power cooperation and collective security to maintain postwar peace. Both the United States and Great Britain were democracies whose foreign policies ultimately had to obtain the electorate's approval, but American leaders had to deal with the legacy of isolationism and the possibility that reliance on *realpolitik* might again turn the American public from increased international involvement. Also, the Anglo-Americans faced the danger that too much political jockeying for postwar power might jeopardize completion of the war on the terms that all the Allies sought: unconditional surrender.[37]

The Berlin controversy lives on, despite the historical studies that have sought to resolve it. When Pres. George Bush decided to halt victorious American forces short of Saddam Hussein's Baghdad in March 1991, a *Wall Street Journal* editorial warned that the Euphrates River might prove to be "George Bush's Elbe." Four years later, in the midst of the commemorations of the fiftieth anniversary of Allied victory, an American journalist who had been stationed at SHAEF recalled the decision, the disbelief with which it had been heard by fellow reporters, and the consensus that the western Allies could have reached Berlin before the Soviets. Thus, the decision to halt at the Elbe will undoubtedly attract the curious and those searching for "lessons" for some time to come.[38]

Although the Berlin decision may not have added a chilling effect to the worsening conditions that produced the cold war, for more than fifty years Eisenhower's decision to halt at the Elbe has aroused an enormous furor in the generation inspired by the promises of the Atlantic Charter and the Four Freedoms. Many in this generation, dissatisfied by the postwar world, sought to discern how or when the "Great Crusade" had fallen short in its struggle for a more peaceful world. In an environment conducive to scapegoating, conspiracy theories, and "what-if" history, the Berlin decision offered abundant room for speculation on how a different course might have changed history. During repeated confrontations over the divided city during the 1940s, 1950s, and early 1960s, the west inevitably brooded on the might-have-beens. The atmosphere affected leaders such as Eisenhower, Churchill, and Montgomery, whose memoirs sought to justify actions they had taken earlier. As historians have gained some distance from cold war passions, they have viewed the Berlin decision in a broader context and with greater detachment. Still today, however, Eisenhower's decision presents so many imponderables that it continues to serve as a productive and provocative subject for debate.

NOTES

I wish to thank my editors, Arnie Offner and Ted Wilson, for many perceptive suggestions, and also Jim Knight for his help with innumerable interlibrary loan requests.

1. Eisenhower to Military Mission, Moscow, March 28, 1945, in *The Papers of Dwight David Eisenhower: The War Years*, ed. Alfred D. Chandler, 5 vols. (Baltimore: Johns Hopkins University Press, 1970), 4: 2551.

2. Forrest C. Pogue, The *Supreme Command, U.S. Army in World War II* (Washington, D.C.: Office of the Chief of Military History, 1954), 249, 253, 435–36.

3. Drew Pearson, "Yanks, at Berlin Edge, Left to Please Reds," *Washington Post*, April 22, 1945, 1; Wes Gallagher, "Elbe Halt 'According to Plan,' Writer Says," *Washington Post*, April 22, 1945, 3; Stephen E. Ambrose, *Eisenhower and Berlin, 1945: The Decision to Halt at the Elbe* (New York: W. W. Norton, 1967), 10–11; Robert Sherwood, *Roosevelt and Hopkins: An Intimate History* (New York: Harper, 1948), 884; David Eisenhower, *Eisenhower at War, 1943–1945* (New York: Random House, 1986), 36–38, 781.

4. Harry C. Butcher, *My Three Years with Eisenhower* (New York: Simon and Schuster, 1946), 788, 799, 804; Ralph Ingersoll, *Top Secret* (New York: Harcourt, Brace, 1946), 314–16, 320–22; Walter B. Smith, "Eisenhower's Six Great Decisions," *Saturday Evening Post*, July 6, 1946, 20, and July 13, 1946, 26; John R. Deane, *The Strange Alliance: The Story of American Efforts at Wartime Cooperation with Russia* (New York: Viking, 1947), 158; Bernard L. Montgomery, *Normandy to the Baltic* (London: Hutchinson, 1947), 328–31; G. E. Patrick Murray, "Eisenhower and Montgomery: Broad Front versus Single Thrust: The Historiography of the Debate over Strategy and Command, August 1944–April 1945" (Ph.D. diss., Temple University, 1991), 22, 39, 53, 66.

5. *Report by the Supreme Commander to the Combined Chiefs of Staff on the Operations in Europe of the Allied Expeditionary Force, 6 June 1944 to 8 May 1945* (Washington, D.C.: GPO, 1946), 103–7; Dwight D. Eisenhower, *Crusade in Europe* (Garden City, N.Y.: Doubleday, 1948), 396–403, 457–59, 473–75; Murray, "Eisenhower and Montgomery," 126–27.

6. Murray, "Eisenhower and Montgomery," 132–35, 184–85; J. F. C. Fuller, *The Second World War, 1939–1945: A Strategical and Tactical History* (New York: Duell, Sloan and Pearce, 1949), 356; Hanson W. Baldwin, *Great Mistakes of the War* (New York: Harper, 1950), 1–13, 53–57; Joseph R. McCarthy, *America's Retreat from Victory: The Story of George Catlett Marshall* (New York: Devin-Adair, 1951), 43–46.

7. Omar N. Bradley, *A Soldier's Story* (New York: Holt, 1951), 513, 517–18, 531–37. After the war, Bradley told his collaborator on the memoir, Col. Chester B. Hansen, that one major consideration in the Berlin decision was a concern that the Red Army not advance into the prearranged American zone because no one was certain of the ability of the western Allies to evacuate them; see Murray, "Eisenhower and Montgomery," 185.

8. Chester Wilmot, *The Struggle for Europe* (New York: Harper, 1952), 640, 685–96, 716.

9. Winston S. Churchill, *The Second World War*, 6 vols. (Boston: Houghton Mifflin, 1948–1953), 6: ix, 455–56.

10. Ibid., 6: 455–68; Murray, "Eisenhower and Montgomery," 185, 213–14.

11. Pogue, *Supreme Command*, 434–36, 441–45; Forrest C. Pogue, "The Decision to Halt at the Elbe," in *Command Decisions*, ed. Kent R. Greenfield, 2d ed. (Washington, D.C.: Center of Military History, 1987), 479–82.

12. Roland G. Ruppenthal, *Logistical Support of the Armies, U.S. Army in World War II*, 2 vols. (Washington, D.C.: Office of the Chief of Military History, 1959), 2: 373–77; John Ehrman, *Grand Strategy*, vol. 6, *October 1944–August 1945*, History of the Second World War: United Kingdom Military Series (London: Her Majesty's Stationery Office, 1956), 131–49.

13. Bernard L. Montgomery, *The Memoirs of Field Marshal the Viscount Montgomery of Alamein, KG* (Cleveland: World Publishing, 1958), 296–97; "Symposium: Who Was Right? Monty or Ike?" *U.S. News and World Report*, June 22, 1959, 78–84; Sir Arthur Bryant, *Triumph in the West, 1943–1946* (London: Collins, 1959), 441–45.

14. Lord Ismay, *Memoirs of General Lord Ismay* (New York: Viking Press, 1960),

392; Sir Francis W. De Guingand, *Generals at War* (London: Hodder and Stoughton, 1964), 202; Lord Tedder, *With Prejudice* (Boston: Little Brown, 1966), 679; Sir Kenneth W. D. Strong, *Intelligence at the Top* (Garden City, N.Y.: Doubleday, 1968), 191–99; Lionel F. Ellis, *Victory in the West*, vol. 2, *The Defeat of Germany*, History of the Second World War: United Kingdom Series (London: Her Majesty's Stationery Office, 1968), 297–302, 326, 351.

15. James M. Gavin, *On to Berlin: Battles of an Airborne Commander* (New York: Viking Press, 1978), 312; "Why Ike Didn't Capture Berlin: An Untold Story," *U.S. News and World Report*, April 26, 1971, 70–73; Dwight D. Eisenhower, "My Views on Berlin," *Saturday Evening Post*, December 9, 1961, 19–20; Dwight D. Eisenhower, *At Ease: Stories I Tell to Friends* (Garden City, N.Y.: Doubleday, 1967), 264, 268; Dwight D. Eisenhower and Alistair Cooke, *General Eisenhower on the Military Churchill* (New York: Norton, 1970), 55–56; Eisenhower, *Crusade in Europe*, 218, 474–75; Stephen E. Ambrose, *Eisenhower: Soldier, General of the Army, President-Elect, 1890–1952* (New York: Simon and Schuster, 1983), 403.

16. Earl F. Ziemke, *The U.S. Army in the Occupation of Germany, 1944–1946*, Army Historical Series (Washington, D.C.: U.S. Army Center of Military History, 1975), 115–26. See also Daniel J. Nelson, *Wartime Origins of the Berlin Dilemma* (Tuscaloosa: University of Alabama Press, 1978).

17. Lucius D. Clay, *Decision in Germany* (Garden City, N.Y.: Doubleday, 1950), 15; Robert Murphy, *Diplomat Among Warriors* (Garden City, N.Y.: Doubleday, 1964), 227; William H. McNeill, *America, Britain, and Russia: Their Cooperation and Conflict, 1941–1946* (London: Oxford University Press, 1953), 482; Ambrose, *Eisenhower and Berlin*, 5–43; McCarthy, *America's Retreat from Victory*, 43; Herbert Feis, *Churchill, Roosevelt, and Stalin: The War They Waged and the Peace They Sought* (Princeton: Princeton University Press, 1957), 119, 358, 364–65; "How Berlin Got Behind the Curtain," *Time*, September 29, 1961, 18; "The Truth About the Berlin Problem," *U.S. News and World Report*, May 18, 1959, 63–66; Forrest C. Pogue, *George C. Marshall: Organizer of Victory* (New York: Viking Press, 1973), 460–65; Ziemke, *The U.S. Army in the Occupation of Germany, 1944–1946*, 115–17; Nelson, *Wartime Origins of the Berlin Dilemma*, 25, 29–31, 41, 143, 154.

18. John Toland, *The Last 100 Days* (New York: Random House, 1965), 307–8, 312, 315–18; Cornelius Ryan, *The Last Battle* (New York: Simon and Schuster, 1966), 199–200, 207; Stephen E. Ambrose, "Refighting the Last Battle: The Pitfalls of Popular History," *Wisconsin Magazine of History* 49 (spring 1966): 294–95; Murray, "Eisenhower and Montgomery," 170.

19. Ambrose, "Refighting the Last Battle," 294–301; Ambrose, *Eisenhower and Berlin, 1945*, 9–10, 20, 24–31, 67–68, 73–80, 88–89, 93, 97–98.

20. John S. D. Eisenhower, *The Bitter Woods* (New York: G. P. Putnam's Sons, 1969), 436–37, 443–44, 449–51, 466–69; Stephen E. Ambrose, *The Supreme Commander: The War Years of General Dwight D. Eisenhower* (Garden City, N.Y.: Doubleday, 1969), 600–603; "Why Ike Didn't Capture Berlin," 70–73; Charles B. MacDonald, *The Last Offensive, U.S. Army in World War II* (Washington, D.C.: Center of Military History, 1973), 340, 406, 480; Charles B. MacDonald, *The Mighty*

Endeavor: American Armed Forces in the European Theater During World War II (New York: Oxford University Press, 1969), 517; Peter Lyon, *Eisenhower: Portrait of the Hero* (Boston: Little Brown, 1974), 330–36; Russell F. Weigley, *Eisenhower's Lieutenants: The Campaigns of France and Germany, 1944–1945* (Bloomington: Indiana University Press, 1981), 685–87; Eric Larrabee, *Commander in Chief: Franklin Delano Roosevelt, His Lieutenants, and Their War* (New York: Harper and Row, 1987), 498–500, 505–7; Merle Miller, *Ike the Soldier: As They Knew Him* (New York: G. P. Putnam's Sons, 1987), 764.

21. Gabriel Kolko, *The Politics of War: The World and United States Foreign Policy, 1943–1945* (New York: Random House, 1968), 373; Edward N. Saveth, "A Decade of American Historiography: The 1960s," in *The Reinterpretation of American History and Culture*, ed. William H. Cartwright and Richard L. Watson Jr. (Washington, D.C.: National Council for the Social Studies, 1973), 18.

22. Gavin, On to Berlin, 269, 275–77, 283, 298, 312–20; David Irving, *The War Between the Generals* (New York: St. Martin's Press, 1981), 398–99; Piers Brendon, *Ike: His Life and Times* (New York: Harper and Row, 1986), 1, 9–13, 180–83.

23. Blanche Wiesen Cook, *The Declassified Eisenhower: A Divided Legacy of Peace and Political Warfare* (Garden City, N.Y.: Doubleday, 1981), 27, 30–34; Ambrose, *Eisenhower*, 401–4.

24. D. Eisenhower, *Eisenhower at War*, 697, 709–13, 727–33, 738–46, 759–61; David Eisenhower, "The Race for Berlin: Why the Allies Held Back," *U.S. News and World Report*, September 1, 1986, 32.

25. Murphy, *Diplomat Among Warriors*, 247–48; Sherwood, *Roosevelt and Hopkins*, 819; Feis, *Roosevelt, Churchill, and Stalin*, 120; Gaddis Smith, *American Diplomacy During the Second World War, 1941–1945* (New York: John Wiley, 1965), 6, 65, 120, 136, 152–53; Robert Dallek, *Franklin D. Roosevelt and American Foreign Policy, 1932–1945* (New York: Oxford University Press, 1979), 533–34; Terry H. Anderson, *The United States, Great Britain, and the Cold War, 1944–1947* (Columbia: University of Missouri Press, 1981), 28, 43, 48, 51; Warren Kimball, *The Juggler: Franklin Roosevelt as Wartime Statesman* (Princeton: Princeton University Press, 1991), 92–93; Randall B. Woods and Howard Jones, *Dawning of the Cold War* (Athens: University of Georgia Press, 1991), 48.

26. William D. Leahy, *I Was There* (New York: Whittlesley House, 1950), 350–51; Eisenhower and Cooke, *General Eisenhower on the Military Churchill*, 58; Pogue, *Organizer of Victory*, 539, 548–51, 555–57, 568–73. See also Henry L. Stimson and McGeorge Bundy, *On Active Service in Peace and War* (New York: Harper, 1948); Geoffrey Hodgson, *The Colonel: The Life and Times of Henry Stimson, 1867–1950* (New York: Knopf, 1950); Walter Millis, ed., *The Forrestal Diaries* (New York: Viking Press, 1951); Henry H. Arnold, *Global Missions* (New York: Harper, 1949); Ernest J. King and Walter M. Whitehill, *Fleet Admiral King: A Naval Record* (New York: Norton, 1952).

27. D. K. R. Crosswell, *The Chief of Staff: The Military Career of General Walter Bedell Smith* (Westport, Conn.: Greenwood Press, 1991), 315–19; Walter B. Smith, *Eisenhower's Six Great Decisions* (New York: Longmans, Green, 1956), 221; Omar N. Bradley and Clay Blair, *A General's Life: An Autobiography* (New York: Simon and

Schuster, 1983), 416–19, 426–27; Martin Blumenson, *The Patton Papers,* vol. 2, *1940–1945* (Boston: Houghton Mifflin, 1974), 685; John Strawson, *The Battle for Berlin* (NewYork: Charles Scribner's Sons, 1974), 118.

28. Rodney G. Minott, *The Fortress That Never Was: The Myth of Hitler's Bavarian Stronghold* (NewYork: Holt, Rinehart andWinston, 1964), xiii, 135–54; Ralph Bennett, *ULTRA in the West: The Normandy Campaign, 1944–1945* (NewYork: Charles Scribner's Sons, 1979), 257–63; Smith, *Eisenhower's Six Great Decisions,* 176; Strong, *Intelligence at the Top,* 187; Stephen E. Ambrose, *Ike's Spies: Eisenhower and the Espionage Establishment* (Garden City, N.Y.: Doubleday, 1981), 150–52; Pogue, *Organizer of Victory,* 557; Butcher, *My Three Years with Eisenhower,* 799, 809; Eisenhower, *Report by the Supreme Allied Commander,* 103; Eisenhower, *Crusade in Europe,* 397; Bradley, *A Soldier's Story,* 536–37; Bradley and Blair, *A General's Life,* 418–19; J. S. D. Eisenhower, *The Bitter Woods,* 449; D. Eisenhower, *Eisenhower at War,* 712, 727; Nigel Hamilton, *Monty: Final Years of the Field Marshal, 1944–1976* (NewYork: McGraw Hill, 1986), 442; Wilmot, *The Struggle for Europe,* 690; Baldwin, *Great Mistakes of the War,* 54; Pogue, *The Supreme Command,* 435; Ehrman, *Grand Strategy,* 133–34; Ellis, *Victory in the West,* 2: 302; Ambrose, *Eisenhower,* 391–92; Ambrose, "Refighting the Last Battle," 299–300; Ambrose, *Eisenhower and Berlin,* 73–79; MacDonald, *The Last Offensive,* 340–41, 407–9; Weigley, *Eisenhower's Lieutenants,* 700–701; Miller, *Ike the Soldier,* 760–62; Gavin, *On to Berlin,* 282; Crosswell, *Chief of Staff,* 319.

29. Roger Parkinson, *A Day's March Nearer Home: The War History from Alamein to VE Day, Based on the War Cabinet Papers of 1942 to 1945* (NewYork: D. McKay, 1974), 463–74; Martin Gilbert, *Winston Churchill,* vol. 7, *Road to Victory, 1941–1945* (Boston: Houghton Mifflin, 1986), 829, 948, 1157, 1235, 1243, 1273–76; Brian Gardner, *The Wasted Hour: The Tragedy of 1945* (London: Cassell, 1963), 90; Robin Edmonds, *The Big Three: Churchill, Roosevelt, and Stalin in Peace and War* (NewYork: Norton, 1991), 419; Tuvia Ben-Moshe, *Churchill: Strategy and History* (Boulder, Colo.: Lynne Rienner, 1992), 225, 299, 307; Wilmot, *Struggle for Europe,* 689–92; Larrabee, *Commander in Chief,* 494–96; Bryant, *Triumph in the West,* 444; Strawson, *The Battle for Berlin,* 16; Toland, *The Last Hundred Days,* 312; Ryan, *The Last Battle,* 235; Smith, *Eisenhower's Six Great Decisions,* 223; Ingersoll, *Top Secret,* 324; Feis, *Churchill, Roosevelt, and Stalin,* 273; Gordon Wright, *The Ordeal of Total War, 1939–1945* (NewYork: Harper, 1968), 229; D. Eisenhower, *Eisenhower at War,* 697, 709–12, 742; J. S. D. Eisenhower, *The Bitter Woods,* 449–51, 466–67; Eisenhower, *Crusade in Europe,* 399.

30. David Fraser, *Alanbrooke* (NewYork: Atheneum, 1982), 451, 485–86; Bryant, *Triumph in the West,* 469; Ronald Lewin, *Montgomery as Military Commander* (New York: Stein and Day, 1972), 252–54, 258; Richard Lamb, *Montgomery in Europe, 1943–1945: Success or Failure?* (London: Buchan and Enright, 1983), 364–65, 371, 416; Hamilton, *Monty,* 3, 413, 430, 435, 438–49, 458.

31. John Erickson, *The Road to Berlin* (London: Weidenfeld and Nicolson, 1984), 473–76, 517, 522, 528–34; Vasili I. Chuikov, *The Fall of Berlin,* trans. Ruth Kisch (NewYork: Holt, Rinehart, andWinston, 1967), 117–20, 140, 180; Earl F. Ziemke, *Stalingrad to Berlin: The German Defeat in the East,* Army Historical Series (Washing-

ton, D.C.: Office of the Chief of Military History, 1968), 439–40, 456–57, 467–70; Daniil Kraminov, "The End of the War in the West," *International Affairs* 11 (1978): 113–22; Wright, *The Ordeal of Total War*, 202; Bryant, *Triumph in the West*, 443; Strawson, *The Battle for Berlin*, 9–11, 69–72, 110–11; Ryan, *The Last Battle*, 243–52; Gavin, *On to Berlin*, 270; Eisenhower, *Eisenhower at War*, 744–46; Lewin, *Montgomery as Military Commander*, 258.

32. H. P. Wilmott, *The Great Crusade*, 3d ed. (New York: Free Press, 1991), 448–50; John Ellis, *Brute Force: Allied Strategy and Tactics in World War II* (New York: Viking Press, 1990), 412–13; Ben-Moshe, *Churchill*, 312; Gerhard L. Weinberg, *A World at Arms: A Global History of World War II* (New York: Cambridge University Press, 1994), 730, 792, 813–14, 816, 821; John Keegan, *The Second World War* (New York: Viking Press, 1989), 519; Stephen E. Ambrose, "Eisenhower's Generalship," *Parameters* 20 (June 1990): 12; Martin Gilbert, *The Second World War: A Complete History* (New York: Holt, 1991), 658.

33. Pogue's argument on military considerations is persuasive; see Pogue, *The Supreme Command*, 434–35, and also 53; Pogue, "The Decision to Halt at the Elbe," 481; Eisenhower to Marshall, March 30, 1945, in Chandler, ed., *The Eisenhower Papers*, 4: 2559–61; Ambrose, *Eisenhower*, 401–3; D. Eisenhower, *Eisenhower at War*, 727; Eisenhower and Cooke, *General Eisenhower on the Military Churchill*, 55; Ellis, *Brute Force*, 412.

34. Churchill to Eisenhower, March 31, 1945, and Churchill to Roosevelt, April 1, 1945, in Ambrose, *Eisenhower and Berlin*, 99–102; Ehrman, *Grand Strategy*, 132–45; Bryant, *Triumph in the West*, 441–45, 448; Parkinson, *A Day's March Nearer Home*, 463–70; D. Eisenhower, *Eisenhower at War*, 709–15, 727–30, 741–42; Fraser, *Alanbrooke*, 451, 482, 485–86; Gavin, *On to Berlin*, 281; Hamilton, *Monty*, 435.

35. For differing views on this subject, see Bradley, *A Soldier's Story*, 537; Wilmot, *The Struggle for Europe*, 685; Ambrose, *Eisenhower and Berlin*, 93–94; Ambrose, *Eisenhower*, 697; MacDonald, *The Mighty Endeavor*, 517; Larrabee, *Commander in Chief*, 506.

36. Toland, *The Last 100 Days*, 315–19; Samuel P. Huntington, *The Soldier and the State: The Theory and Politics of Civil-Military Relations*, 2d ed. (Cambridge: Belknap Press, 1985), 315–44; Ambrose, *Eisenhower and Berlin*, 26–30; Ambrose, *The Supreme Commander*, 600–604; Cook, *The Declassified Eisenhower*, 27; D. Eisenhower, *Eisenhower at War*, 728; Ehrman, *Grand Strategy*, 135; Churchill, *Second World War*, 6: 455; Montgomery, *Memoirs*, 296–97; Harry S. Truman, *Memoirs*, vol. 1, *Year of Decisions* (Garden City, N.Y.: Doubleday, 1955), 211–12; Eisenhower, *Report by the Supreme Allied Commander*, 107; Eisenhower, *Crusade in Europe*, 396; Eisenhower, *At Ease*, 275–76; Pogue, *The Supreme Command*, 441; Gavin, *On to Berlin*, 315–16; Anderson, *The United States, Great Britain, and the Cold War*, 48.

37. Weinberg, *A World at Arms*, 722–24, 737–38; Woods and Jones, *Dawning of the Cold War*, 48; Larrabee, *Commander in Chief*, 494.

38. "George Bush's Elbe," *Wall Street Journal*, March 13, 1991, A16; Joseph C. Harsch, "Why Eisenhower Halted at the Elbe," *Christian Science Monitor*, April 10, 1995, 9.

4. Dublin: The View from a Neutral Capital

Ronan Fanning

For Ireland, World War II was the greatest security crisis since independence was achieved in 1921 and 1922; indeed, it remains the only international crisis to have posed a real threat to Irish independence. After the fall of France in 1940 that threat was twofold. Germany, aware of Ireland's minuscule and poorly equipped armed forces, might be tempted to invade Ireland as a backdoor to Britain. Britain, on the other hand, virtually isolated in 1940 and 1941, wanted Irish bases for the Battle of the Atlantic and might be tempted to invade to get them. No one was more tempted than Winston Churchill, who had passionately opposed the return of the three Irish ports retained by the British under the Anglo-Irish Treaty of 1921 but that had been relinquished under the terms of the Anglo-Irish defense agreement concluded by Neville Chamberlain with Eamon de Valera (the Irish prime minister and minister for external affairs) in April 1938.

But Ireland was advantaged because geographical accident made it the least vulnerable of European neutrals to German invasion. Ireland was also fortunate that occupation of its territory never became absolutely vital, or was thought to become vital, to the security of any of the belligerents. In short, the advantages to be derived from any attempted occupation were not greater than the costs, moral and military, involved in such an operation.[1]

The partition of Ireland—the fact that Northern Ireland, comprising the six northeastern counties of the island, remained part of the United Kingdom—shaped this Allied assessment. Since British and, from January 1942, American forces could operate from Northern Ireland, bases south of the border, however desirable, were not vital. It was "certain," acknowledged a postwar assessment drawn up by the Department of External Affairs in Dublin, "that it would have been more difficult if not impossible to maintain Irish neutrality were it not for British occupation of the Six Counties."[2]

Irish policy throughout World War II rested on twin foundations, one public, the other secret. Public policy was based on the even-handed implementation of neutrality as "the outward and visible sign of absolute sovereignty . . . the mark of independence."[3] By March 1942, noted a perceptive English visitor to Dublin, neutrality had already assumed "an almost religious flavour; it has become a question of honour; and it is something which Ireland is not ashamed of, but tremendously proud."[4]

But there was a second, secret policy designed to safeguard Ireland from the threat of German victory. Unknown to the Irish public, the Irish government, as British Dominions Secretary Viscount Cranborne wrote in a February 1945 memorandum to the war cabinet, "have been willing to accord us any facilities which would not be regarded as overtly prejudicing their attitude to neutrality." Cranborne appended a fourteen-point list that included staff talks between the British and Irish military authorities to plan against the contingency of a German invasion; the Irish government's silent acquiescence in giving free passage to the tens of thousands of southern Irishmen who served in the Allied forces and who won 780 decorations, including eight Victoria Crosses, twice as many as for Northern Ireland and nearly as many as Canada with triple the population;[5] the establishment of a radar station in February 1945 for use against German submarines; and the provision of vital information to British intelligence.[6] Regarding this underground world of espionage and intrigue, Sir John Maffey, the United Kingdom representative in Dublin throughout the war, later observed, "A British authority in Ireland could never achieve what was achieved by a native authority. 'The dog of the country hunts the hare of the country.' "[7] In Washington, the Office for Strategic Services and the Pentagon were equally appreciative of the substantial intelligence results produced by cooperation with the most senior Irish officers and Irish military intelligence.[8]

Compare this reality with America's official line promulgated in *The Pocket Guide to Northern Ireland* issued to GIs stationed there in 1942. "Eire's neutrality is a real danger to the Allied cause. There just across the Irish Channel from embattled England and not too far away from your own billets in Ulster, the Axis legations maintain large legations and staffs. . . . The Ulster border is 600 miles long and hard to patrol. Axis spies sift back and forth across the border constantly." The Southern Irish, reported the intelligence officer to the First Armored Division in September 1942, "are the most treacherous people on earth."[9]

To suggest that secret Irish support for the Allies betokened a hypocritical departure from strict neutrality ignores that such support was designed to preserve the independence for which neutrality was only an expression. The wisdom of such a course was revealed when the German war plans were disclosed after the war ended. Operation SEA LION provided for the occupation of both islands, and German plans drawn up in September 1940 show that Dublin was one of the six administrative centers from which the Third Reich intended to govern the occupied islands.

There was thus a preservationist, as well as an expressionist, purpose underlying neutrality: the first pragmatic, the second principled. Principle demanded that de Valera's government be publicly perceived, internationally as well as nationally, as acting impartially between both blocs of belligerents. Pragmatism demanded whatever retreat from the practice of absolute neutrality might be required for the ultimate preservation of independence. De Valera's pragmatism was of the same order as that displayed by Pres. Franklin D. Roosevelt when, as late as October 1941, he had informed the British ambassador in Washington "that if he asked for a declaration of war, he wouldn't get it, and opinion would swing against him."[10] The same sort of hard-headed realism established the setting in which transpired Irish reactions to the final collapse of Nazi power.

Reaction in Dublin on May 7–8, 1945, to the news of the German surrender mirrored divided opinions about the merits of neutrality, rigidly maintained behind a stifling curtain of censorship. *The Irish Times,* the most anglophile of Dublin's daily newspapers, had conducted a running battle with the censor throughout the war, and on V-E Day the censor paid no attention to a profusion of single-column photographs of Allied war leaders scattered at random through the proofs. But when the final edition appeared, the editor, R. M. Smyllie, had personally laid out the front page, arranging the single-column photographs into an enormous "V for Victory" from the top to the bottom of the page across all seven columns.[11]

Joy and relief at the Allied victory was likewise reflected in the celebrations of students at Trinity College Dublin who flew British, American, Russian, French, and Irish flags from the roof of the university. But crowds in the streets outside took exception to the positioning of the Irish flag at the bottom of the mast and, still more, to reports that the Irish flag had been hauled down and burned. Minor rioting followed and windows were broken in Trinity, in the British and American diplomatic missions, and in Jammet's Restaurant and the Wicklow Hotel (both of which were regarded as pro-British haunts).[12]

Not surprisingly, American and British resentment at the Irish government's refusal to abandon neutrality in the dying days of the war in Europe remained intense. These resentments were rehearsed in the State Department's instructions to their minister in Dublin, David Gray, on how he should respond if questioned as to why Ireland had not been invited to the inaugural conference of the United Nations in San Francisco.

Only those countries who had declared war on the Axis Powers by March 1 had been invited. *Ireland* is not one of the United Nations and therefore has not been invited. We regret that Ireland's adherence to a policy inconsistent with its historic bonds of blood and friendship with this and other United Nations has made necessary this decision. . . .

In December, 1941, the President notified the Irish Government that its freedom as well as the freedom of the United States was at stake and expressed the hope that the Irish people *would know* how to meet their responsibilities. . . . The Irish Government, however, continued to adhere firmly to the policy of neutrality and in February, 1944 refused our request that Axis diplomatic and consular representatives be removed in order that existing *centers* of espionage could not be used by the Axis Powers to harm the cause of the United Nations. More recently we asked for assurance that Ireland *would not* harbor war criminals, to which the Irish Government made an equivocal reply.

Therefore, while membership in the proposed international organization will in due course be open to all peace-loving nations, Ireland, in view of the policy it has chosen to pursue, has no rightful claim to participate in the formation of the organization.[13]

De Valera's government continued refusing publicly to "recognize [the] existence of any moral issue" between the Axis and UN powers. The Irish censor's refusal to permit publication of the horrors uncovered at Buchenwald and Belsen especially incensed David Gray, who telegrammed that as long as de Valera could prevent Irish recognition of moral issues and keep Irish people in ignorance about Axis practices, he could justify his neutrality and count upon support of a virtually united Ireland in his efforts to exploit frictions among the United Nations and use Irish-American pressure groups to attack administration policy and Anglo-American cooperation.[14]

But de Valera's public adherence to neutrality remained unwavering as the Third Reich disintegrated. He gave the American minister short shrift when Gray called on him on April 30 and demanded possession of the premises and contents of the German legation and of all other German property in Ireland. Gray opened the conversation by telling de Valera that he had just received word from General Eisenhower's political adviser, Robert Murphy, that the Irish minister for Germany, along with the Irish personnel of the legation, had been overrun at Babenhausen near the Swiss frontier by American troops but that they were safe and under American guard at the castle they were occupying and that orders had been issued to treat them with distinguished consideration.

Although de Valera did not question Gray's assertion that the German government no longer exercised effective control over Germany and consequently de facto no longer existed, he insisted on consulting his legal advisers about the precedents in international law. When Gray urged him to seize the opportunity "to show some mark of friendliness," de Valera replied "that he refused to discuss that aspect of the matter since Ireland was neutral." Gray persevered:

I said that was all very well but that there was a human side to the matter. If he were struggling in the ditch with an enemy who was trying to kill him and asked me, a bystander, for help as an old friend, I might have the right to say, "I am sorry, but I am neutral," but nevertheless such a reply would not create a favorable impression on him. I added that in this world one got what one gave. If one gave friendship, one received it. He then told me that he refused to go into that, as he had often told me before when I had taken that line with him. He said that they were neutral and would continue to behave entirely correct[ly] as neutrals.[15]

Gray met an equally unyielding response when he spoke to the secretary of the Department of External Affairs, Joseph P. Walshe, on May 1 and again on May 2. Walshe took the view that the war had not yet ended and that there were serious political difficulties for his government in turning over German government-owned property prior to a formal announcement in the British Parliament of general surrender or collapse of the German Reich.[16]

The State Department's reaction was predictably icy. It charged that the Irish government had "missed the boat," and that in consequence the United States did not intend to invite it to abandon its neutrality or to support its efforts to participate in the peace settlement. Rather, America would adopt toward Ireland an attitude as frigidly indifferent as its government had adopted toward the aspirations of the United Nations.[17]

Frigidity turned to fury when, on May 2 (the day that Gray and Joseph Walshe discussed the sequestration of German property in Ireland), de Valera gratuitously offered the most notorious illustration of what he meant when he told Gray that the Irish government "would continue to behave entirely correct[ly] as neutrals." Acting in his capacity as head of the government and minister for external affairs, and accompanied by Joe Walshe, de Valera called upon Dr. Edouard Hempel, the German minister in Dublin, to express official condolences on Hitler's reported death.

De Valera's action, in the words of Frederick Boland, one of his most senior officials in the Department of External Affairs, was "a ghastly mistake. . . . [the] one thing I profoundly disagreed with him about." Joe Walshe was also opposed. Even Hempel, who was never a Nazi sympathizer, "was aghast" at de Valera's visit and "didn't know what to say." But de Valera, backed up by some of his more anglophobic cabinet colleagues such as Frank Aiken (minister for coordination of defensive measures) and Sean T. O'Kelly, and, remembering that he had condoled with the "Americans a fortnight earlier on the death of Roosevelt, feared being accused of being partisan."[18]

Those Americans were predictably outraged. The *New York Herald Tribune* of May 4, 1945, thundered of "neutrality gone mad—neutrality carried into a diplomatic jungle where good and evil alike vanish in the red-tape thickets: where conscience flounders helplessly in sloughs of protocol, and there is no sustenance for the spirit but mouldy forms and desiccated ceremonies." The *Washington Post* of May 5 likewise editorialized under the heading "Moral Myopia." The Irish legation in Washington reported on the "bitter and caustic" American reaction: "Anti-German feeling was never so bitter here as now." British reaction was similar, and de Valera's courtesy call on Minister Hempel provoked a month-long correspondence in the *Times* (London).[19]

Secretary of State Edward Stettinius was so incensed that he wired the State Department from San Francisco, urging that de Valera's action be brought to the special attention of the president.[20] It may even have prompted a mysterious late-night phone call to the White House, when Harry S. Truman, in office less than a month, was called from his bed to speak to his secretary of state.[21] David Gray fanned the flames of American fury when he reported after conferring with his British counterpart, Sir John Maffey, about what he described as the "conspicuous condolence visits" of de Valera and Michael McDunphy (the secretary of Ireland's president, Douglas Hyde). Gray termed these actions a "studied affront" to the United Nations. "No one representing President Hyde called here [at the American legation] when President Roosevelt died," Gray peevishly noted. He also reported that Maffey feared that the British government might act unilaterally and order his immediate withdrawal. Gray rehearsed the case for a dignified joint withdrawal of all UN diplomatic representatives to put de Valera in the wrong with the majority of his people. "As long as de Valera is in power," Gray said, "we can expect no concessions or cooperation."[22]

The initial response of Acting Secretary of State Joseph Grew in Washington was supportive, and he telephoned President Truman to that effect on the morning of May 7. But Grew then set himself the bizarre task of re-examining the steps taken by the Irish government on the deaths of President Roosevelt and Hitler and informing President Harry Truman of them:

President Roosevelt's death—

1. The President of Ireland sent a telegram of sympathy to President Truman.
2. De Valera sent a telegram of condolence to the Secretary of State on behalf of his Government, the Lower House [Dail Eireann], and the people of Ireland.
3. The Irish Minister in Washington sent a message of sympathy to Mrs. Roosevelt.
4. De Valera called in person on Minister Gray on the morning of April 13.

5. The Lower House adjourned out of respect and de Valera in moving the adjournment paid a warm tribute to President Roosevelt. The Upper House [Seanad Eireann] also passed resolutions of condolence.

Hitler's death—

1. The Secretary to the President of Ireland called in person on the German Minister to express condolence on behalf of the President. This action may have been taken because there was no one to whom the President of Ireland could telegraph a personal message as he did in the case of Roosevelt's death.
2. De Valera, accompanied by his Secretary of [the Department of] External Affairs, called on the German Minister.

This apparently is all that was done in the case of Hitler's death. No action was taken by either the Upper or Lower House on behalf of Hitler and no public statement by de Valera was made in the Irish Parliament.

Grew added that the president of Ireland "is a very insignificant figure" and that no great importance should be attached to his secretary's failure to call on Gray since in all other respects the Irish government acted appropriately. The upshot of this quaint exercise in comparative sympathetic calculus was that Grew recommended to President Truman that U.S. diplomatic representation should not be withdrawn from Dublin.[23] The White House agreed, and Gray was informed there was no reason for joint withdrawal of UN representatives, nor would America change its policy of "leaving Ireland severely alone."[24] But the State Department harbored no illusions that this policy would effect a change of heart in Irish government circles, as was made plain by the crisp and hard-headed analysis appended to the report, "British Capabilities and Intentions," prepared for the Joint Chiefs of Staff on May 10, 1945:

Ireland. There is no reason for believing that Ireland's policy of strict neutrality and independence will change in the post-war period, in spite of the fact that Ireland is completely dependent upon Great Britain for its foreign trade and physical protection. Great Britain's policy toward Ireland will also remain the same—that is, resignation, non-interference in Irish domestic affairs, friendly commercial relations, maintenance of the status quo as regards Northern Ireland, and concern over Ireland's strategic position as a possible base of enemy operations against Britain.[25]

The British indictment was no less damning. De Valera, reported Sir John Maffey to the Dominions Office, had "taken a very unwise step. Obstinately and mathematically consistent—stung perhaps by the most recent assault on his principles, i.e. by the request for the possession of German archives before VE day—he decided to get a mention for a conspicuous act of neutrality in the field. He would at least show that he was no 'bandwaggoner.' "

Mahaffey asserted that this aim explained de Valera's call on the German legation in Dublin to express "his personal condolences" on the death of Hitler:

> The public mind was too stunned to react quickly to this unnecessary but
> significant performance, but there came overnight the collapse of the
> Reich and with the sudden end of the censorship there came also atroc-
> ity stories, pictures of Buchenwald, etc. In the public mind Mr. de Valera's
> condolences took on a smear of turpitude, and for the first time, and at
> a critical time, a sense of disgust slowly manifested itself and a growing
> feeling that Mr. de Valera had blundered into a clash with the ideals of
> decency and right and was leading away from realities.[26]

Not long after, de Valera defended himself in a personal letter to Bob
Brennan, a close friend since revolutionary days and then the Irish minister
in Washington:

> I have noted that my call on the German Minister on the announcement
> of Hitler's death was played up to the utmost. I expected this. I could have
> had a diplomatic illness but, as you know, I would scorn that sort of
> thing. . . . So long as we retained diplomatic relations with Germany, to
> have failed to call upon the German representative would have been an
> act of unpardonable discourtesy to the German nation and to Dr. Hempel
> himself. During the whole of the war, Dr. Hempel's conduct was irre-
> proachable. He was always friendly and invariably correct—in marked con-
> trast with Gray. I certainly was not going to add to his humiliation in the
> hour of defeat. . . . It would establish a bad precedent. It is of considerable
> importance that the formal acts of courtesy paid on such occasions as the
> death of a head of a State should not have attached to them any special
> significance, such as connoting approval or disapproval of the policies of
> the State in question, or of its head. It is important that it should never be
> inferred that these formal acts imply the passing of any judgments, good
> or bad.[27]

Even the Canadian high commissioner in Dublin, John Kearney ("a
Catholic of Irish origin . . . [inclined] to take the kindly view of Irish short-
comings"), reported Maffey, interpreted "de Valera's action as a slap in the
face." But Kearney noted that the atmosphere in the Department of External Affairs after the visit was "profoundly depressed" and concluded that
public opinion was rising against de Valera. " 'We had him on a plate,' " said
Kearney to Maffey. " 'We had him where we wanted him.' "[28]

But de Valera swiftly seized an opportunity to swing the tide of public
opinion back in his favor—an opportunity offered him by none other than
Winston Churchill during his prime ministerial victory broadcast on May
13, 1945. A still embittered Churchill engaged first in self-congratulation at
Britain's never having "laid a violent hand" upon Ireland, "though at times

it would have been quite easy and quite natural." Churchill then sneered at Irish neutrality when he spoke of Britain having "left the Dublin Government to frolic with the Germans and later with the Japanese representatives to their hearts' content." The war, said Churchill, had been "a deadly moment in our lives and if it had not been for the loyalty and friendship of Northern Ireland we should have been forced to come to close quarters with Mr. de Valera or perish forever from the earth."[29]

On May 16 de Valera delivered a national broadcast on Irish radio in reply. His measured rebuke to Churchill—pointing out that if Britain's necessity was admitted as a moral code, "no small nation adjoining a great power could ever hope to . . . go its way in peace" and even praising him for having resisted the temptation to add "another horrid chapter to the already bloodstained record" of Anglo-Irish relations[30]—caught the Irish public's imagination and mightily reinforced the national identification of neutrality with pride in independence.

De Valera's broadcast, reported the Canadian high commissioner, was "regarded in Ireland as a masterpiece" that effectively stilled the criticism provoked by his visit to the German minister. Sir John Maffey likewise concluded that it was de Valera's reply rather than Churchill's victory speech "which bore the stamp of the elder statesman."[31]

Churchill subsequently admitted to his son, Randolph, that his speech might have been a mistake, but it had been made in the heat of the moment. "We had just come through the war, and I had been looking around at our victories; the idea of Eire sitting at our feet without giving us a hand annoyed me."[32] Churchill's revulsion over Irish neutrality, notwithstanding his awareness that the Irish government had accorded the Allies any facilities that did not publicly compromise their neutrality, was a classic example of what the Austrian historian, Gerald Stourzh, has identified as two paradoxes that bedevil the foreign policies of neutral states: the affinity paradox and the credibility paradox. Stourzh has observed that "the affinity paradox consists in the fact, pointed out in Machiavelli's 'Principe' that your friends want you to be allies, your enemies want you to be neutral. In other words, neutrality will satisfy a potentially more hostile power or power bloc more than a potentially friendlier power or power bloc." This fact suggests that nations "with whom for whatever reason close ties of sympathy exist may be disappointed or even irritated that the neutral State pursues merely a neutral policy." The second of Stourzh's maxims, the credibility paradox, "consists in the fact that permanent neutrality strictly speaking is but a means to secure the end, independence. *As a means,* it may, *like* all other means, be abandoned in favour of other means better apt to *secure* the end, independence."[33]

British revulsion over Irish neutrality, however benevolent, is a classic example of the affinity paradox, as a comparison with Churchill's charitable treatment of Swiss and Swedish neutrality well illustrates.[34] Likewise, Lord Crewe, writing in the *Sunday Times* in February 1944, had offered an analysis that justified the neutrality of Switzerland, Sweden, Portugal, Spain, and Turkey but argued that "Ireland's unique refusal to stand by the Commonwealth and Empire has shocked public opinion because the issue was not one of disputed rights or wounded pride but of simple right and wrong."[35]

Yet if Churchill was the affinity paradox personified, those working in the cloak-and-dagger world of intelligence had no difficulty understanding the Irish credibility paradox. Indeed even on V-E Day the Office of the British Representative in Dublin was busy communicating the latest in a series of secret messages from their British intelligence contact, Guy Liddell, through Frederick Boland of the Department of External Affairs to Col. Dan Bryan, head of Irish Military Intelligence.[36] These contacts and the intelligence they yielded had proved invaluable to the Allied war effort.

Nonetheless, it was hardly surprising that, for some time after the war in Europe had ended, the residue of resentment over Irish neutrality left a bitter aftertaste in American and British mouths. In July 1945, for example, David Gray personally wrote the new secretary of state, James F. Byrnes, suggesting that they might meet in London if Byrnes intended to go there after the Potsdam Conference. The seventy-five-year-old Gray urged Byrnes that the time had come to find his successor. His only recommendation regarding the qualifications of that successor graphically illustrates his alienation from the great majority of the population of the country to which he had been accredited for the past five years:

> I think the replacement should be a career officer to finish out this present episode in Irish-American relations. An American Catholic of Irish descent is at a great disadvantage here under present conditions. Pressure would be put on him both through the Church and political agencies. If he is loyal to American interests as an appointee of yours would be he will have the heat put on him at home. It is an unfair position in which to put a friend.

Gray entrusted his letter to be hand-delivered by a houseguest who was then en route to London. The identity of that houseguest offers one of those ironies that all too rarely reward the historian for those long hours in the archives. For Gray's houseguest—and this is how he described him to the secretary of state (who was himself a lapsed Catholic who had become an Episcopalian when he married[37])—was none other than "Jack Kennedy, Joe's boy," who fifteen years later was to become the first "American Catholic of

Irish descent" to enter the White House. The irony is compounded by the fact that today, more than fifty years after the end of the war in Europe, "Joe's youngest boy," Sen. Edward Kennedy, is Pres. Bill Clinton's closest confidant on Irish policy and "Joe's girl," Ambassador Jean Kennedy-Smith, until recently occupied the official residence in Dublin's Phoenix Park, then occupied by David Gray.[38]

NOTES

1. T. Desmond Williams, "Ireland and the War" in *Ireland in the War Years and After,* ed. Kevin B. Nowlan and T. Desmond Williams (Dublin: Gill and Macmillan, 1969), 25–26.

2. Undated memorandum (?November 1949), "The North Atlantic Pact and Ireland," 24, Irish National Archives (INA), Department of Foreign Affairs (D/FA), Secretary's Files, A89.

3. F. S. L. Lyons, *Ireland Since the Famine* (London: Weidenfeld and Nicolson, 1971), 548.

4. Harold Nicolson, *Diaries and Letters, 1939–1945* (London: Collins, 1967), 217.

5. Joseph T. Carroll, *Ireland in the War Years, 1939–1945* (Newton Abbot and New York: David and Charles, 1975), 163.

6. Public Record Office (PRO), London, CAB 66/62. February 21, 1945.

7. PRO, London, CAB 129/2/8–10: August 21, 1945.

8. See Ronan Fanning, *Independent Ireland* (Dublin: Helicon, 1983), 123–24, for a fuller account.

9. David Reynolds, *Rich Relations: The American Occupation of Britain, 1942–1945* (London: HarperCollins, 1995), 117–18.

10. Ibid., 11.

11. Tony Gray, *Mr. Smyllie, Sir* (Dublin: Gill and Macmillan, 1991), 160–61.

12. Carroll, *Ireland in the War Years,* 161; Dermot Keogh, *Twentieth Century Ireland: Nation and State* (Dublin: Gill and Macmillan, 1994), 158.

13. Acting Secretary of State Joseph Grew to David Gray, March 5, 1945, National Archives (NA) (U.S.A.) 500, San Francisco Conference, telegram 47.

14. Gray to Secretary of State, April 23, 1945, NA (U.S.A.) 740.00 116 EW/4–2345 telegram 86.

15. David Gray's memorandum of conversations with de Valera (April 30, 1945) and J. P. Walshe (May 2, 1945), May 2, 1945, NA(U.S.A.) 800.414/5–745.

16. Ibid.

17. Joseph Grew to David Gray, May 4, 1945, Gray Papers, Box 3, Franklin D. Roosevelt Library (FDRL), Hyde Park, N.Y.

18. Boland manuscript, quoted in Keogh, *Twentieth-Century Ireland,* 157.

19. Dermot Keogh, "Eamon de Valera and Hitler: An Analysis of International Reaction to the Visit to the German Minister, May 1945" in *Irish Studies in International Affairs* 3, 1 (1989): 69–92.

20. Stettinius to Grew, May 5, 1945, NA (U.S.A.) 711.41 D/5–545.

21. "Daniels told me of receiving a long distance phone call from San Francisco during the night. It was Secretary of State Stettinius. Daniels had to call the President out of bed to talk to him about the matter I had called him about" (diary of Eben A. Ayers, May 5, 1945, Harry S. Truman Library, Independence, MO).

22. Gray to Grew, May 5, 1945, NA (U.S.A.) 711.41 D/5–545.

23. Joseph Grew to President Truman, May 7, 1945, NA (U.S.A.) 711.41D/5– 545.

24. Grew's telegram to Gray, May 16, 1945, NA (U.S.A.) 711.41 D/5–545.

25. See appendix D, p. 29 of the Joint Intelligence Staff Report "British Capabilities and Intentions," May 10, 1945, NA (U.S.A.), RG 218 JCS 000.1, Gr. Britain (5–1045), sec. 1. The appendixes to this report were prepared by the Department of State.

26. Maffey memorandum, May 21, 1945, quoted in Robert Fisk, *In Time of War: Ireland, Ulster and the Price of Neutrality 1939–1945* (London: Andre Deutsch, 1983), 462.

27. De Valera to Bob Brennan, Whit Monday 1945; Lord Longford and Thomas P. O'Neill, *Eamon de Valera* (London: Hutchinson, 1970), 411.

28. Carroll, *Ireland in the War Years,* 166.

29. Winston Churchill, *The Second World Wars,* 6 vols. (London: Reprint Society, 1948), 6: appendix F, 608.

30. See Maurice Moynihan, ed., *Speeches and Statements by Eamon de Valera, 1917–1973* (Dublin: Gill and Macmillan, 1973), 471–77, for the full text of de Valera's speech.

31. T. Ryle Dwyer, *Irish Neutrality and the U.S.A., 1939–1947* (Dublin: Gill and Macmillan, 1977), 205.

32. Keogh, *Twentieth-Century Ireland,* 159.

33. Gerald Stourzh, "Some Reflections on Permanent Neutrality," in *Small States in International Relations,* ed. August Schou and Arne Olav Brundtland. (Nobel Symposium 17, Stockholm, 1971, 90 (italics added). Machiavelli wrote in *The Prince* (chap. 21): "And it will always happen that the one who is not your friend will want you to remain neutral, and the one who is your friend will want you to declare yourself by taking arms."

34. "Of all the neutrals Switzerland has the greatest right to distinction," wrote Churchill in December 1944. "What does it matter whether she has been able to give us the commercial advantages we desire or has given too many to the Germans to keep herself alive? She has been a democratic State, standing for freedom in self-defence among her mountains, and in thought, in spite of race, largely on our side." For Sweden, like Switzerland a neutral neighbor of Germany, Churchill wrote that "the choice was a profitable neutrality or subjugation. She could not be blamed because she did not view the issue from the standpoint of our unready but now eager Island" (*Second World War,* 6: appendix C, 565, and 1, 486).

35. Carroll, *Ireland in the War Years,* 1676–78.

36. Liddell's message thanked Bryan for reports transmitted on some German soldiers who had landed at Gormanstown airfield outside Dublin some days before and

that requested "complete identity particulars and life history of each man," NAI, D/FA, Secretary's Files, A 60.

37. David McCullough, *Truman* (New York: Simon and Schuster, 1992), 297.

38. David Gray to the secretary of state (July 23, 1945, Gray Papers, Box 1). Byrnes replied, July 30, 1945, saying that he was not going to London from Potsdam and that he wanted Gray to remain at his post, which he did, until 1947. Gray had earlier written in similar terms to Assistant Secretary of State Julius C. Holmes: "There is a setup of astute and disingenuous officials here who pulled the wool over my eyes for a considerable period. If an Irish-American Catholic should be sent to succeed me as a goodwill messenger, he would be, I fear, at a disadvantage, no matter how loyal he might be both to the country and to the Department. Mr. de Valera has acquired the habit of expecting to have two Ministers—one in Washington and the other in this Legation. I think the solution is, therefore, a Foreign Service Officer during the postwar period" (May 10, 1945, Gray Papers, box 3). It was about this time that Gray also took "sharp exception" to a proposal that the American military attaché to Ireland be a Roman Catholic on the utterly specious grounds "that there are among the Catholics in Eire several groups who differ radically with each other, and that an M.A. who is a Roman Catholic would be bound to affiliate himself with one or other of the Catholic groups, and hence find himself in the midst of conflicting emotional influences. In Mr. Gray's opinion it would be far better to have a Protestant as our M.A." (intraoffice memorandum from Gen. P. E. Peabody, chief of the Military Intelligence Service to the director of Intelligence, July 4, 1945). Col. Samuel McKee Jr. (chief of the Political Branch of the Military Intelligence Division) took a contrary view and reported that three State Department experts (Patrick Mallon, Eire expert, British Empire Desk; Robert Stewart, former Eire expert, British Empire Desk; and Francis Styles, American consul in Dublin, 1939–1945) saw "no disadvantage in sending a Catholic representative to Eire." McKee also reported that Gray's predecessor in Dublin from 1937 to 1940, John Cudahy, "who was a Roman Catholic, was outstandingly successful and beloved in Eire. Irish officials attribute the high regard accorded him to the fact that he went to church every Sunday and he rode good horses—two highly esteemed activities in Dublin" (Cudahy died following a riding accident near his home in Wisconsin in 1943). Two reliable sources have reported de Valera as saying that had Mr. Cudahy rather than Mr. Gray been the U.S. representative in Eire during the war there was a good possibility that Ireland would have joined the Allies (memorandum for director of Intelligence, July 18, 1945). The opinion elicited from the military attaché then serving in Dublin, Lt. Col. George E. Sprague, was even more dismissive of Gray's prejudices. "The appointment of a Military Attaché to Dublin who is a Roman Catholic is neither desirable nor undesirable. While the majority of the people of this country are members of the Roman Catholic faith, religious intolerance is not rampant and the peoples of all faiths have learned to live together in amity. The undersigned is not a Roman Catholic, nor actively practicing any other faith, but in two and one-half years here has never found his religious status in question nor his official or social life affected by such status. Any adult, intelligent officer who has learned to look upon life objectively and who has proper respect for the faith and

beliefs of others, can, the undersigned believes, successfully perform the duties of a Military Attaché, in Ireland, as in any other country, without regard to his personal religious beliefs or disbeliefs" (Col. Sprague to Gen. Peabody, August 18, 1945). Sprague's views were heartily endorsed by both McKee and Peabody (NA[U.S.A.–Suitland], RG 319, box 779, Ireland 210.681).

5. Military Expediency, the "Hunger Winter," and Holland's Belated Liberation

Hal E. Wert

Whether Europeans under Nazi occupation were starving or merely hungry was a question periodically debated in the United States and Great Britain during World War II. The extent to which each country under Nazi control was plundered varied considerably, but all experienced debasement of their currency; expropriation of their natural resources, food, and labor; and the murder of a significant percentage of their population.[1] Further, British wartime prime minister Winston Churchill insisted on maintaining a blockade of the Continent and prosecuting a campaign of economic warfare.[2] For Churchill and his minister of economic warfare Hugh Dalton, who possessed limited means to carry war to the German enemy, the denial of food was just as much an instrument of war as was bombing.

Representatives of the exiled governments of Belgium, Czechoslovakia, Greece, Holland, Luxembourg, Norway, Poland, and Yugoslavia, as well as the Free French, primarily headquartered in London, took exception to the British approach to blockade. These governments felt obligated to aid fellow citizens under German occupation in any way possible. A legitimate conflict of interest between the British and the governments-in-exile caused continuous difficulties. For the exiled governments, however, their dependency limited their ability either to participate in or to protest decisions made in London or Washington. The overseas London governments continually maneuvered to avoid becoming victims of Great Power expediency. The blockade of Europe posed a tragic dilemma for leaders of these overrun countries. They understood, but were reluctant to accept, that in order to win the war it was unavoidable that the civilian populations of their countries, already suffering Nazi occupation, undergo additional hardships imposed by the Allies.

The governments-in-exile generally accepted these hard realities and assented to blockade and area bombing, another weapon with which the British might reach the enemy. But initially the overseas governments, especially the Belgians, fought hard against the British decision to place food imports on the contraband list. The London governments of Belgium and Holland feared the combined consequences of the British blockade and Nazi occupation policies on their populations. Blockade encountered more resistance than area bombing because starvation threatened larger segments of the population, compared to the smaller number of unfortunate individuals who lived near selected targets. Later in the war, as the Allies undertook round-the-clock bombing of cities and civilian populations, the overseas governments began to voice opposition to area bombing.[3]

The cry from Europeans for U.S. assistance began with the start of the war in September 1939 but reached new heights in summer 1940 after Hitler's conquest of the west. European governments and civilian relief agencies tried to obtain aid unavailable in Great Britain and sought U.S. assistance in breaking the blockade. On August 20, 1940, Churchill forcefully put the British case: "It is our intention to maintain and enforce a strict blockade not only of Germany but of Italy, France and all the other countries that have fallen into the German power."[4] In the House of Commons he thundered, "Let Hitler bear his responsibilities to the full and let the peoples of Europe who groan beneath his yoke aid in every way the coming of the day when that yoke will be broken."[5] Britain, the PM promised, would store food and upon liberation rush supplies to the hungry. "The shattering of Nazi power will bring to them all immediate food, freedom and peace."[6] Though Churchill's remarks fulfilled his immediate purpose, it remained to be seen whether the British and their future ally, the United States, would make good on this grandiose promise. If a significant portion of Europe were liberated by Allied forces, bringing "them all immediate food" was a gargantuan undertaking.

The formal restatement of British blockade policy dealt a serious blow to those who would feed hungry Europeans, and that included representatives of the governments-in-exile who remained convinced that the citizens of their countries were hungry or starving. Franklin D. Roosevelt's administration reluctantly supported British blockade policy, which helped to check efforts by the overseas governments to play off Washington against London or to exploit fissures in the burgeoning Anglo-American alliance. In the Atlantic Charter of August 24, 1941, both Roosevelt and Churchill committed their nations to a peace at war's end that would secure a Europe free from want.[7] Shortly after, on September 29, the Inter-Allied Council—composed of Great Britain and the governments-in-exile—hesitantly endorsed the long-range goals of the Atlantic Charter.[8] This endorsement was a general agreement to accede to Anglo-American policy that provisions would follow liberation. Until liberation, the occupied countries would have to get along as best they could. Meanwhile, public opinion in the United States and Great

Britain, convinced by the arguments that the Nazis would most likely steal food shipments and that aid would unnecessarily prolong the war, increasingly opposed relief proposals for Europeans under Nazi domination and swung their support to the Churchill/Roosevelt policy of blockade.

Yet the hunger issue refused to go away. The British Ministry of Economic Warfare officially posited that hunger was tolerable—even an incentive to resistance—but starvation was intolerable. Facts and figures filtering into various wartime planning agencies and private philanthropic groups in the United States and Great Britain caused concern that periodically reignited the battle over aid versus blockade, hunger versus starvation.[9] If evidence clearly demonstrated that famine was imminent, then the United States and Great Britain promised to consider intervention. Conditions in Greece deteriorated to such an extent in 1941 and 1942 that in Athens over one thousand people a day were dying of malnutrition-related causes. The British, with U.S. concurrence, relaxed the blockade, and an elaborate scheme was worked out among the Allies, the Axis, and the Swedes that provided food for Greece throughout the rest of the war.[10] The Italians and Germans permitted the Allies to feed Greece because it lessened their burden of occupation and prevented the country from slipping into chaos. Much of the food that ended up on Greek tables was of U.S. or Canadian origin.

Feeding the Greeks remained the major exception to British blockade policy, although at Roosevelt's request a few supply ships brought relief to refugees in Vichy, France.[11] Small amounts of aid, gasoline, and food were allowed Fascist Spain in an effort to "decouple" the Franco regime from its Axis partners. But the exception of relief for Greece was seen by those opposed to blockade and in support of a European feeding plan as a precedent—the hoped-for breakthrough. The key to obtaining British consent to relax the blockade was to demonstrate convincingly that Europeans were starving. Herbert Hoover, with support in the U.S. Congress, tried once again in 1943 to rekindle his National Committee on Food for the Small Democracies and to bend Allied policy in favor of a limited feeding plan.[12] Unsuccessful in demonstrating that starvation was prevalent, Hoover focused his attention on the coming peace and on the likely problems of postwar Europe.[13] The Roosevelt administration had at last silenced one of the severest critics of its policy of support for the British blockade.

In July 1944, the overseas governments of France, Belgium, Norway, and the Netherlands, concerned over reports of hunger coming from underground units in their home countries, once again pressed Cordell Hull, U.S. secretary of state, and Anthony Eden, British foreign secretary, to allow the shipment of food through the blockade for children in big cities.[14] The longer the war lasted, the greater was the concern in the west for the captive populations of Europe. Only the retaking of European territory would confirm the condition of the civilian population, though it was known that in certain areas severe food shortages had occurred, that widespread hunger existed, and that death among the elderly, the very young, and the poor had increased dramatically, especially in urban areas.[15]

Whether shortages were caused by a breakdown in the distribution system, by declining production, by widespread combat, by confiscation, or by these combined factors remained an open question. It was assumed that statistical data from occupied Europe was subject to wide variation and that underreporting was most likely quite common.[16] Mass starvation had not occurred, but prior to liberation any downturn in agricultural production, coupled with a natural disaster, could have resulted in famine. Northwest Europe was of particular concern, as countries like Belgium and Holland had experienced a reduction in rations in 1944 and would suffer terribly from another winter under Nazi occupation. The London governments of Holland, Belgium, and Norway persistently argued that unless liberation came soon or intervention occurred as it had in Greece, it seemed likely that the Allies would liberate starving Europeans.

Planning for the coming invasion of Europe began in earnest in spring 1943. President Roosevelt, changing his mind as to whether civilians or the military should administer the liberated areas, on November 10, 1943, charged the army with the responsibility of providing initial civilian relief supplies "necessary to avoid disease and unrest."[17] In order adequately to supply and govern the liberated populations of Northwest Europe, it was necessary to organize and train special G-5 Civil Affairs teams. In the first months of 1944, the army, in response to this new presidential charge, gathered over twenty-five hundred British, Canadian, and American officers at the hastily assembled Civil Affairs and Military Government School in Shrivenham, England. As a working hypothesis the Shrivenham group accepted the "collapse theory" put forward by military planners. In this "end game" scenario it was assumed "that the Netherlands would be totally evacuated after German collapse," and civil administrators would take over the entire country.[18] Civil Affairs officers underwent final training in various specialized facets of military government prior to being assigned to specific military units.[19] Newly trained G-5 units were elements of Allied formations from Supreme Headquarters to battalions and were designated by the letters A through D, based on the size of the unit and the size of the geographic area for which the unit was responsible.[20] G-5 staff officers on all four levels specialized in differing areas of government, for example, food distribution, public health, public safety, public utilities, legal affairs, commerce, industry, and agricultural production. All aspects of regional and city government

would be in the hands of Civil Affairs officers until responsibility was transferred to a civilian or military administration of the liberated nation.[21] Transfer schemes varied from country to country as the United States and Great
Britain negotiated separate agreements with the governments-in-exile.[22]

Reports arriving at Shrivenham in spring 1944 from thousands of sources
painted a confused and often contradictory story of food availability to civilians under Nazi domination. Analysis of available information demonstrated
a general year-by-year decline in food production, but future food stocks
depended on the size of the 1944 harvest, the harshness of the 1944–1945
winter, the ferocity and duration of battle after the cross-Channel landings
in France, and the amount of food and supplies confiscated by the Germans.
To be on the safe side, and to fulfill the Allied promise of provisioning repeatedly made by Churchill and Roosevelt, G-5 planners assumed the worst.[23]
Huge stores of food and equipment were stockpiled in England, and arrangements were made for a sufficient number of ships (an arduous task in itself)
to ferry supplies to the Continent. Shipping was in short supply, but a greater
worry for G-5 planners was that limited port facilities would prevent food
and equipment from reaching those in need.[24]

After the great Normandy invasion of June 6, 1944, the Allied armies
encountered stiff resistance, especially on the left flank as British general
Bernard Montgomery attempted to move into Belgium and capture the
badly needed ports of Antwerp and Ghent. The Germans heavily fortified
the numerous low-lying islands that studded the marshy delta to the north-
west of Antwerp to deny Montgomery this prize.[25] Nazi defenders also
sought to protect V-1 and V-2 launch sites and the V-3 launch sites under
construction in northwest Belgium and in the Netherlands.[26] The Allied high
command, without sufficient port facilities, daily found it more difficult to
provision armies that spread out across Belgium and France in a huge arc.
The problem was complicated by the arrival of more and more troops, the
increased distances of the armies from the beaches, the improvised ports
along the French coast, and by army responsibility for the feeding and care
of the civilian populations.[27] In July, August, and September 1944, after the
successful St. Lo breakout, a lack of port facilities and transportation curtailed Allied supplies and threatened to realize one of the Allies' worst fears—
hunger or famine among those recently liberated.[28] Local French officials
protested to their government and to Allied military authorities that food
distribution was inadequate and that more food had been available under
the Nazis.[29]

By September 5, 1944, the day the Dutch call "Dolle dag" (mad Tues-
day), British and Canadian armies had swept into southern portions of the
Netherlands.[30] The Supreme Headquarters Allied Expeditionary Force

(SHAEF) Mission to the Netherlands and the Netherlands Military Administration, an interim Dutch organization that worked with Allied Army Civil Affairs Units until the Dutch government returned, moved advanced units forward to Brussels. A rear headquarters unit remained in London to coordinate activities with the Dutch government, and on September 19 the main echelons of the SHAEF Mission arrived in Brussels.[31]

Two days earlier, General Montgomery had launched Operation Market Garden, a combined airborne and tank assault, which was to speed across Holland, capture the Rhine River bridges, and drive into the industrial heart of the Reich. If successful, this "left hook" at the northern end of the Allied line promised to bring the war to an early end.[32] Eisenhower had a standing bet that the war would be over by Christmas.[33] Even if a total Nazi collapse did not occur, it was reasonable to expect that an armored thrust into the Ruhr would bring about the surrender or evacuation of German forces in western and northern Holland. If Market Garden was successful, then Montgomery could avoid the military costs of opening the port of Antwerp.

A Civil Affairs Staff was assigned to the invading Allied Airborne Corps to take control behind the lines. Market Garden units found the civilian population in the southeast corner of the Netherlands physically deteriorated and in worse shape than most civilians recently liberated in France and Belgium.[34] Food shortages existed, meat especially was in short supply, and clothing worn threadbare. Though famine had not occurred, it was not far off unless the daily ration was increased. United Press correspondent Walter Cronkite reported from the liberated sector of Holland on September 27, "There is not enough food in the Netherlands. For the last two years . . . they have suffered through excruciating cold without coal. Some families little by little burned their furniture to get some heat. People," continued Cronkite, "are living almost wholly on cabbages, turnips, and backyard vegetables." When asked about the difficulty of surviving under such conditions, many Hollanders responded, "Oh it was not so bad here—at least not so bad as in Amsterdam and Rotterdam."[35]

Civil Affairs worked assiduously to set up new local governments in the areas under Allied control and in regions still contested. The volatile military situation prohibited all but limited feeding. When the British Thirtieth Corp failed in its cross-country drive to reach the advanced airborne units stranded in Arnhem and Apeldoorn, Operation Market Garden collapsed. Half of the Civil Affairs personnel in advanced areas were lost.[36] In an effort to salvage as much military advantage as possible, Thirty Corps turned east and west and attempted to establish a line in southern Holland. In the months that followed, British, Canadian, Czech, French, Polish, and American forces were able to liberate a narrow belt that ran across Holland south of the rivers Maas and Waal.[37]

Though most of the city of Antwerp had fallen to the British on September 4, before Operation Market Garden was launched, the estuaries and key islands that controlled entry into the port were strongly defended by the Germans. The mounting supply crisis, worsened by Market Garden, hampered the advancing armies, threatened the Allies' ability to feed the ever-increasing number of civilians under their control, and made it difficult to stockpile supplies for those Dutch still suffering under German occupation. Continued Allied success depended on opening the port of Antwerp. Montgomery and Eisenhower, unable to bring about the collapse of Nazi Germany in fall 1944, were forced in early October to undertake the dreaded campaign for the Scheldt estuary—a casualty-ridden battle of attrition. On Walcheren Island in the mouth of the estuary and to the south on the mainland in an area known as the Breskens Pocket, the Germans dug in.[38] In an intense effort to dislodge the defenders, the First Canadian Army engaged in some of the toughest fighting to occur in northwest Europe.[39] The town of Breskens capitulated on November 2, but German forces on Walcheren did not surrender until November 6. British and Canadian forces suffered thirteen thousand casualties in opening the approaches to the port of Antwerp.[40]

The Scheldt estuaries were cleared of mines as quickly as possible, and the port facilities repaired; nonetheless, the first Allied convoy did not enter Antwerp harbor until November 28. It was now clear that no rapid advances into Holland would take place for several months, if at all. Both Eisenhower and Montgomery wished to strike into Germany and preferred to bypass Nazi forces in western Holland. A campaign in western Holland not only deviated from the main strategy of defeating the Germans as quickly as possible but also promised to be extremely difficult—a repeat of the operations that had cleared the estuaries. As nearly all of western Holland was below sea level, the Germans needed only to breech the remaining dikes (which they threatened to do), flooding additional countryside, to render Holland all but impassable. For Allied armies to advance on a small number of elevated narrow roads or causeways was a defender's dream.[41] Allied soldiers and Dutch civilians in any attempted advance would take heavy casualties. Large cities like Rotterdam and Amsterdam would be severely damaged in intense street-by-street fighting.[42]

Within the occupied area of the Netherlands the food problem was greatly exacerbated by the Dutch Resistance's call for a general railroad strike throughout the country in support of Operation Market Garden. In anticipation of imminent liberation, the strike continued after the airborne operation failed. As a result, the shipment of food supplies from the eastern half of the country slowed, especially to the larger cities in the western Netherlands— Rotterdam, Amsterdam, Utrecht, and The Hague. In retaliation the Nazis systematically withheld food and further curtailed distribution.[43] Even before the full force of Nazi retaliatory policies were felt, the daily ration in the large cities of the Netherlands declined to around sixteen hundred calories a day— one-third less than what was considered a minimal diet.[44] Further hardship awaited those in the occupied zone, for the Allies controlled Limberg, the source of nearly all of Holland's coal.

On October 6, Premier Pieter S. Gerbrandy summarized the Dutch dilemma at a press conference in London: "I have bad news for you, very bad news. When I last spoke with you some weeks ago, we already knew the situation [inside the Netherlands] was far from cheerful. At the time, however, with the magnificent Allied armies sweeping across France and Belgium and into Holland, it seemed reasonable to believe that the sufferings of our people were almost over. As it turned out, their real ordeal is only just about to begin."[45] Echoing his colleague's dire forecast, the Netherlands foreign minister, Eelco N. van Kleffens, bluntly warned, "Holland is facing famine. This statement is not one iota too strong."[46] Arthur Seyss-Inquart, the Reichskommissar in the Netherlands, affirmed that the German army in "Fortress Holland"—two hundred thousand men strong—would fight.[47] Unforeseen military realities dictated that the majority of Holland remain under Nazi occupation during winter 1944–1945. Allied inability to aid the Dutch imposed severe hardship on a civilian population poised on the brink of starvation. For the population of the western Netherlands, a terrible ordeal, ever after known as the "Hunger Winter," had begun.

Dutch officials who had warned of drastic food and fuel shortages in the Netherlands continued to badger and plead for assistance. To ensure that Dutch inquiries were dealt with at the highest levels, Queen Wilhelmina appealed directly to Roosevelt (himself of Dutch ancestry) and Churchill two days later, on October 8, 1944. The queen additionally requested that the Swedes acting for the International Red Cross be allowed to ship food and medical supplies through the blockade into occupied Holland.[48] The Dutch government's warning of impending disaster was given wide circulation on American radio and in the U.S. and British press. Edward R. Murrow reported from London on the evening of October 8: "Whatever happens, Europe this winter will suffer terrible torment from the shortage of fuel, food, housing, and clothes. . . . It seems highly probable that a lot of it will occur in Holland."[49] That same week a *Times* (London) editorial stated, "The Netherlands nation may suffer a fate which is beyond the power of imagination to conceive."[50] William Shirer, writing in the *Washington Post* on October 22, predicted that "the people of Belgium and France will scrape through. But unless the rest of Holland is liberated by the end of November the Dutch, seven million of them, will face annihilation."[51]

On October 26, Roosevelt reiterated that food and medical supplies would be forthcoming after liberation.[52] The president and the prime minister voiced no opposition to Swedish relief; it was, they stated, a matter of "military responsibility."[53] In other words, the decision lay with Eisenhower. Before Eisenhower had an opportunity to approve the queen's Swedish food proposal, three more plans for aiding the Dutch were forwarded to the general for consideration. The first proposed that a Red Cross food relief ship be sent from Lisbon, Portugal; the second urged that an International Red Cross relief ship be sent down the Rhine from Basel; and a third plan called for free air-dropping of food and medical supplies to those in Holland's main cities.[54]

In late October Eisenhower approved the sending of a Swedish Red Cross or International Red Cross relief ship from either Sweden or Portugal, even though he recognized that some of the supplies might fall into German hands. The supreme commander rejected free air-dropping of food, as there were no controls over distribution; and he rejected allowing an International Red Cross vessel to traverse the Rhine on "operational grounds."[55] Efforts in November to arrange a series of relief ships from Sweden ran into difficulties when it was discovered that the Dutch Red Cross in the occupied zone lacked the transport necessary to distribute large amounts of food. A new plan was concocted in December that proposed that Swedish ships dock in northern Holland.[56] Cargoes would be transferred to canal barges and transported to the food-starved cities of western Holland. The Germans did not consent to this plan until the third week of January 1945. As negotiations dragged on, daily rations throughout the occupied Netherlands further diminished.

While the Dutch government frantically attempted to obtain aid from the Swedish Red Cross and a number of other international relief agencies, SHAEF in October and November made strenuous efforts to increase food rations and to undertake necessary repairs in the liberated sectors south of the rivers Maas and Waal. Twenty-first Army Group, the liberators of southern Holland, assigned four transport companies at a time when most Allied supplies still came from the Normandy Beach area and trucks were in very short supply.[57]

A SHAEF staff member observed that "in spite of the stupendous efforts by the military, the delays in utilizing indigenous resources . . . [led to] a gradual deterioration in the food situation during the first six to eight weeks of liberation."[58] In November 1944, the average ration dropped from around sixteen hundred calories a day to one thousand or lower. When liberated, the Dutch enthusiastically welcomed the Allies, but as the food situation worsened many questioned if the price of freedom were not too high. People "became sullen and listless; men, women, and children were gaunt, many with open sores, the result of malnutrition and dirt. Demonstrations took place in many places."[59] Attempting the care and feeding of the liberated peoples and the basic restoration of their countries while engaging in intense fighting on numerous fronts was proving a far more arduous task than British and U.S. planners had assumed. Allied resources were stretched to the limit.

The opening of the port of Antwerp came to the rescue of the Dutch in the liberated zone. Two food trains arrived on December 4, and for the next several weeks two trains arrived each day carrying approximately five hundred tons of food, medical supplies, and other necessary items. Even more supplies were needed, but a shortage of rolling stock, of storage facilities, and a critical shortage of trucks sorely limited supply and distribution.[60] By late December much progress had been made in solving these complicated logistical problems; that progress was acknowledged by Prime Minister Gerbrandy in a letter to Gen. Walter Bedell Smith, chief of staff to General Eisenhower, on December 16, 1944.[61] But like the French before him, Gerbrandy felt compelled to add "that since the day of liberation our population has, from the material point of view, been far worse off than under the German regime."[62] Week by week the Allies slowly raised daily rations from a low of nine hundred calories in October/November to sixteen hundred calories in December.[63]

Gerbrandy, however, worried that this amount was still insufficient for good health. The Dutch prime minister wrote to Eisenhower the same day he had written to Smith and shared his fears: "If the now occupied part of the Netherlands has to go through the same process as the liberated part, we shall witness a calamity as has not been seen in Europe for centuries, if at all. The calamity would be comparable only with those that have sometimes fallen upon the people of China."[64] Asking for a meeting with Eisenhower before the beginning of the year, Gerbrandy confessed, "My conviction that everything will come right in the end is gone."[65] Moved by the letter but fully engaged with the German surprise attack in the Ardennes, Eisenhower declined to meet with Gerbrandy.[66] Instead, he reminded the prime minister that supplies were stockpiled and reiterated the Allied pledge of providing relief upon liberation.

SHAEF's plans for feeding the population of northern Holland had begun in October 1944 simultaneously with the efforts of the Twenty-first Army Group to feed Dutch civilians in the liberated south. Holland was divided into four areas. Area A comprised territory already liberated. Area B included that portion of the country west of the River Ijssel and Area C all territory east of the River Ijssel and to the north along the Frisian Islands and North Sea Coast. Area B was further divided in the center from north to south into areas B1 and B2. The Netherlands' large cities, Rotterdam, Amsterdam, Utrecht, and The Hague, which faced acute shortages of food, were in the area designated B2.

SHAEF's analysis of available data determined that the large cities in the B2 area would not run out of food until February or March. This projection conflicted with estimates made by the London Dutch government and by the International Red Cross, both of whom anticipated that food stocks would be exhausted a month or two earlier.[67] Nevertheless, SHAEF stuck with its projections and began in November 1944 to stockpile a fourteen-day supply of food and to amass equipment; thirty thousand tons of relief supplies and seventeen hundred three-ton trucks were collected in southern Holland near the towns of Oss and 'sHertongenbosch.[68] Food reserves for seven additional days were warehoused in Antwerp, and longer-range reserves for sixty and thirty days were stockpiled in London and the United States. Plans were also made for evacuating three hundred thousand Hollanders to Great Britain if the Nazis flooded the country.

As stores accumulated in ever-growing quantities, one of the coldest winters on record, a repeat of the devastating winter of 1939–1940, set in. The residents of Holland's major cities grew increasingly hungry. First furniture, then trees, and finally floorboards, wallboards, and window seals were burned in an effort to keep warm and to cook what little food was available. Vacant houses and air-raid shelters often collapsed, as they had been stripped of all wood.[69] Many people, who still possessed the strength to walk long distances, foraged for food and firewood in the surrounding countryside and survived by eating large quantities of boiled tulip bulbs.[70] "Since September more than two thousand persons, mostly women and children, have dropped dead from starvation on one forty-mile stretch of road leading from Amsterdam."[71] After having deported two hundred thousand workers to Germany in October 1944, the Nazis preyed on the hungry in insidious ways in order to fill labor quotas.[72] In areas of severe food shortage, loudspeakers announced that those who reported for labor service would be fed. As an inducement, food carts with steaming caldrons of soup were pushed up and down the streets. Men who surrendered to the pangs of hunger were given hot meals and usually sent off to Germany—many never to return. Press gangs worked the streets, easily rounding up hungry men who had come out of hiding in search of food and were too weak to struggle or run.[73]

The London Dutch government's persistent fears that Allied strategy would end up victimizing the Dutch population were heightened when all but six thousand tons of the forward supplies earmarked for the B2 area was diverted to Belgium to help counter the German thrust in the Ardennes.[74]

On January 15, 1945, Queen Wilhelmina, urged on by the overseas Dutch government, appealed directly to Roosevelt, Churchill, and King George VI for direct intervention into Holland to prevent mass starvation. The queen argued that while plans for feeding her subjects after liberation were all well and good, hunger had advanced to a stage, six hundred calories a day or less in the B2 area, that demanded the Allies act immediately. Challenging the Allied strategy of defeating Germany first, Wilhelmina stated, "It is, that goes without saying, necessary that this war be won, but I assert that it is not necessary for winning the war that conditions are allowed to spread and develop, . . . which will inevitably result in [northwest Holland's] total or partial ruin and extinction."[75]

Roosevelt's response to the queen's entreaty was to appoint Judge Samuel I. Rosenman as his personal representative, charged with conducting a mission to northwest Europe to survey the needs of Great Britain, France, Belgium, and the Netherlands.[76] Rosenman undertook to staff his mission with appropriate experts from the Departments of State, War, and Treasury as well as from the Foreign Economic Administration. During the first week of February, while Roosevelt, Churchill, and Stalin were at Yalta, a series of conferences at the White House set forth mission goals and planned the itinerary.

British representatives in Washington also met with Rosenman to outline areas of joint concern and cooperation. In fact, the Richard Law Mission to the United States had brought word from the British cabinet to the U.S. secretaries of state, war, and navy in December 1944 that the stability of northwest Europe was "getting a little out of hand and there is a danger of political disturbance."[77] To counter this precarious situation, the British recommended increased economic aid, including food, raw materials, transportation vehicles, coal, gasoline, and electric power.

The United States agreed that more aid was necessary, but where these supplies would come from was a matter of debate. In a disagreement reflective of Washington's and London's differing views about postwar policy, the Roosevelt administration argued that increases should come from stocks in Great Britain. The British, worried that shipments from the United States would dramatically decrease or altogether cease at war's end, opposed taking supplies from British stores. The United States maintained that war supplies be used for war-related purposes, and that included feeding the inhabitants of northwest Europe. The immediacy of winning the war, the "wait-and-see" attitude of the United States, and the uncertain shape of the postwar world produced a reluctance among the Washington planners to enter into any long-term aid agreements.[78]

On February 9 the Rosenman Mission, armed with much advice, left by air for Britain, flying the southern route through Bermuda and the Azores.

Shortly after his envoy's arrival in London, Roosevelt, in Algiers, en route home from Yalta, requested that Rosenman join him to discuss a special assignment.[79] Rosenman returned to England on March 5 and began a series of meetings with Queen Wilhelmina and the Dutch government that carefully reviewed Dutch needs. These discussions went beyond the immediate crisis in the B2 area and undertook an estimation of Holland's overall postwar reconstruction needs.[80] Dutch officials were gratified that a comprehensive investigation was under way, but as Rosenman and his mission prepared to leave for France, Stanley Hornbeck, the American ambassador to the Dutch government-in-exile, handed him a memorandum that underscored the worsening hunger situation in western Holland and pleaded for a high-level commitment.[81]

As spring approached, no immediate solutions were forthcoming, although at the end of January the International and Swedish Red Cross at last succeeded in bringing a modicum of relief when two small ships, the *Noreg* and the *Dagmar Brat,* unloaded thirty-two hundred tons of food and supplies at Delfzijl. Due to poor port facilities, frozen canals, and lack of transportation, Red Cross food did not reach Amsterdam until mid-February. The Germans had insisted on the port of Delfzijl, which was near the German border and far from the cities of western Holland, in an effort to break the ongoing railroad strike.[82] If the rail workers went back on the job, then the starving would more quickly receive supplies. Dutch obstinacy prevailed, and the strike continued. In February Swedish and Swiss aid provided 3 million Dutch citizens in the B2 area with an increase in rations of fourteen ounces a day for two weeks.[83] In early March a third Red Cross ship reached Holland, and the Germans shipped in twenty-six hundred tons of rye from the eastern provinces. Red Cross aid, from which everyone received a twenty-ounce loaf of white bread and four ounces of margarine, increased morale and enabled urban dwellers to stave off famine for several more weeks; but given long-term needs the shipments were woefully inadequate.[84]

Eisenhower underscored his position on the Dutch food crisis in a message to the Combined Chiefs of Staff on March 27, 1945. The quickest means of relieving the suffering in western Holland, he stated, "may well be the rapid completion of our main operations."[85] Eisenhower and Montgomery contemplated no change in strategy, and both counted on International Red Cross aid to sustain the Dutch population to war's end. The fastest way to Rotterdam and Amsterdam was from somewhere deep in Germany after the Nazi surrender. Allied armies had crossed the Rhine on March 23, four days before Eisenhower's letter to the Combined Chiefs of Staff; however, the First Canadian Army, which began to drive into northern and eastern Holland on

March 28, was carefully instructed not to attempt the liberation of the B2 area.[86] Montgomery ordered Canadian forces to halt at the old Dutch Grebbe Line—a series of fortifications that ran north to south from the Ijsselmeer to the Rhine.[87] But how long the Germans might hold out in both Holland and Germany remained an open question in spring 1945. As food supplies in Holland continued to dwindle, famine might be only weeks, perhaps days away. Time was the enemy. Political and humanitarian considerations mandated a more direct means of alleviating Dutch hunger and would not allow the Allies to tie the fate of 3,664,500 Dutch civilians in the western Netherlands to the success of military operations in the heart of Germany.

Updated plans called for food and other critical supplies to be rushed into Holland by truck from huge forward supply depots near Arnhem, by barge through the inland waterways to Rotterdam, and by ship from Belgium. Air supply was to be undertaken from England, and as the coast and channels of Holland's ports to the north of Rotterdam were cleared of mines, food would arrive directly from England or the United States.[88] Holland's major cities were to become supply depots that stocked thirteen Civil Distribution Centers intended to supply fuel and soup ingredients to some three hundred soup kitchens. Uncooked food and supplies were to be distributed from 972 Issue Points to be established in 507 towns and 465 rural locations.[89] Plans called for feeding all inhabitants in the B2 area. By April 1945 three huge warehouses in Eindhoven bulged with food packages and gifts from individuals and from private relief agencies worldwide: condensed milk and orange concentrate from Curaçao and Aruba and food packages from the American Queen Wilhelmina Fund, the Belgians, the Swedes, the Swiss, and the previously liberated parts of Holland.[90]

In the interim between the German surrender and the arrival of the Allies, plans called for feeding the Dutch population by air-dropping supplies, Operation Manna, at designated sites on the outskirts of major cities.[91] As supplies had not been previously free-dropped, the RAF and the U.S. Air Force repeatedly tested various containers that would withstand the impact of falling from fifteen hundred feet without damaging the food bombs' contents: large cement bags worked best.[92] B-17 and Lancaster bombers were fitted with special carrying slings hung in the bomb bays. Each aircraft carried seventy-one food bombs that would feed approximately 3,280 a day. Each British food bomb contained sacks of canned meat, vegetables, flour, yeast, milk, cheese, margarine, sugar, eggs, tea, salt, and pepper.[93] American food bombs contained "10-in-1" rations that included sausage, bacon, corned beef, baked beans, cereal, vegetables, coffee, condensed milk, sugar, preserved butter, cigarettes, and sundry items.[94]

To deal with acute cases of starvation, a British-American-Dutch nutrition committee established by SHAEF recruited and trained fifty-one medical feeding units. Each of these units comprised one doctor, six nurses, and five welfare workers. Mobility was of extreme importance, so each unit was assigned an ambulance and other necessary vehicles.[95] Treatment of the most severe cases of starvation included the most advanced medical techniques, and huge quantities of predigested proteins and vitaminized glucose were manufactured in England. This "factory food," known as F-treatment, was a yellow-brown liquid that came in pint bottles like those used for blood and could be fed orally or injected.[96] Eventually seventy thousand people were treated with these new starvation cures, which doctors hoped would drastically reduce recovery time to twenty-four to forty-eight hours; but complications and side effects reduced their effectiveness.[97] All necessary supplies and transport had been accumulated, and medical teams and Civil Affairs units were at the ready, prepared to rush to the assistance of the starving Dutch when the signal was given.[98]

But German troops, one hundred thousand strong under Gen. Johannes Blaskowitz, still took orders from Berlin and refused to lay down their arms. Famine stalked the cities of Rotterdam, Amsterdam, Utrecht, and The Hague as the Nazis once again reduced the daily ration to a low of 230 calories per day.[99] International Red Cross aid increased at the end of March and the beginning of April, but this aid did not offset the drastic reductions made by the Nazis. The death toll increased dramatically. Because of a lack of coffins and transport, corpses remained unburied and were stacked in rows inside churches. One church in Amsterdam contained approximately fifteen hundred dead bodies.[100]

By early April 1945, the B1 and C areas had been liberated, and massive feeding programs were under way. But in the B2 area the London Dutch government emphatically stated that all "supplies in occupied Holland will be used up by 28 April."[101] On the evening of April 8, Rosenman, just returned from his food and supply survey, explained to Churchill the famine conditions in the western Netherlands, the extent of war-related destruction, and the need for an extensive rehabilitation program throughout northwest Europe. The mission recognized that food shortages, lack of supplies, destruction of infrastructure, and general economic problems were not of short duration.[102]

Churchill and Rosenman talked until three o'clock in the morning. The prime minister emphasized that the British would not make additional cuts in their meager diet to feed Axis satellites while U.S. Army personnel and American civilians continued to "live on their present gigantic diet."[103] As Rosenman well knew, asking the American people for continued and additional sacrifice in the postwar period was a risky political proposition.

The following morning, Churchill, at last convinced that the Dutch would starve in large numbers before Germany collapsed, cabled Roosevelt and strongly advocated immediate Allied intervention.[104] The prime minister recommended negotiations with Seyss-Inquart and the Dutch Nazi government to allow the passage of food into the B2 area under the sponsorship of the International Red Cross. If the Nazis refused they should be warned that they "brand themselves as murderers before the world, and we shall hold them responsible with their lives for the fate which overtakes the people of Holland."[105] Roosevelt responded the next day, April 10, and agreed with Churchill's suggestion to open negotiations with the German government in Holland; however, he cautioned that before any agreements were reached with the International Red Cross, Stalin should be notified.[106]

April 14 witnessed the first meeting between a representative for the Free Dutch government, Secretary General of Economics Dr. Koert Hirschfeld, and the Nazi occupiers.[107] Seyss-Inquart revealed that his orders were to continue resistance and that he was authorized by Berlin to undertake whatever steps were necessary to maintain a defense, including massive flooding. The hated Reichskommissar, called *Rot Moffen* (rotten kraut) by the Dutch, explained that as long as Germany had not surrendered he would neither surrender Nazi forces in Holland nor enter into a formal truce. Nonetheless, if the Allies promised not to inform Berlin of their negotiations and ceased their advance, he would agree to an informal truce, open the port of Rotterdam to shipments of food and coal, cease executing political prisoners, and curtail the Gestapo.[108]

Seyss-Inquart's offer of a truce set off a week-long flurry of discussions among Churchill, Eden (in Washington and on his way to San Francisco for the founding meeting of the United Nations), Secretary of State Edward Stettinius, and Army Chief of Staff George Marshall. On April 18 Marshall sent a cable to Eisenhower asking his opinion on air-dropping of supplies to the starving Dutch. Later that same day, Churchill cabled Marshall of the possibility of arranging a truce with Seyss-Inquart.[109] The next day Marshall again cabled Eisenhower and explained in detail the Nazi offer of a truce, and Churchill proposed that a solution to the Dutch problem was to declare the B2 area neutral. Marshall, speaking for the U.S. Chiefs of Staff, rejected Churchill's "neutrality proposal," as they feared altering the unconditional surrender doctrine. The chiefs also warned that the Russians might take offense and needed to be consulted. No action would be taken until a reply was received from Eisenhower.[110]

Eisenhower responded the following day—April 20—that Allied food relief for the B2 area was now a necessity and that Seyss-Inquart's proposal for a halt at the Grebbe Line was a military advantage. Holding the line would require minimal numbers of troops and would release more forces to Montgomery for the final push across northern Germany.[111] "Consequently, from both the humanitarian and military viewpoints I concur with the Prime Minister's proposal, subject always to the necessity for securing Russian concurrence."[112] Eisenhower stressed that the best solution was to reach an agreement with Seyss-Inquart.

Meanwhile, in Washington, Stettinius and Eden sought Russian support from Foreign Minister Mikhail Molotov. Official Washington was in a state of confusion due to Roosevelt's death on April 12 and the ascendency of the new president—Harry Truman, and in the middle of a whirlwind of preparation for the upcoming charter meeting of the United Nations in San Francisco.[113] Before a Russian response was obtained, Eisenhower signaled the Combined Chiefs of Staff and the British Chiefs of Staff on April 23, requesting "as free a hand as possible owing to the urgency of the problems that confront us."[114] He also proposed sending a strongly worded message to the German general Blaskowitz, pointing out the hopelessness of his position and demanding his cooperation in feeding Dutch civilians starving under his command. If Blaskowitz continued to open dykes and to undertake action that resulted in the loss of Dutch lives, he and his officers would be considered war criminals "who must face the certain consequences of their acts."[115]

Eisenhower was granted his "free hand" by the Combined Chiefs on April 24, 1945. That same day the Russians consented to the proposed negotiations with Seyss-Inquart and Blaskowitz.[116] Stalin appointed Maj. Gen. Ivan Susloparov, chief of the Soviet Military Mission to France, to represent him in all surrender negotiations in the west.[117] Events moved rapidly forward. On the evening of April 24 and continuing through April 26, the Allies repeatedly broadcast messages to Holland that the free air-dropping of food would soon commence and that German units were not to interfere. British Bomber Command and U.S. Eighth Air Force were asked by SHAEF to assign two hundred bombers to the Dutch food-drop mission. The War Office, which had been gathering food for several months, had 8 million individual ration packages ready to drop and would have 4 million more ready by May 14 and an additional 6 million on May 21.[118]

Eisenhower also sent a message through Dutch underground channels to Seyss-Inquart on April 24, requesting a meeting with the Nazi senior military commanders in Holland. The message stated as well that free air-dropping would start soon and that Allied aircraft were not to be fired on.[119] Allied troops would halt just short of the Grebbe Line and bombing of German installations would cease. Seyss-Inquart and Blaskowitz responded the following day. The Nazi leaders accepted the proposal that food be allowed to move through

German lines but rejected free air-dropping, as in their judgment it would only aid black marketeers and other small groups. As an alternative, Seyss-Inquart proposed the use of ships and trains. The following morning, April 27, Eisenhower sent Blaskowitz a telegram informing him that the Allies would go forward with free dropping; if interference occurred, then Blaskowitz and his commanders would be charged as war criminals. As the message was being sent from SHAEF headquarters, a message arrived from the Germans that designated drop zones for free dropping and agreed to a meeting on April 28 that would work out the details of an enlarged relief program.[120] Free airdropping was to commence that same morning, but inclement weather forced cancellation of the mission.[121]

On the night of April 27 verbal orders were passed up and down the Canadian line that a cease-fire would take effect at eight o'clock the following morning. For soldiers near the Grebbe front World War II was at an end on April 28. Crossing into Canadian army lines under a white flag of truce, German representatives listened as Allied officers of the Twenty-first Army Group outlined relief proposals. When Allied officers discovered that the Reichskommissar's delegates were not granted the authority to enter into negotiations, they demanded that those with the authority to treat come forward within forty-eight hours.

Weather cleared on the morning of April 28, the day planners had calculated that western Holland would run out of food. Two hundred and fifty-three Lancaster heavy bombers braved a freak blizzard above the English Channel and swooped low over the Dutch countryside at an altitude of fifteen hundred feet, dropping thousands of "mercy bombs." As the planes approached The Hague, the marked targets, large circles of green flares with red lights in the center, were plainly visible as were large crowds of people "madly waving flags, bed sheets and other white articles."[122] Major Tinley, G-5 SHEAF Mission to the Netherlands, reported: "The civilian population went mad with joy to see low-flying Allied planes dropping food from the skies—manna from heaven." Hundreds of Allied planes streamed over Holland for the next ten days and dropped approximately 14.5 million individual rations packages to crowds of hungry and enthusiastic Dutch.[123]

At the sight of vapor trails or the sound of aircraft engines, people spilled into the streets and moved off en masse to the drop zones. Although repeatedly warned of the dangers associated with free dropping, hundreds of people ran onto the drop sites to retrieve food packages and tragically were hit by food bombs released from the oncoming waves of aircraft. Although the drops were largely symbolic in that the rations supplied only a few days' food, Dutch spirits soared with the sure knowledge that liberation would occur shortly.[124]

Eisenhower chose not to meet with Seyss-Inquart and his party of high-ranking Nazi generals on April 30 in the little village of Achterveld but sent instead a group of Allied officers headed by Lt. Gen. Walter Bedell Smith, his chief of staff. Smith's group included Russian general Susloparov and the Netherlands' commander in chief Prince Bernhard. (Comically, Bernhard arrived in a Mercedes-Benz that been captured just a short while before from Seyss-Inquart by the Dutch underground and bore the license plate RK–1.) Dutch civilians responsible for distributing relief and traveling with the German delegation refused to ride in cars with the Nazis and packed into one automobile so tightly that even the floor space was occupied.[125]

The two delegations coldly eyed one another, exchanged salutes, and proceeded to work out an agreement on limited air, land, and sea routes over which relief supplies would travel safely, with details left to committees that met later the same day. Seyss-Inquart revealed that he had not contacted Berlin, as he feared a refusal. At the conclusion of the general meeting, Smith, Susloparov, and two other Allied generals met with Seyss-Inquart and two of his aides in an effort to convince the Reichskommissar to surrender all German forces in Holland.[126]

Smith pushed hard, commenting that further resistance was pointless and that at some future date Seyss-Inquart would be shot. The Reichskommissar replied in a soft voice, "That leaves me cold." Smith quickly retorted, "It will."[127] Nonetheless, the Germans refused to surrender. Smith, agreement in hand, immediately ordered relief supplies into Holland by barge, ship, and truck. Five days later, at 8:00 A.M., May 5, 1945, all German forces in Holland surrendered. Relief supplies and medical units poured into western Holland's major cities.[128] After fleeing Holland by speedboat, Seyss-Inquart attempted to return to Germany by car and was arrested by a British MP in Hamburg.

Even after liberation, many of those suffering from advanced cases of starvation died. Working diligently, the Allies were able slowly to increase Dutch rations. In the first week after liberation a 760-calorie-per-day-level was achieved, and in each succeeding week large increases were possible. By early June a level of twenty-one hundred calories per day was reached, and the following month the daily ration climbed to a high of twenty-two hundred calories. Most people were able to add 100 to 150 extra calories a day to this basic diet, and those with more money were able to buy fruits and vegetables on the black market. Fresh produce was rationed locally, and fresh fish was rationed sectionally. As more and more food became available, black market prices plummeted.[129] The high level of daily rations was continued into the summer to allow the population to recover from months of severe food shortages and to restock depleted pantries. June witnessed the return of differential rationing and the lowering of the percentage of canned meat in favor of an increase in bread, flour, and occasionally, fresh meat. By September, uniform rationing was in place throughout the country.[130]

In late May a fierce controversy was touched off by Maj. Gen. Warren Draper, chief of the Public Health Branch of Supreme Allied Headquarters, who commented to a Reuters reporter that in Holland, "there were some cases of advanced malnutrition, but no cases of starvation."[131] A flood of statements countering Draper's remarks poured forth from SHAEF Civil Affairs officers, from journalists who had traveled widely in the B2 area, and from Dutch government officials. Statistics gathered in the B2 area clearly demonstrated an increase in the death rate, with 933 deaths directly attributed to starvation. Many others died of diseases indirectly related to starvation. For example, a comparison of deaths from all causes in April 1944 with those in April 1945 shows an increase of 162.5 percent.[132] SHAEF medical teams also established that the average weight of adults was down by thirty to forty pounds and that approximately 10 percent of the urban population (200,000 to 250,000 people), mostly men and mostly from the lower class, suffered hunger-edema, a starvation-induced disorder that causes the stomach to distend grossly and the joints to swell.[133] While General Draper and others may have felt that the situation was not as bad as "had been feared," the Dutch in April 1945 hovered on the edge of mass famine. Had Seyss-Inquart and his fellow Nazis hunkered down in Fortress Holland, refused the passage of food through the German lines, and fought tenaciously, the hunger winter of 1944–1945 would have had a radically different outcome. In fact, had the Allies successfully intervened only a few weeks later, tens of thousands of additional deaths would have occurred.

Conversely, had Operation Market Garden been a success and brought the war to a quick end in late 1944, the hunger winter would never have occurred. Even had Germany collapsed, a brief period of hunger might have transpired, for the Allies were severely short of supplies and transportation in fall 1944. Given the almost unassailable military position of the Nazis in the B2 area of western Holland, Eisenhower and Montgomery's strategy of attempting to end the war by a quick drive into Germany made sense. That strategy was derailed a second time by the German surprise attack in the Ardennes.

Internal Dutch food supplies, coupled with International Red Cross aid, might have done more to provision those in the B2 area in the first quarter of 1945, but abnormally cold weather froze the canals and prevented the transport of available food. How long Eisenhower and Montgomery might have stuck with their "Germany first" strategy is an unanswerable question. Credit must go to Queen Wilhelmina, Prime Minister Gerbrandy, and

Samuel I. Rosenman, whose persistence finally captured Winston Churchill's attention, and perversely, to Seyss-Inquart, who signaled his willingness to negotiate. Churchill's letter of April 9, 1945, to Roosevelt started the often hesitant and clumsy process that resulted in Operation Manna on April 29. Once Eisenhower was convinced that the Dutch would starve before Germany surrendered, he moved decisively to avert the impending tragedy.

Eisenhower and Montgomery were perhaps too close to events, involved in the rush of happenings, both anticipated and inadvertent, associated with the end of the war in Europe, to see in the Dutch food crisis the emerging postwar world. The Rosenman Mission grasped the appalling level of destruction visited upon Europe and glimpsed the future when its members foresaw that northwest Europe's need for aid would extend long beyond the end of the war. Washington planners and politicians were loathe to hear Rosenman's call for longer-range aid commitments and were slow to relinquish the self-serving World War I economic model that predicted that Europe would suffer a year of hard times and then steadily move toward recovery.[134]

Americans, victorious and affluent after years of depression and self-sacrifice, were in no mood in summer 1945 to accept the burdens of global responsibility. The Dutch had been rescued from the Nazis and at the last minute from starvation. Though liberated Europe may not have been free from want, Churchill, Roosevelt, and Truman had fulfilled their pledge that "the shattering of Nazi power would bring to them all immediate food, freedom, and peace." Responsible government officials in Washington and London reasoned that surely the substantial economic aid provided by the Allies throughout 1945 would enable the liberated nations of Western Europe to go forward on their own.

NOTES

1. See Karl Brandt, *Management of Agriculture and Food in the German-Occupied and Other Areas of Fortress Europe* (Stanford: Stanford University Press, 1953); Jan T. Gross, *Polish Society Under German Occupation* (Princeton: Princeton University Press, 1979); and Raphael Lemkin, *Axis Rule in Occupied Europe* (Washington, D.C.: Carnegie Endowment for International Peace, 1944).

2. W. N. Medlicott, *The Economic Blockade*, 2 vols. (London: Her Majesty's Stationery Office [HMSO], 1952).

3. Forest C. Pogue, *The Supreme Command* (Washington, D.C.: GPO, 1989), 334.

4. "Extract from the Prime Minister's Speech," August 20, 1940, Foreign Office (FO) 371/25195, W11802/8156/49, Public Records Office (PRO), Kew Gardens, London.

5. Ibid.

6. Ibid.

7. Theodore A. Wilson, *The First Summit* (Boston: Houghton Mifflin, 1969), 205–7.

8. H. V. Morton, *Atlantic Meeting* (London: Methuen, 1943), 151.

9. Boris Shub, *Starvation over Europe* (New York: Institute of Jewish Affairs, 1944), and Brandt, *Management of Agriculture and Food in the German-Occupied and Other Areas of Fortress Europe*.

10. Mark Mazower, *Inside Hitler's Greece* (New Haven: Yale University Press, 1993), 32–48; Shub, *Starvation Over Europe*, 38–39; and Brandt, *Management of Agriculture and Food in the German-Occupied and Other Areas of Fortress Europe*, 238–48.

11. Shub, *Starvation over Europe*, 41; "France and the Blockade," October 1941, Box 3, John G. Winant Papers, Record Group (RG) 84, National Archives (NA), Washington, D.C., and "Following for President from Former Naval Person (Churchill to Roosevelt)," January 3, 1941, Premier 3/74/6, PRO.

12. See "In the Name of Humanity," "Feed the Starving Now," "Food for Europe's Children," "The Food Situation," and "Our Food Front," in Herbert Hoover, *Addresses upon the American Road, 1941–1945* (New York: D. Van Nostrand, 1946), 305–41.

13. Herbert Hoover and Hugh Gibson, *The Problems of Lasting Peace* (Garden City, N.Y.: Doubleday and Doran, 1942).

14. "A Plea for Food Shipments," *Netherlands News Digest* 3, 9 (July 15,1944): 335, and Pogue, *The Supreme Command*, 334–35.

15. "Report to the Director General," May 8, 1946, Farm and Agriculture Organization (FAO), United Nations (UN), RG 83, NA.

16. Brandt, *Agriculture and Food in the German Occupied and Other Areas of Fortress Europe*, 438.

17. "Report to the President by Samuel I. Rosenman on Civilian Supplies for the Liberated Areas of Northwest Europe," January 20, 1945, Samuel I. Rosenman Papers, Franklin D. Roosevelt Library (FDRL), Hyde Park, N.Y., and Harry L. Coles and Albert K. Weinberg, *Civil Affairs* (Washington, D.C.: GPO, 1976), x–xi.

18. Coles and Weinberg, *Civil Affairs*, 821–23.

19. Maj. Gen. John J. Maginnis, *Military Government Journal* (Amherst: University of Massachusetts Press, 1971), 2–3.

20. Ibid., 2–3, and James Madison Tinley, "Wartime Food Problems of the Netherlands," James Madison Tinley Papers, Herbert Hoover Archives (HHA), Hoover Institution (HI), Stanford University, Stanford, Calif., 29.

21. Tinley, "Military Preparations for Civilian Relief," 29–30, part 2 of Tinley, "Wartime Food Problems of the Netherlands," Tinley Papers, and Maginnis, *Military Government Journal*, 2–3.

22. Coles and Weinberg, *Civil Affairs*, 654–55.

23. Col. C. P. Stacey, *The Victory Campaign*, 3 vols. (Ottawa, Queen's Printer, 1960), 3:582.

24. "F.E.A. [Foreign Economic Administration] Studies Holland," *Knickerbocker Weekly* 5, 5 (March 26, 1945): 14, and "Note on Shipping for Liberated Areas, U.M.E.B. Paper 1/8," Office of War Mobilization and Reconversion (OWMR), spring 1945, RG 250, NA.

25. See Stacey, *The Victory Campaign*, 3:3; C. P. Stacey, *The Canadian Army, 1939–1945* (Ottawa: King's Printer, 1948), 210–19; and Charles B. MacDonald, *The Siegfried Line Campaign* (Washington, D.C.: GPO, 1990), 215–30.

26. F. S. V. Donnison, *Civil Affairs and Military Government North-West Europe, 1944–1946* (London: HMSO, 1961), 131, and Stacey, *The Canadian Army, 1939–1945*, 212–14.

27. Dwight D. Eisenhower, *Crusade in Europe* (Garden City, N.Y.: Doubleday, 1948), 290–92, and Roland G. Ruppenthal, "Logistics and the Broad-Front Strategy," in *Command Decisions*, ed. Kent Roberts Greenfield (Washington, D.C.: GPO, 1960), 419–27.

28. On the St. Lo breakout, see Stephen E. Ambrose, *The Supreme Commander* (Garden City, N.Y.: Doubleday, 1970), 459–78, and John Keegan, *Six Armies in Normandy* (New York: Viking, 1982), 231–34. On the decline in rations after liberation, see Tinley, "Wartime Food Problems of the Netherlands," Tinley Papers, and "European Inland Transport Problem," March 16, 1945, Minutes of Meetings Folder, Box 29, Rosenman Papers.

29. On French complaints, see Pogue, *The Supreme Command*, 335. On the role of SHAEF in relationship to French shortages, see W. B. to Livingston T. Merchant, April 10, 1945, "Comment on Merchant Report," Memos and Corres. Folder, Box 19, Rosenman Papers.

30. Henri van der Zee, *The Hunger Winter* (London: Jill Norman and Hobhouse, 1982), 17–26, and "Living on the Rations of the Dead," *Knickerbocker Weekly*, 5, 8 (April 16, 1945): 3.

31. Donnison, *Civil Affairs and Military Government North-West Europe, 1944–1946*, 131–34.

32. Sir John Hackett, "Operation Market Garden," in M. R. D. Foot, ed., *Holland at War Against Hitler* (London: Frank Cass, 1989), 157–69; Ambrose, *The Supreme Commander*, 516–26; van der Zee, *The Hunger Winter*, 27–42; and Stacey, *The Canadian Army, 1939–1945*, 217–19.

33. Eisenhower made the bet with Montgomery on October 23, 1943, while the Allied armies were in Italy. See Capt. Harry C. Butcher, *My Three Years with Eisenhower* (New York: Simon and Schuster, 1946), 722.

34. On Dutch civilians see Piet Kamphuis, "Caught Between Fear and Hope," in Foot, ed., *Holland at War Against Hitler*, 175.

35. Walter Cronkite, United Press story, September 27, 1944, in "Occupied Holland—German Measures," *Netherlands Digest*, 3, 15 (October 15, 1944): 579–80.

36. Donnison, *Civil Affairs and Military Government North-West Europe, 1944–1946*, 132.

37. Tinley, "Wartime Food Problems of the Netherlands," 31.

38. Donnison, *Civil Affairs and Military Government North-West Europe, 1944–1946*, 134–37, and *The Papers of Dwight David Eisenhower, The War Years*, ed. Alfred D. Chandler Jr., 5 vols. (Baltimore: Johns Hopkins University Press, 1970), 4:2200–2201, 2208, and 2215.

39. Stacey, *The Canadian Army, 1939–1945*, 220–29; Donnison, *Civil Affairs and*

Military Government in North-West Europe, 1944–1946, 135; and Pogue, *The Supreme Command,* 298–301.

40. MacDonald, *The Siegfried Line Campaign,* 229.

41. Charles B. MacDonald, *The Last Offensive: The United States in World War II* (Washington, D.C.: GPO, 1986), 460–61, and Eelco N. van Kleffens, "If the Nazis Flood Holland," reprint from *Foreign Affairs* (July 1944): 1–11, the Netherlands, 1942–1944, Box 310, Stanley K. Hornbeck Papers, HHA, HI.

42. Stacey, *The Victory Campaign,* 3:584.

43. "Dutch Resistance," October 21, 1944, *Washington Post,* in the Netherlands, 1942–1944, Box 310, Hornbeck Papers; Donnison, *Civil Affairs and Military Government North-West Europe, 1944–1946,* 141–42, and Kamphuis, "Caught Between Hope and Fear," 175–76.

44. Donnison, *Civil Affairs and Military Government North-West Europe, 1944–1946,* 141, and Report, "Urgent Food Problems," May 14, 1946, FAO, UN, RG83, NA.

45. "Occupied Holland—German Measures," 575.

46. Ibid., 574.

47. Coles and Weinberg, *Civil Affairs,* 830.

48. Van der Zee, *The Hunger Winter,* 88–96.

49. "Occupied Holland—German Measures," 580.

50. Ibid., 581.

51. William L. Shirer, "Free Face Grim Days," *Washington Post,* October 22, 1944, in the Netherlands, 1942–1944, Box 310, Hornbeck Papers.

52. Stacey, *The Victory Campaign,* 582, and Pogue, *The Supreme Command,* 334–35.

53. Pogue, *The Supreme Command,* 334–35.

54. Van der Zee, *The Hunger Winter,* 175–80, and Pogue, *The Supreme Command,* 334–35.

55. Pogue, *Supreme Command,* 334–35.

56. Stacey, *The Victory Campaign,* 583.

57. "Wartime Food Problems of the Netherlands," 57, Tinley Papers.

58. Ibid., 35.

59. Ibid.

60. Ibid., 60.

61. Coles and Weinberg, *Civil Affairs,* 827.

62. Ibid.

63. The figure for a low of 900-calories-a-day ration or even lower is to be found in Coles and Weinberg, *Civil Affairs,* 823. Other caloric figures come from "Wartime Food Problems in the Netherlands," 35, Tinley Papers. In February and throughout spring 1945 the daily ration climbed to 1,750 calories per day.

64. Coles and Weinberg, *Civil Affairs,* 827.

65. Ibid., 828.

66. On the Battle of the Bulge, see Trevor N. Dupuy, *Hitler's Last Gamble* (New York: HarperCollins, 1994); Charles B. MacDonald, *A Time for Trumpets* (New York: William Morrow, 1985), and Eisenhower, *Crusade in Europe,* 342–65.

67. Precisely when the B2 area would run out of food was a question to which there were many answers. The SHAEF Mission to the Netherlands Report, "Wartime Food Problems of the Netherlands," Tinley Papers, states the end of December 1944. An International Red Cross Report of March 27, 1945, claims the B2 area had been without since the middle of November 1944, and the London Dutch government revised its figures several times over winter 1944–1945 and finally concluded that the entire occupied sector would exhaust all supplies by April 28, 1945. See Coles and Weinberg, *Civil Affairs*, 830. Unable to resolve these discrepancies with any accuracy I assume that ration levels in the B2 area continually declined during winter 1944–1945 and that by late March they reached lows of between 600 and 320 calories per day.

68. Donnison, *Civil Affairs and Military Government North-West Europe, 1944–1946*, 142, and Coles and Weinberg, *Civil Affairs*, 826.

69. Van der Zee, *The Hunger Winter*, 146–58, and " 'We Want More Fatness, Less Wetness,' " *Knickerbocker Weekly* 5, 5 (March 26, 1945): 6–11.

70. Stacey, *The Victory Campaign*, 583.

71. "First U.S. Food Shipped to Holland," *Knickerbocker Weekly* 5, 2 (March 5, 1945): 4.

72. "Freeing Holland," April 5, 1945, London *Times*, in the Netherlands, 1944–1945, Box 310, Hornbeck Papers, and van der Zee, *The Hunger Winter*, 53–59.

73. "Memorandum of Conversation," March 13, 1945, in the Netherlands, 1944–1945, Box 29, Rosenman Papers.

74. Donnison, *Civil Affairs and Military Government North-West Europe, 1944–1946*, 143.

75. Coles and Weinberg, *Civil Affairs*, 829, and Stacey, *The Victory Campaign*, 3:583.

76. Norway and Denmark were added subsequently to Rosenman's itinerary. See Rosenman, "Civilian Supplies for the Liberated Areas of Northwest Europe," May 1, 1945, History of the Rosenman Mission, 3, Rosenman Papers.

77. "Notes for Meeting December 27, 1944, Secretaries State, War and Navy," December 26, 1944, Committee of Three: State, War, Navy, Entry 74A, Henry L. Stimson "Safe File," July 1940–September 1945, RG167, NA.

78. See R–710 in Warren F. Kimball, *Churchill and Roosevelt*, 3 vols. (Princeton: Princeton University Press, 1984), 3:540.

79. Ibid., 5.

80. Rosenman, "Civil Supplies for the Liberated Areas of Northwest Europe," History of the Rosenman Mission, 9; "Memorandum of Meeting," March 12, 1945, in the Netherlands, 1944–1945, Box 29, Rosenman Papers; and J. J. Llewellin to Samuel I. Rosenman, March 13, 1945, in Memorandum and Correspondence, Box 29, Rosenman Papers.

81. See memorandum by the ambassador of the Netherlnads Government in Exile (Hornbeck), SDDF 856.48/3–1945, *Foreign Relations of the United States* [*FRUS*], *1945*, 8 vols. (Washington, D.C.: GPO, 1968), 5:12–13.

82. Van der Zee, *The Hunger Winter*, 176–80, and "Memorandum of Conversation," March 13, 1945, the Netherlands, Box 29, Rosenman Papers.

83. Van der Zee, *The Hunger Winter*, and "Red Cross Aid for Holland," *Knickerbocker Weekly* 5, 10 (April 30, 1945): 18, 24–25.

84. Van der Zee, *The Hunger Winter*, 253–54; " 'We Want More Fatness, Less Wetness,' " 6–11; and "Allies Sweep Through Northern Holland," *Knickerbocker Weekly* 5, 7 (April 9, 1945): 4–7.

85. Supreme Commander to Combined Chiefs of Staff, March 17, 1945, in Stacey, *The Victory Campaign*, 3:584.

86. Jeffrey Williams, *The Long Left Flank* (Toronto: Stoddart, 1988), 280–81, and Stacey, *The Canadian Army, 1939–1945*, 256–72.

87. Williams, *The Long Left Flank*, 284.

88. Donnison, *Civil Affairs and Military Government North-West Europe, 1944–1946*, 143.

89. Ibid., 144.

90. "The Queen Appeals for Aid to Holland," *Knickerbocker Weekly* 5, 2 (March 5, 1945): 4–5; "Red Cross Aid for Holland, *Knickerbocker Weekly* 5, 10 (April 30, 1945): 24–25; "R.A.F. Drops Food to Holland, *Knickerbocker Weekly* 5, 11 (May 7, 1945): 4–11; and "Telephone Conversation with Colonel Rowell, 21 Army Group," March 20, 1945, War Office (WO) 32/11704, PRO.

91. Van der Zee, *The Hunger Winter*, 247–57.

92. "R.A.F. Drops Food to Holland," 4–11.

93. Ibid.

94. "Food for Holland," 10–12.

95. G. C. E. Burger, H. R. Sandstead, and Sir Jack Drummond, "Starvation in Western Holland: 1945," *Lancet* (September 1, 1945), 282–90, Tinley Papers, Box 310.

96. "R.A.F. Drops Food to Holland," 4–11, and London *Times*, May 28, 1945, in the Netherlands, 1945–1946, Box 310, Hornbeck Papers.

97. London *Times*, May 28, 1945, and Donnison, *Civil Affairs and Military Government North-West Europe, 1944–1946*, 144.

98. Charles F. Egan, "Food Is Assembled to Build up Dutch," April 10, 1945, *New York Times* in the Netherlands, 1945–1946, Box 310, Hornbeck Papers.

99. "Amsterdam Health Position," June 13, 1945, and "Report on Washington Press Conference," April 11, 1945, *Anep-Aneta Bulletin*, in the Netherlands, 1945–1946, Box 310, Hornbeck Papers.

100. "Northeastern Holland Liberated," *Kickerbocker Weekly*, 5, 9 (April 23, 1945): 6–9, and *Anep-Aneta Bulletin*, April 13, 1945, and May 3, 1945, in the Netherlands, 1945–1946, Box 310, Hornbeck Papers.

101. Coles and Weinberg, *Civil Affairs*, 830, and "Wartime Food Problems in the Netherlands, 49, Tinley Papers.

102. "Civilian Supplies for the Liberated Areas of Northwest Europe," May 1, 1945, Rosenman Papers.

103. John Colville, *The Fringes of Power* (New York: W. W. Norton, 1985), 586, and Martin Gilbert, *Road to Victory, 1941–1945*, 8 vols. (Boston: Houghton Mifflin, 1986) 8: 1286.

104. Winston Churchill to Franklin Roosevelt, April 9, 1945, *FRUS, 1945,* 5:19–20; "Churchill to Roosevelt," April 9, 1945, C–938, and "Churchill to Roosevelt," April 10, 1945, C–939, Kimball, *Churchill and Roosevelt,* 3:621–22.

105. Kimball, *Churchill and Roosevelt,* 3:621–22.

106. Gilbert, *Road to Victory, 1941–1945,* 1286, and "Roosevelt to Churchill," R–740, Kimball, *Churchill and Roosevelt,* 3:623. The president and the prime minister exchanged only a few more telegrams, for Roosevelt died in his sleep the night of April 12, 1945, in Warm Springs, Georgia.

107. Sir Francis De Guingand, *Operation Victory* (London: Hodder and Stoughton, 1947), 445–53, and Pogue, *The Supreme Command,* 457.

108. Van der Zee, *The Hunger Winter,* 258–67; De Guingand, *Operation Victory,* 445–53; and Donnison, *Civil Affairs and Military Government North-West Europe, 1944–1946,* 144.

109. Chandler, ed., *The Papers of Dwight David Eisenhower,* 4:2630–31.

110. Ibid.

111. Ibid., 4:2630, and Pogue, *The Supreme Command,* 457–58.

112. Chandler, ed., *The Papers of Dwight David Eisenhower,* 4:2630–31.

113. See *The Diaries of Edward R. Stettinius, Jr., 1943–1946,* ed. Thomas M. Campbell and George C. Herring (New York: New View Points, 1975), 322–25.

114. Chandler, ed., *The Papers of Dwight David Eisenhower,* 4:2638–39.

115. Ibid.

116. Donnison, *Civil Affairs and Military Government North-West Europe, 1944–1945,* 144.

117. Chandler, ed., *The Papers of Dwight David Eisenhower,* 4:2642.

118. Coles and Weinberg, *Civil Affairs,* 830–31.

119. Chandler, ed., *The Papers of Dwight David Eisenhower,* 4:2653 and 2654.

120. Ibid.

121. Coles and Weinberg, *Civil Affairs,* 831.

122. Van der Zee, *The Hunger Winter,* 247–57 and "R.A.F. Drops Food to Holland," 4–11.

123. Coles and Weinberg, *Civil Affairs,* 831; Donnison, *Civil Affairs and Military Government North-West Europe, 1944–1945,* 145; and "R.A.F. Drops Food to Holland," 4–11.

124. Later in May the air drops would be the subject of many children's drawings and thank-you notes that were sent to Eisenhower's headquarters, to Ambassador Hornbeck, and to others associated with the relief efforts. In printed documents there were few references to injuries caused by free dropping, but injury is a common theme in many of the children's drawings and must have been a reasonably common occurrence. See Tinley Papers; Vernon C. Manfred Papers, HHA, HI, and for report of one casualty, see van der Zee, *The Hunger Winter,* 247–57.

125. "Food for Holland," 10–12; van der Zee, *The Hunger Winter,* 263; and De Guingand, *Operation Victory,* 445–55.

126. Eisenhower, *Crusade in Europe,* 416–17; van der Zee, *The Hunger Winter,* 262–67; and De Guingand, *Operation Victory,* 450–53.

127. Sources consulted all confirm that Seyss-Inquart was cooperative and sub-dued, but versions of the exchange that took place between Seyss-Inquart and Smith vary considerably. De Guingand, who was in the meeting, reports the Reichskom-missar's reply was, "I am not afraid—I am a German." See De Guingand, *Operation Victory*, 452. The version of the Seyss-Inquart/Smith exchange in this chapter is taken from Coles and Weinberg, *Civil Affairs*, 834, and varies only slightly from van der Zee's version in *The Hunger Winter*, 265.

128. Coles and Weinberg, *Civil Affairs*, 831–34; Stacey, *The Victory Campaign*, 3:606–7; Donnison, *Civil Affairs and Military Government North-West Europe, 1944–1945*, 145–46; Chandler, ed., *The Papers of Dwight David Eisenhower*, 2666–67; and van der Zee, *The Hunger Winter*, 276–86.

129. "Wartime Food Problems of the Netherlands," 51–52.

130. Ibid.

131. London *Times*, May 23, 1945, Hornbeck Papers.

132. Zena Stein, Mervyn Susser, Gerhart Saenger, and Francis Marolla, *Famine and Human Development* (New York: Oxford University Press, 1975), 52–53.

133. "Wartime Food Problems in the Netherlands," 52–53.

134. Report to the president by Samuel I. Rosenman, May 1, 1945 and *Washington Dispatches, 1941–1945*, ed. H. G. Nicholas (Chicago: University of Chicago Press, 1981), 557.

6. Allies or Adversaries?
The Joint Chiefs of Staff and
Soviet-American Relations,
Spring 1945

Mark A. Stoler

Throughout World War II the U.S. Joint Chiefs of Staff (JCS) and their planners devoted much time and attention to relations with the Soviet Union. They did so within the context not only of the war effort but also of the probable shape of the postwar world.

Such concerns might seem odd for officers whose training and traditions had previously led them to leave such matters to their civilian superiors and to insist that their own functions were "purely military." But alliance and postwar political assessments proved to be inseparable from wartime strategic planning in a global, coalition war. They were also prerequisite for the extensive postwar military planning that took place in the United States during the final years of the war, which the Joint Chiefs considered mandatory in order to avoid any repetition of the prewar politico-military lack of preparedness and coordination that had culminated at Pearl Harbor. This chapter focuses on assessments of the Soviet Union during the early months of 1945, and analyzes the struggle that took place within the armed forces during the German collapse and surrender over a proposed revision of the military and foreign policies governing U.S. relations with the Soviets.

Throughout 1942 and 1943 the JCS and their planners had consistently emphasized the importance of the Soviet Union to the Allied war effort. They had bluntly warned that victory over Germany depended on continued Russian participation in the war and that this required early initiation of cross-Channel rather than the Mediterranean operations being proposed by London. They also emphasized the vital importance to the United States of eventual Soviet participation in the war against Japan as a means to minimize U.S. casualties. One high-level paper bluntly stated in mid-1943 that such participation was "the most important factor the United States has to consider in relation to Russia."[1]

By mid-1943 the JCS and their planners had also begun to explore the probable shape of the postwar world, assuming the Grand Alliance would defeat the Axis, an exploration that intensified in 1944. Their conclusions once again focused on Soviet power. Allied victory, the Joint Chiefs' senior military advisers on the Joint Strategic Survey Committee (JSSC) maintained, would cause the greatest shift in the global balance of power since the fall of the Roman Empire fifteen hundred years earlier. In truth, defeat of the Axis powers and a severe decline in British military power would destroy any traditional balance. Rather, two superpowers, the United States and the Soviet Union, would dominate the world.

British military decline was the result of numerous long-term factors whose impact World War II had greatly accelerated, including loss of industrial and war-making capacity, changes in warfare that negated the importance of seapower, and continued revolt within the British Empire. Paralleling Britain's decline was an enormous increase in the power of both the United States and the Soviet Union, an "epochal" and "phenomenal" development that would give the USSR "assured military dominance" after the war in Eastern and Central Europe, the Middle East, and northeast Asia. Similarly, the United States would have ensured dominance in the Western Hemisphere and the Atlantic and Pacific Oceans. Neither power would be able successfully to challenge the other within its respective sphere or to defeat the other in a war—even if aligned with Great Britain.

Given these projections, as well as wartime military realities and fears of a postwar Axis revival should the Grand Alliance collapse, the JSSC argued that U.S. policy should be to minimize friction with the Soviets and to try to erase Russian suspicions and hostility so as to make possible postwar as well as wartime collaboration. In particular, Washington should under no circumstances support British proposals for military or political involvement in Eastern Europe, which was to be within the Soviet sphere of influence, or even begin any postwar territorial discussions since simply raising the issue could lead to Allied conflict.[2]

Such conclusions were not unanimous within the armed forces. Numerous high-ranking officers rejected the JSSC assessments. JCS chair Adm. William D. Leahy, the chief of staff to the commander in chief, consistently argued that only civilians should discuss such issues. Others warned that postwar collaboration with the USSR might not be possible and that Soviet power could threaten U.S. security. They also maintained that the proposed policy constituted appeasement, that Britain would remain powerful and America's "natural" ally in the postwar world, and that the Soviets respected only force and hard-bargaining.

As early as November 1940, the army and navy chiefs of staff and their planners had emphasized the importance of the balance of power to U.S. security;[3] acceptance of Soviet domination of most of the Eurasian landmass was not consonant with such an emphasis. Moreover, even older anti-Soviet sentiments existed that had never disappeared and that were now strengthened by Soviet military victories and expansive definitions of postwar security. There was also a belief that Soviet security claims were no different from those Adolf Hitler had made for Germany and that the USSR viewed western cooperation as a sign of weakness.

As early as February/March 1943, some high-level army planners had argued for a tough, quid pro quo policy on Lend-Lease aid. By late 1944–early 1945 these arguments had expanded into attacks on the entire cooperative approach and calls for a new policy based on viewing the Soviets as a major postwar threat. Within the army, such attacks were centered in the Intelligence Division (G-2), the Strategy and Policy (S&P) Group of the Operations Division (OPD), and air force postwar planners whose air-age geopolitical "map" of the world envisioned the USSR as a potential threat. Russian lack of seapower led postwar naval planners to take a more optimistic view of postwar Soviet-American relations, but this optimism declined rapidly in late 1944, due largely to the impact of the new secretary of the navy, James Forrestal, who was rapidly coming to view the USSR as a postwar ideological as well as a geopolitical menace.[4]

High-level U.S. officials in Moscow reinforced these anti-Soviet sentiments within the War and Navy Departments. Throughout 1944 Soviet behavior led to increasing calls from Ambassador Averell Harriman for a reversal of policy and the use of economic aid as "one of the most effective weapons at our disposal to influence European political events in the direction we desire and to avoid the development of a sphere of influence of the Soviet Union over Eastern Europe and the Balkans." Russian behavior during the Warsaw Uprising led him to warn in August–September 1944 that Soviet leaders had become "bloated with power" and now "expect that they can force their will on us and all countries." This was partially the result of Washington's "generous attitude," which had been "misinterpreted . . . as a sign of weakness, and acceptance of their policies," and which now needed to be reversed. Otherwise, the Soviets would "become a world bully wherever their interests are involved."[5]

Air force and embassy officers, as well as Gen. John R. Deane, head of the U.S. Military Mission to Moscow, joined Harriman in calling for a reversal of policy. By December 1944 Deane was bluntly informing Army Chief of Staff Gen. George C. Marshall that he had "sat at innumerable Russian banquets and become gradually nauseated by Russian food, vodka and protestations of friendship. It is amazing how these toasts go down past the tongues in the cheeks." The Russians, Deane insisted, "simply cannot understand giving without taking, and as a result our giving is viewed with suspicion." Moreover, Russians looked upon any foreigner as "either a shrewd trader to be admired or a sucker to be despised." American policy had placed the United States in the latter category and needed to be reversed. Confrontation was not inevitable, Deane maintained, but "we must be tougher if we are to gain their respect and be able to work with them in the future." One month later he reiterated these warnings and recommendations and sent the JCS a fifty-four-page memorandum filled with thirty-four case histories of Soviet noncooperation.[6]

Despite this growing chorus, the Joint Chiefs and their senior military advisers on the JSSC continued to support a cooperative policy. During spring and summer 1944, the JCS rejected all proposals calling for retaliation and for rejection of the JSSC assessments. Instead, they approved the assessments with minor modifications and forwarded them to the State Department as their official position papers. These papers reappeared in the State Department's briefing books for the 1944 Quebec Conference and the 1945 Yalta and Potsdam Conferences. The JCS and JSSC sustained this policy during the early months of 1945, despite the pleas of Deane and others. Indeed, as late as April 7 they bluntly rejected Deane's request for retaliation through cancellation of a Lend-Lease convoy.[7]

Numerous factors account for the JCS position. Primarily, there was the constant fear that a confrontation could lead the Russians to cease military operations against the Germans, sign a separate peace, or both, thereby endangering the war effort. This possibility had been abundantly clear in 1942 and 1943, when the Red Army was engaging the overwhelming bulk of the Wehrmacht and Anglo-American forces had not yet landed in Europe. Even after the June 1944 Normandy invasion and subsequent liberation of Western Europe, however, and well into 1945, the Red Army continued to inflict the overwhelming majority of casualties on the Germans.[8] Furthermore, the 1943 War Department decision to create no more than ninety divisions meant that this disparity and reliance on the Red Army would continue for the duration of the war, a fact reinforced when the German Ardennes counteroffensive of late 1944 led to the commitment of the last U.S. reserves and requests for the early launching of a Russian offensive in the east. Without such an offensive, Gen. Dwight D. Eisenhower bluntly informed Marshall, "a quick decision cannot be obtained."[9]

The JCS also worried that a confrontational policy would preclude Soviet entry into the war against Japan. Absence of the Soviets in the Far East would not threaten Allied victory, but it would lengthen the war and make victory much more costly, a matter underscored in early 1945 by new Japanese suicide tactics and the ensuing heavy U.S. casualties during the Iwo Jima and Okinawa campaigns.[10] Furthermore, the success of the Japanese offensive in China during summer 1944 had led to the virtual collapse of that theater and recognition that Chiang Kai-shek's forces were incapable of tying down the Japanese army on the Asian mainland. Only the Red Army could do so.

The JSSC insisted as well that Eastern Europe was *not* a vital postwar security concern for the United States but that it *was* vital for the Soviets, whose intentions there were largely defensive. Along with such conclusions went the important complementary belief that the most likely cause of future Allied conflict was a revival of the old Anglo-Russian clash in the Balkans and that the weakened British were attempting to involve the United States in this conflict.

Such suspicions were not new. U.S. military planners had long believed that British Mediterranean strategy had been at least partially motivated by a desire to manipulate U.S. forces into conflict with the Soviets and defense of British interests in the Balkans. They further argued in 1944 that Soviet behavior was partially a response to British machinations. Clearly implied was the belief that Soviet and American postwar interests did not collide but that British interests did conflict with both nations and that London constituted a threat both to wartime collaboration and to postwar peace. "Our past efforts to effect closer liaison with the Russians have always been sandbagged by the British," one planner bluntly concluded in late 1944. "Our future efforts . . . must not be similarly obstructed by British national interests." Correspondingly, a poll taken in late 1944 revealed that 54 percent of the public blamed the British and only 18 percent blamed the Soviets for Allied problems.[11]

The JCS and their planners also knew that a major Axis objective was to create Allied discord and that avoidance of such a break was the cornerstone of Pres. Franklin D. Roosevelt's wartime and postwar policies. Indeed, JSSC proposals as accepted by the JCS echoed the president's policies. Whether military policy followed or led presidential policy remains a question, however. Roosevelt's beliefs regarding the USSR had been well known in the armed forces since 1941 and might very well have influenced JCS/JSSC assessments, but it is equally likely that those assessments enormously influenced the president's policies.[12] In all probability, the relationship was mutually reinforcing.

A notable example of this relationship could be seen in the armed forces' recommendations to Roosevelt prior to the February 1945 Yalta Conference and then in their positive reaction to the Crimean accords. From the military's perspective, that conference succeeded brilliantly in resolving Allied differences and in guaranteeing both continued military cooperation against

Germany and the quick Soviet entry into the war against Japan that the Joint Chiefs desired. "For what we have gained here," Marshall stated at the end of the conference, "I would have gladly stayed a whole month." A few weeks later he further noted in preparation for an off-the-record press talk that the Yalta accords had foiled Axis hopes for Allied conflict. "They have always planned on a split of the Allies," he noted. "They never for one moment calculated that the Allies could continue to conduct combined operations with complete understanding and good faith."[13]

Marshall and his JCS colleagues had an additional reason to be pleased with the Yalta results and to oppose a policy shift: they desired to avoid confronting the Soviets in contests they could not win and that could promote an equally unwinnable World War III. Soviet power, the JSSC had previously made clear, could not be successfully challenged in Eastern Europe. Furthermore, any effort to do so could lead to a war in which the Red Army could conquer Western Europe, an area critical for U.S. security. Yet the American public would be unlikely to support the massive military buildup and involvement necessary to defend this area. In effect, Western Europe was a hostage to avoiding conflict with the Soviets and winning them over to postwar collaboration.

This conclusion was based not on naive trust of the Soviets but on recognition of the severe limits to U.S. power vis-à-vis the USSR. As Army Operations Division Chief Gen. Thomas Handy noted in October 1944, maintaining U.S. forces in Europe after German defeat "to impress the other victorious Allies" would not work because the Russians "can always outnumber us in divisions."[14] Nor did military officials think that the American people would support long-term military involvement in Europe. As one scholar has correctly noted, Roosevelt's comments at Yalta that American forces could not be expected to stay in Europe for more than eighteen months clearly placed the president "in agreement with his senior military advisers, especially General Marshall."[15]

The armed forces' conception of postwar Soviet-American cooperation did not leave the United States defenseless, however. Despite their lip service to the concept of international security and organization, the JCS and their planners had effectively opposed all proposals to base postwar U.S. security on such an organization and to create an international police force. Instead, the military had focused on an informal Great Power division of the world into areas of "regional" responsibility. Within this system, they demanded that the United States control an extensive series of air and naval bases that could maintain postwar peace in conjunction with Britain and Russia against Axis resurgence or that could defend the United States and project U.S. power against the Soviets if Allied postwar cooperation failed.[16]

In late March 1945, the JSSC forwarded to the JCS an extraordinary memorandum that highlighted the need for such an umbrella policy vis-à-vis the Soviets. Written by seven scholars who had worked for the armed forces, State Department, and/or the Office of Strategic Services (OSS) during the war, the memorandum asserted that British power had previously shielded the United States from Continental aggression but had seriously declined and that preventing any power from controlling all of Europe now had to become a "continuous" U.S. concern. Only Germany and Russia could pose such a threat, and then only in the event of Soviet-American conflict. Preventing such a conflict must therefore be a cardinal U.S. policy.[17]

The scholars were not ready either to trust the Soviets or to treat them as adversaries without solid evidence that they were. "Soviet Russia is a power whose good intentions must be assumed until there is incontrovertible evidence to the contrary," they asserted, "but its intentions are sufficiently unclear so that the United States must in no case place sole reliance for security on Soviet good will." Yet "while the United States can afford to make no concessions which leave its security or vital national interests at the mercy of the Soviet Union, there is almost no other concession which it can afford not to make to assure Soviet collaboration in the maintenance of security." Without such collaboration there would be no security, only another catastrophic, and perhaps unwinnable, world war. Admittedly, the United States needed to define "the limits of permissible concessions" to the Soviets and make sure that Moscow was willing to cooperate. But the scholars saw the Yalta accords on Poland as fulfilling remaining Russian territorial demands, and the Crimean Declaration on Liberated Europe provided a clear test of Soviet sincerity in regard to future collaboration.[18]

Ironically, those accords were breaking down just when this memorandum was being circulated in Washington, leading to calls from numerous quarters for a dramatic change in U.S. policy. And over the next few months many of the reasons previously given for continuing to cooperate either disappeared or were severely modified. The result was a gradual reversal of JCS policy toward the Soviets, beginning just a few weeks before German surrender, which would reach its logical conclusion a year later.

Confronting the JCS by early April 1945 were extensive complaints about Soviet violations of the Yalta accords and calls for a firm American response from U.S. military representatives on the Allied Control Councils for Romania, Bulgaria, and Hungary as well as from General Deane. Roosevelt, Churchill, and Stalin also engaged in bitter exchanges over Soviet behavior in Poland and Soviet charges of bad faith regarding Anglo-American negotiations for the surrender of German forces in northern Italy. On April 3 General Marshall formally informed his JCS colleagues of a series of reports "indicating increasing Russian non-cooperation with U.S. military authorities" and violation of the Yalta military accords. These included the grounding of U.S. aircraft behind Russian lines, refusal to repair U.S. aircraft forced to land behind those lines, a prohibition on further air entries, refusal to allow a naval survey party to enter the USSR or Poland, problems with American POWs, and obstruction of the strategic bombing survey in Russian-occupied areas. Deane recommended immediate retaliation through a halt in Lend-Lease aircraft shipments to Russia, cancellation of the next northern convoy to the USSR, and similar treatment for Russian POWs; the American control commissioner in Hungary recommended suspension of Soviet flights to Italy. Soviet actions might be "indicative of [an] increasing non-cooperative attitude," though they might also be "the result of unrelated causes" or a reflection of diplomatic problems "intended to invite retaliation which could be used as an excuse by [the] Soviets to abrogate commitments." Consequently, Marshall and his JCS colleagues agreed to submit the matter to the JSSC for study and policy recommendation "as a matter of priority."[19]

On the same date, April 3, the President's Soviet Protocol Committee forcefully rejected Deane's call for retaliatory cancellation of a northern convoy on the grounds of its impracticality and "departure from established policy" that the president had reasserted as recently as January 6, regarding the importance and priority to be accorded supplies to Russia. Two days later the JSSC concurred, albeit for far more extensive reasons. "The maintenance of the unity of the Allies in the prosecution of the war," it stated,

> must remain the cardinal and over-riding objective of our politico-military policy with Russia. The instances of Russian refusal to cooperate. . . , while irritating and difficult to understand if considered as isolated events, are of relatively minor moment. They would assume real importance in themselves only if their occurrence should cause our Government to adopt retaliatory measures in kind, and these in turn should be followed by further Russian measures, and thus lead in the end to a break in Allied unity.[20]

Russian actions, the JSSC implied, were the result of their extreme suspicion in areas of primary interest such as Eastern Europe and continued Allied disagreement over the future of these areas. U.S. retaliation against Russian moves would only provoke further Russian measures and break Allied unity. Furthermore, the episodes cited might reflect a "very grave misunderstanding" resulting from the negotiations in Bern for the surrender of German forces in northern Italy that had caused Stalin to accuse his allies of trying to negotiate a separate peace. The committee warned that this could be the result of a German ploy to divide the Allies. Consequently, it recommended no retaliatory action against the Soviets but suggested that Roosevelt settle these matters personally with Stalin at the proper time. It even drafted a message for the president to send to Moscow, inviting Soviet military officials to visit the western front and see for themselves that no separate peace was being negotiated. The JSSC did recommend, however, that the JCS restudy all present bilateral projects and Soviet requests and drop those not essential to the war effort.[21]

At the same time the JSSC members were publicly reasserting the broader conclusions they had reached in 1943 and 1944 regarding Soviet-American postwar cooperation. On April 4, for example, committee member Adm. Russell Willson informed the Academy of Political Science that the postwar world would exhibit changes so profound as to be comparable with those occasioned by the fall of Rome, that British power was in decline while the Soviet Union and the United States would emerge as the two superpowers, and that the key to future peace was not the United Nations but the unity of the Big Three. Failure to retain that unity would lead to war between the victors or a revival of Axis strength and aggression. Thus, "The three great powers must see to it that they maintain control over their former enemies, and find no new enemies among themselves."[22]

The Joint Chiefs considered the April 5 JSSC recommendations amid extraordinary secrecy and on April 7 agreed with the committee that no retaliation should be undertaken. Significantly, however, Admiral Leahy prodded his colleagues to add the words "at the present time" to this conclusion and to veto the proposed Roosevelt letter to Stalin on the grounds that the president had already affirmed American good faith to the Soviet leader.[23] Such caveats may have reflected underlying JCS concerns or continued anger over Stalin's accusations of a separate peace. The JSSC had warned that these might be part of a German ploy to divide the Allies, and Roosevelt, in his final message to Churchill on April 11, soft-pedaled what had taken place. During the first week of April, however, he and the JCS were enraged by Stalin's accusations, which Marshall and his staff labeled "vile misrepresentations" causing "bitter resentment"—terms Leahy and Roosevelt incorporated into the president's April 4 message to Stalin.[24]

Increased suspicion of the Soviets was then asserted in a twenty-two-page OSS Research and Analysis Branch paper, circulated within the JCS and the army staff and then forwarded to the White House, that bluntly warned of a postwar Russia "more powerful than Germany or Japan has ever been" creating a situation "potentially more dangerous than any preceding one."[25] If the United States took no counteraction, Moscow would be able to dominate all of Eurasia and perhaps even "outrank the United States in military potential." With this enormous military capability went intentions that remained uncertain, and intense Soviet suspicion based on history and ideology, that might "easily lead Russia to interpret as aggressive the most pacific security measures of the other powers, and then herself to embark upon 'preventive' aggression" to control all of Eurasia. If successful, it would then become "a menace more formidable to the United States than any yet known." U.S. policy should continue to aim at convincing Russia of Washington's pacific intentions but "at the same time demonstrat[e] our determination to safeguard our own interests." A world security system and organization should continue to be pursued, but the United States must also prepare for possible failure by simultaneously creating a multitiered postwar defense system to include a West European bloc as the preferred "first line" of defense, an extensive series of Atlantic and Caribbean bases, and a "common defense system for all the Americas" in case these first two tiers failed.

Hemispheric defense alone would be insufficient to halt an attack from a Soviet Union able to harness Eurasian resources, however. "This is the crux of the problem," the OSS memorandum maintained, "and it dictates the urgent necessity of taking all measures to prevent or delay the domination of Europe and/or Asia by a power already so formidable as Russia." Such measures included the formation of a strong "Western-European-Mediterranean-American bloc," support for noncommunist forces in Asia to re-create an Asian balance of power, unilateral control of the Pacific through a series of air and naval bases, and maintenance of the British, French, and Dutch empires. On this last point the United States had "at present no interest in weakening or liquidating these empires or in championing schemes of international trusteeship which may provoke unrest and result in colonial disintegration, and may at the same time alienate from us the European states whose help we need to balance the Soviet power."[26]

In effect, the OSS memorandum directly challenged the JCS/JSSC belief that Soviet aims were limited and defensive. Instead, it argued that Soviet policy might be aimed at domination of Eurasia, that Russia clearly possessed the military ability to achieve this, and that the United States had to take immediate countermeasures, including support of European colonialism. The memorandum's author was not alone in his conclusions. At least one member of the S&P Group of Army OPD simultaneously attacked the March scholars' memorandum urging cooperation as "wishful thinking" and concluded that the "greatest danger to U.S. is Soviet Power Politics which includes giving in its sphere of influence [sic]."[27]

This challenge to a pillar of the JCS position on Soviet-American relations occurred just when German forces in the west were collapsing and the need for continued military collaboration in Europe was dissipating. On April 2, one day after Eisenhower's forces had completed their envelopment of Wehrmacht forces in the Ruhr, Marshall informed Roosevelt and Secretary of State Edward Stettinius of the War Department's estimate that by month's end military operations would probably be at a final, "mopping up" stage.[28]

Then on April 12 Roosevelt died. Simultaneously, U.S. forces reached the Elbe. On April 16 the Soviets began their final drive on Berlin, and three days later 325,000 German forces in the Ruhr pocket surrendered. In the space of a few weeks, two of the major reasons for continuing cooperation with Russia—its necessity in defeating Germany and presidential insistence on such a policy—disappeared. At the same time, Allied conflict increased dramatically; and the validity of a third reason for cooperation, the limited and defensive nature of Soviet aims, was directly challenged.

The impact of these dramatic changes could be seen as early as April 16, only four days after Roosevelt's death, when General Deane once again requested revision of JCS Russian policy. Germany, he argued, was already defeated, and the Soviet Union was so sure of its strength and contemptuous of Washington and London that it was breaking the Yalta accords and assuming an intolerable "attitude of dominance" toward its allies. This situation, he said, had "reached a climax" since the Yalta Conference and was at least partially the result of a Soviet mind "that can only look for ulterior motive behind our liberality. Failing to find one they conclude that our cooperation springs from fear." Soviet entry into the war against Japan admittedly remained a cardinal U.S. policy, but Deane insisted that Moscow would enter that war in its own interests no matter what the state of Soviet-American relations and that America's cooperative policy was only convincing the Soviets to demand more concessions.

Little of this was new—but what was new was the international environment, the absence of Roosevelt, the level of JCS suspicion of Soviet intentions, and the specifics of Deane's recommendations. Again he requested a reversal of the cooperative policy; but perhaps recognizing that his superiors simply would not engage in retaliation, he and Ambassador Harriman proposed instead that the United States "cease forcing ourselves on the Soviet Union" and instead "wait for the Soviet authorities to come to us" on collaborative matters. "Only in this manner," they insisted, "can we regain Soviet respect." Specifically, the JCS should withdraw from all Soviet-American military projects not essential to the war effort, wait for Soviet initiatives, and approach Moscow only on important issues and "only" when they were prepared, in instances of refusal, to take "positive and effective action to force Soviet cooperation." Deane also listed the specific projects from which the United States should withdraw.[29]

On the following day the Joint Chiefs approved the first four steps Deane had proposed to implement this new policy and referred the rest to the Joint Staff Planners (JPS) as a "matter of priority." Simultaneously, Leahy ordered the White House Map Room Secretariat to prepare major briefing papers, giving emphasis to the Polish and Italian surrender disputes, for the new president. On April 19, he presented these memos to Harry Truman, stressing Stalin's "insulting language." The next day Harriman weighed in with a warning to Truman about Russia's "barbarian invasion of Europe"; and Deane explained his proposals to the Anglo-American Combined Chiefs of Staff, with Marshall implying that the April 17 U.S. withdrawal from projects reflected a new firmness in U.S. policy vis-à-vis the Soviets. On April 23 the senior members of the Joint Planning Staff recommended JCS approval of Deane's broad proposals; that approval was forthcoming on the following day.[30]

These actions, completed less than a week before Hitler's suicide and two weeks before Germany's unconditional surrender, clearly modified the Joint Chiefs' policy toward Russia and marked a turning point in Soviet-American relations. They were not a complete reversal of policy, however. Deane had not recommended, nor the Joint Chiefs endorsed, confrontation or retaliation. Furthermore, the partial withdrawal from collaborative projects was similar to JSSC recommendations in April; and in accepting Deane's more moderate recommendations on April 23 the JPS both toned down his anti-Soviet language and reaffirmed opposition to retaliation. Moreover, JCS agreement to these recommendations on April 24 followed acceptance only three days earlier of a JSSC report that assumed any U.S. action on possible Italian participation in the war against Japan would be "coordinated" with Russia as well as with Britain.[31]

What appears in retrospect to be confusion in JCS views regarding the Soviet Union and appropriate U.S. policy was most likely the result of uncertainty and divided counsel within the armed forces and the new administration of Pres. Harry S. Truman. Furthermore, some of the major reasons for continuing the cooperative policy still existed. Roosevelt was dead, the war in Europe all but over, and Soviet intentions were no longer perceived as defensive and limited. But the fear of Britain manipulating a Soviet-American conflict still remained, as did the desire for Soviet entry into the war against Japan and the concern over starting an unnecessary and unwinnable World War III.

The most important matter for the armed forces was probably Soviet participation in the war against Japan, although they also inclined to emphasize British manipulation and an unwinnable third world war. Interestingly, these factors were generally cited by the individuals most interested in Soviet entry into the war against Japan—members of the War Department.

Spring 1945 found the Joint Chiefs and their planners divided over whether Soviet entry was still necessary. By this time the utter destruction

of Japanese naval and airpower, combined with the highly effective subma-
rine campaign against Japanese shipping and the strategic bombing campaign against Japanese cities, had led numerous naval and air force planners
to conclude that Japan would soon be forced to surrender and that Soviet
aid was therefore unnecessary. Numerous army planners disagreed; for
despite the hopelessness of their situation, Japanese forces continued to fight
relentlessly and suicidally, and by early 1945 they had perfected a new series
of suicide tactics designed to take as many Americans with them as possible. The casualties on Iwo Jima in February were appalling and were even
worse in the ongoing battle for Okinawa that began in April.[32]

In June the Joint Chiefs agreed on plans to invade Kyushu, the south-
ernmost of the Japanese home islands, but this accord masked disagreement
as to whether additional invasions and Soviet entry would then be necessary,
or whether bombing and blockade could by themselves force Japan to surrender. On May 11, three days after V-E Day, chief naval planner Adm.
Charles Cooke informed Navy Secretary Forrestal that "the necessity for
Russia's early participation was very much lessened as a result of recent
events, although the Army didn't share that view."[33] Army officials would
thus continue to object to a confrontational approach vis-à-vis the Soviets
as both unnecessary and dangerous, despite navy, State Department, and
even presidential comments to the contrary.

As late as April 16 Secretary of War Henry L. Stimson had reiterated in
his diary the JCS/JSSC belief that "our respective orbits do not clash geo-
graphically and I think that on the whole we can probably keep out of clashes
in the future."[34] At a critical April 23 White House meeting, he and General
Marshall, supported to an extent by Admiral Leahy, directly challenged the
belief expressed by President Truman, Stettinius, Forrestal, Harriman, and
Deane that the Soviets had broken the Yalta accords, that this was part of a
pattern of domination in Eastern Europe and contempt for U.S. objections,
and that Washington must respond firmly even if it meant a showdown and
a break.

Stimson bluntly asserted that "in the big military matters the Soviet Government had kept their word and that the military authorities of the United
States had come to count on it." Indeed, the Russians "had often been better than their promise." He also reminded those present that "twenty-five
years ago virtually all of Poland had been Russian" and that "without understanding how seriously the Russians took this Polish question we might be
heading into very dangerous water." Indeed, "the Russians were perhaps
being more realistic than we were in regard to their own security." Although
he was anything but favorably inclined toward the Soviets and the Yalta
accord on Poland, Leahy admitted that "in his opinion the Yalta agreement

was susceptible to two interpretations" and warned that breaking with the Russians "was a very serious matter." Marshall explained why. Though the military situation in Europe could be labeled "secure," the planners still hoped for Soviet entry into the war against Japan "at a time when it would be useful to us. The Russians had it within their power to delay their entry," he warned, "until we had done all the dirty work."[35]

What may have been as extraordinary as this blunt rejection of the definition of reality being proposed by the new president and some of his top advisers were the strong counterarguments of Stettinius, Harriman, and Deane. Directly challenging the conclusions of his superior General Marshall, Deane asserted that the Soviets would declare war against Japan in their own interests and as soon as possible, "irrespective of what happened in other fields"; and he reiterated his previously expressed belief that "if we were afraid of the Russians we would get nowhere." Truman continued to agree with this point of view and in effect ended the debate by concluding "he was now satisfied that from a military point of view there was no reason why we should fail to stand up to our understanding of the Crimean agreements."[36]

Such presidential comments clearly had an impact on the Joint Chiefs, who approved Deane's recommendations on the following day. They were far from ready, however, to move beyond this limited response. Nor was Stimson. Indeed, on April 26 he reasserted in his diary the belief that "our position in the western hemisphere and Russia's in the eastern hemisphere could be adjusted without too much friction"; and on April 30 he instructed Marshall to make sure the new president was informed of past differences with London—particularly British balance-of-power machinations and efforts to create an anti-Soviet bloc. He also warned Undersecretary of State Joseph Grew of these dangers in regard to the looming crisis with Marshal Tito in Yugoslavia, a crisis in which the State Department's desire for toughness "very much troubled" Marshall and his staff and over which the JCS consistently urged caution.[37]

German surrender did not alter this JCS/War Department position. Indeed, on May 13 the JSSC reiterated that Russia could not be successfully opposed militarily in the Balkans and warned that any effort to do so could result in an increase in U.S. forces in Europe that would "adversely affect the war effort against Japan." A week later Stimson, with Forrestal's concurrence, warned Grew of the continued importance of Soviet entry into the war against Japan, that the Russians could unilaterally conquer most of the Far Eastern territorial concessions they had been granted at Yalta, and that therefore "not much good" would come of a proposed "rediscussion" of the Yalta accords. Simultaneously, the secretary of war reasserted his belief that no conflict of vital geographic interests existed between the United States and the Soviet Union and that Roosevelt's policy of mediating between London and Moscow was wiser than supporting the British.[38]

As the war in Europe ended, the armed forces had thus begun to reassess their view of postwar relations with the Soviet Union. They had not moved very far in that direction, however, and they remained divided both between and within the services. Not until July would the Joint Chiefs shift and begin to support those who opposed Soviet territorial demands, and not until October/November would internal differences disappear and a new Soviet threat be fully enunciated.

Continuing divisions were vividly illustrated in June and July when the JSSC itself as well as army planners split before the Potsdam Conference on questions regarding Soviet and American acquisition of postwar naval and air bases. In June, Gen. Stanley Embick, army member of the JSSC, argued against U.S. acquisition of unilateral base rights on Iceland as not essential to U.S. security but likely to arouse Russian suspicions. A month later both he and air force representative Gen. Muir S. Fairchild proposed no objections to Soviet demands for base rights and treaty revisions regarding the Kiel Canal, Bear Island, Spitsbergen, and the Dardanelles. To support these recommendations, Embick once again cited Russian security interests and history, previous Anglo-Russian antagonism, and the need for postwar cooperation and peace. Once again members of the S&P Group of OPD objected to this policy as appeasement and warned that acceptance would endanger U.S. security. This time, however, they were joined by the entire JPS as well as Admiral Willson of the JSSC, who now fully accepted Deane's position that the "preferred treatment" previously granted the USSR had only resulted in additional demands. Those demands should be resisted, he argued, as "untimely," unnecessary for Soviet security, and contrary to American security considerations. "This war has been fought to prevent an aggressive nation from dominating Europe," Willson warned, "and ultimately threatening the Western Hemisphere." Consequently, the United States should "resist demands and policies which tend to improve [the] Soviet position in Western Europe." The State Department and the Joint Chiefs concurred, with the latter accepting Willson's minority report over the majority one signed by Embick and Fairchild.[39]

Nevertheless, with the war against Japan still in progress and postwar Soviet policy far from clear, the Joint Chiefs and their planners remained unwilling in July to propose confrontation with the Soviet Union. By October, however, the situation had changed dramatically. The detonation of atomic bombs over Hiroshima and Nagasaki in August and the subsequent surrender of Japan negated the need for any additional military assistance from the Soviet Union. Simultaneously, Soviet postwar demands continued to increase and Soviet-American relations continued to deteriorate, culminating in the total failure to reach accord at the London Foreign Ministers' Conference in September. One month later the JSSC unanimously warned the JCS that Soviet policy now appeared bent on world domination rather than on merely defensive control of contiguous areas, that this posed a mortal threat to American security, that rapid demobilization was precluding any capacity to check this threat, and that nuclear weapons posed a serious future threat to the United States, despite its present nuclear monopoly. Consequently, the committee called for a thorough reexamination of U.S. military policy and position so as to be able in the future to "draw the line" on Soviet aggression, maintenance of the U.S. nuclear monopoly for as long as possible, and a "well advanced" definition of "defensive frontiers" through extensive Atlantic, Pacific, and Arctic bases so as to be able both to project atomic airpower against the Soviets and to preclude them from projecting such power against the continental United States.[40]

Only at this stage did the Joint Chiefs and their planners clearly define the Soviet Union as an adversary rather than as an ally in the postwar world. Given the previous statements and actions of the State Department and the president, one can hardly conclude that they were early cold warriors. Indeed, in many ways they were belated converts to this new global crusade. Although individual officers had throughout World War II called for a confrontational policy, the Joint Chiefs strongly supported the cooperative approach until at least April 1945. The collapse and surrender of Germany, combined with the death of Roosevelt and increasing Soviet-American friction, began a reconsideration and modification of this policy. With the war against Japan still in progress and Soviet intentions still uncertain, however, no reversal took place for another six months. Yet once the Joint Chiefs and their planners did conclude that the USSR constituted a threat, the reversal was quite dramatic; by early 1946 the planners had produced their first contingency plan for nuclear war against the Soviet Union.

NOTES

1. *Foreign Relations of the United States [FRUS]: The Conferences at Washington and Quebec, 1943* (Washington, D.C.: GPO, 1970), 624–27. See also Mark A. Stoler, *The Politics of the Second Front: American Military Planning and Diplomacy in Coalition Warfare, 1941–1943* (Westport, Conn.: Greenwood Press, 1977).

2. JCS 838/1, "Disposition of Italian Overseas Territories," May 6, 1944, ABC

092 Italy (April 27, 1944), Record Group (RG) 165, Records of the War Department General and Special Staffs; and JCS 973, "Fundamental Military Factors in Relation to Discussions Territorial Trusteeships and Settlements," July 28, 1944, CCS 092 (7-27-44), RG 218, Records of the Joint and Combined Chiefs of Staff, National Archives and Records Service (NA), Washington, D.C. Portions of these papers as modified, approved, and forwarded by the JCS to the State Department can be found in *FRUS, 1944,* 1: 699–703; *FRUS: The Conference at Quebec, 1944,* 190–92; *FRUS: The Conferences at Malta and Yalta, 1945,* 107–8; and *FRUS: The Conference of Berlin, 1945,* 1: 264–66. See also JCS 778/1, "Withdrawal from the War of Hungary, Rumania and Bulgaria," March 27, 1944, ABC 384 Hungary Rumania; JCS 779/1, "Proposed Procedure for Surrender of Rumanian Forces," March 28, 1944; JCS 812/1, "Rumanian Armistice Terms Proposed by USSR," April 10, 1944; Notes of Embick-Roberts Telephone Conversation, April 10, 1944; JCS 1954, "Allied Control Commission for Rumania," September 26, 1944, all in ABC 336 Rumania, sec. 1A (9–26–43), RG 165, NA; JCS 577/12–14, "Occupation of Certain Areas in the Mediterranean Theater Under Rankin 'C' Conditions," May 18–26, 1944, ABC 384 NW Europe (August 20, 43), sec. 5A, RG 165, NA; JCS 958 and 958/1, "Severance of Diplomatic Relations Between Germany and Turkey," July 15 and August 1, 1944, ABC 384, Sweden-Turkey (October 25, 1944), sec. 4, RG 165, NA.

3. Memos, Chief of Naval Operations to Secretary of the Navy, November 4–12, 1940; and Joint Planning Commitee to Joint Board, "National Defense Policy of the United States," December 21, 1940, reproduced in *American War Plans, 1919–1941,* vol. 3, *Plans to Meet the Axis Threat,* ed. Steven T. Ross (New York: Garland, 1992), 225–300.

4. Stoler, *Politics of the Second Front,* 87; informal notes on JCS 812 and 812/1, "Rumanian Armistice Terms Proposed by USSR," April 9, 1944, ABC 336 Rumania, sec. 1A (September 26, 43), RG 165, NA; memos, Caraway to Chief, S&P, and Lincoln to Handy, "JCS 838/1," May 13 and 15, 1944, ABC 092 Italy (April 27, 44); memo, Bissell and Weckerling, G-2, to Director, SPD, "Navy's Basic Demobilization Plan no. 3," July 27, 1944, SPD 370.01, RG 165, NA; Perry McCoy Smith, *The Air Force Plans for Peace, 1943–1945* (Baltimore: Johns Hopkins University Press, 1970), 68–69, 80–81; Alan Henrikson, "The Map as an 'Idea': The Role of Cartographic Imagery During the Second World War," *American Cartographer* 2 (April 1975): 19–53; James Forrestal Diary, August 18 and September 2, 1944, James Forrestal Papers, Princeton University, Princeton, N.J.; Arnold A. Rogow, *James Forrestal: A Study of Personality, Politics, and Policy* (New York: Macmillan, 1963), 126–27, 134, 151–52, 162–63; and Vincent Davis, *Postwar Defense Policy and the U.S. Navy, 1943–1946* (Chapel Hill: University of North Carolina Press, 1962), 101–2, 107–8, and 292–96, nn. 5 and 7.

5. *FRUS, 1944,* 3: 1389, n. 11; *FRUS, 1944,* 4: 951, 988–90, 992–98. See also W. Averell Harriman and Elie Abel, *Special Envoy to Churchill and Stalin, 1941–1946* (New York: Random House, 1975), 335–49,; and Deborah Welch Larson, *Origins of Containment: A Psychological Explanation* (Princeton: Princeton University Press, 1985), 93–106.

6. Letter, Deane to Marshall, December 2, 1944, reprinted in *FRUS:Yalta*, 447–49, and in John R. Deane, *The Strange Alliance:The Story of Our Efforts at Wartime Cooperation with Russia* (NewYork:Viking Press, 1947), 84–86; memo, Deane to JCS, "Present Relations Between the United States Military Mission, Moscow, and the Soviet Military Authorities," January 22, 1945, reproduced on microfilm, *Records of the Joint Chiefs of Staff, Part 1, 1942–1945:The Soviet Union* (Frederick, Md.: University Publications of America), reel 2.

7. See the discussion of this issue in RG 218, NA and RG 165, NA.

8. Between June and September 1944, for example, the Red Army inflicted nine hundred thousand casualties on the Germans, a figure exceeding by two hundred thousand the total number of German troops engaged against Anglo-American forces in Western Europe during their most dramatic advances of the war. See Russell Buhite, *Decisions at Yalta:An Appraisal of Summit Diplomacy* (Wilmington, Del.: Scholarly Resources, 1986), xv–xvi.

9. Forrest C. Pogue, *George C. Marshall*, vol. 3, *Organizer of Victory, 1943–1945* (NewYork:Viking Press, 1973), 508. See also Maurice Matloff, "The 90-Division Gamble," in *Command Decisions*, ed. Kent Roberts Greenfield (Washington, D.C.: GPO, 1960), 365–81.

10. See JCS1308, "Italian Participation in the War Against Japan," April 11, 1945, with supporting documents, ABC 380 Italy (April 1, 1945), RG 165, NA.

11. Unsigned memo for Carter, "Machinery for U.S.–USSR Collaboration in the War Against Japan," December 19, 1944, ABC 384 USSR (September 25, 1944), sec. 1-A, RG 165, NA; Robert M. Hathaway, *Ambiguous Partnership: Britain and America, 1944–1947* (NewYork: Columbia University Press, 1981),97–98;Terry H. Anderson, *The United States, Great Britain, and the Origins of the Cold War, 1944–1947* (Columbia: University of Missouri Press, 1981), 1–27. See Stoler, *Politics of the Second Front,* for earlier fears in this regard.

12. See GeoffreyWarner, "From Tehran toYalta: Reflections on F.D.R.'s Foreign Policy," *International Affairs* 43 (July 1967): 530–36.

13. Michael Charlton, "The Eagle and the Small Birds," *Encounter* 1 (1983): 24–25, quoted in David Dimbleby and David Reynolds, *An Ocean Apart:The Relationship Between Britain and America in the Twentieth Century* (NewYork: Random House, 1988), 174; notes for off-the-record talk to Overseas Press Club in NewYork City, March 1, 1945, Pentagon Office File, Box 111, Folder 49, George C. Marshall Papers, George C. Marshall Research Library, Lexington,Va.

14. Memo, Handy to CofS, "Composition of USAAF for the Occupation of Germany," October 17, 1944, ABC 381 SS Papers (January 7, 1943) (nos. 314–26), SS 323, RG 165, NA.

15. D. C.Watt, "Every War Must End:War-Time Planning for Post-War Security in Britain and America in the Wars of 1914–1918 and 1939–1945:The Roles of Historical Example and of Professional Historians," in *Transactions of the Royal Historical Society*, 5th series (London: Butler andTanner, 1978), 28: 170.

16. See JCS 183 and 570 series, "Air Routes Across the Pacific and Air Facilities for International Police Force" and "U.S. Requirements for Post-War Air Bases,"

CCS 360 (2–9–42), sec. 1 and (12–9–42), sec. 2, RG 218, NA; Thomas M. Campbell, *Masquerade Peace: America's UN Policy, 1944–1945* (Tallahassee: Florida State University Press, 1973); William Roger Louis, *Imperialism at Bay: The United States and the Decolonization of the British Empire, 1941–1945* (New York: Oxford University Press, 1978), 259–73; James F. Schnabel, *The History of the Joint Chiefs of Staff: The Joint Chiefs of Staff and National Policy, vol. 1, 1945–1947* (Wilmington, Del.: Michael Galzier, 1979), 299–346; Melvyn P. Leffler, *A Preponderance of Power: National Security, the Truman Administration, and the Cold War* (Stanford: Stanford University Press, 1992), 55–59; and Lester J. Foltos, "The New Pacific Barrier: America's Search for Security in the Pacific, 1945–1947," *Diplomatic History* 13 (summer 1989): 317–42.

17. JCS Memorandum for Information no. 382, "A Security Policy for Post-War America," March 29, 1945, CCS 092 (7–27–44), RG 218, NA.

18. Ibid. The seven scholars were Edward M. Earle and Harold Sprout of Princeton; Frederick S. Dunn, William T. R. Fox, David Rowe, and Arnold Wolfers of Yale; and Grayson Kirk of Columbia. The original memorandum was dated March 8 and appears to have been drafted at a January weekend conference in Rye, New York. Information on this conference can be found in the Edward M. Earle Papers, Princeton University, Princeton, N.J.

19. JCS 1301, "Arrangements with the Soviets," April 3, 1945, CCS 092 USSR (3–27–45), aec. 1, RG 218, NA.

20. JCS 1301/1 and 1301/2, "Cancellation of Convoy to North Russia" and "Arrangements with the Soviets," April 3 and 5, 1945, CCS 092 USSR (3–27–45), sec. 1, RG 218, NA.

21. Ibid., JCS 1302.

22. Willson speech before Academy of Political Science, April 4, 1945, Box 25, Adm. Willson Speech folder, Forrestal Papers.

23. April 6–7, 1945 memos attached to JCS 1301–1301/2, CCS 092 USSR (3–27–45), RG 218, NA.

24. Warren F. Kimball, ed., *Churchill and Roosevelt: The Complete Correspondence* (Princeton: Princeton University Press, 1984), 3: 609–12, 630; Pogue, *Marshall*, 3: 565–66.

25. This memorandum was written by OSS Research and Analysis (R&A) Branch director William Langer and OSS Russian section chief Geroid Robinson, as noted by Betty Dessants, "The American Academic Community and United States–Soviet Union Relations: The Research and Analysis Branch and Its Legacy, 1941–1947" (Ph.D. diss., University of California–Berkeley, 1995), 145–46.

26. OSS R&A Paper, "Problems and Objectives of United States Policy," April 2, 1945, copies in ASW 336 Russia, RG 165, NA, and Pentagon Office File, Box 67, Folder 41, Marshall Papers. Additional documents in this folder reveal that during the first ten days of April General Embick of the JSSC brought this memorandum to the attention of Leahy and Marshall and that Marshall sent it to his strategic planners in the Operations Division. OSS head Col. William Donovan sent it to Leahy or Truman or both on May 5. See Anderson, *United States, Great Britain and the Cold War*, 76.

27. Comments of Col. Paul Thompson on JCS Memo for Information no. 382, ABC 334.8 Intl. Sec. Org. (August 9, 1944), RG 165, NA.

28. Memo, Marshall to president, "Probable Developments in the German Reich," April 2, 1945, Map Room File, Box 167, Franklin D. Roosevelt Papers, Franklin D. Roosevelt Library, Hyde Park, N.Y.

29. JCS 1313, "Revision of Policy with Relation to Russia," and JCS 1313/1, "Specific Actions to be Undertaken Under Revised Policy with Russia," April 16, 1945, CCS 092 USSR (3–27–45), sec. 1, RG 218, NA.

30. JCS 1313/2, April 23, 1945; tel., Marshall to Deane, April 19, 1945; memo, "Revision of Policy with Relation to Russia," McFarland to JPS, April 17, 1945; U.S. Secretariat Notes of Closed CCS Meeting, April 20, 1945; tel., Wilson to CCS, April 20, 1945, CAB 122/936, PRO; *FRUS 1945*, 5:231–34.

31. Ibid., JCS 1313/2; JCS 1308, "Italian Participation in the War Against Japan," April 11, 1945, with supporting documents, ABC 380 Italy (April 1, 1945), RG 165, NA. The JPS explained the seeming contradiction in its approval of Deane's recommendations and continued opposition to retaliation by asserting that retaliation was already being practiced by the Russians and *might* be practiced by the United States in the future but that for the present it was "important that the U.S. become dependent on the Russians only when necessary in the furtherance of vital interests of the U.S." For greater detail with differing conclusions as to the extent of the JCS shift in April, see Diane S. Clemens, "Averell Harriman, John Deane, the Joint Chiefs of Staff, and the 'Reversal of Co-Operation' with the Soviet Union in April 1945," *International History Review* 14 (May 1992): 277–301.

32. On Iwo Jima, twenty-five thousand entrenched Japanese troops killed eight thousand Americans, wounded an additional twenty thousand, and fought virtually to the last man. On Okinawa four times as many Japanese soldiers as well as kamikaze pilots fought similarly, at a cost to the United States of twelve thousand five hundred dead, thirty-six thousand wounded, twenty-one ships sunk, and sixty-seven damaged.

33. Walter Millis, ed., *The Forrestal Diaries* (New York: Viking Press, 1951), 55.

34. Henry L. Stimson Diary, April 16, 1945, Henry L. Stimson Papers, Yale University, New Haven, Conn.

35. *FRUS, 1945*, 5: 252–54.

36. Ibid., 253–55. See also Millis, ed., *Forrestal Diaries*, 49–51.

37. Stimson Diary, April 26, 1945; Hathaway, *Ambiguous Partnership*, 137; *FRUS, 1945*, 4: 1129–30; Roberto Rabel, *Between East and West: Trieste, the United States, and the Cold War, 1941–1954* (Durham, N.C.: Duke University Press, 1988), 47, and "Prologue to Containment: The Truman Administration's Response to the Trieste Crisis of May 1945," *Diplomatic History* 10 (spring 1986): 147; Water S. Poole, "From Conciliation to Containment: The Joint Chiefs of Staff and the Coming of the Cold War, 1945–1946," *Military Affairs* 42 (February 1978): 12–13.

38. JCS 1350, "The Current Situation in Rumania and Bulgaria," May 13, 1945, ABC 336 Rumania (September 26, 1943), sec. 1-B, RG 165, NA; Poole, "From Conciliation to Containment," 12–13; Rabel, *Between East and West*, 56; Department of Defense, "The Entry of the Soviet Union into the War Against Japan: Military

Plans, 1941–1945" (1955 typescript), 68–71; McCloy memo of telephone conversation with Stimson, May 19, 1945, ASW 336 Russia, RG 165, NA.

39. JCS 1418/1, "United States Policy Concerning the Dardanelles and Kiel Canal," and "Decision Amending JCS 1418/1, July 12–22, 1945, ABC 093 Kiel (7–6–45), sec. 1-A, RG 165, NA; JCS 1443/1 and 1443/2, "Soviet Demands with Respect to Bear Island and the Spitsbergen Archipelago," July 17–22, 1945, ABC 386 Spitsbergen (7–14–45), RG 165, NA; memo, Embick to Hickerson, June 8, 1945, ABC 686 (11–6–43), sec. 18, RG 165, NA; *FRUS: Berlin*, 2: 649–50, 1420–22; *FRUS, 1945*, 5: 96–97; Poole, "From Conciliation to Containment," 13; Mark A. Stoler, "From Continentalism to Globalism: General Stanley D. Embick, the Joint Strategic Survey Committee, and the Military View of American National Policy During the Second World War," *Diplomatic History* 6 (summer 1982): 314–19.

40. JCS 1445, "Military Position of the United States in the Light of Russian Policy," October 9, 1945, CCS 092 USSR (3–27–43), RG 218, NA; JCS 1471/2, "Military Policy as to Secrecy Regarding the Atomic Bomb," October 19, 1945, and JCS 1477/1, "Overall Effect of Atomic Bomb on Warfare and Military Organization," October 30, 1945, ABC Atom (8–17–45), secs. 2 and 3; JCS 1518, "Strategic Concept for the Employment of United States Armed Forces," September 19, 1945, ABC 092 (7–18–45), RG 165, NA. See also Poole, "From Conciliation to Containment," 13, and Stoler, "From Continentalism to Globalism," 319–20.

7. Congress and the Roots of Postwar American Foreign Policy

Randall Woods

The legacies that World War II left to the United States are significant and varied. Massive government spending laid the basis for twenty years of postwar prosperity, and that prosperity in turn changed the nature of American politics. Working-class Americans were pulled up into the middle class and suddenly became concerned with preserving the status quo rather than with overturning it. Federal bureaucracies, already swollen by the New Deal, grew geometrically under the impact of war. Indeed, the government intervened into every walk of life, setting prices, allocating manpower, rationing tires, and taxing on a massive scale. That trend would continue. Out of European Fascism came the Holocaust, an evil stunning in scope and intent. The systematic extermination of 6 million Jews generated a pessimism concerning the human condition that pervaded religion, philosophy, and politics. And, of course, World War II introduced America and the world to the atomic age, creating among other things the anxiety that served as a vehicle for Sen. Joseph McCarthy and the second red scare. Finally, the struggle between the Allies and the Axis transformed American foreign policy, producing an activism that would have monumental consequences for the nations of the world.

Foreign affairs was, not surprisingly, much on the minds of the U.S. Congress, particularly the Senate, as the war drew to a close. Franklin Roosevelt had paid almost as little attention to that body as he had to the State Department in the years following Pearl Harbor. He had bypassed the Senate, relying on executive agreements rather than on treaties in the conduct of wartime diplomacy. The president bullied and cajoled Congress into creating dozens of new bureaucracies, such as the War Production Board, which in effect usurped congressional prerogatives. Although it had made significant gains in the midterm elections in 1942, the Republican party had been out of power for twelve years. GOP leaders were determined not to let the Democratic party monopolize the peacemaking. That determination was reinforced by the defeat of Thomas Dewey's "me-too" presidential candidacy in 1944. Though southern Democrats were as offended by the growth of the federal bureaucracy and presidential power as members of the GOP, the Democratic leadership in Congress had little problem arousing partisan sentiment among the rank and file and persuading them to support first Roosevelt and then Pres. Harry Truman's diplomatic initiatives. In the wake of the Yalta Conference in February 1945, then, the halls of Congress rang with debate over America's proper role in the postwar international community.

There existed in 1945 three clearly identifiable foreign policy impulses or alternatives around which legislators coalesced: traditional isolationism, or noninterventionism, as its defenders referred to it; conservative internationalism; and liberal internationalism. A fourth option, which historian Justus Doenecke has labeled liberal isolationism, existed but was given very little credence in 1945.[1] It is worth noting, however, that this latter approach provided the foundation for the New Left/revisionist critique of U.S. diplomacy that was to play such an important role in American intellectual and political life during the 1960s.

There were those in Congress who refused to acknowledge that World War II had forever changed the world and the role that America would be able to play in it. Hard-core isolationists had come to terms with the fact that German, Italian, and Japanese Fascism constituted an authentic threat to American interests and that war had been necessary. But in 1945 as they turned their eyes to the future, they continued to see Britain rather than the Soviet Union as the primary threat to U.S. independence and sovereignty. The isolationists were staunchly anticommunist, but they believed that Europe was a European problem. They feared that the Europeans, particularly the British, would once again attempt to use the United States as a cat's paw, expending American blood and treasure to maintain a Continental balance of power—"perpetual war for perpetual peace," to use Harry Elmer Barnes's phrase. They insisted that internationalism, and, specifically, the administration's campaign in behalf of a collective security organization, was simply a mask for a policy of realpolitik conducted exclusively by the executive. This new activism would allegedly bankrupt the nation, destroy free enterprise, and lead to the creation of a police state.

The personification of isolationism, or noninterventionism, was Robert A. Taft. The junior senator from Ohio was the eldest but not the favorite son of William Howard Taft. He worshiped his father, who much preferred Robert's handsome, outgoing, athletic younger brother, Charles, to the dour, intense young man that Robert became. Following his graduation from Harvard Law School, he returned to Cincinnati to a career in law and politics. The embodiment of Republican orthodoxy, Taft rose through the ranks to occupy a seat in the Senate and became a regular challenger for the presidency from 1940 through 1952.

Taft shared his father's reverence for the Constitution. The greatest threat facing the United States in the late 1930s, he believed, was not disintegration of the international order but growth in executive authority. The primary reason he opposed an active foreign policy was that such a course inevitably augmented the power of the executive.

Congressional acquiescence in Rooseveltian "internationalism," which Taft saw as merely a desire by the president for complete freedom of action in foreign policy making, was a threat to the balance of power within the federal system and to the liberties of the people. In 1939 he tried to cut funds for the Export-Import Bank, which he said "could finance a European war without Congress knowing anything about it." As early as January 1942 Taft was complaining about the postwar expectations of what he referred to as the "war crowd." He railed against Republicans such as Wendell Willkie, Thomas E. Dewey, and the other members of the eastern establishment who wanted to "out-intervention" the Democratic interventionists. The GOP should no more do this than it should try to "out-New Deal" the New Dealers.[2]

Not surprisingly, the Roosevelt administration feared and resented Taft's "loyal opposition" during World War II. Citing considerations of national security, Secretary of State Cordell Hull, Dean Acheson, Vice President Henry Wallace, and others insisted that he "get on the team." Taft would not. As a matter of general principle, he proclaimed, there could be no doubt that criticism of the administration in time of war was essential to the maintenance of democratic government. "The duties imposed by the Constitution on Senators and Congressmen certainly require that they do not grant to the President every power that is requested . . . they require that they exercise their own judgment on questions of appropriations to determine whether the projects recommended have a real necessity for the success of the war," he told a reporter.[3]

Some of his opponents attributed Taft's hypercriticism to obtuseness. Dean Acheson once accused the senator of being a "re-examinist," "like farmers who pull up their crops each morning to see how they had done during the night."[4] Others gave him credit for being bright but insisted that he was virtually devoid of a social conscience. Taft, however, regarded himself as the true guardian of conservatism, the most humanitarian of all doctrines because of its emphasis on individual liberty.

Taft's commitment to congressional independence was rooted not only in his background and education but also in a broader philosophy that encompassed the conservative Republicans' commitment to the putative halcyon days of yesteryear. The GOP's attachment to the nineteenth-century political and economic system as perceived by conservatives dictated its posture on foreign policy. It aligned Republicans against big government and a strong executive, which they feared would result in dictatorship and destroy political and civil freedom; against large-scale expenditures, which would allow the government to impose "socialist" controls over prices, wages, and the free enterprise system; and against high taxation, which crushed the initiative of the private sector.

Yet as political scientist John Spanier and others have pointed out, internationalism in the 1940s, even more than the New Deal, required these elements—a powerful government capable of negotiating with other powerful governments; a strong president who could act decisively and vigorously; and huge outflows of cash to sustain military establishments and to finance foreign aid. In that sense, orthodox Republican philosophy seemed to make active participation in world affairs incompatible with the preservation of political democracy and free enterprise. Thus did the Taft Republicans oppose the view put forward by the British government and American internationalists—that Europe was vital to American security and that both Great Britain and the nations of the Continent, devastated by the war, had to be nursed back to health and strength by the United States.[5]

These views prompted Taft to become the most articulate and effective opponent of Anglo-American efforts to create an interdependent world economy—multilateralism—in the United States. "The Capital is full of plans of all kinds," the Ohioan told a group gathered to celebrate William McKinley's one hundredth birthday in January 1943. "Every economic panacea any long-haired crank ever thought of is being dusted off and incorporated in a magnificent collection of glittering landscapes supposed to lead to Utopia. Nearly every one of them rests on the huge expenditure of Government without telling us where the money is coming from, when we already face a debt of over $200 billion."[6] In spring 1944 he attacked specifically the proposed International Monetary Fund and International Bank for Reconstruction and Development. Both institutions were based on the fallacious assumption that underlay all administration foreign policies, "that American money and American charity shall solve every problem."[7]

Committed to the notion that America was and could continue to be economically and strategically self-sufficient, Taft opposed foreign aid in the immediate postwar period, and he voted against ratification of the charter of the North Atlantic Treaty Organization (NATO). As a staunch anticommunist, the junior senator from Ohio did vote for the Truman Doctrine, but only reluctantly. He was careful to observe at the time that "I do not regard this as a commitment to any similar policy in any other section of the world." America should "withdraw as soon as normal economic conditions are restored."[8]

Taft stood in the wings and cheered on Sen. Joseph McCarthy of Wisconsin as he conducted his anticommunist witch-hunt during the early 1950s. Taft saw the campaign against alleged subversives as helpful to the

Republican cause. But in supporting McCarthy, he acted only partly out of political opportunism. Because McCarthyism represented a variety of isolationism, it buttressed Taft's views on foreign policy. If the real threat to American security came from traitors within, there was no need for alliances, foreign aid, or the United Nations.

Taft also sympathized with the Asia Firsters in his party, those politicians who eschewed engagement in Europe but advocated an aggressive policy in Asia, especially in opposition to Communism. He supported U.S. participation in the Korean War and in so doing acknowledged that America had legitimate economic and strategic interests in the Pacific as well as in the Caribbean. But that was as far as he would go.

During his campaign for the Republican presidential nomination in 1952, Taft articulated an approach to foreign affairs that Spanier has labeled unilateralism. First, Taft proposed that the United States should withdraw from the United Nations and enter no "entangling alliances" such as NATO. Second, America should stress Asia over Europe, although Taft and his supporters believed that the United States should rely for defense of its interests in the area on island bases and anticommunist allies. Indeed, the third mainstay of the unilateralist position was that the United States should never become bogged down in a war on the Asian landmass. America's resources were limited, and the world was full of nations willing to use the United States for its own purposes.[9]

Robert Taft, however, spoke for only one sector, perhaps the more orthodox, of the conservative community. World War II converted a number of former isolationists into conservative internationalists. Japan's attack on Pearl Harbor destroyed the myth of impregnability that the America First movement had worked so assiduously to disseminate in the early 1940s. The Atlantic and Pacific were not great barriers protecting "Fortress America" from attack, as the isolationists had argued, but were highways across which hostile ships and airplanes could move and assault the Western Hemisphere. Led by *Time-Life* publisher Henry Luce, longtime America Firsters decided that if America could not hide from the rest of the world, it must control it. They would support foreign aid, alliances, and a massive military budget but not out of any Wilsonian desire to improve the lot of other members of the global village. These nationalists sought not to save the world but to safeguard American strategic and economic interests by creating, and dominating, interlocking spheres of influence.

Arthur H. Vandenberg of Michigan, who succeeded to the chair of the Senate Foreign Relations Committee when the Republicans won control of Congress in 1946, was the leader of these conservative internationalists. Vandenberg shared most of Taft's conservative attitudes toward the Constitution—the role of the federal government in society, the budget, free enterprise, and individual liberty—and he was a thoroughgoing nationalist in foreign affairs. But he became convinced in 1945 and 1946 that the United States could not return to the past and that the best way to preserve the status quo in a dangerous world was to dominate that world.

Interestingly, despite his interwar isolationism, Vandenberg had begun public life as a disciple of Theodore Roosevelt, and his conversion to conservative internationalism at the close of World War II does not now appear as surprising as it did then. Still, it was no less powerful. Vandenberg was an overachiever who emerged from a working-class background—his father ran a boardinghouse and made harnesses—to work his way through the University of Michigan in the waning years of the nineteenth century. Following his graduation he became a journalist. While editor of the *Grand Rapids Herald*, he endorsed the Open Door policy, annexation of the Philippines, and the Roosevelt Corollary to the Monroe Doctrine. During the years prior to America's entry into World War I, Vandenberg was an outspoken interventionist, branding pacifists and noninterventionists as cowards. He supported membership in the League of Nations and during the red scare of 1919 proved himself to be as ardent a Bolshevik-baiter as any person in America.[10]

First elected to Congress in 1928, Vandenberg supported the presidential policies of both Calvin Coolidge and Herbert Hoover. Though evidencing some of the midwestern Progressives' distrust of Wall Street, the Michigan legislator showed himself to be devoted to the domestic conservative agenda. He opposed the New Deal and joined with members of the conservative American Liberty League in castigating Franklin Roosevelt as a would-be dictator and a stalking horse for the forces of collectivization. From 1939 through 1941 he fought against Roosevelt's interventionist proposals. War would destroy the free enterprise system; Lend-Lease, he declared, constituted nothing less than the "suicide of the Republic."[11]

After America entered World War II, Vandenberg, like Taft, quickly accommodated himself to the new circumstances. He supported the war effort and paid tribute to the Atlantic Charter. As the war neared its end, however, he turned his gaze not backward to the putative days of economic self-sufficiency and Fortress America but forward to a postwar world filled with danger and uncertainty. As a thoroughgoing nationalist, Vandenberg believed that the United States had legitimate interests abroad. He concluded that with the destruction of the balance of power in Europe and Asia, the United States would have to don the mantle of world leadership. In January 1945 Vandenberg shocked his colleagues by endorsing membership in a collective security organization: "I do not believe that any nation hereafter can immunize itself by its own exclusive action," he told the Senate. "Our oceans have ceased to be moats which automatically protect our ramparts. Flesh and blood now compete unequally with winged steel. War has become an all consuming juggernaut. . . . I want maximum American cooperation, consistent with legitimate American self-interest, with constitutional process and with collateral events which warrant it, to make the basic idea of Dumbarton Oaks [i.e., collective security] succeed."[12]

As a legislator with a huge Polish constituency, however, Vandenberg was deeply upset by the February 1945 Yalta settlement regarding Eastern Europe. Vandenberg perceived the Soviet Union as head of an international Communist conspiracy bent on ruling the world. As Doenecke has pointed out, as a delegate to the San Francisco Conference during spring 1945, he was much more concerned with curbing Russian ambitions and securing the right of nations to act within regional collective security organizations than with fostering international community per se.

Vandenberg's journey from isolationist to conservative internationalist culminated in his dramatic speech to the Senate delivered in February 1946. "What is Russia up to now?" he asked. After reviewing Soviet activities in the Balkans, in Manchuria, and in Poland, he announced that the world had become divided between two rival ideologies: democracy and Communism. Peaceful coexistence was possible only if the United States was as vigorous and firm as the Soviet Union in defending its interests. The United States must establish limits beyond which it would not compromise.[13] The Truman administration responded with Secretary of State James F. Byrnes's Overseas Press Club speech—the second Vandenberg concerto, as one reporter dubbed it. Byrnes indirectly denounced Soviet activities in Eastern Europe and promised that henceforward the United States could not and would not permit aggression "by coercion or pressure or by subterfuges such as political infiltration."[14]

Vandenberg's views on foreign policy were determined not only by his nationalism but also by his ambition for both himself and the Republican party. He had closely followed the party line under presidencies from Theodore Roosevelt through Franklin Roosevelt. In late 1945 and early 1946 he sensed that President Truman was politically vulnerable on Yalta specifically and on foreign policy in general.[15] Vandenberg and the Republicans came to the conclusion that a hard line toward the Soviets would earn them kudos with the electorate and enable them to recapture control of the White House in 1948. Yet when Truman and Byrnes adopted a confrontational stance toward Moscow in 1946 and 1947, Vandenberg proved to be the epitome of bipartisan cooperation. The former isolationist from Michigan supported the Truman Doctrine and the Marshall Plan in 1947 and U.S. membership in NATO in 1949, but not because he wanted to bring the blessings of American civilization to the Greeks and Turks or because he believed that the United States had the duty to promote socioeconomic justice abroad. The purpose of alliances and bases was to establish a Pax Americana that would ensure a stable world and serve America's vested interests. The conservative internationalism that he espoused would remain one of the cornerstones of postwar American foreign policy.

Joining the neoimperialists in pushing for an activist American role in world affairs were Wilsonian internationalists, who believed that if the United States had joined the League of Nations and acted in concert with the western democracies after World War I, aggression could have been nipped in the bud. Many of these Wilsonians were veterans of William Allen White's Committee to Defend America by Aiding the Allies, formed in 1941, and were supporters of the New Deal who believed that the state had an obligation to help the less fortunate and to intervene in the private sector to ensure equality of opportunity. Their efforts in behalf of internationalism culminated in spring 1945 when the United States led the way in establishing a new collective security organization whose stated goals were to prevent armed aggression and to promote prosperity and human rights throughout the world. When subsequently the UN proved incapable of guaranteeing the political and economic security of Western Europe, these liberal internationalists supported foreign aid and anticommunist alliance systems as mechanisms that would not only protect America from Soviet aggression but would also bring social justice and economic security, first to Europe and then to the less fortunate peoples of the developing world.

Despite his segregationist voting record and his opposition to organized labor, first-term senator J. William Fulbright of Arkansas accurately represented the liberal internationalist philosophy. The junior senator had grown up in Fayetteville, Arkansas, a college community situated in the foothills of the Ozark mountains. Fulbright's father was a successful businessman and banker and his mother, Roberta, published the local newspaper. It was she who instilled in her son an appreciation of education and a sense of public duty. Shortly before his graduation from the University of Arkansas in 1924, where he had been active in athletics and campus politics, Fulbright won a Rhodes scholarship. After a full diet of tutorials, rugby, lacrosse, and the Oxford Union, the young Arkansan graduated from Pembroke College with a concentration in modern history. He returned to America and earned a law degree from George Washington University. He subsequently taught there until his return to Arkansas, where he ran successfully for the House in 1942 and the Senate in 1944.[16]

Fulbright's commitment to internationalism was in part an offshoot from his years at Oxford as a Rhodes scholar. The most important acquaintance he made at Pembroke College was his young tutor, Ronald Buchanan McCallum, whose guidance and instruction were crucial in shaping the young American's intellect and worldview. The two men maintained a close personal and intellectual relationship until McCallum's death in 1973. In 1944 McCallum, a liberal and an ardent admirer of Woodrow Wilson, published *Public Opinion and the Lost Peace,* in which he challenged the long-standing view of John Maynard Keynes that the peace structure worked out at the Versailles Conference in 1919 was predestined to fail. The concept of the League was sound; the organization had not worked because political figures on both sides of the Atlantic had never been willing to make a true commitment to the principles that underlay it and had attempted to use it for their own selfish political purposes. McCallum concluded his book with an appeal to Americans and Britons to rediscover and rededicate themselves to the fundamentals of Wilsonian internationalism, at the core of which was a willingness by nation-states to surrender part of their sovereignty in behalf of the common good.[17] Meanwhile, in the United States, first-term congressman J. William Fulbright, the practicing politician, began to develop and promulgate his own version of Wilsonian internationalism. In 1943 Fulbright had coauthored with Sen. Tom Connally of Texas a resolution placing Congress on record as favoring membership in an international organization dedicated to keeping the peace. Impressed by the subsequent outpouring of public support for the idea of collective security that followed, the Roosevelt administration boarded the internationalist bandwagon. The upshot was American leadership in the creation of the United Nations. No senator was more active in speaking and lobbying for ratification of the UN Charter than the junior senator from Arkansas.[18]

Central to Fulbright's philosophy was the assumption that there existed a body of ideas and a constellation of economic and political institutions that together defined Western civilization, that the United States shared in these ideals and institutions, and that therefore it had an obligation to defend them. The United States had not been willing in the past to acknowledge its debt to this common culture, much less its obligation to preserve it, he told the Senate in 1945.[19] Fulbright, like most internationalists, was reacting to a particular interpretation of the immediate past. No less than Harry Truman, Dean Acheson, and so many others of his generation, Fulbright accepted what historian Gaddis Smith has called a great cycle theory of history. According to this view, the story of the twentieth century was largely a recurring pattern of American isolation, European aggression, and American intervention.[20] It was up to his generation, Fulbright believed, to break that cycle.

Time and again the former Rhodes scholar attempted to demonstrate that isolationism was merely a facet of old-fashioned nationalism. Those of his contemporaries who posed as defenders of national sovereignty were in fact advocating a return to the policies of the interwar period when the United States refused to acknowledge that its fate was linked to the fortunes of other democracies. National sovereignty was a trick, an illusion, especially in the world of airplanes, submarines, and atomic weapons. Having equated isolationism with obsessive nationalism, Fulbright observed that both led to a narcissistic attitude toward international affairs. Abnegation, in turn, made possible oppression and poverty, the twin seeds of war.[21] Horrified by pictures of the destruction wrought by the atomic bombs at Hiroshima and Nagasaki, Fulbright called upon Congress, the nation, and the world to develop a mechanism capable of restraining blood-and-soil nationalism and channeling modern technology into peaceful uses.

What the freshman senator had in mind was an authentic international federation run on democratic principles. In a speech to the American Bar Association in 1945, Fulbright outlined his vision: "The history of government over the centuries, which is largely the chronicle of man's efforts to achieve freedom by the control of arbitrary force, indicate [sic] that only by the collective action of a dominant group can security be obtained."[22] The hope of the world rested with the establishment of a global organization with a collective security mandate and a police-keeping force sufficient to enforce that mandate. Once the UN Charter was ratified, it should be clearly understood that the president through his delegate would have the authority to commit American troops to military action authorized by the Security Council.

Fulbright was an economic as well as a political internationalist; he fully shared the multilateralist views of his friend, Assistant Secretary of State for Economic Affairs, Will Clayton. Unlike Taft, who believed that the United States could remain economically self-sufficient and that economic conditions elsewhere in the world had no bearing on American interests, these intellectual heirs of Adam Smith believed that the line between national and international economics was disappearing and that prosperity was infinitely expandable. They looked forward to the creation of an economically interdependent world free of tariffs, preferences, quotas, and exchange controls. To this end Fulbright helped lead the fight in the Senate in 1945 for approval of the Bretton Woods Agreements and in 1946 for passage of the British loan, a $3.5 billion credit designed to rehabilitate Britain's economy and to enable that country to abandon imperial preference and exchange controls.[23]

Fulbright understood the residual strength of traditional isolationism and the implications of conservative internationalism. As early as summer 1945 he began to express doubts about America's commitment to authentic internationalism. The junior senator wondered aloud to the Senate why there was unanimous support for ratification of the UN Charter while only weeks before, economic nationalists and neoisolationists had fought vigorously against the Bretton Woods Agreements and the British loan. Could it be, he asked, that they believed that the Charter did not impinge on the nation's sovereignty and that despite its membership in the United Nations, the United States still retained absolute freedom of action?[24]

In the years that followed, Fulbright continued to preach the internationalist creed; but his globalism, unlike Henry Wallace's, acknowledged the threat posed to the security of Central and Western Europe by Stalinism. He readily admitted that Soviet Communism was totalitarian, aggressive, and autarkic. Indeed, like historian Arthur Schlesinger, Sen. Hubert Humphrey of Minnesota, and other members of the Americans for Democratic Action (because of his stance on civil rights the Arkansan was not a member of this organization, but he was friends and sympathized with most of its founders), Fulbright was an active cold warrior. In the immediate postwar period, he supported the Truman Doctrine, the Marshall Plan, and foreign aid in general.

During the 1950s he criticized Pres. Dwight David Eisenhower and Secretary of State John Foster Dulles not only for the rigidity of their thinking but also for their lack of imagination in dealing with the Communist threat in the developing world and for the general ineffectiveness of their policies. As chair of the Senate Foreign Relations Committee, Fulbright was a vigorous supporter of the presidency of John F. Kennedy. In fact, no figure in Washington was more visible in articulating the liberal, activist philosophy that characterized that administration's foreign policies. Effective resistance against the forces of international Communism involved not only military strength, he told the Senate, but also a willingness to help developing nations "toward the fulfillment of their own highest purposes."[25] America could be truly secure, he seemed to be saying, only in a community of nations whose institutions and values closely resembled its own.

By the time of President Kennedy's death in 1963, Fulbright had come to have doubts about America's ubiquitous confrontation with the forces of international Communism. In spring 1964 he delivered his famous "old myths and new realities" speech on the floor of the Senate. He declared that coexistence with the Soviets and even with Cuban leader Fidel Castro was possible. He called for a realistic assessment of U.S. policy toward Latin America and the Far East based on recognition that there were limits to American power as well as pressing domestic needs that demanded attention. In anticipation of the inevitable overthrow of "feudal oligarchies" in Latin America, the United States should consider opening communications with the revolutionary movements that would replace them. America should be ready to adopt a more "flexible" attitude toward Communist China and, indeed, the entire Communist world.[26] Inevitably, given this new perspective, Fulbright broke with Pres. Lyndon Johnson in 1965 over U.S. intervention in the Dominican Republic and escalation of the war in Vietnam.

Though it was considered more of a political philosophy and a historical interpretation than a viable foreign policy option, and that only by a handful of legislators in 1945, a fourth approach—liberal isolationism—existed as World War II came to a close. This perspective did not have as conspicuous a spokesperson as the other three; probably its most influential proponent was Robert M. LaFollette Jr. "Young Bob," a studious, conscientious public servant authentically dedicated to improving the welfare of his fellow human beings, had succeeded his famous father, Robert M. LaFollette Sr., in the Senate in 1925.[27] A Progressive from Wisconsin, the younger LaFollette came from a political tradition that viewed Wall Street, that is financiers and corporate executives, as avaricious exploiters of the farmers and artisans of the American heartland. The political and economic systems were controlled absolutely by these plutocrats, who set the prices of agricultural commodities and labor at artificially low levels and of manufactured items, especially farm implements, at artificially high levels. The liberal isolationists, which included individuals such as economist-historian Charles Beard and progressive-populist Sen. William Langer (R-N.D.), believed that Wall Street had formed an unholy alliance with British financiers to spread monopoly capitalism abroad and that they were exploiting the labor and markets of the developing world as well as those of their respective homelands.

The younger LaFollette was convinced that wars were caused by imperialism and power politics, that is, the struggle between national corporate elites to dominate various regions of the world. Like his father, who had voted against the Treaty of Versailles, young Bob opposed any peace settlement that perpetuated an unjust status quo or that denied all peoples of the earth the right of self-determination. He opposed American intervention in Nicaragua during the Hoover administration and was an outspoken champion of disarmament during the 1930s. LaFollette supported the Neutrality Acts, pushed for heavy taxation of war profits, and fought tenaciously to keep the United States out of the European war.[28] Though he supported the administration after Pearl Harbor, LaFollette expressed grave doubts about the Yalta accords, and he voted against the British loan on the grounds that it would dangerously deplete America's resources.[29]

In essence, LaFollette and the other liberal isolationists believed that America's first priority should be social justice and democracy at home; that an activist foreign policy was a diversion from that great objective; and that as long as the political and economic systems were dominated by Wall Street, an activist foreign policy would result in economic exploitation and political oppression overseas. LaFollette was a great defender of the New Deal and even went so far as to advocate nationalization of the railroads and banking system. His desire, like Charles Beard's, was that America build a social democracy that would stand as an unobtrusive example to the rest of the world.

Building on this tradition, academics, student activists, and a handful of politicians emerged in the 1960s to articulate a scathing indictment of the cold war, U.S. foreign policy, and American society in general. Focusing on the twin evils of discrimination and imperialism, these reformers denied the efficacy of traditional electoral politics and decried established institutions— universities, churches, and government bureaucracies—as inherently corrupt. New Left activists called for the people to resume control of their destinies through direct, "participatory" democracy.[30] By the mid-1960s the great Satan of the New Left had become "corporate liberalism," a phrase coined by Carl Oglesby, president of the Students for a Democratic Society. The term was not new to the movement, but Oglesby's linking it to American foreign policy was. The men who engineered the war in Vietnam "are not moral monsters," he said. "They are all honorable men. They are all liberals." The American corporate machine they oversaw was the "colossus of history," taking the riches of other nations and consuming half of the world's goods. Being decent men, corporate liberals rationalized their rapacity and their policy of counterrevolution with the ideology of anticommunism, defining all revolutions as Communist and Communism as evil.[31] Isolationism was implicit in the New Left/revisionist indictment. America should dismantle its huge network of bases, disinvest in developing areas, and halt the endless round of military interventions that punctuated U.S. foreign policy during the twentieth century. Without justice and equity at home, an interventionist foreign policy could only be an abomination.

In the years following World War II, two of the foreign policy approaches articulated in Congress in 1945—conservative and liberal internationalism— came together to produce an activism that committed the United States to fighting Communism on every front, to use historian Thomas Paterson's phrase.[32] Conservative anticommunists preoccupied with markets and bases backed by a burgeoning military-industrial complex argued that the only way America could be safe in a hostile world was to dominate that world through a network of alliances and overseas bases and through possession of the largest nuclear arsenal in the world. Joining them were liberal internationalists, many of whom were domestic reformers, who saw America's welfare as tied to that of the other members of the international community. To a degree they supported alliances and military aid; but in addition, the liberal internationalists wanted to eliminate the social and economic turmoil that they perceived to be a breeding ground for Marxism and an invitation to Soviet imperialism. They wanted to do nothing less than spread the blessings of liberty, democracy, and free enterprise and to guarantee stability and prosperity to peoples threatened by Communist imperialism. The blending of these two strains led to the creation of an empire the likes of which had not been seen since Rome ruled the world. It also led to America's tragic involvement in Vietnam. It was ironic that J. William Fulbright, liberal internationalist par excellence, borrowed from both the traditional and liberal noninterventionist approaches to frame a critique of that war and the assumptions that underlay it.

NOTES

1. Justus D. Doenecke, *Not to the Swift: The Old Isolationists in the Cold War Era* (Lewisburg, Pa.: Bucknell University Press, 1979), 27.

2. See Geoffrey Matthews, "Robert A. Taft, the Constitution and American Foreign Policy, 1939–1953," *Journal of Contemporary History,* 17, 3 (July 1982): 507–22, and James T. Patterson, "Alternatives to Globalism: Robert A. Taft and American Foreign Policy, 1939–1945, *The Historian* 36, 4 (August 1974): 670–88.

3. Quoted in Richard E. Darilek, *A Loyal Opposition in Time of War: The Republican Party and the Politics of Foreign Policy from Pearl Harbor to Yalta* (Westport, Conn.: Greenwood Press, 1976), 28.

4. Ibid.

5. John Spanier, *The Truman-MacArthur Controversy and the Korean War* (Cambridge, Mass.: Belknap Press, 1959), 158–59.

6. *New York Times,* January 30, 1943.

7. Address of Robert A. Taft to War Veterans Club of Ohio, May 6, 1944, Box 802, R. Taft Papers, Library of Congress.

8. James T. Patterson, *Mr. Republican: A Biography of Robert A. Taft* (Boston: Houghton Mifflin, 1972), 371.

9. Spanier, *Truman-MacArthur Controversy,* 156–59.

10. Doenecke, *Not to the Swift,* 45.

11. Ibid.

12. John L. Gaddis, *The United States and the Origins of the Cold War, 1941–1947* (New York: Columbia University Press, 1972), 168.

13. Gaddis, *U.S. and Origins of Cold War,* 296.

14. Quoted in Randall B. Woods and Howard Jones, *Dawning of the Cold War: The United States' Quest for Order* (Athens: University of Georgia Press, 1991), 109.

15. Public opinion polls indicated that before Potsdam while Truman was still in his honeymoon period, 87 percent of those questioned approved of the way he was handling his job. A year later, with Soviet-American relations strained to the break-

ing point, that figure had more than halved, dropping to 43 percent. See Terry H. Anderson, *The United States, Great Britain and the Cold War, 1944–1947* (Columbia: University of Missouri Press, 1981), 107.

16. See Haynes Johnson and Bernard M. Gwertzman, *Fulbright: The Dissenter* (Garden City, N.Y: Doubleday, 1966), 17–64.

17. George Herbert Gunn, "The Continuing Friendship of James William Fulbright and Ronald Buchanan McCallum," *South Atlantic Quarterly* 83, 4 (autumn 1984): 417–19.

18. J. William Fulbright (hereafter JWF) to Edward J. Meeman, March 19, 1945, BCN24, Folder 29, Fulbright Papers, University of Arkansas, Fayetteville.

19. U.S. Congress, Senate, *Congressional Record,* 79th Cong., 1st sess., 1945, 91, pt. 3, 2898.

20. Gaddis Smith, *Dean Acheson* (New York: Cooper Square Publishers, 1972).

21. U.S. Congress, Senate, *Congressional Record,* 79th Cong., 1st sess., 1945, 91, pt. 3, 2899, and U.S. Congress, House, *Congressional Record,* 78th Cong., 1st sess., 1943, 8, pt. 9, A477.

22. U.S. Congress, Senate, *Congressional Record,* 79th Cong., 1st sess., 1945, 91, pt. 13, A4652–53.

23. See U.S. Congress, Senate, Committee on Banking and Currency, *Anglo-American Financial Agreement: Hearings,* 79th Cong., 2d sess., 1946.

24. U.S. Congress, Senate, *Congressional Record,* 1st sess., 1945, 91, pt. 6, 7962–64.

25. U.S. Congress, Senate, *Congressional Record,* 1st sess., 1951, 97, pt. 1, 520–22.

26. U.S. Congress, Senate, *Congressional Record,* 2d sess., 1964, 110, pt. 5, 6227–34.

27. Wayne S. Cole, *Roosevelt and the Isolationists, 1932–1945* (Lincoln: University of Nebraska Press, 1983), 30.

28. Doenecke, *Not to the Swift,* 27–28.

29. Ibid., 65.

30. Allen J. Matusow, *The Unraveling of America: A History of Liberalism in the 1960s* (New York: Harper and Row, 1984), 310.

31. Ibid., 319.

32. Thomas G. Paterson, *On Every Front: The Making of the Cold War* (New York: Norton, 1979).

8. Commoners, Commissars, and Spies: Soviet Policies and Society, 1945

Vladimir V. Pozniakov

This chapter explores what the Soviet people thought, hoped for, and expected during Russia's last months of the Great Patriotic War, and especially their concerns on the eve of V-E Day. I do not examine Soviet public opinion, or governmental policies, or Soviet intelligence activities per se. Rather, I reveal how the Soviet government perceived world conditions in spring 1945, more precisely, how Stalin and his subordinates reacted to the situation confronting the USSR and to the hopes of their people as the war drew to a close.[1] Indeed, what hopes for the future were embraced by the Russian people, and how and why did the Soviet leadership deal with these aspirations?

The war's outcome became a source of deep concern for the Soviet government during winter 1944–1945. Despite the liberation of occupied territories and the imminent defeat of Germany and its tight control over the predominant part of East and East Central Europe, the Kremlin felt far from secure. First, the new Soviet borders in the west were still in dispute, and the policy pursued by the Soviet Union in Poland, Romania, Bulgaria, Hungary, and Germany was producing serious tensions with its western Allies. Second, the situation within the Soviet borders was no better. According to a report submitted to the Soviet leadership by the Extraordinary State Commission, headed by Nikolai A. Voznesensky, the country had lost at least 30 percent of its national wealth: 1,170 cities, towns, and townships had been destroyed; about 70,000 villages and hamlets had burned to the ground; and some 32,000 factories were blown up or rendered unusable. More than 25 million people were homeless, struggling for survival in barns, dugouts, and temporary shelters.[2]

Notably, neither the staggering totals of economic losses, nor the famine in a number of regions,[3] nor the growing rate of crime[4] represented the principal concerns of J. Stalin and his entourage. They were much more worried about what the people were thinking and doing, believing that such thoughts and actions posed a direct challenge to the regime. One of Stalin's greatest concerns was the situation in the newly acquired Soviet territories of Western Ukraine and Belorussia, Lithuania, Latvia, and Estonia. The liberation of these territories, seized by the Soviet Union in 1939 and 1940 according to the terms of the Molotov-Ribbentrop Pact, again brought under Soviet rule vast numbers of people who had no desire to be Soviet. In these areas and in many Russian and Ukrainian cities occupied by the Germans from 1941 through 1944, Soviet authorities confronted at least several hundred thousand Poles, Ukrainians, Belorussians, and Baltic nationals, many of whom were members of various nationalist societies and organizations fighting for the freedom of their countries and accustomed to underground activities. Many of these people also belonged to paramilitary formations and armed groups, some of which had collaborated with the Germans and fought local Soviet guerrillas; others, such as the Polish Army of Homeland (AK, *Armia Krajowa*) and a part of the Ukrainian Insurgent Army (UPA, *Ukarain'ska Povstancheska Armiia*), had fought the German regular army and counterinsurgent troops. Their military expertise and weaponry posed a serious security problem for the NKVD and local authorities.

Judging by a vast number of reports sent by the NKVD/NKGB leadership personally to Stalin and Molotov, these organizations and their armed branches fought for the reestablishment of "independent bourgeois . . . states and [for the] overthrowing of the Soviet power by the force of arms, by the way of preventing internment and deportation" of local nationals to the inner regions of the USSR. They also were charged with "carrying out acts of terror against Soviet and Party activists" and conducting "active agitation aimed at prevention of drafting locals" for service in the Red Army.[5] On the eve of the German retreat from the Baltic countries, some of those groups and organizations even tried to form national governments (as in Estonia in September 1944)[6] and had strong ties with their governments-in-exile[7] or other representatives abroad.[8] Alarmingly, several maintained forms of liaison with Allied intelligence agencies.[9] These ties were a constant headache for Moscow. With the legal status of the Baltic countries still unsettled, Stalin and his lieutenants worried that some day the United States and Britain might consider these organizations the legitimate representatives of their nations. They also feared the possible impact of these nationalist movements and the armed struggle they were waging against the Soviet authorities upon the bulk of the Soviet population, believed by Stalin to be ripe for disaffection.

The struggle by partisan groups did look impressive. According to the NKVD/NKGB statistics, in Latvia alone there were at least three major organizations fighting Soviet authorities.[10] During the period from July 1944 through January 20, 1945, the NKVD and NKGB arrested 5,223 persons— 962 of whom were taken into custody in Riga and 542 in the First Baltic Front rear. Among those arrested were ten Lutheran ministers and Roman Catholic and Russian Orthodox priests; the rest, reflecting the customary categories employed by Soviet security organizations, were "agents of intelligence and counterintelligence services" of Germany, "enemy intelligence and counterintelligence organs officers," "members of Latvian nationalist organizations," "traitors and collaborators," "participants in various bandit formations," and "various anti-Soviet elements."[11]

A similar struggle was also going on in Lithuania and Estonia. The only distinction was that in Lithuania the NKVD/NKGB had to fight two underground armies—the Polish AK and the Lithuanian LLA (Lithuanian Liberation Army).[12] In Estonia, however, they faced various organizations and groups that had not been able to unite within a national liberation front or coalition.

Even though the war waged against the Soviets by the Polish and Lithuanian underground became an ongoing headache for the Kremlin until at least the very end of the 1940s and proved a costly affair for both sides, it was doomed to failure from the outset. The traditional animosity between the Poles and the Lithuanians, dating back to the days of a united Polish-Lithuanian state and exacerbated during the interwar period by the Polish seizure of Vilnius (which both nations considered to be an integral part of their territory) and by widespread Lithuanian collaboration with German occupational authorities from 1941 through 1944,[13] prevented any meaningful cooperation against Moscow and local Communists. This rivalry helped the NKVD/NKGB to crush first their principal opponent—the AK—and then to concentrate their efforts against the less numerous and poorly armed Lithuanian Resistance.[14] The same tactics were used by the Soviet authorities later in Western Ukraine, especially in the Lvov region where Ukrainian and Polish guerrilla forces had been fighting each other since the middle of the war,[15] and in those parts of Western Belorussia with a substantial Polish population.[16]

Notwithstanding the scope of resistance in the Baltic countries, a much bigger war was being waged in Western Ukraine. The core of the Ukrainian resistance fighters was composed of seasoned veterans of the OUN (Organization of Ukrainian Nationalists) and the UPA, many of whom had had lengthy experience in underground work against Polish authorities in prewar Poland, later had served in the SS "Galizien" Division fighting Soviet partisans, and then turned their arms against both their former masters and the advancing Red Army troops. Soon after the German retreat, the NKVD reported to Stalin than in "Lvov District" alone "there is an apparent growth of activities on the part of the OUN bandits," and in several "woodland areas of the district" its officials "have registered appearance of bands each 300 to 500 in number."[17]

The OUN/UPA groups were well trained and impressively armed. According to a report from Beria sent to Stalin, Molotov, and Malenkov some eight months later: "All in all, during 13 months [from February 1944 through March 1945] in order to liquidate the UPA bands" the Ukrainian NKVD "undertook 11,357 military operations. 81,470 bandits were killed and 83,902 more have been captured alive." Beria noted that "62,685 bandits and those dodging the draft have given themselves up voluntarily."[18] Among the trophies captured by the NKVD special detachments were light aircraft, field artillery pieces, armored vehicles, communications equipment, many modern weapons, and more than one thousand stockpiles of ammunition.[19]

The OUN/UPA fighters proved no easy prey for the NKVD troops. Throughout that period from February 1944 through March 1945, NKVD special detachments as well as the Red Army regular units supporting them lost 1,879 men and officers killed, 2,312 wounded, and 319 missing in action.[20] The Ukrainian underground's activities, along with overt operations undertaken by its armed formations and with mass support from the bulk of the local population, virtually paralyzed local Soviet government activities.[21] Despite mass reprisals and deportations of the locals to Siberia, Kazakhstan, and other distant areas,[22] the NKVD/NKGB were not able to secure complete control of Western Ukraine until the very end of the 1940s.[23] According to a report sent to Stalin and other Soviet leaders by the minister of interior, Sergei N. Kruglov, from March 1947 through February 1948 his ministry had "liquidated in Western districts of Ukraine 78 [underground] organizations of the OUN and 62 UPA bands, killing or detaining several thousand bandits."[24]

There was less fighting in Western Belorussia, where the situation was closer to that of neighboring Lithuania than to Western Ukraine. The forces confronting Soviet authorities—the Polish AK, the Belorussian "National Labor Alliance of New Generation (NTS), the Belorussian Alliance," the Belorussian Youth Union (BYU), and the Lithuanian LLA[25]—were split by national and factional controversies, and their rivalries allowed the NKVD/NKGB to smash them one by one. Some of these organizations and groups were heavily compromised by collaboration with German occupational authorities, as in the case of the NTS and some armed self-defense groups in small towns and rural areas.[26] Further, these groups and bands were constantly facing a natural foe, for Belorussia teemed with former Soviet partisans, seasoned guerrilla fighters who had fought the Germans and those who had collaborated with them for many years.

The most important factor underlying the measures undertaken by the NKVD/NKGB to crush the anti-Soviet underground in Belorussia was the area's crucial military importance to the Soviet war effort: the railroad lines crossing the country from east to west provided the shortest route to Poland

and Germany. Thus, Moscow paid special attention to Belorussia and neighboring Lithuania. To crush its principal opponents—the Polish AK and the Lithuanian LLA—the NKVD dispatched thirteen special regiments to Belorussia and five to Lithuania.[27] Two of Beria's chief deputies, Generals S. Kruglov and Amayak Kobulov, were sent to Minsk and Vilnius to head the operations.[28]

The majority of those in the Baltic countries, Western Ukraine, and Western Belorussia who fought the NKVD and Red Army troops did so chiefly to express their opposition to Soviet rule. Other forms of resistance also surfaced, affirming the deep disaffection of the local populations. These same people engaged in draft dodging, desertion, and sheltering AWOLs. Judging by some of the NKVD reports, all these forms of opposing Soviet rule were widely practiced in these areas.[29] According to a memorandum to Moscow in December 1944, during just two months 1,001 privates of the Fiftieth Lithuanian Reserve Rifle Division, stationed in Vilnius, Kovno, and Ukmerge Districts, left their units.[30] Other reports revealed that particular operations undertaken by the NKVD/NKGB special detachments against local guerrillas entrapped large numbers of draft dodgers hiding in the nearby woodlands and countryside.[31]

The other ways of expressing animosity toward the Soviet regime used by local populations included demonstrations, dissemination of various leaflets, and organization of numerous patriotic societies and groups.[32] Though such activities were habitual and legal in any democratic society, they were deemed illegal and subversive by Soviet officials. Overall, the methods used by many people in the Baltic countries, Western Ukraine, Western Belorussia, and in other newly acquired Soviet territories included a complex and sometimes bizarre combination of nonviolent opposition, guerrilla warfare, and acts of terrorism and sabotage against Soviet and Communist officialdom.[33]

These territories constituted only a small part of the Soviet Union, and the people living there represented a small minority of the total Soviet population. Much more important for J. Stalin and his entourage were the opinions and behavior of those who lived in other parts of the huge country, despite the regime's claims that their people were unfailingly loyal to the Soviet government and social system.[34]

Stalin was manifestly amazed by the astonishing courage and loyalty demonstrated by the Soviet people throughout the war. The Soviet dictator's stupefaction perhaps found its best reflection in his toast—stressing the sacrifices and character of the Russian people, "the most remarkable of all the nations of the Soviet Union"—at the grand Kremlin reception on May 24, 1945, Victory Parade Day.[35] Stalin always feared his people. He was especially fearful, even paranoid, about what they might do after the war's end.

The personal impressions of East and Central Europe, brought home by millions of Soviets in 1945, became the poisoned fruits of victory over Germany for Stalin's regime. When the Red Army entered Europe—especially Germany—its soldiers were astounded by its wealth and prosperity (despite the wartime devastation) and continually asked themselves and each other the same question: "Why did they invade our country? They did live so well!"[36] This unavoidable comparison of European standards of living with those of the USSR dealt a mighty blow to one of the principal myths created by prewar Soviet propaganda—that life under capitalism was unbearable. The soldiers of the victorious Red Army came through four long years of war more sure of themselves and less scared of the authorities. Moreover, 2 million ex-POWs who had survived German concentration camps,[37] several million Soviet civilians sent west by the Germans to work for the Third Reich, and several hundred thousand Russian émigrés who, prior to World War II, lived in Germany, Czechoslovakia, France, and other European countries, were also voluntarily or compulsorily returning home.[38]

These millions of Soviet citizens, as well as those who fought the Red Army on the side of the Germans (General Vlasov's "Russian Liberation Army," Pyotr Krasnov's Don Cossacks, and so forth),[39] posed a serious problem for the Soviet government and the Communist party; how to silence them and thereby prevent them from passing along their experiences before the information they possessed became common knowledge. Stalin considered several solutions to this problem. Vlasov's and Krasnov's men, as well as the other captured collaborators, were tried and sent to the labor camps. Red Army soldiers could be disciplined and indoctrinated, ordered not to talk about the things they had seen in Europe. The former POWs, though in Stalin's view virtual traitors, had to be dealt with more carefully. Predictably negative popular reactions to summary imprisonments had to be considered.[40] The same was true regarding those Soviet civilians who had been taken to Germany against their will, for their plight was generally known. Also, as huge as it had become by the end of war, the Gulag was still too small to absorb all those millions of former POWs and civilians. The big question, then, was what to do with all of them.

Stalin employed the tried and tested tactics of divide and rule. All the "repatriats" had to go through a series of so-called "filtration camps," in which experienced NKVD/NKGB and officers of Smersh (Stalin's murderous counterespionage apparatus) separated "lambs" from "wolves," sending the latter to expiate their sins in Siberia and other distant places. According to the draft resolution of the State Defense Committee prepared by the NKVD, along the Ukrainian and Belorussian borders with Poland eleven such camps capable of accommodating from fifteen thousand (five to be built in Belorussia) to twenty thousand repatriates (six camps planned for the Ukraine) were required. The People's Commissariat of Defense had to transfer 1,500 enlisted men and 250 officers to the NKVD for manning three new battalions of the agency's guard troops. While undergoing filtration, the camp inmates were to be fed rations similar to those adopted for the regular Gulag labor camps and colonies.[41]

Besides these filtration camps for displaced civilians, the NKVD, according to Stalin's decree of May 11, 1945, had to build a huge system of similar camps for the former Soviet POWs. Stalin's order stipulated one hundred camps, each accommodating ten thousand persons.[42] After passing through these purgatories, those who were deemed suspicious by the NKVD/NKGB and Smersh overseers were to be tried by so-called Special Conferences *(Osobye Soveshchaniia)* and sent to regular Gulag camps. The rest were to be freed and given special domestic passports forbidding them to reside in border areas and many big cities and preventing them from holding "important" positions in industry, local administration, and education. All were virtually condemned to hard manual labor. The whole procedure of filtration was "not to take longer than one or two months."[43]

Nevertheless, it was not Ukrainian, Polish, and Baltic nationalist guerrillas, former Soviet POWS and displaced persons, or the former Vlasovites and other collaborators who most frightened Stalin and his entourage. They believed that the main source of possible trouble was the Soviet people themselves—those whose courage, stamina, and self-denial had been so crucial for winning the war. But fighting and winning the war had changed the peoples of the USSR in many ways. They were less intimidated by the authorities, much more sure of themselves, proud of what they had done in the war, and proud of their country and its great history. As Marshal Leonid A. Govorov observed, "Folk got smarter and it's beyond the doubt."[44] A substantial element of the population became more religious—a phenomenon noted by many domestic and foreign observers,[45] as well as by the NKVD and Communist party officials.[46] The people apparently also realized that they constituted a nation. "Never before had that feeling of fellowship been as strong as it was during the war," noted Veniamin Kaverin, a well-known Russian writer, in his memoirs.[47] These changing attitudes and the possible implications deeply worried Stalin.

Despite being dissatisfied with their standard of living and with the poor performance of local authorities, the Soviet people apparently still believed that these matters had nothing to do with the existing political and social system.[48] The Soviet government, Communist party, and Stalin as the personification of the supreme power were still held in high esteem.[49] During the war against Nazi Germany, while working to exhaustion on the home front, people nurtured the faith that the peace to come would bring something better than the circumstances they had known before June 22, 1941. They expressed the hope that the postwar years (despite the enormous work needed to rebuild and restore all that had been destroyed) would be "different," "more reasonable," that "all the mistakes made during the prewar years would be acknowledged," and that "everyone has understood" that the "country just would not be able to live under unlimited and unrestrained centralization of power, red tape and distrust toward its own people."[50]

Many people, including numerous intellectuals, had almost no doubts that the Soviet political system and social life "were undergoing profound changes" and that after the war Soviet society would inevitably go through "moral, political and ideological restructuring." Some of these people were convinced that the Soviet government "would have to change its [internal] policy" and that this would lead to democracy.[51]

Substantial numbers, including many industrial workers, hoped that political concessions made by the Soviet government to its western Allies might lead to changes in the economic system, such as dissolution of collective farms and partial restoration of private retail trade.[52] Then—at some future time—there might emerge a multiparty political system.[53] Similar ideas were held by the members of secret organizations formed by students in Moscow, Chelyabinsk, Voronezh, and other Soviet cities.[54]

No wonder that numerous NKVD/NKGB reports on the state of public opinion worried Stalin. He recognized that Soviet society was entering a period of profound crisis, threatening in the long run to destroy the very political and social system he had devoted his entire life to create. But what exactly was Stalin seeking to establish as his chief legacy?

The innovations introduced across the spectrum of Soviet society from 1943 to 1945 offered some idea of what was intended. New uniforms and shoulder straps in the Red Army and Navy; the newly adopted and rigid "Table of Ranks" (dear to many Soviet generals and senior officers); new uniforms for lawyers, railroadmen, miners, geologists, and other professions being introduced; the different rhythm and melody of a new Soviet national anthem; reintroduction of the system of separate education of males and females in Soviet high schools; a protectionist policy toward the Russian Orthodox Church; reestablishment in early 1946 of discarded ministries; new medals—novelties large and small—all had one thing in common.[55] They were exact replicas, or nearly so, of those old imperial traditions. Consciously or subconsciously, Joseph Stalin was building a new Russian Empire, which was destined, he thought, to become greater than that of the czars. Victory over Germany convinced him of the permanence of the Soviet system and its social institutions, the profound might of the state he had created during the prewar years, and the basic correctness of his domestic and foreign policies. Victory in Europe also strengthened his conviction that the greater and more majestic the state, the more grand and imperious should be its material and psychological facades.

Stalin had long identified himself with the state. As chairman of the Council of People's Commissars, he was accustomed to speak in the name of the Soviet people. In the first months after the war he approached the apogee of his domestic and world fame, personal power, and the maturation of that cult seeking to deify him and his works.[56] Stalin always held democracy in deep contempt and wanted none of it in his country. Soon after V-E Day he made it plain that there were to be no changes in the internal life of the Soviet Union. His later address to the voters of the Stalin District in the election to the Supreme Soviet on February 10, 1946, contained not a single mention of democracy.[57] In Stalin's opinion, the people should work to reconstruct the devastated national economy according to rules determined by him and only by him. Hence, all talk about expanding democracy and impending changes had to be silenced once and forever.

To launch a crusade against his own people, however, demanded that Stalin must have new images of an "enemy," both internal and external. Those old ones, used during the prewar years and wartime, could not be exploited. Nobody would believe that after the defeat of Hitler's Germany and the impending collapse of Japan that Nazi-style Fascists or "Japanese militarists" and their agents in the USSR still posed any threat to the Soviet Union.

Although knowing who his real opponents were (Stalin never believed in longtime collaboration with his wartime allies[58] and even feared that cooperation might undermine his regime[59]), he could not exploit the image of "world imperialism" because the United States and Britain remained as the Allies. Stalin also realized that the Soviet people were deadly tired of wartime privations and hardships and that the industrial and military potential of the Soviet Union was vastly inferior to that of the United States and Britain.[60] To prepare his country and people for a new round of confrontation with the west, he had to buy time. As events have shown, it took him about two years to start this new crusade, both at home and abroad.

Meanwhile, Stalin had to lay the groundwork for this new offensive. Recently discovered documents generated by Soviet intelligence provide an interesting perspective regarding the regime's activities in pursuit of that goal. The Soviet intelligence community—the NKVD/NKGB First Chief Directorate (FCD), the Fourth Department of the Red Army General Staff (later GRU), the Comintern's Division of International Communication (DIC), and the Red Navy Main Staff's Intelligence Department (RNRU)—by the beginning of World War II had built a formidable network abroad. Actually, there were four separate networks whose activities were coordinated by the Kremlin. Though severely decimated during the Great Terror,[61] they proved adequate to their tasks of supplying Stalin and their immediate superiors with information needed to fight the Axis.[62] Major networks such as the *Rote Kapelle* (Red Chapel), headed by Leopold Trepper;[63] the Sandor Rado group in Switzerland;[64] Rihard Sorge's ring working in Tokyo;[65] the Burgess-Philby-Blunt group in Britain;[66] and those operating in the United States survived throughout the war.[67] During the period from 1939 to 1944, these operatives supplied their Moscow centers with precious political, military, economic, scientific, and technical information. According to a report sent to Stalin by L. Beria in late 1944: "During the Patriotic war the employees of the 1st [Intelligence] Directorate . . . sent abroad for the illegal work 566 officers, recruited 1,240 agents and informers, obtained by the means of intelligence 41,718 various materials, related to intelligence, including a big number of documents. Out of 1,167 documents obtained by the technical intelligence 616 have been used by our country's industries."[68] Among those officers who, in the opinion of Beria, deserved government awards, was NKGB Commissar III (roughly equal to a major general) Gaik B. Ovakimyan, First Chief Directorate (FCD) who, working undercover as an official of Amtorg, the Soviet state-run trading company, was arrested by the FBI in April 1941 and later expelled from the United States by the Franklin D. Roosevelt administration. Caught red-handed, he was not prosecuted, the Soviet Union and the United States having become somewhat allied by that time.[69]

Several other names mentioned in Beria's list will be familiar to those interested in Soviet espionage in America: NKGB Maj. Stepan Z. Apresyan, who in 1944 replaced Vasili M. Zarubin as the Soviet resident in Washington; Maj. Leonid R. Kvasnikov, deputy resident in New York City and the chief of scientific and technical intelligence in the United States; Capt. Semyon M. Semyonov, another Amtorg official, also a part of sci/tech intelligence, who later played an important role in atomic espionage; Lt. Col. Grigory G. Dolbin, later to become the Washington, D.C., resident; Capt. Alexandr S. Feklisov of the New York City network and future resident (1960–1964), who from 1947 to 1949, while posted in Britain, ran Klaus Fuchs; and Senior Lt. Constantine A. Chugunov, also a part of the New York City NKGB group.[70]

Among those who, according to Beria, deserved to be decorated with the Red Star Order were Elizabeth Bentley, a liaison agent, assigned by her Soviet controller and the other Red Star nominee, Joseph Katz, to collect information from some of the Washington rings; Harry Gold, a courier for Klaus Fuchs; and George Silvermaster, a high-level official of the Department of Treasury and one of the most successful and productive of the Soviet agents in the United States, who by the time of Pearl Harbor had gathered together "a group of ten government officials working for various parts of Roosevelt's wartime administration."[71] All these spymasters and spies, according to Beria and V. Merkulov, then people's commissar of state security, deserved decorations "for successful realization of the Government's tasks of safeguarding state security during the period of the Patriotic War."[72]

The tasks assigned these operatives were determined by Stalin personally during a private meeting with the NKGB FCD chief, Commissar III Pavel M. Fitin. Secondhand testimony lists these assignments: "to watch for Churchill and Roosevelt to learn whether they are going to reach a separate peace agreement with Hitler and then go to war against the Soviet Union together; to obtain Hitler's plans of war against the USSR which the Allies might possess; to learn any secret goals and plans of the Allies related to the war; to make attempts of finding out when exactly the Allies are going to open the second front in Europe; to obtain information on the latest secret military equipment designed and produced in the U.S.A., England and Canada." Further, according to the instructions received by the FCD resident in the United States, Vasili M. Zarubin, Stalin had requested information related to the "Allies' secret plans on postwar global settlement."[73]

The broad spectrum of tasks thus facing Soviet intelligence in the United States required additional Soviet and American personnel. The staff of the regular NKGB and GRU residencies in the United States was rather modest—for example, in the New York City Consulate and in the Amtorg there were only thirteen intelligence officers (three doing clerical work), and most of the group were well known to the FBI.[74] Having in mind the fact that the USSR and the United States had become allies, both branches of Soviet intelligence had to limit the usage of clandestine structures of the American Communist party (at least, in most important operations, such as those related to the Manhattan Project).[75] The use of local Communists was also limited in two other ways: many of them were known to the FBI, and many others after Pearl Harbor had been drafted into the U.S. Army and Navy[77] or interned, as was the case with a number of Communist party USA (CPUSA) members of Japanese extraction on the U.S. West Coast.[77]

The lack of trained personnel characteristic of 1941 and early 1942 was soon compensated for by the torrent of Soviet military and civilian specialists coming to the United States to work in the Soviet Purchasing Commission (SPC) and other agencies that mushroomed when the USSR became a part of the Lend-Lease program. According to Alexander Feklisov, by 1944 the staff of Amtorg and SPC in New York City had reached some twenty-five hundred; and an equal number of officials, engineers, and other specialists were working at the SPC in Washington, D.C.[78] The majority of these people reported directly or indirectly to the FCD or GRU.[79] Too, the limitations imposed on employment of CPUSA members did not mean that Soviet intelligence stopped recruiting other people—both Americans and aliens. Judging by the testimony of former intelligence officers and other sources, both major branches of intelligence and their junior partners—the RNRU and the Comintern's DIC, the latter later merging with the first two services—kept busy with this dimension of their work.[80]

Further, although the actual number of agents recruited by the Soviet intelligence officers operating in the United States throughout and immediately after the war will probably never be known, according to British estimates, out of twelve hundred cryptonyms that "littered the traffic" of the New York City/Moscow and Washington/Moscow channels of the FCD and GRU, "more than 800 were assessed as recruited Soviet agents."[81] The amount of information collected by Soviet networks in the United States was impressive. A report of March 28, 1944, of an investigation made in Great Falls, Montana (where the air route from Alaska to Russia originated), by a special agent of the U.S. Counterintelligence Corps indicated that aboard three C-47 aircrafts bound for the USSR between January 29 and February 28, 1944, the amount of "diplomatic mail" protected from censorship totaled 10,600 pounds, or 5.03 tons. And those were just three flights.[82] It is hardly possible to estimate the number of military, industrial, and scientific secrets that were actually shipped to Moscow, especially since the Alaskan air route was not the only channel used by Soviet intelligence. In fact, the most urgent and sensitive information was immediately transmitted to the USSR from radio stations operating in New York City and Washington, D.C.[83] What sort of information was sent to Moscow? According to the testimony of A. Feklisov, from 1942 to 1946 he managed seven agents working at the laboratories and plants of RCA, Western Electric, Westinghouse, General Electric, and two "leading aircraft building companies." He had obtained "more than 20,000 pages of secret documental information" dealing with various types of radars, sonars, gun- and bombsights, computers, and so forth, including the schematics and maintenance manuals for the P-81, the first American jet fighter.[84] Information collected with the help of American nuclear physicists resulted in speedier creation of the first Soviet A-bomb.[85]

No less successful was Soviet intelligence in obtaining classified political and economic information crucial for policy planning and decision making. The three major wartime summits where Stalin was present and many other meetings of Soviet and western representatives were exploited. Besides the preliminary data obtained through agents in the State Department and Whitehall, the FCD and the Second Chief Directorate–counterintelligence (SCD) recorded all conversations between the participants of the U.S. and British delegations both inside and outside the rooms where they lived and worked.[86] At the same time, officers of Soviet signals intelligence were busily recording all messages sent and received by the American and British delegations.[87]

Moreover, because the FBI and army counterintelligence agents were preoccupied with the Axis network operating in the United States in 1941 and 1942, the attitude toward known Soviet agents was lenient.[88] Soviet intelligence by the end of World War II and during the immediate postwar period proved capable of providing the Soviet government with almost any kind of information needed for policy planning and decision making.

A similar process of penetration of governmental, military, intelligence, and public structures was at the same time going on in other parts of the world—in Eastern, East Central, and Western Europe and in Asia. In Western Europe it was rather manifold—the FCD and GRU were trying to use the old network, which did survive the war, reinforcing it with new agents and recruiting new informers.[89] The FCD and GRU were also acting under the guise of Soviet repatriation or military mission personnel in France and Italy.[90] Of course, they continued to use local Communist parties' apparatuses; the increased influence of these parties in postwar Europe and the direct participation of their functionaries in the local and national governments of France and Italy provided the FCD and GRU with a host of new opportunities.[91]

No less active were both major branches of Soviet intelligence in Asia, especially in the Middle East[92] and China. In the latter, the FCD alone was running at least three major networks: one operating in Chungking and informing Moscow on the Nationalist government's political and military activists;[93] the second stationed with Chinese Communists in Yenan, which closely watched the interparty struggle, especially the one going on between the Mao Ze-dong and the Vang Ming factions;[94] and the third working in Manchuria and other regions occupied by the Japanese.[95]

There was also a special NKGB operation in Sinkiang. It was a large-scale one aimed at exerting pressure on the Chinese Nationalist government through the use of separatist movements of local Uighur, Uzbek, and other Turkic peoples in the province headed by Ali Khan Tyuria. The NKGB operation probably hoped to establish a Soviet stronghold in this isolated part of Northwest China.

In 1944 and 1945 the NKVD/NKGB not only supplied the troops of the self-proclaimed Eastern Turkestan government with captured rifles, machine guns, and mortars but also sent them two NKGB "special operational groups" totaling twenty-seven hundred officers and men. After signing the Soviet-Chinese treaty in August 1945, the Soviet government assumed the role of mediator between Chungking and Kuldzha and pressured the rebels to halt operations against the Chinese army. The NKVD/NKGB also withdrew its Takhtamysh and Altaic operational groups and took back all the weapons provided to the rebels in order to "prevent the Chinese from learning about" the Soviet aid.[96] On NKGB advice, the Soviet government decided to grant Soviet citizenship to Russians and former Soviets living in Sinkiang and to evacuate them to the Soviet Union.[97]

The NKVD/NKGB operations in America, Western Europe, and Asia were, nevertheless, rather modest in comparison to those undertaken in Soviet-controlled parts of Eastern, East Central, and Central Europe, especially in neighboring Poland, Romania, and Bulgaria. It is noteworthy that both major branches of Soviet intelligence as well as the Comintern's DIC[98] had in these countries prior to 1941 vast networks that, despite the ongoing efforts of the German *Abwehr*, the SD, the Gestapo, the Romanian *Siguranta*, and Bulgarian counterintelligence, survived the war and were then reinforced by many new agents and by local Communist parties.[99]

Soviet intelligence and counterintelligence had new opportunities in Eastern Europe from their own networks, from the newborn intelligence and counterintelligence forces of the Polish Provisional Government,[100] and from the purged and reorganized security structures of Bulgaria and Romania.[101] In Poland, for example, the NKVD/NKGB assisted with manning the local security forces; and the *Urzad Bezpieczenstwa* (UB) undertook, along with the Red Army's Smersh, its own operations against the Polish AK and oppositionist political parties and groups.[102]

In countries such as Hungary, Yugoslavia, Czechoslovakia, and Finland, the NKVD/NKGB operated a vast network of informers and local agents, ranging from ministers, senior civil servants, police, and security officials to ordinary citizens. Thus, the NKVD/NKGB obtained a huge amount of information about political, military, and economic life in these regions.[103] In sum, during the second half of 1944 and through 1945, Soviet intelligence and counterintelligence services secured almost total control over the newborn governments of Poland, Bulgaria, and Romania; heavily penetrated those of Czechoslovakia, Hungary, Finland, and Albania; and operated wide networks in Yugoslavia, Greece, Iran, and Turkey.[104] Thus, Soviet intelligence services—the FCD, GRU, and RNRU—were capable of supplying Stalin and the Soviet political and military leadership with all kinds of political, strategic, economic, and scientific information.[105] How all this vast information was used is another story.

The evidence presented in this chapter leads to several conclusions. First, the paramount goal of Stalin, his immediate entourage, the vast Soviet party and state bureaucracy, and the military and security establishment was to preserve and strengthen the Soviet system as it had evolved by the end of World War II. But the fact that the predominant part of Soviet society believed itself entitled to some version of a "better life" caused a dilemma for Stalin and those who supported and depended on him. There were two ways to improve the lot of the Soviet people.

The first choice was political and economic cooperation with the Allies and with the west in general. This approach could lessen tensions that had surfaced in interallied relations by the end of the war, lower the level of military expenditures, and thus allow more rapid restoration of the Soviet national economy and higher living standards in the Soviet Union. But this cooperation required compromises on both the domestic and international stages, which neither Stalin nor his lieutenants found acceptable. In their view, any such compromises would cause the Soviet Union to depend on the west. Further, in the long run, this choice would undermine their power base.

The second choice was to impose tighter control over the Soviet people, crushing hopes for changes in the Soviet political and social system. Following this course would ensure the Soviet Union's international position vis-à-vis the west by forging an empire consisting of the USSR within its new borders, along with a new "sphere of influence" in Eastern, East Central, and Central Europe. Stalin would also have to arm the Red Army and Navy with new weapons and military technology and infuse the Soviet people with a new form of "siege mentality." Cooperation with the wartime Allies would end, and confrontation would ensue.

Stalin preferred the second choice because it was familiar and had already been used successfully in the late 1920s and early 1930s. A policy of confrontation with the west could also help to solve many domestic problems; by creating new images of enemies both abroad and at home, Stalin could easily explain and justify the necessity of maintaining strict control over domestic life, suppression of real and imaginary opposition, and inevitable privations for the population. He could also justify maintaining strict military and political control over neighboring states, which he always considered essential for the security of the Soviet Union.

Judging by the steps the Soviet government took during 1945 and 1946, the die already had been cast. The deportation of large groups of several nationalities, the policy toward former Soviet POWs and displaced persons, the subtle and silent support of anti-Semitic sentiments spreading across the USSR, along with propaganda about Great Russian values and virtues—in sum, all sorts of big and small manifestations of government domestic policy—lead to the conclusion that by mid-1945 the principal outlines of Soviet postwar domestic political culture had been set.[106]

One cannot resist the same judgment based on the Soviet government's actions abroad. These included unilateral recognition of the Polish Provisional Government and the NKVD/NKGB crackdown on the Polish underground and political opposition; overt support of Communists in Romania and Bulgaria; the Soviet military buildup in Iran and along the USSR border with Turkey; the perpetual and growing penetration of the west by Soviet intelligence services; and a rush to build the A-bomb.[107] Clearly, Soviet leaders were preparing their country and their people to confront the west long before the iron curtain speech by Winston S. Churchill in Fulton, Missouri, in 1946.

Further, the fact that Stalin and his cohorts probably realized that they could not afford a large-scale conflict with their wartime Allies did not mean that they sought to avoid an apocalypse. As true Communists, Stalin and his entourage were unable to imagine long-term, peaceful relations with imperialist or capitalist powers. Nor did they believe that their wartime Allies sought civilized relations with the Soviet Union. The Soviet leaders never believed in or had respect for any international compact or declarations; they adhered to such agreements only as long as those accords served their interests. When on the eve of signing the Declaration on Liberated Europe in 1945, Molotov voiced reservations with regard to the draft submitted by the American delegation, Stalin reassured him, saying, "We shall implement it our own way. It's correlation of forces which really matters."[108] Seeing their principal and ultimate objective as undermining capitalism and establishing a world Communist system, they could not help but confront their temporary Allies.[109] Thus, cold war was inevitable.

NOTES

1. This chapter is based on the documents found recently in the so-called Stalin and Molotov's Special Files. These are huge collections of various reports sent to the principal figures in the Soviet state and party hierarchy by numerous high-ranking officials of the NKVD and NKGB, including People's Commissars of Interior and State Security Lavrenti Beria and Vsevolod N. Merkulovk; their deputies, Generals Serei N. Kruglov and Pavel M. Fitin; and many other high-ranking officers of State Security, military intelligence and counterintelligence, and functionaries of the Communist party and the state apparatus. All those documents were transferred several years ago from the Archive of the President of the Russian Federation (the Kremlin Archive) to the State Archive of the Russian Federation (SARF). I have also used a number of documents collected in the Comintern File, primarily Georgy Dimitrov's correspondence with the heads of military and NKVD intelligence, and in the files of some departments, divisions, and subdivisions of the Communist party's Central

Committee, constituting immense collections of the Russian Center for Storage and Study of Contemporary History Documents (RCSSCHD)—the former Central Party Archive.

2. N. A. Voznesensky, *Izbrannye Proizvedenia* (The selected works) (Moscow, 1979), 584.

3. In late 1944 and early 1945, several regions of the USSR were plagued by famine, which was especially severe in Eastern Siberia where, judging by the NKVD reports, there were even some cases of cannibalism—Portnov, Chief, Chita District Department of the NKVD, to L. Beria, March 1, 1945, typewritten copy. In Tatar Autonomous Soviet Republic (mid-Volga area) more than 46,000 persons needed "urgent medical treatment suffering malnutrition"—Gorbulin, People's Commissar of Interior, Tatar ASR, to L. Beria, April 7, 1945, no. 407/b, t/w copy—State Archive of the Russian Federation (SARF), Fond 9401 (Stalin and Molotov's Special Files), Opis 2, Delo 94, list 74, 383.

4. Judging by Sergei Kruglov's report during the period from 1942 through 1945, the number of murders had grown from 4,485 in 1942 to 8,656 in 1945 while the total number of crimes committed throughout the period was 515,159 (1942), 622,575 (1943), 675,889 (1944), and 558,912 (1945). S. Kruglov, Col. General, Minister of Interior, USSR, to J. Stalin, V. Molotov, L. Beria, N. A. Voznesensky, March 6, 1947, no. 7267k, Top Secret, t/w copy—ibid., F. 9401, Op. 2, D. 168, 1. 426–28.

5. Bartashunas and Guziavichus, People's Commissars of Interior and State Security, Lithuanian SSR, to L. Beria, January 26, 1945, no. 108/b, t/w copy—ibid., D. 92, 1. 229. See also Vsevolod N. Merkulov, People's Commissar of State Security, USSR, to L. Beria, January 27, 1945, no. 122/b, t/w copy—ibid., D. 92, 1. 269–75; Belichenko and Yesaulov, People's Commissars of Interior and State Security, Belorussian SSR, to L. Beria, January 29, 1945, t/w copy, sent by high frequency telephone—ibid., d. 92, 1. 278–82.

6. L. Beria to J. Stalin, V. Molotov, G. Malenkov, October 19, 1944, no. 1109/b, t/w copy—ibid., D. 67, 1. 9. This report of Beria's was a detailed account of the investigation of the activities of the Omakaitse group (a paramilitary organization of prewar Estonia) and its attempts to unite other local anti-Soviet groups into a broad national coalition. The Estonian government formed on the eve of German withdrawal from Tallin, reported Beria, readopted the prewar Estonian constitution and "was looking for guidance to the U.S. and Britain . . . and had its representatives in London and Washington." The report was based on the testimony of several of the government's members arrested by the local NKVD in mid-October 1944.

7. For example, Polisyh AK. L. Beria to J. Stalin, V. Molotov, G. Malenkov, Col. General Antonov, August 3, 1944, N. 841/b, t/w copy—SARF, F. 9401, Op. 2, D. 66, 1. 124.

8. For example, the "Lithuanian Committee," established in 1944 in Sweden and headed by the former Lithuanian minister to this country, Gilis, or "Mezha Kati" (Forest Cats) group, whose leadership emigrated to Sweden or the Estonian underground previously mentioned. L. Beria to J. Stalin, V. Molotov, G. Malenkov, September 19, 1945, no. 1106; L. Beria to J. Stalin, V. Molotov, G. Malenkov, September

21, 1945, no. 1117, t/w copies; L. Beria to J. Stalin, V. Molotov, G. Malenkov, October 19, 1944, no. 1109/b—ibid., D. 99, 1. 199, 355–56; D. 67, 1. 9.

9. In January 1945, while "cleansing the rear of the 1st Ukrainian Front, the NKVD arrested three British officers: Major Sollyflad, Captain Tickeranton, and Lieutenant Morgan, who, along with two other British officers, were parachuted in to Eastern poland to make a contact with the AK troops operating in the area." L. Beria to J. Stalin, V. Molotov, January 24, 1945, no. 97/b, t/w copy—ibid., D. 92, 1. 190. According to Ivan Serov's report, British intelligence formed in Poland a group called "Musketeers" to supply the SIS with information related to the military and political situation in Poland and Germany. The group was headed by Captain Vitkovski and consisted of the AK fighters recruited by the SIS. I. Serov, NKVD Special Commissioner for the First Belorussian Front, to L. Beria, March 17, 1945, no. 307, t/w copy—ibid., D. 94, 1. 89–90.

10. L. Beria to Stalin, V. Molotov, G. Malenkov, January 26, 1945, no. 106/b, t/w copy; V. N. Merkulov to L. Beria, January 27, 1945, no. 122/b, t/w copy—ibid., D. 92, 1. 215–18.

11. L. Beria to J. Stalin, V. Molotov, G. Malenkov, January 24, 1945, no. 97/b, t/w copy—SARF, F. 9401, Op. 2, D. 92, 1. 214.

12. According to the report by the People's Commissars of Interior and State Security, Lithuanian SSR, from July 1944 and through January 20, 1945, both the NKVD and the NKGB arrested in this Baltic republic 22,327 persons. During the incomplete week of January 15 to January 20, 1945, alone, both agencies arrested 1,388 persons, including sixty "participants of Lithuanian nationalist underground." Ibid., D. 92, 1. 226–27. The bulk of arrested Lithuanians were soldiers of the LLA enlisted in local groups of Lithuanian Resistance; one should mention the "Freedom Fighters" of Panevezhis District, the LPC (Union of Lithuanian Guerrillas) and the "Kiargitas ouzh Tevine" (Revenge for the Motherland) formations, which fought Soviet authorities in the Pokon' District and Kovno (Kaunas). L. Beria to J. Stalin, V. Molotov, G. Malenkov, September 19, 1945, no. 1106/b, t/w copy—ibid., D. 99, 1. 195–201. According to the other report, dated November 15, 1945, during the period from July 1 through November 1, 1945, both the NKVD and the NKGB "liquidated 312 bandit groups, killed in action 3,925 bandits and captured 5,251 of those alive." L. Beria to V. Molotov, G. Malenkov, A. Mikoyan, November 15, 1945, no. 1284, t/w copy—ibid., D. 105, 1. 97. The Polish underground in Lithuania was represented by the AK and the "Polish Underground" group (named by the NKVD/NKGB interrogators). Bartashunas and Guziavichus to L. Beria, January 20, 1945, no. 85/b—ibid., D. 92, 1. 157. Judging by the NKVD report, they were well-armed and -manned: during the initial phase of disarming of the AK troops alone Soviet army and NKVD special detachments collected 5,500 rifles, 370 submachine guns, 12 light field-artillery pieces, 27 cars and trucks, 7 radio transmitters and 270 horses. The number of the AK officers and men detained during the operation was 7,924. Some 4,400 of them were sent to local draft commissions of Wojsko Polske—the Polish Liberation Army formed in the USSR by the Polish Committee of National Liberation; 2,500 were sent home and the rest, 1,024, were arrested. L. Beria

to J. Stalin, V. Molotov, G. Malenkov, Col. General Antonov, August 3, 1944, no. 841/b, t/w copy—SARF, F. 9401, Op. 2, D. 66, 1. 124.

13. L. Beria to J. Stalin, V. Molotov, G. Malenkov, Col. General Antonov, August 3, 1944, no. 841/b, t/w copy—ibid., D. 66, 1. 125.

14. L. Beria to J. Stalin, V. Molotov, November 3, 1944, no. 1178/b, t/w copy— ibid., D. 67, 1. 191–92.

15. L. Beria to J. Stalin, V. Molotov, G. Malenkov, N. Khrushchev, Col. Gen. Antonov, August 19, 1944, no. 901, t/w copy; L. Beria to J. Stalin, V. Moltov, G. Malenkov, April 10, 1945, no. 411/b, t/w copy—ibid., D. 66, 1. 238; D. 94, 1. 388–92.

16. Belichenko and Yesaulov, people's commissars for interior and state security, Belorussian SSR, to L. Beria, January 29, 1945, no. 123/b; L. Beria to J. Stalin, V. Molotov, December 1, 1944, no. 1297, t/w copy—ibid., D. 92, 1. 276–82; D. 68, 1. 59–60.

17. L. Beria to J. Stalin, V. Molotov, G. Malenkov, N. Khrushchev, Col. Gen. Antonov, August 19, 194, no. 901/b, t/w copy—ibid., D. 66, 1. 234.

18. L. Beria to J. Stalin, V. Molotov, G. Malenkov, April 10, 1945, no. 411/b— ibid., D. 94, 1. 388.

19. Ibid., 1. 388–89.

20. Ibid., 1. 389.

21. Though any attempt to abstain from any kind of election campaign in the Soviet Union was considered to be an anti-Soviet act, it is noteworthy that the 1946 Supreme Soviet elections met mass boycott in the Western Ukraine. S. V. Kuleshov, O. V. Volobuev et al., *Our Fatherland. An Experiment in Writing a Political History*, 2 vols. (Moscow, 1991), 2: 435.

22. Robert Conquest estimates the number of Ukrainians deported by the Soviet authorities during and after World War II to be close to 1 million (Conquest, *The Nation Killers: The Soviet Deportation of Nationalities* [London, 1970], 64–66). Unfortunately, I could not find any reliable summary report related to mass deportations of the Western Ukrainians among the papers of Stalin and Molotov's Special Files.

23. Throughout 1947, for example, according to the MVD report, Soviet border troops had seized along the western border of the USSR 1,792 Ukrainians who had tried to flee to Poland and 157 "bandits and their accomplices." S. Kruglov, minister of Interior, USSR, to J. Stalin, V. Molotov, L. Beria, January 21, 1948, no. 375/k, t/w copy—SARF, F. 9401, Op. 2, D. 199, 1. 80.

24. S. Kruglov, minister of interior, USSR, to J. Stalin, V. Molotov, G. Malenkov, L. Beria, Z. Zhdanov, February 27, 1948, no. 357/k, t/w copy—ibid., D. 199, 1. 314.

25. L. Beria to J. Stalin, V. Molotov, G. Malenkov. "On the Situation in Liberated Areas of the Belorussian SSR and the Karelian-Finnish SSR," July 27, 1944, no. 809/b, t/w copy—ibid., D. 66, 1. 54–56.

26. Ibid., 1. 56.

27. L. Beria to J. Stalin, V. Molotov, December 1, 1944, no. 1297/b—ibid., D. 68, 1. 59–60.

28. Ibid., D. 68, 1. 60.

29. L. Beria to J. Stalin, V. Molotov, G. Malenkov, Col. Gen. Antonov, August 3,

1944, no. 841/b, t/w copy; Bartashunas and Guziavichus to L. Beria, January 26, 1945, no. 108/b, t/w copy; L. Beria to J. Stalin, V. Molotov, G. Malenkov, September 19, 1945, no. 1106/b; L. Beria to J. Stalin, V. Molotov, G. Malenkov, September 21, 1945, no. 1117/b, t/w copy—ibid., D. 66, 1. 124, 128; D. 92, 1. 226; D. 99, 1. 195, 356.

30. S. Kruglov, deputy people's commissary of interior, USSR; Tkachenko, commissar of state security, NKVD/NKGB commissioner for Lithuania, to L. Beria, December 15, 1944 (marked: "To be sent to: Comrades Stalin, Molotov, Malenkov, Bulganin")—ibid., D. 68, 1. 180–81.

31. Starting with the liberation of Belorussia in July and through December 21, 1944, the number of Belorussian and Polish deserters and draft dodgers detained by the NKVD/NKGB during several "cleansing" operations was 15,685 and 60,236. In Lithuania during the period of July 1 through September 15, 1945, according to an NKVD report, some 31,360 "deserters and draft dodgers voluntarily have given themselves up." Similar data could also be found in some other NKVD/NKGB reports. Amayak Kobulov, deputy people's commissar of state security, USSR, to L. Beria, December 25, 1944; L. Beria to J. Stalin, V. Molotov, G. Malenkov, September 19, 1945, no. 1106, t/w copy—ibid., D. 68, 1. 260; D. 99, 1. 195.

32. For example, the nonviolent mass demonstration organized by the Polish population of Vilno on All Saint's Day (November 1, 1944) at a military cemetery, in the course of which, even according to the NKVD report, "No anti-soviet speeches and appeals have been delivered." L. Beria to J. Stalin, V. Molotov, November 3, 1944, no. 1178. The other example was that of resisting by entirely legal means the joint Soviet-Polish program of resettlement in Poland of the Poles living in Western Ukraine, Belorussia, and Lithuania. People used any excuse to postpone their enlistment into that program. L. Beria to J. Stalin, V. Molotov, October 15, 1944. All these acts as well as, for instance, a meeting of Tauragen high school teachers and students held on the eve of Lithuania's Independence Day (February 16, 1945) were considered by Soviet authorities to be counterrevolutionary and anti-Soviet manifestations. Rodionov, NKVD/NKGB commissioner for Lithuania, Guziavichus, people's commissar of state security, Lithuanian SSR, to L. Beria, February 27, 1945, no. 196/b, t/w original—SARF, F. 9401, Op. 2, D. 67, 1. 191–92; D. 66, 1. 395–97; D. 67, 1. 191–92; D. 66 1. 395–97; D. 93, 1. 216.

33. These acts of terrorism and sabotage were fairly common for all newly acquired territories of the USSR. Thus, for example, in Riga on December 27, 1944, one of the local military commandants, Col. Shetsel'nikov, was shot in broad daylight in front of the movie theater by a local student, Petrovskis, a member of the underground "Briva Latija" group. V. N. Merkulov, people's commissar of state security, USSR, to L. Beria, January 27, 1945, no. 122/b. In Lithuania, the Kiargitas ouzh Tevine (Revenge for the Motherland) group had in its structure a special subdivision responsible for carrying out acts of terrorism called "Department of Execution." L. Beria to J. Stalin, V. Molotov, G. Malenkov, September 19, 1945, no. 1106/b. Yet especially active terror was practiced by the OUN/UPA battle groups in Western Ukraine. During just some two weeks (July 26 to August 11, 1944) in the Lvov District alone they killed and wounded 143 persons, including 96 civilians, 41 Red Army

officers and men, and 6 NKVD/NKGB officials. Sixty more, both military and civilian, just disappeared and were officially considered MIA. L. Beria to J. Stalin, V. Molotov, G. Malenkov, N. Khrushchev, Col. General Antonov, August 19, 1944, no. 901/b, t/w copy—SARF, F. 9401, Op. 2, D. 92, 1. 272; D. 99, 1. 199; D. 66, 1. 234.

34. This loyalty has been noted both by domestic and foreign observers. See, for example, I. Ehrenburg, *People, Years, Life,* vols. 5 and 6 (Moscow, 1966), 278; T. Leshchenko-Sukhomlina, *Long Future* (Moscow, 1991), 171; V. Kaverin, *Epilogue. Memoirs* (Moscow, 1989), 290; and S. E. Frisch, *Through the Prism of Time* (Moscow, 1992), 303. This phenomenon was also reported by American intelligence. See, for instance, *The Soviet Union* (an analytical report), prepared by Intelligence Division, WDGS, War Department, Washington, D.C., 1947, 16, Papers of Harry S. Truman, President Secretary File: Foreign Affairs (Russia–2), Box 188, Harry S. Truman Library, Independence, Mo. (hereafter PHST, PSF).

35. I. V. Stalin, *Works,* ed. R. H. McNeed, 3 vols. Hoover Institution on War, Revolutions and Peace (Stanford, 1967), 2: 204.

36. Ehrenburg, *People,* 243.

37. S. V. Kuleshov, O. V. Volobuev et al., *Our Fatherland,* 2 vols. (Moscow, 1991), 2: 427.

38. The NKVD laid the groundwork for their reception and mass "filtration" as early as August 1944 when a draft resolution of the State Defense Committee regulating their admittance to the USSR was sent to V. Molotov by the agency. The State Defense Committee Resolution (a Draft), " . . . " August 1944—SARF, F. 9401, Op. 2, D. 69, 1. 349–51. It is noteworthy that similar arrangements for mass "filtration" of the ex-POWs had been made much later, in early May 1945, and the decree related to their reception and containment was signed by J. Stalin on May 11. D. Volkogonov, *Stalin. Triumph and Tragedy* (New York, 1988), 491–92.

39. For more details, see N. Tolstoy, *Stalin's Secret War* (London, 1981), 295–327.

40. Volkogonov, *Stalin,* 427.

41. The State Defense Committee Resolution (a Draft), " . . . " August 1944—SARF, F. 9401, Op. 2, D. 69, 1. 349–51. The draft resolution also specified which People's Commissariat had to provide these camps with transportation, fuel, foodstuff, drugs, and medical service. All the camps had to be financed by the Ukrainian and Belorussian governments, not by the NKVD.

42. Volkogonov, *Stalin,* 492.

43. Ibid.

44. Ehrenburg, *People,* 291. The same change was also noted by the other Soviet Marshal, Pavel A. Rotmistrov (ibid., 192).

45. Leshohenko-Sukhomlina, *Long Future,* 235.

46. Amazing data on the religious sentiments of Penza District peasants as well as some excerpts from their petitions for reopening of local churches and a description of their rallies and demonstrations may be found in the NKVD/NKGB reports. See, for example, chief, Special Department, Penza District Committee, Communist party, to Kuznetsov, chief, Propaganda Group, Central Committee, Communist party, July 28, 1943, no. 011/877, t/w copy; Nikolaev, Col. of State Security, chief,

Penza District Dept. of NKGB (PDD of NKGB), to Morshchinin, secretary, PDD, Communist party, n.d., May 1943; Davydov, major of state security, deputy chief, PDD of NKGB, and Klimashev, chief, 2d Dept., PDD of NKGB, to Morshchinin, secr., PDD, Communist party, June 5, 1945—Russian Center for Storage and Study of Contemporary History Documents (RCSSCHD), f. 17 (Central Committee, Communist party), Op. 125 (Department of Propaganda and Political Agitation), D. 181, 1. 9–12, 12 reverse.

47. Kaverin, *Epilogue*, 297.

48. Sometimes it was more than just dissatisfaction, for example, a hunger strike in Nizhne-Shachtama Gold Mine, Chita Dist., Siberia, in early 1945, or a mass walk-out of railroadmen in Karaganda and Akmolinsk Railroads, Kazakhstan, in September 1944. For details, see Portnov, chief, Chita Dist. Dept. of NKVD, to L. Beria, "One Economic Situation in Chita District," March 1, 1945; L. Beria to J. Stalin, V. Molotov, G. Malenkov, no. 7, 1944, no. 1200/b, t/w copies—SARF, F. 9401, Op. 2, D. 94, 1. 74; D. 67, 1. 297–99. On peasants' attitudes, see L. Beria to V. Molotov, G. Malenkov, May 25, 1945, no. 596/b (summary of a report sent by Sverdlovsk Dist. Dept. of NKVD); L. Beria to V. Molotov, G. Malenkov, August 22, 1945, no. 966/b, t/w copies (summary of a report sent by Tyumen Dist. Dept. of NKVD). Soviet workers' dissatisfaction related to their food rations, wages, taxes, housing, and clothing was also reported by American intelligence. See, for example, Brig. General Frank N. Roberts, U.S. Military Attaché, Moscow, to Gen. Clayton Bissell, WDGBI (G-2), Washington, Memorandum of Conversation with an Informant, December 7, 1945, Papers of W. Averell Harriman, Special File: Public Service, World War II Files, Moscow Files, Box 184, Chrono File, December 1–7 (hereafter PWAH. MF), Library of Congress, Manuscript Division.

49. Ehrenburg, *People*, 278; Leshchenko-Sukhomlina, *Long Future*, 171; Kaverin, *Epilogue*, 290; Frisch, *Prism*, 303. This attitude toward Soviet leadership was also reported by American intelligence (see Soviet Union . . . , 14, 16, and PHST, PSF: FA, Box 188, HSTL).

50. Ehrenburg, *People*, 197; Frisch, *Prism*, 303.

51. Some of the changes they did explain in that the Soviet Union had become a part of the Grand Alliance and thus its government had to make some compromises with the United States and Britain. See the statements by Professor Tereshchenko (Kharkov Polytechnical Institute), Bogdanov (Kharkov Institute of Agriculture), and Assistant Professor Segileev (Kharkov University), reported to the party's Central Committee by the special propaganda group sent to Kharkov soon after its liberation in late summer 1943. I. Fomina, chief, Dept. of Propaganda and Political Agitation Group, to G. F. Aleksandrov, chief, Department of Propaganda and Political Agitation, Central Committee, Communist party, n.d., late summer, 1943—RCSSCHD, F. 17, Op. 125, D. 181, 1. 51–52. Similar views were expressed by a number of the Academy of Sciences' scholars in Sverdlovsk as early as November 1942. See M. Borschev, Sverdlovsk Dist. Dept. of NKVD, to G. F. Aleksandrov, November 17, 1942, no. 24839, Sverdlovsk Distr. Dept. of NKVD Special Report "On Political Attitudes of Mind of the Academy of Sciences' Intelligentsia"—ibid., D. 84, 1. 5.

52. A. Petrosian, chief, Dept. of Propaganda and Political Agitation Group, to G. F. Aleksandrov and Yovchuk, Division of Propaganda, Central Committee, Communist party, May 26, 1943, "On Political State of Mind Related to the Recent Executive Committee of Comintern"—ibid., D. 181, 1. 4–5.

53. Ibid., 1. 4–5. The same ideas and especially that of the dissolution of collective farms were also very popular among a substantial number of Siberian peasants. See L. Beria to V. Molotov, G. Malenkov, May 25, 1945, no. 596/b; L. Beria to V. Molotov, G. Malenkov, August 22, 1945, no. 966/b—SARF, F. 9401, Op. 2, D. 103, 1. 180, 322–24. See also Davydov, major of State Security, deputy chief, PDD of NKGB, and Klimashev, chief, 2d Dept., PDD of NKGB, to Morshchinin, secr., Penza Dist. Committee, Communist party, June 5, 1943—RCSSCHD, F. 17, Op. 125, D. 181, 1. 12–13.

54. The idea of a "party of intellectuals and civil servants" was popular among the members of a students' group, Dept. of Philosophy, Moscow University, arrested by the NKGB in late 1943—Vasilii F. Nozdrev, secretary, Communist Party Committee, Moscow University, to Aleksandr S. Shcherbakov, secretary, Central Committee, Communist party, n.d., 1944—RCSSCHD, F. 77 (Andrei A. Zhdanov Personal Papers), Op. 1, D. 895, 1. 121. For details on other youth groups in other Soviet cities, see Kuleshov et al., Our Fatherland, 2: 433–34.

55. All those innovations and novelties worried many Soviet people and especially intellectuals. The "Red Army and especially its units in the rear," wrote Sergei Frisch, a prominent Soviet physicist, served as a perilous example for civil agencies. This "Generalina" malady ("generals' disease," as it was popularly called then) penetrated even the scholarly community, starting to convert it into some "rank and title" system." Frisch, Prism, 322–23. See also Ehrenburg, People, 164, and Leshchenko-Sukhomlina, Long Future, 265.

56. Volkogonov, Stalin, 501.

57. Ibid., p. 503.

58. According to the memoirs of Victor Kravchenko, an employee of the Soviet Purchasing Commission in the United States, on the eve of his departure for Washington, D.C., in mid-1943, the Assistant People's Commissar of Foreign trade Lebedev told him, "America . . . is just a temporary ally." The same line was also pursued by a high-ranking Central Committee official who instructed Kravchenko earlier. V. I. Kravchenko, Choose Freedom. The Personal and Political Life of a Soviet Official (New York, 1946), 443, 445. Talking to Georgy Dimitrov in January 1945, Stalin told his interlocutor, "The crisis of capitalism manifested itself dividing capitalists into two groups—the fascist faction and democratic one. . . . Now, we are [fighting] along with one of them against the other and in future we shall be against the former." M. M. Narinsky, Soviet Foreign Policy and the Origins of the Cold War, a Retrospective, 1917–1991, ed. A. O. Chubarian and Gorodetsky (Moscow, 1993), 122.

59. Regularly reading reports submitted by the NKVD/NKGB, Stalin knew that a substantial number of people belonging to various strata of Soviet society pinned their hopes for postwar liberalization of Soviet domestic policy on the applied policy toward the USSR. Such hopes were reported by many district Communist party

committees. See, for example, information reports by Voronezh Distr. Committee (May 21) and Rostov-on-Don Dist. Committee—RCSSCHD, F. 17, Op. 88 (Dept. of Organizational Affairs, Central Committee, Communist party), D. 469, 1. 32, 140.

60. Judging by the reports of many local and district party committees, the people after V-E Day started complaining of tiredness, bad state of health, lack of basic foodstuff, and so on. See Moscow City Committee, Communist party, to the Central Committee, Information Report, May 21, 1945; "Questions Asked by the Working People of the Omsk District at Meetings," June 28, 1945; Novosibirsk Dist. Committee, CP, to the Central Committee, "Information on the Working People Attitudes Toward the End of the War and the Address by Comrade Stalin," May 19, 1945—RCSSCHD, F. 17, Op. 88, D. 469, 1. 98; D. 421, 1. 20; D. 469, 1. 113.

61. In early 1937 NKVD/NKGB chief Nikolai I. Ezhov sent to the United States and Britain a special agent (code-named Journalist) to investigate supposed penetration of the U.S. and British Communist parties' apparatus by the Trotskyites as well as by American and British counterintelligence. Though the investigation was focused on "Trotskyist functionaries and their entourage" it could have led to accusations of a number of Soviet illegals working within the underground structures of those CPs having some ties with Trotsky and his followers. See Minaev, NKGB commissar III rank, deputy chief, 3d Dept. of State Security Chief Directorate, NKVD, to Georgy Dimitrov, secretary general, Comintern, April 23, 1937, no. 191740, t/w original—RCSSCHD, F. 495 (Communist International), Op. 74 (G. Dimitrov's Secretariat), D. 465, 1. 1–4. Anyway, soon after this mission (as well as possibly a number of similar ones) had been accomplished, many Soviet residents and agents abroad were charged with being a part of a widespread Trotskyist conspiracy, summoned to Moscow, and executed. Among them were such outstanding intelligence officers as, for example, Theodor Maly; Ignace Poretsky (aka Reiss), who refused to return and was subsequently killed in Switzerland; and Walter Krivitsky and Alexander Orlov (the last two chose to defect). For details, see E. Poretsky, *Our Own People* (Ann Arbor, MI, 1969), 214–16, 231; A. Orlov, *The Secret History of Stalin's Crimes* (New York, 1953), 231; B. Starkov, *The Tragedy of Soviet Military Intelligence,* and the foreword to W. Krivitsky, *I Was Stalin's Agent* (Moscow, 1991), 3–52 (in Russian).

62. On the early warnings about the impending German attack, see G. K. Zhukov, *Recollections and Reminiscences* (Memoirs of Marshal Zhukov) (Moscow, 1970), 241–42 (in Russian); V. A. Novobranets, *On the Eve of the War. Memoirs* (Znamya, June 1990) (in Russian); P. Sudaplatov and A. Sudoplatov, *Special Tasks. The Memoirs of an Unwanted Witness—A Soviet Spymaster* (Boston, New York, 1994), 116–20; A. Foote, *Handbook for Spies* (London, 1964), 88–90; L. Trepper, *The Great Game* (New York, 1989), 126, 136–37; and S. Rado, *Codename Dora* (London, 1990), 53–59. On Soviet wartime intelligence focused on Germany, see Sudaplatov and Sudoplatov, *Special Tasks,* 126–71; Trepper, *Great Game,* 140–97; Rado, *Codename,* 61–114, 130–51, 196–211; C. Andrew and O. Gordievsky, *KGB: The Inside Story of Its Foreign Operations from Lenin to Gorbachev* (New York, 1991), 270–79, 305–11.

63. For details on this network, see Trepper, *Great Game*, especially 96–329; D. J. Dallin, *Soviet Espionage* (New Haven, 1955), 234–72.

64. See Rado, *Codename, passim;* Foote, *Handbook*, 37–148; Dallin, *Espionage,* 182–233.

65. For details, see C. A. Willoughby, *Shanghai Conspiracy. The Sorge Spy Ring: Moscow–Shanghai–Tokyo–San Francisco–New York* (New York: 1952), *passim;* Andrew and Gordievsky, *KGB*, 239–40, 264–65, 270–72; G. W. Prange et al., *Target Tokyo: The Story of the Sorge Spy Ring* (New York, 1985), *passim*.

66. The most important works are J. Costello, *Mask of Treachery* (New York, 1988), *passim,* esp. 367–506; P. Knightley, *Philby: KGB Master Spy* (London, 1988), *passim*.

67. Save for the biggest part of *Rote Kapelle*, crushed by the German Gestapo by the end of 1942 (see: Trepper, *Great Game*, 191–251, and Andrew and Gordievsky, *KGB*, 276–77), the Sorge group, caught by the end of 1941 (see Willoughby, *Shanghai*, 117–19); and a substantial part of Sandor Rado network arrested by the Swiss authorities in late fall 1943 (see: Rado, *Codename*, 240–75, and Foote, *Handbook*, 104–31).

68. L. Beria and V. N. Merkulov to J. Stalin, November 4, 1944, no. 1186, t/w copy—SARF, F. 9401, Op. 2, D. 67, 1. 275.

69. Ibid., D. 67, 1. 276. For details on G. Ovakimyan's activities, see A. Feklisov, *Beyond the Ocean and on the Island. Notes of an Intelligence Officer* (Moscow, 1994), 24, 51; R. J. Lamphere, *The KGB–FBI War. A Special Agent's Story* (New York, 1986), 25–27, 164–65.

70. L. Beria, V. N. Merkulov to J. Stalin, November 4, 1944, no. 1186—SARF, F. 9401, Op. 2, D. 67, 1. 277–81. For details of these officers' careers, see Feklisov, *Beyond the Ocean,* 50–67, 72, 100–107, 139–73.

71. "Silvermaster" was the apparent misprint of a Moscow typist. L. Beria, V. N. Merkulov to J. Stalin, November 4, 1944, no. 1186—ibid., D. 67, 1. 278–79; for details, see Dallin, *Espionage*, 440, 464–65; Lamphere, *KGB–FBI*, 181; and Andrew and Gordievsky, *KGB*, 281–83.

72. L. Beria, V. N. Merkulov to J. Stalin, November 4, 1944, no. 1186—ibid., D. 67, 1. 275.

73. Feklisov, *Beyond the Ocean,* 51–52.

74. Ibid., 50, 60–63.

75. Sudoplatov and Sudoplatov, *Special Tasks,* 186–87.

76. Ibid., 187. Also see information from "Brother" and "Son" (code names of unidentified American Communist functionaries for Georgy Dimitrov, approximately January 1943, photocopy of the original typewritten report in English—RCSSCHD, F. 495, Op. 74, D. 480, 1. 1–3.

77. Information from "Brother" and "Son" for G. Dimitrov, approx. January 1943—ibid., 1. 3–4.

78. Feklisov, *Beyond the Ocean,* 32; Kravchenko, *Choose Freedom,* 465.

79. Feklisov, *Beyond the Ocean,* 100–101; Kravchenko, *Choose Freedom,* 445, 461, 465; Dallin, *Espionage,* 428–32.

80. Feklisov, *Beyond the Ocean,* 65–105; M. Vorontsov, Capt. 1st rank, chief Red

Navy Main Staff, Intelligence Department, and Petrov, military commissar, RNMS, ID, to G. Dimitrov, August 15, 1942, no. 49253ss, t/w original; G. Dimitrov to Pavel M. Fitin, November 20, 1942, no. 663, t/w copy; P. M. Fitin to G. Dimitrov, May 6, 1943, no. 1/3/5354; P. M. Fitin to G. Dimitrov, March 16, 1944, no. 1/6/3787; P. M. Fitin to G. Dimitrov, July 14, 1944, no. 1/3/10987, t/w copies; P. M. Fitin to G. Dimitrov, September 29, 1944, no. 1/3/16895; P. M. Fitin to G. Dimitrov, October 19, 1944, no. 1/3/18161. All these documents are RNMS, ID, and FCD chiefs' requests for information related to the Americans and naturalized American citizens working in various U.S. government agencies and private corporations, some of whom could have been in the past the CPUSA members. The last two are related to a certain Donald Wheeler (an OSS official), Charles Floto or Flato (who in 1943 worked for "Dept. of Economic Warfare"), and Harry Magdoff (War Production Board)—the request dated September 29—and to Judith Coplon (who according to the FCD information worked for the Dept. of Justice)—RCSSCHD, F. 495, Op. 74, D. 478, 1. 7; d. 484, 1. 34; D. 485, 1. 10, 4, 17, 31, 44.

81. P. Wright, *Spy Catcher. The Candid Autobiography of a Senior Intelligence Officer* (New York, 1987), 182.

82. Dallin, *Espionage*, 436–37.

83. Feklisov, *Beyond the Ocean*, 63. A certain amount of information related to the political, industrial, military, and sometimes even the intelligence activities of the U.S. government was obtained by Soviet intelligence as before from the underground structures of CPUSA. See information from "Brother" and "Son" to G. Dimitrov; P. M. Fitin to G. Dimitrov, July 23, 1943, no. 1/3/3163, t/w original (information on Earl Browder's meeting with President Roosevelt and the latter's statement that "the Communist party USA should understand that the Sicilian campaign is just a prelude to a big invasion of the European continent in summer of this year")—RCSSCHD, F. 495, Op. 74, D. 480, 1. 2–6; d. 484, 1. 32–33.

84. Feklisov, *Beyond the Ocean*, 105–6.

85. For the controversial story of stealing American atomic secrets, see Sudoplatov and Sudoplatov, *Special Tasks*, 172–220; Feklisov, *Beyond the Ocean*, 101–2, 139–78; Dallin, *Espionage*, 453–73; S. Beria, *My Father Lavrenti Beria* (Moscow, 1994), 257–306; E. Knight, *Beria, Stalin's First Lieutenant* (Princeton, N.J., 1993), 132–40; A. Yatskov, "Vopprosy Istorii Estestvoznaniia i Tekhniki" (Questions of history of natural science and technology) (Moscow, 1992), no. 3, 101–6; Y. Khariton and Y. Smirnov, "The Khariton Version," *Bulletin of Atomic Scientists*, May 1993.

86. Feklisov, *Beyond the Ocean*, 106–7; Dallin, *Espionage*, 441–49; J. Burnham, *The Web of Subversion. Underground Networks in the U.S. Government* (New York, 1954), 70–71; Andrew and Gordievsky, *KGB*, 332, 335–37; Sudoplatov and Sudoplatov, *Special Tasks*, 222.

87. The amazing data and details on the NKVD/NKGB preparations for the Yalta Conference may be found in General Kruglov's report to Beria and the latter's report to J. Stalin, including information on bugging Yusupov, Livadia, and Vorontsov Palaces. See S. Kruglov to L. Beria, January 27, 1945, no. 115/b; L. Beria to J. Stalin, January 27, 1945, no. 114/b, t/w copies—SARF, F. 9401, Op. 2, D. 92, 1. 238–40;

D. 94, 1. 15–27. For personal recollections on the Yalta and Tehran Conferences, see: Beria, *My Father,* 231–56.

88. Feklisov, *Beyond the Ocean,* 65, 83–91; Dallin, *Espionage,* 424; Lamphere, *KGB–FBI,* 26; Dallin, *Espionage,* 425; Andrew and Gordievsky, *KGB,* 280.

89. Foote, *Handbook,* 140; Costello, *Mask,* 473–75.

90. Foote, *Handbook,* 137–40; SACMED to AGWAR, Washington; U.S. Military Mission, Moscow; Troopers, London, October 22, 1945—PWAH, MF, Box 183, Chron. Files, October 21–25. MD. According to the telegram, the personnel of the Soviet delegation to the Advisory Council for Italy, the Soviet representation to the Allied Commission (Italy), and the Soviet Military Mission numbered within Italy 101 officers and civilians. These people "traveled widely throughout Italy, opening unofficial offices in various towns and carrying on extensive propaganda under the guise of caring for displaced persons of which very few can now remain." They were also very interested in the "area where Polish troops are located." The FCD had also used its network in Italy to recruit agents for work in Yugoslavia. See L. Beria to V. Molotov, June 26, 1945, no. 745/b, t/w copy (the report deals with the unsuccessful attempt to recruit a certain Ranko and Italian movie actress Larisa Vernati by the officials of the Soviet embassy, Rome). In France one of the FCD's networks, headed by its resident "Kir" (a code name), was closely watching Russian and Georgian émigrés who also succeeded in penetrating French intelligence. See P. A. Sharia to L. Beria, n.d. (approx. May 1945), no. 180/b, t/w copy. Earlier, by fall 1944 the NKGB Sigint Department had broken a cipher used by the Foreign Ministry of France, thus enabling it to supply the Kremlin with top secret information related to Charles de Gaulle's forthcoming visit to Moscow. See L. Beria to J. Stalin, November 29, 1994, no. 1285/b, t/w copy—SARF, F. 9401, Op. 2, D. 103, 1. 215; D. 93, 1. 67–73; D. 68, 1. 24–25.

91. Costello, *Mask,* 441; Foote, *Handbook,* 140; Dallin, *Espionage,* 315–16.

92. Besides the fact that the area was always considered by Moscow to be one of vital importance for the Soviet Union's security and was the focus of attention of the NKGB/NKVD, with the outset of World War II it became by far the most important route for sending agents into the Balkan states, East Central, and Central Europe, including Germany, as well as into North Africa, Portugal, Spain, and France. See "On the Elaboration of Using Iran and Turkey for Transfer of Groups of Brother Parties' Members into Their Countries," unsigned memorandum, n.d. 1943, t/w original; "The Bulgarian Group's Transfer," unsigned memo, n.d., 1943—RCSSCHD, F. 495, Op. 73, D. 182, 1. 34–36, 37; Beria, *My Father,* 238–39. By the end of the war the area once again acquired its prewar role: according to the British "War Office intelligence," the NKGB became "increasingly interested in penetrating Near East in effort to weaken strategic position of British in area" (Dean Acheson, acting secretary of state, to W. Averell Harriman and Gen. Roberts, Moscow, January 15, 1946, PWAH, MF, Box 186, Chron Files, January 13–16. MD).

93. The FCD used both the Comintern and its own network. See, for example, P. M. Fitin to G. Dimitrov, June 13, 1944, no. 1/4/8799 (a report on the political and military situation in Nationalist government-controlled territories and negotiations between Chiang Kai-shek and the Chinese Communist mission); P. M. Fitin to G. Dimitrov,

November 15, 1944, no. 1/4/19566 (a report on P. Hurley's return to Chungking from Yenan)—RCSSCHD, F. 495, Op. 74, D. 340, 1. 8, 26.

94. See, for example, P. M. Fitin to G. Dimitrov, 29 September 1943, no. 1/4/6678 (a report on conflict between Mao Zedong and Vang Ming's groups in the Communist party politbureau)—ibid., D. 340, I. 19.

95. The GRU had in Manchuria its own network and was trying to keep it for itself. When in late 1942 the Comintern's Division of International Communication tried to get the GRU's assistance for transferring a group of the DIC agents into the region, the military intelligence did not cooperate. See Cohgan, Comintern representative in Mongolia, to G. Dimitrov and I. A. Morozov, chief, DIC, November 8, 1942, t/w original; Cohgan to I. A. Morozov, November 9, 1942, "The 1st Division's Plan of Work in China for November and December 1942," t/w original—RCSS-CHD, F. 495, Op. 73, D. 182, 1. 6, 2.

96. Vladimir S. Yegnazarov, Alexander I. Langfang, commissars of state security, Alma-Ata, to L. Beria, December 4, 1945, no. 409, t/w copy; L. Beria to Usman Yusupov, first secretary, Uzbek Communist Party Central Committee, Tashkent, September 20, 1945, t/w copy—SARF, F. 9401. Op. 2, D. 105, 1. 337, 235.

97. L. Beria to V. Molotov, G. Malenkov, November 29, 1945, no. 1339/b—ibid., D. 105, 1. 236–40.

98. Judging by the content of the "Brief Note on the Tasks and Forms of Active Assistance to the USSR in a Case of War with the Bordering Countries of the West," a long memorandum prepared by the DIC officials in the early 1930s and found within the huge collection of Dimitry Z. Manuilsky's Secretariat papers, by this time the DIC had possessed in Poland and Romania a vast underground network penetrating virtually all defense industry, transportation infrastructures and at least a part of the local administration of these countries. See RCSSCHD, F. 495, Op. 10a (D. Z. Manuilsky's Secretariat), D. 480, 1. 1–6, 7-12, 20–27.

99. For details, see "The Bulgarian Group's Transfer." Unsigned memo, n.d., 1943—ibid., F. 495, Op. 73, D. 182, 1. 34–37; I. Vinarov, *The Silent Front's Fighters. Recollections of an Intelligence Officer* (Sofia, Bulgaria, 1981), 333–50; 357–61 (in Russian).

100. Training of officers and noncoms for the Communist Polish government and army security forces had been started by the NKVD/NKGB in May 1944 with the sending of 218 Polish officers and men selected by the Red Army Smersh and NKVD Department of Personnel to a special crash course program (2.5 months long). L. Beria to Molotov, August 2, 1944, no. 833/b, t/w copy—SARF, F. 9401, Op. 2, D. 69, 1. 339–42. Later, Gen. N. N. Selivanovsky and M. A. Mel'nikov of the NKGB, with the staff of ten officers, were assigned to serve as official Soviet advisers on counterintelligence matters with the Polish government. V. Chernyshev, deputy people's commissar of interior, commissar of state security 2d Rank, and Army Gen. A. Khruliov, chief, the Red Army Rear, to V. Molotov, June 20, 1945, no. 1/12351, t/w copy; "The Regulations of the Rights and Duties of the Adviser with Ministry of Public Security, Poland," March 16, 1945—ibid., D. 103, 1. 205–6; 109-11. See also Andrew and Gordievsky, *KGB*, 346–49.

101. On the reorganization of Bulgarian security forces, see L. Beria to V. Molotov, February 13, 1945, no. 278/b; A. Yugov, minister of interior, Bulgaria, to L. Beria, January 30, 1945, t/w copies—SARF, F. 9401, Op. 2, D. 103, 1. 95–96.

102. See N. N. Selivanovsky, NKVD adviser with Ministry of Public Security, Poland, to L. Beria, October 10, 1945, no. 1269/b; A. Leontiev, chief, Main Department of Fighting Gangsterism, NKVD, to L. Beria, November 10, 1945, no. 1270/b, t/w copies—ibid., D. 105, 1. 5–9, 10–11; L. Beria to V. Molotov, March 19, 1945, no. 308/b, t/w copy (report on the arrest and deportation to Moscow of Prince Janusz Radziwill and his son as well as Counts Zamoiski, Bronicki, and Krasicki with their families)—ibid., D. 103, 1. 112–13.

103. See, for example, reports on Yugoslavian politics supplied by a leader of the Serbian People Peasant Party Naidenovic; data on underground activities of former Finnish Army intelligence officers, obtained through an NKGB agent in the Finnish police; information on King Michael of Romania's contacts with the Allied Military Missions in Bucharest. P. M. Fitin to L. Beria, November 29, 1945, no. 1334/b; P. M. Fitin to L. Beria, November 28, no. 1333/b; G. Ovakimyan, Timofeev, and Kuznetsov, NKGB Representatives in Bucharest, to L. Beria, March 5, 1945, no. 226/b—SARF, F. 9401, Op. 2, D. 105, 1. 225–27, 223–24; D. 93, 1. 268–72.

104. In May 1944 L. Beria and the people's commissar of shipbuilding, I. Nosenko, addressed V. Molotov, urging him to issue a directive providing the NKVD/NKGB with industrial facilities for production of a vast number of new sophisticated ciphering and deciphering machines "for the Government high frequency communications and special needs of NKVD and NKGB," designed by NKVD's Special Designs Bureau. The first order for 192 machines of various types had to be filled by the end of 1944. L. Beria, I. Nosenko to V. Molotov, May 15, 1944, no. 452/b, t/w copy—SARF, F. 9401, Op. 2, D. 69, 1. 257–61.

105. After the dissolution of the Comintern in May 1943, its Department of International Communications was also disbanded. The DIC infrastructure in the USSR—several radio stations, special radio operators school, shops producing radio equipment and counterfeited documents and IDs—as well as their staffs and personnel were divided between the FCD and the GRU. One can assume that at least part of the DIC's networks abroad was also split between those two agencies. "The Commission on Comintern's Affairs Settlement Resolution," n.d., approximately June/July 1943—RCSSCHD, Fond 495, Op. 73, D. 174, 1. 78–82; Il'ichev (no rank noted), GRU, to G. M. Dimitrov, June 18, 1943, no. 208199, t/w original—ibid., D. 175, 1. 13–17; memorandum, no address, no signature, May 14, 1943 (a list of Comintern's DIC facilities)—ibid., D. 182, 1. 16–27. Some of the DIC functions and primarily that of operational communications between national Communist parties and their representatives in Moscow have been delegated to the newly established Research Institute–100—a new branch of the Central Committee, Communist Party, International Department. "The Commission on Comintern's Affairs Settlement Report," 1. 79.

106. Condemning the Holocaust, the Soviet government during the war paid little attention to the apparent growth of anti-Semitic sentiments in the USSR and

frowned upon the attempts of the Soviet Jewish Antifascist Committee to defend the Jews from acts of discrimination they suffered. Receiving this kind of tacit support on the part of governmental and Communist party officials, many anti-Semites in the Soviet bureaucracy felt fairly secure, and by the end of the war anti-Semitic sentiments and practice became widespread in local government, the Red Army, and various public agencies. See Solomon Michoels, deputy chairman, Schashno Epstein, Itzik Fefer, secretaries, Soviet Jewish Anti-Fascist Committee, to J. Stalin, February 15, 1944, t/w copy—SARF, F. 8114 (Soviet Jewish AFC), Op. 1 (Correspondence with Stalin, Soviet and Party Agencies), D. 792, 1. 34; V. Kruzhkov, executive secretary, Soviet Information Bureau, to Aleksandr S. Shcherbakov, secretary, Central Committee, Communist party, May 11, 1943—ibid., D. 792, 1. 9; S. Michoels, Sh. Epstein to L. Beria, May 26, 1944, t/w copy—ibid., 1. 56.

107. Many facts on the Soviet military buildup in Iran and along the Soviet border with Turkey were reported by American military intelligence in the USSR. See, for example, Brig. Gen. F. Roberts to Gen. Bissel, WDGBI (G-2), November 30, 1945 (a report on Soviet units disposition in North Perisa), and W. A. Harriman to Brig. Gen. F. Roberts, December 30, 1945 (a report on the increasing number of Soviet troops in Leninakan area), PWAH, MF, Box 184, Chron. Files, November 27–30, Box 185, Chron. Files, Dec. 30–31.

108. F. Chuev, *One Hundred and Forty Conversations with Molotov. From the Diary of Felix Chuev* (Moscow, 1991), 76.

109. Ibid., 14, 63, 67, 86, 90, 498.

9. Churchill, the Americans, and Self-Determination

Warren F. Kimball

World War II's proximate cause had been the Nazi determination to crush Poland and the belated commitment of Britain and France to champion Polish aspirations for national self-determination and independence. As World War II wound down, the question of self-determination again advanced to the forefront. Poland's ability to determine its own fate remained an open question, the status of those nations that had attained nationhood in the aftermath of World War I was in jeopardy, and the receding tide of Japanese conquest was making plain both the strength of Asian nationalism and the enervation of European colonial rule. Africa, too, was witnessing manifestations of hunger for self-determination. A pivotal personage in these matters was the intrepid yet anachronistic figure of Britain's wartime leader, Winston S. Churchill.

During World War II, the president of the United States, Franklin D. Roosevelt, and his close advisers routinely expressed concern that his British counterpart, Prime Minister Winston Churchill, held an outmoded and even dangerous worldview. At the root of FDR's distrust was the belief that Churchill, like most British leaders, represented and defended a class-structured society that militated against reform and fairness. British politics might have democratic forms, but class divisions caused that democracy to lack substance.

That conclusion by the Roosevelt administration underlay its concern about two of Churchill's policies: his inclination to think in terms of "spheres of influence" or "power politics" and his outspoken defense of the British Empire—both policies that the Americans often labeled "Victorian."

Even before the two leaders held their first conference, the president expressed concern about the Englishman's antiquated, Victorian views and his excessive drinking. To be fair, Churchill expressed concern—horror might be a better word—about Roosevelt's drinking habits as well, though in this case it was the president's custom of concocting what he called martinis, a mixture of gin with both dry and sweet vermouth, stirred vigorously by FDR himself. Churchill loathed such mixed drinks, once going so far as to spit out a mouthful of what FDR's cousin, Polly Delano, labeled a Tom Collins.[1]

More substantive were Roosevelt's concerns about Churchill's old-fashioned, nineteenth-century views. The prime minister ruefully admitted that "in the White House, I'm taken for a Victorian Tory." Fittingly, when Churchill stayed in the White House he slept in a room decorated with prints of the court of Queen Victoria. New Dealers and Roosevelt himself frequently spoke critically about Churchill's unsympathetic attitude toward the progressive reforms they felt were necessary in the United States—and throughout the world. According to Harry Hopkins, Roosevelt's closest adviser, the president "loves Winston as a man for the war, but is horrified at his reactionary attitude for after the war." Even though Roosevelt balanced that apprehension with the comment, "Isn't he a wonderful old Tory to have on our side," the unmistakable conclusion was that Churchill posed a barrier to the kind of postwar world FDR sought. That certainly was the belief of Eleanor Roosevelt, who told their daughter, Anna, "I like Mr. Churchill, he's lovable and emotional and very human but I don't want him to write the peace or carry it out." But then Eleanor Roosevelt also thought that Franklin was "much in the nineteenth century."[2]

That nineteenth-century image of Britain invariably began with colonialism. Americans opposed European colonialism for two connected but different reasons. One (which, despite its importance, I will only mention in passing) was the conviction that British trade policy, particularly the much-vilified Imperial Preference System, created dangerous and unfair restrictions on international commerce. Little did it matter that World War II had already demonstrated that imperial preference was dying if not dead; Roosevelt and the State Department assumed (in an inheritance from the French philosophers) that international economic interdependence would prevent war. Eliminating empires fit American desires to open all the world to commercial access—"free markets" in the political jargon of the 1990s. "Roosevelt did not confine his dislike of colonialism to the British Empire alone," wrote Anthony Eden, "for it was a principle with him, not the less cherished for its possible advantages."[3] Even in the midst of the Yalta Conference, Roosevelt prodded Churchill to open serious official talks on the matter. The prime minister responded with a vague statement about the usefulness of current informal talks and suggested that the entire question be postponed.[4] That economic liberalism promised tangible benefits for the United States, but Americans had pursued economic liberalism since their Revolution—and the urge cannot be dismissed as merely two centuries of cynicism, whatever American domestic squabbles over tariffs.

Their second objection to colonialism was its denial of self-determination. The American image of Churchill's Victorianism received early confirmation shortly after the announcement of the Atlantic Charter in August 1941, with its call for territorial changes to have "the freely expressed wishes of the peoples concerned" and for "the right of all peoples to choose the[ir] form of government." In each instance, democratic choice was part of the process. For FDR, that included European colonies. Churchill, his attention focused on getting the Americans into the war, had initially assumed that self-determination referred to nations under Hitler's yoke. But he quickly exempted the British Empire, even if Clement Attlee said the Charter applied to "coloured peoples, as well as white." Stalin quickly recognized that self-determination posed a threat to more than just the colonial world. Whatever the extent of his territorial ambitions, the Baltic states and a westward shift in the Soviet-Polish boundary were his "minimum demands," and he excluded the Soviet Union from the self-determination provisions of the Charter.[5]

From the outset of the Grand Alliance, British policy makers understood that Soviet demands for frontiers as negotiated in the Nazi-Soviet Pact gave the USSR territory in violation of the Atlantic Charter—just as the Germans asserted.[6] In late 1941, Eden traveled to Moscow in an attempt to reach an accommodation with Stalin. At the start of the talks, the British foreign secretary tried to avoid recognition of Soviet territorial demands, but once Stalin explained that his nation's western frontier and the Baltic states "[are] really what the whole war is about," Eden decided to support recognition of Soviet claims to those lands, even though the British cabinet had instructed otherwise.[7]

Churchill opposed Eden's proposals and suddenly found the Atlantic Charter and self-determination a convenient way to avoid specific postwar commitments that might give the Soviets something they did not deserve and could not earn. Then, for reasons that must be inferred, in early March 1942 the prime minister told Roosevelt that the Atlantic Charter should not be interpreted to deny the Soviet Union the boundaries it had when Germany attacked since that was the understanding when Stalin accepted the Charter. Perhaps the explanation for Churchill's reversal is found in the final paragraph of his cable to the president where, with seeming casualness, he raised the issue of India.[8]

The joining of the two themes was neither new nor accidental. A few months earlier one of Churchill's favorites, Lord Beaverbrook, had made a similar connection. After labeling the Baltic states "the Ireland of Russia"— an analogy pregnant with hints of disloyalty and vexations for Churchill— Beaverbrook argued that the "strict application" of the Atlantic Charter "would be a menace to our own safety as well as to that of Russia. It would involve us among other things in the surrender of Gibraltar to the Spaniards," a reference designed to play on Churchill's contempt and anger toward Spain, just in case the Irish ploy failed to work.[9]

Whatever Roosevelt's preference for self-determination, he also had to deal with a wartime alliance and the hope of a postwar "family circle," as he later termed the Great Power relationship. At least briefly in spring 1942, FDR considered letting the Soviets get the Baltic states, eastern Poland, Bukovina, and Bessarabia, musing that he would not mind if that happened. Reminded that the Atlantic Charter might have something to say about that, he took the thought no further.[10]

Churchill, uncomfortable with anything that expanded Soviet influence, soon changed his mind again. In May 1942, he summarized his talks in London with Soviet Foreign Minister V. M. Molotov, assuring Roosevelt that Britain had avoided making any territorial concessions to the Russians. The proposals for an Anglo-Soviet treaty are, wrote Churchill, "entirely compatible with our Atlantic Charter."[11] But an issue that was "really what the whole war is about" would not go away so easily.

Ultimately, Roosevelt and Churchill themselves undermined the self-determination principle of the Atlantic Charter by agreeing that the Soviet Union retain the basic shape of its Nazi-Soviet Pact boundaries. That process began as soon as Stalin heard of the Charter and continued throughout the war, culminating in the Churchill-Stalin (Tolstoy) talks of October 1944, the famous percentages deal whereby Churchill found a way to justify and arrange a spheres-of-influence settlement in Eastern Europe, from Greece to the Baltics—arrangements Roosevelt accepted. Yalta merely added some cosmetics to the agreement. Roosevelt's praise of plebiscites as "one of the few successful outcomes of the Versailles Treaty" may have been sincere in 1941, but by the end of the war, plebiscites had become a convenient means of providing the image of self-determination without having to confront the Soviets in Eastern Europe. Even Cordell Hull, disinclined to get involved in what he called the "piddling little things" of Eastern Europe, publicly stated in April 1944 that the major postwar goal was to provide security and to prevent aggression, and "the Atlantic charter did not prevent any step including those relating to enemy States to achieve these goals."[12]

The other side of self-determination, decolonization, came up in Anglo-American relations even before the United States entered the war. In spring 1941, Hull suggested self-government for India; then the Atlantic Charter with its promise of self-determination indirectly raised the issue a few months later. The United States, with its own colonies, certainly practiced (what one historian has called) a "combination of populism and arrogance" regarding European empires, even if Roosevelt had scheduled independence for the Philippines as soon as the war ended (as FDR constantly reminded Churchill). But that did not stop Americans from believing that colonialism, with its closed economic systems and political repression, would generate future wars.[13]

The intensity of American views prompted FDR to raise the issue with Churchill even while the U.S. Pacific Fleet still lay burning in Pearl Harbor. When Churchill visited Washington immediately after the Japanese attack, Roosevelt directly confronted him about a timetable for Indian independence. We have only Churchill's boast on the substance of the remarks: "The President . . . discussed the Indian problem with me, on the usual American lines. . . . I reacted so strongly and at such length that he never raised it verbally again."[14] The prime minister claimed to have responded as he did whenever such proposals surfaced, with angry arguments that the Americans did not understand the bitter Muslim-Hindu feud, that only the Muslims (the minority) had proved effective as soldiers, and that he would resign before he would "yield an inch of the territory that was under the British flag."[15]

At times, Churchill played the British bulldog more as a terrier, substituting angry barking and bravado in an attempt to cover weakness. The president may not have raised Indian independence again with him face to face—FDR later told Stalin that discussing India with the Englishman was a waste of time. But Roosevelt, convinced that colonialism's day was over, never quit trying to push and persuade the British to beat the inevitable to the punch—to choose devolution over revolution. He insisted in January 1942 that India sign the wartime alliance pact, grandly titled the Declaration by the United Nations—a title that FDR took credit for, particularly once it became the name for the United Nations Organization.[16] Shortly thereafter, he unleashed Chinese leader Chiang Kai-shek, who visited India and suggested that the Indians would fight more effectively against Japan if Britain promised independence. At the same time, the president opened a second front against colonialism by instructing his representatives in London, Averell Harriman and "Gil" Winant, to "get a slant" on Churchill's thinking about a changed relationship between India and Britain. All this came in the wake of the humiliating British defeat at Singapore—to an army of "little yellow men." When later talks with Indian Congress leaders collapsed, Churchill "danced around the Cabinet room. No tea with treason [he said], no truck with American or British Labour sentimentality, but back to the solemn—and exciting—business of war."[17]

Of course Britain was not without sin. In Syria, a French protectorate since World War I, Britain encouraged the Free French to make commitments to independence so as to prevent popular uprisings and to promote Syrian opposition to German schemes. Free French leader Charles de Gaulle rejected British interference and accused the English of having designs on the French

Empire. When his officials arrested Syrian nationalists elected to office on an independence platform, the prime minister piously told FDR that "there is no doubt in my mind that this is a foretaste of what de Gaulle's leadership of France means. It is certainly contrary to the Atlantic Charter and much else that we have declared."[18] One French historian put the dispute in words that could have come from the general himself: "Even after Free French administrations were installed in French territories like Syria, Lebanon or North Africa, relations with the British were less than cordial. This was not only because local would-be Lawrences harboured secret designs of supplanting the French, or even because the British military . . . never quite understood de Gaulle's political importance. . . . It was above all because . . . it could well be necessary to thwart the French in order to propitiate the natives."[19] Neither then nor later in the war could Churchill or Roosevelt solve, or dismiss, the twin dilemmas of self-determination—Eastern Europe and colonial empires. Even postponement had its perils.

The problem of Soviet intentions crystallized around the issue of self-determination. Self-determination for European colonies was awkward and menacing to the British but did not threaten the Great Power cooperation that FDR hoped for, since Britain's stake in postwar cooperation with the United States was too crucial to jeopardize. Moreover, colonial boundaries seemed clear (even if that proved deceptive). But by 1943, with the Germans stopped and the tide about to turn on the Russian front, European frontiers and self-determination became a major issue. As Woodrow Wilson had learned at Paris, Europe's boundary questions came burdened with irreconcilable pieces of historical baggage. At the same time, persuading Stalin to be a cooperative player in the postwar world required that he feel secure, satisfied, and sure of Anglo-American reliability. But self-determination for Lithuanians, Latvians, and Estonians—not to mention significant elements of Poles, Bulgarians, Finns, Hungarians, and Romanians—was quite a different story, for Stalin had made clear from the outset that his territorial demands included large groups of those peoples.

If self-determination meant independence for the Balts and the establishment of an anti-Soviet government in Warsaw, then how could one avoid the obvious? By February 1943, the Stalingrad battle had demonstrated the possibility, even the likelihood, of Red Army occupation of the territory Stalin demanded. What recourse was left to London and Washington? Military confrontation was no option, at least not with Anglo-American forces still struggling in North Africa and an invasion of Western Europe fifteen months away. More to the point, British and American military leaders had long since concluded that the defeat of Germany, as opposed to merely halting Hitler's expansion, required the Soviet army.[20]

And what long-term hope for peace existed if the United States and Britain chose to confront the Russians? Perhaps the atomic bomb eventually changed that calculation, but that weapon was two years away. Then there was Japan waiting in the wings.

Thus the Americans and British agreed, despite their significant differences about tactics, to make the best of the situation. Rather than fruitlessly opposing any expansion of Soviet power in Eastern Europe, they opted to continue to promote long-term cooperation. As Roosevelt and Undersecretary of State Sumner Welles told Eden in 1943, "The real decisions should be made by the United States, Great Britain, Russia and China, who would be the powers for many years to come that would have to police the world." Self-determination would, quite obviously, be a gift from the Big Four, assuming they could agree on the details.[21]

FDR's Four Policemen would also act as trustees for colonial societies not ready for full independence (a category that Roosevelt seemed to apply to almost every colony). The Pacific islands held by the Japanese (usually former League of Nations mandates), Korea (despite its being independent for centuries before the United States existed), and Indochina were his favorite examples. When he spoke to Eden of trusteeships for Japan's Pacific island empire, French Indochina, and Portuguese Timor, the foreign secretary knew the president meant all European empires. With Hong Kong in mind, Eden was dubious about Chinese intentions, commenting that "he 'did not much like the idea of the Chinese running up and down the Pacific,'" and he questioned whether Kuomintang leader Chiang Kai-shek would survive the civil war that would surely follow Japan's defeat.[22]

Nor was Churchill prepared to elevate China to world-power status. Not only did that fly in the face of reality—China was far from a modern power and faced civil war—but that would provide [Churchill wrote] "a faggot vote on the side of the United States in any attempt to liquidate the overseas British Empire."[23] The mirage of an Anglo-American world that had appeared briefly at the Churchill-Roosevelt talks in Casablanca was fading.

That is not to say, as some have, that Roosevelt's "hopes for his brave new world rested largely on the Soviets, not upon the fading and reactionary power of the British Empire."[24] Roosevelt did not dismiss Britain as some sort of minor player. If Britain was a "junior partner," it was still a partner in what was a very limited partnership. FDR's thinking about the postwar world required that the British exercise the responsibilities of a great power. In fact, Roosevelt and the Americans routinely exaggerated the wealth of Great Britain and its empire. Britain's military image had suffered during World War II, but economic strength and political savvy would be the elements of power in the disarmed world Roosevelt imagined.

Churchill concluded, paradoxically, that the Americans would act too vigorously to defend self-determination in Asia and too weakly to defend it in Eastern Europe. As he saw it, that was an old American pattern: activism in Asia, isolationism in Europe. Roosevelt's calls for Britain to grant independence to its empire posed as great a threat to British interests as Soviet expansion into Eastern Europe. That conclusion brought Churchill to make not only the "percentages" deal at the Tolstoy talks in Moscow in autumn 1944 but also to raise with Stalin the issue of Britain's place in East Asia, specifically China.

The prime minister sought Stalin's support, or at least neutrality, in a region of intensifying nationalism, by suggesting concessions that should go to the Soviet Union in the Far East. The deal between Stalin and Churchill was implied, not the sort of explicit, spheres-of-influence arrangement they had made over Greece and Romania; but the approach was the same. The Soviet Union should have "effective rights at Port Arthur," said Churchill. Why worry about Soviet naval power in the Far East, he told his Chiefs of Staff; the Soviet fleet was "vastly inferior" and would be "hostages to the stronger Naval Powers." More important, he said, "Any claim by Russia for indemnity at the expense of China, would be favourable to our resolve about Hong Kong." The Hong Kong issue led Churchill quickly to instruct that no agreements be reached with the United States to oppose a "restoration of Russia's position in the Far East," and the Americans were, apparently, not apprised of the understanding.

Churchill's fears that the Americans would oppose such territorial deals proved groundless. Four months later at Yalta, Roosevelt worked out a Far Eastern settlement with Stalin that paralleled the quid pro quo Churchill had floated at Moscow, but FDR's reasons were a bit different. Primarily, the Soviet Union's entry into what everyone expected to be a long and bloody war against Japan had always been framed to include something for Russia. Roosevelt had no doubt Stalin would live up to his promise, so long as the United States and Great Britain lived up to theirs. Beyond that, FDR was, like Churchill, concerned about China. But it was the impending conflict between Mao and Chiang, not the decolonization of Hong Kong, that worried the president. He hoped to persuade Stalin not to support the Chinese Communists, thereby giving the Kuomintang a chance to consolidate its rule. The danger was that Chiang's chance would come at the expense of Chinese sovereignty and territory—elements of self-determination—running the risk of alienating the nationalism that Chiang had to harness in order to survive. It may be that Roosevelt sought to eliminate British influence from northern China when he suggested privately to Stalin that they exclude Britain from the occupation of Korea. But that latter proposal was more likely aimed at preventing Britain from being a "trustee" responsible for tutoring Korea (or any other nation) to be independent. Stalin, careful to follow his arrangements with Churchill, warned that "the Prime Minister might 'kill us' " and suggested consulting him.[25] But whatever the differences in motives between Roosevelt and Churchill, and despite Churchill's later denials, they both gave positive endorsement to the commitments made to Stalin in return for Soviet entry into the war against Japan.[26]

But China was only part of the challenge raised by Asian nationalism. Roosevelt had steadily pursued his campaign against European colonial empires throughout the war, Churchill's braggadocio to the contrary notwithstanding. In countless ways, FDR kept the pressure on Churchill and the leaders of other European colonial powers to begin the process of decolonization. Roosevelt pushed one of his favorites, Dutch Queen Wilhelmina ("Minnie" he called her, with militant casualness), to begin the process of granting self-government to the Netherlands East Indies. But she would have none of it. She told FDR that Java could, perhaps, become independent in something between fifteen and fifty years, but anything for the backward areas was "'sheer speculation.'" The president did not push the issue, leading the Dutch to believe that he agreed to a restoration of their control.[27]

But the Dutch confused politeness with agreement. Roosevelt was convinced that the pressure of self-determination in the European empires was a most serious threat to postwar peace. Yet he believed that the Europeans had time—perhaps as long as twenty-five or thirty years—to prepare for colonial independence, so long as they made public commitments to self-determination and established some sort of schedule for devolution. He more than once offered the British a history lesson based on the American experience with their Articles of Confederation after the American Revolution. Churchill mocked the analogy, but missed the point (as have so many historians). Decolonization was inevitable, Roosevelt believed. "India is not yet ready for home government," he told the Pacific War Council. "That takes time. The training of thousands of persons over a number of years is necessary for good government." That, he explained, the United States had learned through trial and error during the era of the Articles of Confederation.[28]

American policy did not create the desire for self-determination. General de Gaulle gave the United States too much credit (or blame) when he claimed it had forced the Dutch "to renounce their sovereignty over Java." Independence for India, Indonesia, and most of the colonial world came primarily from the demands of the native peoples, not because of anything done or said by the United States. By the end of World War II, the Asian colonies were neither Europe's to lose, nor America's to win—or to destabilize. Nationalism could not be denied—though it could be delayed.[29]

But Churchill remained adamant in his defense, arguing that "the British alone had managed to combine Empire and Liberty." In December 1944, he instructed Eden that " 'Hands off the British Empire' is our maxim, and it must not be weakened or smirched to please sob-stuff merchants at home or foreigners of any hue." Holding on to the empire was part of why Britain had gone to war. Hitler had challenged British interests in Europe, but Japan was a direct rival for empire in Asia. Moreover, Japan's conquests had given Indian nationalists an opportunity to use the war as leverage for independence. Churchill's contempt for the Indians, heightened by what he viewed as treasonous demands that Britain "quit India" as the price of support for the war, only strengthened his resolve. India was the very symbol of the empire, and he would not negotiate that symbol away. A number of other British leaders had begun to rethink the question of empire, but Churchill and Eden invariably blocked American efforts to conduct direct Great Power discussions about colonialism.[30]

With the instincts of a politician, Roosevelt had focused his attack against colonialism on two very visible examples—British India and French Indochina. Churchill and the British government had rejected FDR's prompting about India ("pitiless publicity" was how the president described his own tactic), although the ruthless suppression of Indian nationalists, which had required over fifty battalions in addition to police forces, had the effect Roosevelt expected—heightened and angry nationalism.

That left Indochina, which, as early as May 1942 the president had held up as an example of colonial mismanagement. Exploitation and indifference had, he told the Pacific War Council, left the natives unprepared for self-government and in need of major reform. He and Stalin had agreed at Tehran that the colony should not be returned to French rule, and FDR made sure that Churchill learned of that conversation.[31]

But the prime minister and his government would have no part of a piece-meal attack on colonial empires. If France could be kept out of Indochina, then India, Burma, and other parts of the British Empire were next. Moreover, the Foreign Office argued strenuously, Britain needed a strong and co-operative France in order to have a secure position in Europe—and General de Gaulle's conditions for cooperation began with retention of the French Empire. Churchill counseled against any discussions with Roosevelt about Indochina until after the presidential election of November 1944, but the British military had already that summer begun to integrate French military and political personnel into their Southeast Asian Command, headed by Adm. Louis Mountbatten. The president refused to recognize the French presence and rejected proposals to provide transport or supplies for the French in Indochina. But he could not force them out without British cooperation.[32]

Had empire been the only thing at stake, Roosevelt could have put near-irresistible pressure on the British to block the French in Indochina and to make specific commitments to the Indian nationalists—commitments that would have set a powerful precedent for other independence movements. But FDR's first prerequisite for avoiding another world war was Great Power cooperation—his Four Policemen—and Britain was to be one of those policemen. Without the British playing that role, the system the president imagined could not work. He had managed to use agreements on postwar economics and international organization (Bretton Woods and Dumbarton Oaks) to keep cooperation as an option, but alienating the British over empire in Southeast Asia, particularly with Churchill openly emotional on the issue, might push them toward the narrow regionalism that FDR feared would only re-create the tensions that had led to two world wars.

Had China been ready and able to play the role of Great Power, Roosevelt would have had more options. But that society was about to plunge into civil war. Moreover, Roosevelt's designated policeman, Chiang Kai-shek, seemed all too inclined himself to expand into Southeast Asia at the expense of Britain and France. With FDR believing that "three generations of education and training would be required before China could be a serious [political] factor," he was left with little faith in the willingness or ability of either Chiang or Mao to play a "responsible" role. With no American military force scheduled to move onto the continent in East or Southeast Asia, and with China needing "tutelage" before it could play the role of responsible policeman, Roosevelt's only option was to have the Europeans reclaim their empires. Self-determination in Eastern Europe had to be postponed in order to bring the Soviet Union into the "family circle." Now expediency seemed to require a similar compromise in Southeast Asia.[33]

FDR was, in his own way, as stubborn as Churchill. For the president, decolonization had always been a process, not an immediate act. His patience and belief in the superiority of American institutions brought him to conclude that most colonies would need long periods of benevolent guidance (what he called trusteeships) before they could govern themselves. He agreed, for example, with State Department arguments that Korea might require a forty-year training period because the thirty-five-year Japanese occupation had politically "emasculated" Koreans and left them without experience in self-government. The idea of lengthy trusteeships tended to be FDR's catch-all answer for any difficult territorial problem, as in the case of the Croatians and Serbs.[34] That kind of paternalism did not take into account the intensity of nationalism, but FDR's willingness to wait for the internal development of what Americans call democracy distinguishes Roosevelt's foreign policy from the experiments in nation-building promoted by his cold war successors.

These considerations led Roosevelt to a tactic. He had long proposed that the lengthy process of preparation for self-government be done under the supervision of international "trustees." He could modify that to allow the Europeans back into their Asian empires but only if their actions as "trustees" would be monitored by the new international organization—the United Nations. FDR backed away from any strenuous confrontation with Britain, or with France by proxy, lest that jeopardize his plans for Great Power cooperation; but he consistently argued for the colonial masters to become colonial trustees, accountable to an international community in which the United States would be a dominant force. What Roosevelt feared, and with good historical reasons, was that if the colonial powers were left to decide when their colonies were "ready" for self-government, they would act the way "Minnie" had spoken: the Europeans would drag their feet, set one ethnic group against another, and do whatever they could to spin a web of control around their colonies before granting even the facade of self-determination.[35]

But Roosevelt never backed away from believing that a smooth, nonviolent transition from empire to independence for Europe's colonies was key to creating a peaceful world, even if he could not prevent the Europeans from reclaiming their Asian empires. He spoke patronizingly of the Asians: "The Indochinese were people of small stature," he told Stalin, "and were not warlike." But that silly statement did not mean he abandoned them to colonialism. When the British secretary of state for colonies, Oliver Stanley, visited Washington late in the war, Roosevelt restated his conviction that European empires would disappear. Indochina would not be returned to France, he said, but would be "administered by a group of nations selected by the United Nations." The movement toward self-determination was irresistible, thought FDR, whether in Burma, the Netherlands East Indies, or even British Gambia and French Morocco. And the United States would support that movement.[36]

Asian nationalism—East European nationalism: here were two movements in the same symphony. Stalin had good reason to fear that the people of Eastern Europe (as he put it) "all wanted something of their own."[37] The Red Army may often have been greeted as liberators, but as Soviet political commissars moved in that welcome faded quickly—sometimes because they were Communists but *always* because they were agents of a "foreign" government in Moscow.

The Pacific war, fought where colonial empires were at issue, complicated the European question—more for Roosevelt than for Churchill. British concerns were defensive: hold on to India, "liberate" Singapore and Malaya, keep Hong Kong, and insulate Britain's Asian empire from any sort of international accountability. Over time, Stalin's crude behavior in Poland and

Eastern Europe would only have helped Churchill's campaign to persuade Roosevelt that British colonialism was far preferable to Soviet domination—as indeed happened in the decade following World War II when the United States "gave priority to anti-communism over anti-colonialism," helping the Europeans to spin the very webs of control that FDR had tried to prevent.[38]

During the Yalta talks, the Soviets accepted the trusteeship principle and wanted it included in the Charter of the United Nations Organization. But when the president brought up the general concept, Churchill predictably exploded in protest: "I absolutely disagree. . . . After we have done our best to fight in this war and have done no crime to anyone I will have no suggestion that the British Empire is to be put into the dock and examined by everybody to see whether it is up to their standard."[39] The president had Stettinius explain to the prime minister that the whole system was "voluntary" except for the defeated Axis nations. But Roosevelt's notion of "voluntary" was different from Churchill's. When it came to trusteeships, FDR told a group of reporters, "Stalin liked the idea. China liked the idea. The British don't like it. It might bust up their empire, because if the Indo-Chinese were to work together and eventually get their independence, the Burmese might do the same thing to the King of England." But there was a bit of bluster in those comments, for he quickly added that "it would only make the British mad. Better to keep quiet just now." Britain was a Great Power, and the Great Powers had to get along.[40]

Nationalism frequently incorporated social reform as part of its appeal, often making it seem revolutionary to the Anglo-Americans. In Greece, republicanism and the "left" expropriated nationalism.[41] In France, it coalesced in the person of Charles de Gaulle, who, with single-minded intensity, rekindled French pride and self-respect after the debacle of 1940. In the colonial world, particularly in South and Southeast Asia, Japanese and American propaganda reinforced long-repressed desires for self-determination. In China, while the civil war between Chiang and Mao remained in suspended animation, both protagonists worked to don the mantle of Chinese nationalism. In Eastern Europe, Polish self-determination became for many in the west the litmus test of Soviet intentions. Even in Italy, where British-sponsored and American-sponsored politicians vied for power, the maneuvering took on the cloak of republicanism and self-determination.

Republicanism, pride, independence, self-determination—all were expressions of the nationalism that challenged Great Power cooperation and control. Power at the service of ideology, and vice versa, would come to dominate the Soviet-western relationship after World War II; but nationalism, particularly in its guise of self-determination, played a crucial role in preventing the extension of wartime cooperation into the postwar world. In

Eastern Europe and, more briefly, in Asia, that self-determination was frustrated, in the process helping to create and solidify the Soviet-western split. Thus the last months and weeks of World War II in Europe witnessed the visible widening of that chasm between nationalistic aspirations and Great Power preoccupations that was to signify for more than four decades what became known as the cold war.

NOTES

1. Churchill's Victorianism is discussed in W. F. Kimball, *The Juggler: Franklin Roosevelt as a Wartime Statesman* (Princeton: Princeton University Press, 1991), 66–67, and seen as an asset by David Jablonsky in *Churchill, the Great Game and Total War* (London: Frank Cass, 1991). On FDR's fears of Churchill's drinking habits, see Michael Beschloss, *Kennedy and Roosevelt* (New York: Norton, 1980), 200. When Roosevelt and Canadian prime minister Mackenzie King met in April 1940, they spent much of the time gossiping about Churchill's drinking; J. L. Granatstein, *Canada's War* (Toronto: Oxford, 1975), 117. When Churchill became prime minister, Roosevelt commented he "supposed Churchill was the best man that England had, even if he was drunk half of his time" (David Reynolds and David Dimbleby, *An Ocean Apart* [New York: Random House, 1988], 136). Wendell Willkie, asked by Roosevelt in 1941 if Churchill was a drunk, replied that he had as much to drink as Churchill did when they met, "and no one has ever called me a drunk." See Kimball, *The Juggler*, 225–26, n.6. The Roosevelt martini is described with distaste by Charles Bohlen, *Witness to History, 1929–1969* (New York: Norton, 1973), 143. See Robert Sherwood, *Roosevelt and Hopkins*, rev. ed. (New York, 1950), 115, for some other "vile" concoctions, and G. Ward, ed., *Closest Companion: The Unknown Story of the Intimate Friendship Between Franklin Roosevelt and Margaret Suckley* (Boston and New York: Houghton Mifflin, 1995), 163, for a story of Churchill spitting out a mouthful of what FDR's cousin, Polly Delano, made with different kinds of rum and labeled a Tom Collins.

2. Lord Moran, *Churchill: Taken from the Diaries of Lord Moran* (Boston: Houghton Mifflin, 1966), entry for February 5, 1945, 240. See also Ted Morgan, *FDR* (London: Collins, Grafton Books, 1986), 759. Averell Harriman claimed that Roosevelt saw Churchill as "pretty much a nineteenth century colonialist" (Averell Harriman and Elie Abel, *Special Envoy to Churchill and Stalin, 1941–1946* [New York: Random House, 1975], 191). Sherwood describes Churchill's White House quarters (*Roosevelt and Hopkins*, 203). For the concerns of New Dealers see, for example, the diaries of Henry Morgenthau Jr., at the Franklin D. Roosevelt Library (FDRL) Hyde Park, N.Y., or the diaries of Assistant Secretary of State Adolf Berle, *Navigating the Rapids*, ed. Beatrice Bishop Berle and Travis Beal Jacobs (New York: Harcourt Brace Jovanovich, 1973). See also Fraser Harbutt, *The Iron Curtain* (New York: Oxford University Press, 1986), esp. 15–19. FDR's "wonderful old Tory" comment is from John Gunther, *Roosevelt in Retrospect* (New York: Harper, 1950), 16; Doris Goodwin, *No*

Ordinary Time (New York: Simon and Schuster, 1994), 312, quotes Mrs. Roosevelt's letter to Anna; Frank Freidel, *Franklin D. Roosevelt* (Boston: Little Brown, 1990), quotes Eleanor Roosevelt's quip about FDR in the nineteenth century; Oliver Harvey, *The War Diaries of Oliver Harvey*, ed. John Harvey (London: Collins, 1978), 228 (March 11, 1943).

3. Anthony Eden, *The Reckoning* (Boston: Houghton Mifflin, 1965), 593.

4. See Randall Woods, *A Changing of the Guard* (Chapel Hill: University of North Carolina Press, 1989); and W. F. Kimball, "U.S. Economic Strategy in World War II," in *American Unbound*, ed. W. F. Kimball, (New York: St. Martin's Press, 1992; W. F. Kimball, ed., *Churchill and Roosevelt*, 3 vols. (Princeton: Princeton University Press, 1984), 3: R–707/1 (February 10, 1945) and C–899/3 (February 13, 1945).

5. The Charter began with the declaration that neither the United States nor Britain sought additional territory—a disavowal of the kind of secret treaties that had stimulated the territorial scramble following World War I. But while that injunction against self-aggrandizement aimed at quieting the American anti-interventionists, it also fell under the broad rubric of self-determination. The Atlantic Charter is printed in U.S. Department of State, *Foreign Relations of the United States [FRUS]* (Washington, D.C.: GPO, 1862–) 1941, 1: 367–69. Attlee's comments are from the *London Daily Herald*, August 16, 1941, as quoted in William Roger Louis, *Imperialism at Bay* (New York: Oxford University Press, 1978), 19–20.

6. John J. Sbrega, *Anglo-American Relations and Colonialism in East Asia, 1941–1945* (New York: Garland, 1983), 29.

7. Lloyd C. Gardner puts the negotiations for an Anglo-Soviet Treaty in perspective in "A Tale of Three Cities: Tripartite Diplomacy and the Second Front, 1941–1942," in *Soviet–U.S. Relations, 1933–1942*, ed. G. Sevost'ianov and W. F. Kimball (Moscow: Progress Publishers, 1989), 104–20. Some have suggested that Eden's policy of accommodation toward Stalin was what Cadogan, who had drafted portions of the Atlantic Charter, sarcastically labeled the "Volga Charter." See Gabriel Gorodetsky, "Origins of the Cold War," *Russian Review* 47 (1988): 166, for the "Volga Charter" as proposed by Eden. However, it may be that the phrase refers to Eden's initial plan to avoid discussions of frontiers and reparations in favor of British promises to aid in reconstructing the USSR after the war. Eden's notion of having the major powers agree not to dominate the nations of Central and Eastern Europe—a "self-denying ordinance"—may also have been part of those early proposals. See Gardner, "Tale of Three Cities, and references in Harvey, *War Diaries*, 63; and David Dilks, ed., *The Diaries of Sir Alexander Cadogan* (New York: G. P. Putnam's Sons, 1972), 414. See also G. Gorodetsky, *Stafford Cripps' Mission to Moscow, 1940–1942* (Cambridge: Cambridge University Press, 1984), 271. The "self-denying ordinance" was part of Eden's diplomacy at the Moscow Foreign Ministers Conference in autumn 1943(See Kimball, *The Juggler*, 94–95).

8. By January 1942, Eden had enlisted the British ambassador in the United States, Edward Lord Halifax, into a campaign to convince Churchill to agree to letting the Soviets have the Baltic states. See Halifax to Churchill, January 11, 1942; Halifax to Eden, January 18, 1942; and Eden to Halifax, January 22, 1942, all in FO

954/29xc/100818 (US/42/5–7), United Kingdom, Public Record Office (PRO), Kew, England. The story, called "A Dismal Tale," is told by Steven M. Miner, *Between Churchill and Stalin* (Chapel Hill: University of North Carolina Press, 1988), 194–213 (for Stalin's comment about the importance of his frontiers, see 190). Miner argues that repossessing the Baltic states was one of Stalin's basic policy goals; see his "Stalin's 'Minimum Conditions' and the Military Balance, 1941–1942," in Sevost'ianov and Kimball, eds., *Soviet–U.S. Relations*, 72–87. Churchill's message is in Kimball, ed., *Churchill & Roosevelt*, 1: C–40, March 7, 1942. Martin Gilbert, *Road to Victory* (Boston: Houghton Mifflin, 1986), 72, attributes the prime minister's shift on Soviet domination of the Baltic states to the pressure of British military defeats, particularly the abandonment of Rangoon, Burma, on March 6. Those setbacks made the prime minister "fully aware" of the need to have good relations with the Soviet Union. Alfred Duff Cooper, then a member of the cabinet as chancellor of the Duchy of Lancaster, warned that recognition of Soviet incorporation of the Baltics would "tear into ribbons the Atlantic Charter and brand us as the arch hypocrites of the world" (Duff Cooper to Eden, April 22, 1942, FO 954/25A/100731, PRO).

9. Memo to the War Cabinet, "Policy Towards Russia," January 31, 1942, FO 954/25A/100731, PRO. Beaverbrook was British minister of supply at the time.

10. Berle and Jacobs, eds., *Navigating the Rapids*, April 30, 1942, 412. This may be the source of the charge that FDR had been ready in early April to accede to Soviet territorial demands but that Hull persuaded him to wait until war's end, as argued by Robert A. Divine, *Roosevelt and World War II* (New York: Penguin Books, 1970), 89–91: "Hull's insistence on adhering to the Atlantic Charter, laudable in principle, undermined Roosevelt's efforts to assuage Russian distrust of the West and strengthen the wartime alliance. . . . In 1942, Roosevelt seemed to be indecisive and hesitant in his diplomacy, allowing others to impose their will on him. As a result, he failed to achieve a sound basis for wartime relations with the Soviet Union." Hugh Phillips, "Mission to America: Maksim M. Litvinov in the United States, 1941–1943," *Diplomatic History* 12, 3 (summer 1988): 269, quotes a message from Litvinov to Narkomindel March 12, 1942 (published in Russian) to the effect that FDR would not object to an arrangement between the USSR and the U.K., presumably (according to Phillips) on the border issue regarding the Baltics, so long as the arrangement was informal and not public. Roosevelt's reference to the "family circle" is in *FRUS, Tehran*, 487.

11. Kimball, ed., *Churchill and Roosevelt*, 1: C–89, May 27, 1942.

12. See Kimball, *The Juggler*, quotes on 95, 183; Lloyd C. Gardner, *Spheres of Influence* (Chicago: Ivan Dee, 1993); Sbrega, *Anglo-American Relations and Colonialism*, 30. During the British intervention in Greece in late 1944/early 1945, Churchill complained that Americans did not understand that British actions were, in fact, securing the ideals of the Atlantic Charter for the Greeks, who were threatened by a Communist dictatorship (Gilbert, *Road to Victory*, 1147). The cosmetic value of plebiscites was recognized by Anthony Eden in December 1941, when he suggested "arranging the necessary vote" in the Baltic states to sanction Soviet control (Miner, *Between Churchill and Stalin*, 194–97).

Soviet frontiers were not the only barrier to reconciling Atlantic Charter practice and principle. Roosevelt recommended to his military chiefs of staff to consider that Churchill's proposal for dealing with a collapse of the Italian regime failed to mention self-determination, and the basic American argument (often with Churchill in agreement) regarding de Gaulle was that the Frenchman had not secured public support in any formal way. But those were side issues, however illustrative of the dilemma.

13. D. C. Watt, "American Anti-Colonialist Policies and the End of the European Colonial Empires, 1941–1962," in *Contagious Conflict: The Impact of American Dissent on European Life*, ed. A. N. J. Den Hollander (Leiden: E. J. Brill, 1973) 93–125, condemns American hypocrisy. John Charmley, *Churchill's Grand Alliance* (London: Hodder and Stoughton, 1995), agrees but is more concerned with condemning the prime minister for supposedly subordinating British interests to an alliance with the Americans. Robert Vitalis, "The 'New Deal' in Egypt: The Rise of Anglo-American Commercial Competition in World War II and the Fall of Neocolonialism," *Diplomatic History* 20 (spring 1996): 211–39, offers Egypt as an exception where American anticolonialism provided Egyptian commercial leaders an opportunity to throw off British economic control.

14. Winston S. Churchill, *The Hinge of Fate* (Boston: Houghton Mifflin, 1950), 209.

15. Churchill used those words when, talking to the American ambassador to China in March 1945, the prime minister defended British control over Hong Kong (Louis, *Imperialism at Bay*, 548).

16. *FRUS, Tehran*, 486. Samuel Rosenman, *Working with Roosevelt* (New York: Da Capo, 1972), 316–17; Ward, ed., *Closest Companion*, 384–85; Sherwood, *Roosevelt and Hopkins*, 453.

17. David Reynolds, *The Creation of the Anglo-American Alliance, 1937–1941* (Chapel Hill: University of North Carolina Press, 1982), 249; Christopher Andrew, *For the President's Eyes Only* (New York: HarperCollins, 1995), 121–22; John Dower, *War Without Mercy* (New York: Pantheon, 1986), 100–102, 105. Churchill is quoted in Kimball, *The Juggler*, 134.

18. Kimball, ed., *Churchill and Roosevelt*, 2: C–504, November 13, 1943.

19. Francois Kersaudy, "Churchill and de Gaulle," in *Winston Churchill: Studies in Statesmanship*, ed. R. A. C. Parker (London and Washington: Brassey's, 1995), 127.

20. See W. F. Kimball, "Stalingrad: A Chance for Choices," *Journal of Military History* 60 (January 1996): 89–114.

21. *FRUS, 1943*, 3: 39.

22. Eden, *The Reckoning*, 437; Sherwood, *Roosevelt and Hopkins*, 716; Llewellyn Woodward, *British Foreign Policy in the Second World War*, 5 vols. (London: HMSO, 1970–1976) 5: 36. For additional discussions of China, see *FRUS, 1943*, 3: 36–38; Eden, *The Reckoning*, 440.

23. Churchill, *The Hinge of Fate*, 562.

24. Charmley, *Churchill's Grand Alliance*, 74.

25. Diane Clemens, *Yalta* (New York: Oxford University Press, 1970), 244–52; *FRUS, Yalta Conference*, 770; Soviet troops entered Korea before Japan surrendered. The United States agreed to dividing occupation duties (thus dividing the country),

although Truman thought about trying to exclude the Russians (William Stueck, *The Road to Confrontation* [Chapel Hill: University of North Carolina Press, 1981], 21); Bruce Cumings, *The Origins of the Korean War* (Princeton: Princeton University Press, 1981).

26. Churchill minute to Eden and the COS Committee, October 23, 1944, M.1024/4, Churchill Papers; Winston S. Churchill, *The Second World War*, 6 vols. (Boston: Houghton Mifflin, 1946–1954), 6: 389–90; *FRUS, Yalta Conference*, 984. Churchill makes no mention of this quid pro quo in his war memoirs, though he discusses Stalin's commitment to join the war against Japan; *WSC*, 6: 236–37. I have found no evidence of a Churchill-Roosevelt agreement (or disagreement) prior to the Yalta talks regarding Far Eastern concessions to the USSR.

27. Albert E. Kersten, "Wilhelmina and Franklin D. Roosevelt: A Wartime Relationship," *FDR and His Contemporaries: Foreign Perceptions of an American President*, ed. Cornelis A. van Minnen and John F. Sears (New York: St. Martin's Press, 1992), 85–96.

28. Minutes, Seventeenth Pacific War Council meeting, August 12, 1942, Map Room Papers, FDRL; Kimball, ed., *Churchill and Roosevelt*, 1: R–116, R–132, C–68, draft A (not sent); *FRUS, 1945*, 1: 210; Louis, *Imperialism at Bay*, 492, and chaps. 30 and 32. For full details on Roosevelt's thinking about colonialism, see Fred Pollock and Warren F. Kimball, " 'In Search of Monsters to Destroy': Roosevelt and Colonialism," in Kimball, *The Juggler*, 127–57. FDR's reference to the Articles of Confederation may well have come from a 1939 best-selling book, *Union Now* (New York: Harper, 1939), by Clarence Streit, in which he called for a world federation dominated by the Anglo-Saxons and referred to the League of Nations as a learning experience, just as the Articles of Confederation had been for the United States. Now, Streit concluded, the time had come to write a constitution for the world, as the United States had done for itself in the 1780s (courtesy of Douglas Brinkley).

29. Charles de Gaulle, *The Complete War Memoirs of Charles de Gaulle* (New York: Simon and Schuster, 1972), 530.

30. Churchill to Eden, December 31, 1944, FO 371/50807, PRO; Randolph Churchill as quoted by Colville in John Wheeler-Bennett, ed., *Action This Day* (London: Macmillan, 1968), 74; Kimball, *The Juggler*, 140–41; Louis, *Imperialism at Bay*, and Christopher Thorne, *Allies of a Kind* (New York: Oxford University Press, 1978), both discuss growing British awareness that decolonization was necessary.

31. *FRUS, Tehran*, 485–86; Eighth PWC meeting, May 23, 1942, Map Room, FDRL; Moran, *Churchill*, 144–45; Kimball, *The Juggler*, 144–46.

32. Stein Tønnesson, *The Vietnamese Revolution of 1945: Roosevelt, Ho Chi Minh, and de Gaulle in a World at War* (London: Sage/PRIO monographs, 1991), 34–72; Kimball, *The Juggler*, 147–48.

33. Ronald Spector, *Eagle Against the Sun* (London: Penguin Books, 1987), 494; Tønnesson, *The Vietnamese Revolution*, 167–69, 274; *FRUS, Yalta Conference*, 544–45; Kimball, *The Juggler*.

34. Kathryn Weathersby, "Soviet Aims in Korea and the Origins of the Korean War, 1945–1950: New Evidence from Russian Archives," working paper no. 8

(November 8, 1993), Cold War International History Project, Woodrow Wilson International Center (Washington, D.C.) 6, n. 16; U.S. Department of State, *Post World War II Foreign Policy Planning: State Department Records of Harley A. Notter* (microform) (Bethesda, Md.: 1987), 548–51, summary dated March 18, 1943, of a White House meeting on February 22, 1943.

35. Louis, *Imperialism at Bay*, 436–40. The American military pushed hard for the United States to imitate the very nation they were fighting in the Pacific and to acquire a series of islands that seemed essential to American military security (if it was to fight World War II once again). Roosevelt agreed on the need for overseas bases but insisted that those territories maintain sovereignty instead of being incorporated into the United States. A few days before he died he set up a meeting just with delegates headed for the United Nations Conference in San Francisco to reinforce his insistence on international trusteeships for the colonial world, including the Pacific islands (Kimball, *The Juggler*, 155).

36. *FRUS, Yalta Conference*, 770. Not all historians agree. The debate is very well summarized in Tønnesson, *The Vietnamese Revolution*, 13–19.

37. Minutes of the Tolstoy Conference as quoted in Gilbert, *Road to Victory*, 1026.

38. See William Roger Louis and Ronald Robinson, "The Imperialism of Decolonization," *Journal of Imperial and Commonwealth History* 22, 3 (September 1994): 462–511.

39. James F. Byrnes, *Speaking Frankly* (New York: Harper, 1947), x. Even the understated official conference record caught Churchill's anger and outrage: "The Prime Minister interrupted with great vigor to say that he did not agree with one single word of this report on trusteeships. He said that he had not been consulted nor had he heard of this subject up to now. He said that under no circumstances would he ever consent to forty or fifty nations thrusting interfering fingers into the life's existence of the British Empire. As long as he was minister, he would never yield one scrap of their heritage." The less inflammatory State Department phrasing is in *FRUS, Yalta Conference*, 844.

40. Franklin D. Roosevelt, *Complete Presidential Press Conferences of Franklin D. Roosevelt*, 25 vols. (New York: Da Capo Press, 1972), 25:70–73 (February 23, 1945); Lloyd C. Gardner, *Approaching Vietnam* (New York: Norton, 1988), 51–52.

41. The "left" is an inclusive term that defies precise definition. It always encompassed the extreme—Communism—and thus was a powerful political pejorative that often blurred significant distinctions, frequently driving moderates and extremists together. For example, many people in the United States, including a few members of Roosevelt's cabinet, viewed the British Labour party as part of the "left," yet party leaders like Attlee and Ernest Bevin were adamant anticommunists. In Greece, the British used the term to describe any element opposed to a restoration of the monarchy or some sort of British-sponsored regency.

10. From Reims to Potsdam: Victory, Atomic Diplomacy, and the Origins of the Cold War

Arnold A. Offner

Harry S. Truman awoke early on May 8, 1945. "I am sixty-one this morning," and about to receive a wonderful birthday present, the new president wrote. Twenty-four hours earlier the German government of Adm. Karl Doenitz, successor to Chancellor Adolf Hitler, had capitulated to Gen. Dwight D. Eisenhower at Allied headquarters in Reims. Now, at 9:00 A.M. on this "historical day," Truman, Prime Minister Winston Churchill in London, and Marshal Joseph Stalin in Moscow would simultaneously announce Germany's surrender. Truman also noted that despite Churchill's insistent phone calls since daybreak urging an Anglo-American statement to preempt the Russians, he would not renege on their agreement. Events had been moving at a terrific pace since he had succeeded Pres. Franklin Roosevelt on April 12, Truman concluded, but he had been lucky so far and hoped only that when the inevitable mistake came, "it would not be hard to remedy."[1]

It was unlikely that Truman would commit one mistake that would fracture the Grand Alliance that had just earned victory in Europe and stood near triumph in the Pacific. Indeed, sharp conflict had already arisen after the Big Three summit at Yalta in February 1945, and shortly before he died Roosevelt had written Churchill that advancing Anglo-American armies in Germany would soon permit them to get "tougher" with the Russians than the war effort had allowed.[2]

Nonetheless, from V-E Day through the Potsdam Conference in July 1945, Truman's diplomacy and policies differed markedly from Roosevelt's. In particular, Truman administration policy toward defeated Germany, combined with the decision to drop atomic bombs on Japan without warning or modifying the demand for unconditional surrender, increased Soviet-American conflict. Truman and his secretary of state, James F. Byrnes, believed that use of atomic bombs would not only end the Pacific war swiftly but also advance American aims in Europe and Asia and perhaps make the Soviets more "manageable." As Secretary of War Henry L. Stimson noted during the Potsdam Conference, "The program for S-1 [the atomic bomb] is tying in what we are doing in all fields.[3]

*   *   *

Truman inherited a complex legacy of wartime diplomacy. In the 1930s Roosevelt had favored efforts to create a "post-Versailles" European order to satisfy Germany and as late as October 1939 contrasted German bourgeois culture to Russian "brutality." But after Germany invaded Western Europe in spring 1940, FDR concluded that the "totalitarian" Nazi state sought global conquest and that the United States had to provide all possible aid to its opponents.[4]

Roosevelt regarded Hitler's assault on the Soviet Union in June 1941 as a major error that augured "the liberation of Europe from Nazi domination," whereas Russia posed no such threat. America had time to mobilize, and if Russia could be sustained until winter, a German offensive would be delayed until 1942, ensuring Hitler's defeat. And "to cross this bridge, I would hold hands with the Devil," FDR added.[5]

The "centerpiece" of Roosevelt's world strategy, especially after America entered the war in December 1941, was to sustain Russia against Germany. FDR had a "horror" of committing American forces to a major ground war, and he hoped that Soviet armies would fight the Wehrmacht until America had built enough airpower to defeat Germany through strategic bombing. Further, Eisenhower said in 1942, America would be "guilty of one of the greatest military blunders of all history" if it allowed Germany to eliminate an Allied army of 8 million men.[6]

Stalin, meanwhile, pressed Britain for wartime-postwar accord, including acceptance of Russia's 1941 borders and a Germany dismembered and paying reparations. The British vacillated, but after Singapore fell in February 1942 Churchill was inclined to restore Russia's "czarist" borders. Roosevelt was of like mind, but State Department officials objected that this would invite further Russian demands, undermine the Atlantic Charter proscription on territorial aggrandizement, and rouse public ire.[7]

Roosevelt compromised by accepting the counsel of his military advisers, who wanted an early invasion of the Continent. In May 1942 he promised the Russians a "second front in Europe" by the year's end. But Churchill resisted a cross-Channel attack, and FDR acceded to the prime minister's preferred North African invasion in November, despite American military planners' warnings that this would delay a European invasion until 1944 and Stalin's bitter complaints.[8]

Thus at Casablanca with Churchill in January 1943, FDR enunciated the Allied demand for the Axis powers' "unconditional surrender" to ensure that neither the Anglo-Americans nor the Russians signed a separate peace and to preclude World War I–style ambiguity over Germany's defeat. The Germans "understand only one kind of language," FDR said, and he wanted them to be rid of "Hitler and the Nazis," the "Prussian military cliques," and their "war breeding gangs." Privately he spoke even more viscerally about castrations and thin diets from army soup kitchens for the Germans, until the whole nation assumed responsibility for its "lawless conspiracy."[9]

Roosevelt's tough peace, or "retributive justice," related to his view of the postwar order. In early 1943, he told the British that Germany would have to be occupied and partitioned into several states; and in November at Tehran the Big Three agreed in principle to partition, or to "dismember," Germany, to extract reparations, and to compensate Poland with German territory in return for retroceding former Russian land. In September 1944 Roosevelt supported Secretary of the Treasury Henry Morgenthau's Program to Prevent Germany from Starting a World War III, which proposed to divide Germany into two states, dismantle heavy industry, and take reparations from existing resources. FDR and Churchill initially endorsed this idea of German pastoralization, but the president (and the prime minister) then retreated, following news leaks as well as State and War Department and British cabinet attacks on the Morgenthau Plan as too vengeful and destructive of German productivity, deemed vital to world prosperity.[10]

At Yalta in February 1945 the Big Three shelved German dismemberment, but Roosevelt and Stalin agreed on $20 billion as a basis for discussion of German reparations, which would include resources and annual production and be taken from all of Germany—with 50 percent going to the Russians. This amount would compensate the Russians for Germany's ravaging their nation, and FDR would not have to ask Congress for a huge postwar loan for the Bolsheviks. The Russians agreed to France's gaining an occupation zone (drawn from the Anglo-American sectors) and a seat on the Four Power Allied Control Council (ACC), which would set occupation policy. The Polish-Soviet border would follow the 1919 Curzon Line, with Poland compensated by "substantial accessions" of German territory in the north and west.[11]

The Yalta decisions, prefigured at Tehran, reflected political-military reality, including Russia's "Great Patriotic War" in the east of Europe and the Anglo-American invasions in North Africa and the west of Europe. Reality was also reflected in Eisenhower's concurrent decision that the Red Army, encamped at the Oder River near Berlin (deep in the intended Soviet occupation zone), should pay the bloody price of capturing the German capital while Anglo-Amerian forces moved rapidly to north German ports and the Baltic to seal off Denmark. Thus the emergent "Yalta system" sought to accommodate differing historical traditions and national security concerns and to sustain postwar accord—with the Pacific war yet to be won.[12]

Stalin quickly strained the Yalta system by imposing a Communist-led government in Romania in March and insisting on veto power over the choice of

Polish leaders who would negotiate a governing coalition with the Russian-backed Communist regime in Warsaw. But Roosevelt and Churchill recognized that Romania—which had attacked Russia in 1941—was not a good "test case," and FDR told Stalin that a "thinly disguised" continuance of the Warsaw Communists would cause Americans to regard Yalta as a failure.[13]

In turn, from mid-March to early April Stalin bitterly protested Russian exclusion from talks led by Allen Dulles, head of the Office of Secret Services in Switzerland, with SS Gen. Karl Wolff about possible surrender of German forces in northern Italy. Roosevelt insisted that the talks were only preliminary, to establish contact with German officials with authority to surrender their armies at Allied headquarters in Italy, where Russian officials would be present. But Stalin alleged that the meetings were to forge an Anglo-American separate peace or else a German maneuver to shift forces eastward. FDR deplored these "vile misrepresentations," and Stalin disclaimed doubting FDR's (or Churchill's) honesty.[14]

Perhaps Stalin's protests were intended to deflect criticism of his Polish policy or to spur his armies to take Berlin. Still, German efforts at separate surrender in the west were current (if rebuffed) in spring 1945; Dulles wanted Anglo-American forces to reach Trieste before Communist forces did; and FDR, who worried that the Russian presence at initial talks might scare off the Germans, regarded Italy as within America's sphere of influence and apparently was moved by advisers who felt that the Russians were seeking to "dominate" on German matters. The result was clumsy diplomacy, which gained only Soviet hostility, because Wolff could not get German army officials to surrender until April 29–May 2, when the war was already at an end.[15]

Despite the discord, Roosevelt told Churchill on April 11 that they should minimize their problems with the Soviets because, like the Bern incident, they usually straightened out—although "we must be firm, however, and thus far our course is correct." FDR also told Stalin that since the Bern incident had faded, he hoped no such "minor misunderstandings" would mar future relations. The next afternoon, FDR died. Enter Truman.[16]

Truman combined parochial nationalism and Wilsonian internationalism. Young Harry's self-tutelage in history derived chiefly from didactic biographies that enhanced his vision of the globe but provided little sense of nuance and instilled an exaggerated belief that "true facts" could resolve any conflict. Thus the new president was "amazed" that the Yalta accords were so "hazy" and fraught with "new meanings" at every reading—which probably added to his "lackluster" adherence to them.[17]

Captain Truman's World War I military service was exemplary, but he deplored Europe's politics and social mores and never sought to revisit the Continent. He also remained convinced that Germany's aggressiveness derived partly from its need to find resources and markets for "60 millions of people" and that the Anglo-French "conqueror theory" of making the defeated pay the victor undermined the postwar order and the League of Nations.[18]

In the 1930s, Senator Truman backed military preparedness, neutrality revision, Lend-Lease for Britain and then Russia, and rightfully said "I am no appeaser." He disdained Nazism and Communism and "Hitler-Stalin tactics"; and after Germany attacked the Soviet Union, he hastily remarked that they should be left to destroy one another—but he opposed Germany's winning—and then likened Soviet leaders to "Hitler and Al Capone." During wartime he supported a second front and aid for America's "brave ally"—the Russians were saving American lives by killing Germans.[19]

As president, Truman immediately pledged to continue FDR's policies, although "they didn't tell me anything about what was going on." His discomfort with diplomacy led to exaggerated decisiveness—"to decide in advance of thinking," a cabinet member said—and his emphasis on "loyalty" spurred disdain for policy critics. He interpreted the Russians in an American vein: they were akin to bad-mannered people from across the tracks. He naively likened Stalin to Kansas City political boss Tom Pendergast, who allegedly always kept his word, and then he took great umbrage at the thought that the Soviet leader was breaking his agreement.[20]

Thus when in late April senior advisers warned of a Russian "barbarian invasion" of Europe, Truman asserted he was not afraid of them and that they "needed us more than we needed them." He would be firm but fair, but he expected to get "85 percent" on important matters. American adherence to the Yalta accords could not continue to be "a one-way street," he warned Soviet Foreign Minister Vyacheslav Molotov, and allegedly gave the Russian the harshest dressing-down of his life. "It was the straight one-two to the jaw," Truman boasted."[21]

Truman worried a little. "Did I do right?" he asked a diplomat. In early May he refused Churchill's proposal to keep Anglo-American forces in Germany advanced beyond their occupation zones, agreed upon in 1944, as a bargaining lever. He also held to their accord on a tripartite announcement of Germany's surrender. The Russians insisted on a second surrender at their Berlin headquarters on May 9, perhaps to delay the war's end by a day to strengthen their forces in Czechoslovakia. More likely, the Russians sought to stage a "super-Hollywood" ceremony—as described by an Eisenhower aide present at the Berlin surrender—to celebrate their role in defeating Germany.

Eisenhower himself deplored skillful German propaganda seeking to promote an anti-Soviet coalition and on May 10 arrested key German High Command officials for prolonging fighting on the eastern front.[22]

Truman said he was anxious "to keep all my engagements with the Russians because they are touchy and suspicious of us." But he approved "getting tough" on Lend-Lease by restricting shipments, as the law required, to goods under contract or necessary for the Pacific war. Washington officials, however, imposed drastic cutoffs (including recalling ships at sea), causing a Russian-British diplomatic storm. The president promptly countermanded the cutbacks and later blamed himself for allowing "anti-Russian" bureaucrats to mislead him. But he and his advisers had given no forewarning of their action because they intended to send the Russians a firm message.[23]

Truman sought to be even firmer regarding Germany. On May 11 he issued the War Department directive, Joint Chiefs of Staff (JCS) 1067, for governing the American occupation zone. Long subject to State-War-Treasury wrangling, this directive, signed by Roosevelt in March 1945, gave the military commander great authority but delimited Germany's economy and living standard and made the Germans responsible for reparations obligations. An exultant Morgenthau hoped that no one would recognize his handiwork. But Truman did; he issued JCS 1067 mainly to establish immediate military authority. Otherwise, this student of history's "lessons" opposed repeating the World War I "conqueror theory," viewed Germany as part of Europe's vital industrial center, and disliked the Morgenthau Plan.[24]

In effect, Truman wanted to revise the Yalta accord on German reparations and dispel any lingering thought of dismemberment. In May he told Morgenthau that he still had to meet with Churchill and Stalin, "and when I do I want the bargaining power—all the cards in my hands, and the plan on Germany is one of them. . . . I am studying this myself." Indeed, he had already ordered FDR's reparations negotiator, White House economist Isidor Lubin, to delay going to Moscow. He then named conservative oil entrepreneur Edwin Pauley—with the rank of ambassador and charged with reporting to the president—to head negotiations.

Truman wanted Pauley to be "as tough as Molotov," and Pauley did not disappoint. He brushed off Russian references to Yalta's $20 billion (and the State Department's proposed $12 to $14 billion) and insisted that reparations had to be calculated as the remainder of German production minus the costs—or "first charge"—of occupation, German consumption, and imports. This led to Pauley's conclusion in July that it was too early to agree to any fixed sum; they could set only each power's percentage share of reparations.[25]

Meanwhile Stimson, who held that Europe depended on German production, trade, and resources, made his summary case to Truman on May

16. German occupation had to include reconstruction and reindustrialization, and the balance of power—and peace—depended on not driving the Germans into a "nondemocratic and predatory habit of life." Similarly, the State Department stressed the need to avert a "Treaty of Versailles" history, to restrain the French from their "obsession" to detach western Germany's coal and industrial regions, and to preclude a "poor house" living standard that would spur German revolt—again—against weak and divided Allies.[26]

The War–State Department consensus was predominant by July. It was "unthinkable" to destroy Germany and "inconceivable" to occupy it permanently. Thus it was necessary to create a new German state and mind that was demilitarized, denazified, democratic—not Communist, as was the alleged Russian intent—and reintegrated into world trade. Moderate reparations would be paid only if this did not require—as after World War I—heavy foreign borrowing or American lending. Germany would be reconstituted along its 1937 frontiers, with Poland to gain its Yalta-pledged territorial accessions from Germany up to the Oder–eastern Neisse River, not to the western Neisse, which would include Polish-occupied Silesia and its coal.[27]

Truman agreed with these plans. In mid-June he instructed Morgenthau neither to testify to Congress on his plan nor to travel to France and in early July forced his resignation by refusing to assure him that he could remain in the cabinet until the Pacific war ended. The president and Byrnes then sailed for Potsdam. En route Truman approved Pauley's "first charge" principle, shortly writing that "Santa Claus is dead" and that America would never again "pay reparations, feed the world, and get nothing for it but a nose thumbing." The president vowed to fight at Potsdam solely for American interests: "Win, lose or draw—and we must win." And his key to winning, his "ace in the hole" as he would say, was the atomic bomb, or atomic diplomacy—but not "blackmail."[28]

Throughout the war Roosevelt and Churchill sought to maintain "utmost secrecy" about Anglo-American atomic development to ensure against leaks, "particularly to the Russians," and agreed that after "mature consideration" they might use atomic bombs against Japan.[29] Truman first learned of the atomic bomb on April 13, 1945, from Jimmy Byrnes, his former close Senate colleague and head of wartime mobilization, who formally became secretary of state in July 1945 and who, at the Potsdam Conference, would earn Stalin's praise as "the most honest horse thief he had ever met."[30] The president later wrote that Byrnes told him in April 1945 that the atomic bomb "might well put us in position to dictate our own terms at the end of the war"; but atomic physicist Leo Szilard, who talked to Byrnes in May about the bomb, recalled being "flabbergasted" by his assumption that "rattling the bomb might make Russia more manageable."[31]

Moreover, in May Stimson believed that America's industrial strength and "unique" weapon constituted a "royal straight flush and we mustn't be a fool about how we play it." If it became necessary to "have it out" with the Russians over Manchuria, "the bomb would be dominant." Stimson opposed a summit with the Russians without knowing whether the bomb would be "a weapon in our hands"; it seemed "terrible" to "gamble with such big stakes in diplomacy without having your master card in your hand." The next day, May 16, Truman told him that is why he had postponed meeting Stalin, and the secretary concurred, "We shall probably have more cards in our hands later than now." Truman soon confided to a diplomat that he had delayed a summit to await atomic bomb test results.[32]

The president, to be sure, never specified the country to which Byrnes intended to dictate terms, and Szilard had paraphrased—not quoted—Byrnes, who also expressed a politician's concern that failure to use the bomb would cause it to be seen as a failure and spur Congress to question its $2 billion expenditure. Further, Stimson at that point opposed a showdown with Russia, and Truman had several reasons to postpone Potsdam, including the need for diplomatic briefings to avert being made "the paw of the cat" of either Churchill or Stalin. Nonetheless, repeated American references to their "unique weapon" and "master card" reflected growing belief that the atomic bomb would not only shorten the war but also determine "big stakes" diplomacy.[33]

Truman did express interest in Acting Secretary of State Joseph Grew's proposal on May 28 to induce Japan to surrender by publicly stating that they might retain their dynasty. Grew, however, sought not just to expedite the war's end but to preclude Russia's entry and its share in Japan's postwar occupation and perhaps deny Russia its Yalta concessions of Port Arthur and Dairen in Manchuria. Truman, however, referred Grew to Stimson and his military advisers, who opposed making any statement before they knew when the bomb would be ready.[34]

Thus Stimson and Byrnes, as chairman and as the president's representative on the Interim Committee, recently created to assess atomic policy, were chiefly responsible for the recommendation on June 1 of that body (and its Scientific Panel and military advisers) that atomic bombs be dropped on Japan as soon as possible and without warning. Although all members apparently assumed use of the bomb, it is noteworthy that when physicist Robert Oppenheimer asked if sudden use might harm postwar relations with Russia, Byrnes insisted that they continue atomic research in secret and "make certain to stay ahead."[35]

Truman approved the Stimson-Byrnes reports of the meeting. Further, when Stimson stressed on June 6 that S-1 should not be revealed until "the first bomb had been successfully laid on Japan" but worried what might be said in advance at Potsdam, the president reiterated that he had delayed the meeting until July 15 "to give us more time." He agreed not to offer Stalin atomic "partnership" without political "quid pro quos." He also noted a cable from his special emissary to Moscow, former FDR confidant Harry Hopkins, that the Russians, as agreed at Yalta, would enter the Pacific war when they concluded their treaty with China and would seek only their agreed-upon concessions in Manchuria.[36]

The bomb's use still seemed inevitable, however, when the Scientific Panel reported on June 16 that it could not propose any demonstration that would induce Japan's surrender. Grew again raised his negotiated surrender proposal, but Truman deferred this "guesswork" to the Potsdam meeting and seemed convinced that an invasion would be required even after use of the bomb and Russian entry. That view emerged at the president's meeting with his Joint Chiefs on June 18, when Truman approved the invasion of Kyushu (Operation Olympic) in November but reserved decision on invading Honshu and the Tokyo Plain (Operation Coronet) in early 1946. Truman did approve exploring Assistant Secretary of War John McCloy's last-minute idea to end the war without an invasion by warning Japan of the impending use of a "terrifyingly destructive weapon" and by ensuring the emperor's status, but Stimson persisted that this "last chance warning" still required "an attack of S-1."[37]

On June 21 the Interim Committee reconfirmed its original recommendation to use the bomb, although it now proposed to forewarn the Russians but to give no atomic information. Stimson held on June 26 that Japan had to be "sufficiently pounded, possibly with S-1," before it would surrender; and Truman and Stimson shelved Undersecretary of the Navy Ralph Bard's suggestion to give Japan assurances about the emperor and a warning of the intent to use the bomb. Stimson then drafted a Potsdam Declaration that demanded unconditional surrender of Japan's military but that implied a post-occupation constitutional monarchy under the current dynasty. The declaration was not to be issued, however, until Japan's "impending destruction" was "clear beyond per adventure." And although Stimson proposed to ask the Russians to sign if their entry was imminent, the declaration and the bomb's use were to come before the Russian attack had "proceeded too far."[38]

Truman accepted this strategy on July 2–3; Stimson added that if relations with Stalin at Potsdam seemed good, the president should say that the Americans were working on an atomic bomb—but to offer no more except for hope of postwar security talks. Truman and Stimson thus agreed to use the bomb to subdue Japan swiftly and perhaps avert the need for an American invasion; they also agreed that they might ask the Russians to sign the Potsdam Declaration as an additional "warning," but only if a Russian attack seemed imminent. Regardless, the bomb was to be dropped before that attack had "proceeded too far," thereby containing Russian advances. The bomb thus served military and political purposes.[39]

Truman's knowledge of the atomic bomb greatly affected his psychology and diplomacy at Potsdam. As Stimson noted while bringing him the New Mexico test reports during July 16–21, the president was "highly delighted," "very greatly reenforced," and "tremendously pepped up"; "It gave him an entirely new feeling of confidence." After his first meeting with Stalin on July 17, Truman wrote that he was unafraid of the Russian's "dynamite" agenda because "I have some dynamite too which I'm not exploding now." The next day he added that he had "several aces in the hole which I hope will help on results."[40] Byrnes too was "immensely pleased" by the bomb test. He was determined, his chief aide noted, to "outmaneuver Stalin on China" and believed that use of the bomb meant that "Russia would not get in so much on the kill" of Japan—or its occupation. And when negotiations over Germany grew testy, Byrnes insisted "that the New Mexico situation has given us great power, and that in the last analysis it would control."[41]

This mindset influenced policy. By July 13–16 American officials knew from diplomatic intercepts that Japan's leaders recognized Soviet intervention was imminent and that the "last obstacle" to peace was unconditional surrender. Stimson no longer thought that Japan had to be "pounded" with S-1. On July 16–17 he urged Truman and Byrnes to issue "prompt and early warnings" that might preclude atomic and ground attacks. But they indicated that they had a different timetable. The next day, when Stalin asked Truman about replying to a Japanese peace feeler conveying the emperor's belief that unconditional surrender left "no alternative" to war, the president accused the Japanese of "bad faith" diplomacy. Byrnes, meanwhile, instructed the State Department that there would be no early warnings or a guarantee for the emperor.[42]

Truman's strategy seems evident. Although Stalin had assured him on July 17 of Russian intervention by August 15—"Fini Japs when that comes about," Truman noted—the next day he wrote confidently that "the Japs will fold up" before the Russian attack, "when Manhattan appears over their homeland." He rebuffed both Churchill's suggestion to modify unconditional surrender to permit Japan to quit the war and Eisenhower's view that the bomb was unnecessary because Japan was already defeated. When Stimson brought an "accelerated timetable" for the bomb on July 22, Truman was "intensely pleased." He had Chief of Staff Gen. George Marshall queried about the need for Russian entry but was told this could not be precluded, although Stimson and Marshall thought "our new weapon" made it unnecessary. Truman also urged the Chinese to continue treaty negotiations on the Yalta concessions, but to give no more, largely to forestall a preemptive Russian strike in Manchuria.[43]

The president said he had exactly what he wanted, however, when he learned on July 24 that the bomb could be ready for use by August 4–5 and not later than August 10—before Russian entry. He knew too that he had to inform the Russians to avoid recrimination; thus he purposely went without his State Department interpreter to remark casually to Stalin that America had a new and unusually destructive weapon. Stalin replied only that he hoped it would be used well against Japan. Truman exulted that his deception had worked, but Byrnes—rightly—thought that the words would soon sink in.[44]

Byrnes also redrafted the Potsdam Declaration to excise all references to the emperor, Russian forces, and the atomic bomb. Japan was left to choose between unconditional surrender or "utter destruction." The British and Chinese signed quickly, and on July 25 Stimson and Marshall approved the directive for the Strategic Air Force to drop an atomic bomb on one of the four designated targets about August 3 and for "additional bombs" as soon as they were available. Truman said the order would stand unless Japan accepted the Potsdam Declaration, which was issued July 26.[45]

Perhaps "domestic politics" influenced Truman and Byrnes not to guarantee the emperor's status or to modify unconditional surrender otherwise. Many government officials and a significant sector of public opinion viewed the Japanese and their emperor harshly and opposed any "appeasement" or softening of surrender terms. But by omitting mention of the emperor, the Russians (their attack was imminent), and the atomic bomb, the Americans prevented the Potsdam Declaration from serving either as a conciliatory device to induce surrender or as an ultimatum to coerce surrender. Thus it did not offer Japan a "rational choice." Further, when the Russians protested at not being shown the declaration, Byrnes lamely replied that Truman did not want to embarrass them because they had not yet declared war. In fact, Secretary of the Navy James Forrestal wrote on July 28, Byrnes was "most anxious to get the Japanese affair over with before the Russians got in" and thus to forestall their Manchurian claims.[46]

That same day the Japanese stated that they had no choice but to "ignore" the Potsdam Declaration. Truman did not explore Japan's ambiguous response and rejected Stalin's request to be invited into the war, despite knowing that Japan was desperately seeking Russian mediation to surrender. But Truman had his reason. On July 30 Stimson cabled from Washington that S-1 was proceeding so swiftly that immediate approval for its use was required. The president hastily scrawled his July 31 approval on the back of the cable: "Release when ready but not sooner than August 2. HST." By then, he knew, he would have departed Potsdam, having just given Stalin an "ultimatum" on Germany with a forty-eight-hour deadline. The bomb would "control," Byrnes had said.[47]

The destruction Truman saw in Germany appalled him, and the Russians' ravaging heightened his concern. He believed he could do business with Stalin, despite worry about a coup by a "demagogue on horseback," but most officials soon concluded that ideology precluded cooperation. Byrnes in particular lamented that "somebody" had made an "awful mistake" by allowing the Russians to emerge from the war with so much power.[48]

The president pressed America's German program at the first meeting on July17. Stalin acceded to Germany's 1937 borders as the "starting point" for its reconstitution, but Truman refused his proposal to set Poland's border with Germany at the Oder–western Neisse line to include Polish-occupied Silesia. They agreed to give a Four Power ACC paramount authority over a decentralized German political-economic structure, with each military commander predominant in his zone. Germany, as agreed at Yalta, would be treated as an economic whole when reparations were extracted, with 56 percent going to the Russians. The Americans insisted, however, on their "first charge" on the German economy for occupation costs, foodstuffs, and imports, likening occupied Germany to a corporation in receivership with creditors having first claim on revenue. The Russians insisted on first priority for their reparations, holding that capitalists always wanted foreign trade profits but cared nothing about reparations for war victims.[49]

Truman quickly grew "sick of the whole business." But after Stimson brought the full atomic report on July 21, the president firmly told the Russians that he would not recognize their proposed Polish-German border or agree to "carving up" Germany, whose loss of coal and food-producing lands jeopardized any reparations agreement. Truman would hear no Soviet protests about economic necessity or security, and he declared an "impasse."[50]

"The President's best day so far," the British exulted. Churchill, having just read the atomic bomb report, said he understood why Truman was "a changed man," who had told the Russians "just where they got on and off and generally bossed the whole meeting." As Stimson noted, the atomic bomb was tying together what the Americans were doing in every field.[51]

Bitter debate continued over reparations and the Polish-German border. Byrnes soon hinted that each power should take reparations from its own zone, thus denying Russian access to Ruhr industry, and he brushed off Molotov's effort to discuss reduced reparations. Truman said he would not agree to set the Polish border at the Oder–western Neisse "yesterday . . . today, and . . . tomorrow." Churchill was exultant again: "If only this had happened at Yalta."[52]

By the last days of July, Truman knew that Potsdam hinged on the two most difficult issues: the German-Polish border and reparations, which had "poisoned" the meeting, one diplomat told him. Truman deplored the "Bolsheviki land grab" in Silesia but realized that the Soviet-backed Poles could not be removed from the territory they occupied "unless we are willing to go to war." That left "old man reparations," with Byrnes convinced by recent reports on the atomic bomb that its use would induce the Russians to comply with American demands.[53]

Byrnes then insisted that each power take reparations from its own zone, despite Molotov's retort that this would produce the same result as not reaching an agreement. "Yes," Byrnes said, as he withdrew the Yalta accord, alleging that dramatically changed conditions in Germany had made it impractical; and he insisted that the agreement to discuss $20 billion "does not mean I am going to write a check for it." That ruled out any fixed sum—even the current Soviet low bid for $4 billion.[54]

Having wiped the bargaining slate clean, on July 29 Byrnes broached his solution: Russian accord on zonal reparations, with some exchange of western zone industry for eastern zone foodstuffs and coal, and American acceptance of Polish administration of German Silesia up to the eastern Neisse. Molotov wanted a guarantee of $2 billion for Russia in Ruhr industry and Poland's border set at the western Neisse. Byrnes again refused a fixed reparations figure; he offered only 25 percent of "available" western industry, prompting Molotov's rejoinder that 25 percent of an unknown sum meant very little.[55]

The next day Byrnes acceded to the western Neisse and a higher percentage of available Ruhr industry but with the critical proviso that the military commander in each zone—not the ACC, as previously agreed—would have final authority over reparations transfers. The Russians balked; and Byrnes, knowing that Japan had just refused the Potsdam Declaration and that atomic bombs would soon be dropped, decided that it was time to "strike a bargain" or go home.[56]

Byrnes spelled out his proposal on July 30–31: zonal reparations with industry-foodstuffs exchanges; Polish administration of Silesia to the Oder–western Neisse; and a new, third element—Italy, then under Anglo-American aegis, admitted to the United Nations in return for America's reconsidering recognition of the governments in East Europe, where Soviet influence lay heavy. But the three issues were inseparable and had to be resolved at once, Byrnes stipulated, or else the president and his delegation would depart the next day.[57]

"Mr. Stalin is stallin'," Truman wrote hours before the climactic plenary session on July 31, but that would not help the Russian leader because "he doesn't know it but I have an ace in the hole and another one showing—so unless he has three or two pairs (I know he has not) we are sitting all right." Stalin was unmoved by the aces but understood what he called the "calculation of forces" in Germany. Bargaining thus moved swiftly to an agreement on zonal reparations, with the exchange of 15 percent of western zone industry, considered "not necessary" for Germany's subsistence economy, for eastern zone foodstuffs and raw materials and with another 10 percent of western industry given free of exchange. Transfers were to be completed within two years.[58]

America had prevailed: there was no mention of a specific sum of reparations; none would be taken from current production until Germany had a balanced economy; and, most important, military commanders in each zone had final authority over reparations transfers. America could thus drop its first-charge principle, and the Soviets had no direct access to the Ruhr. Still, the Big Three agreed to treat Germany as a single economic unit, with the ACC to determine its level of industry and to establish unifying political-administrative systems but not a central government. Accord on Germany sped agreement on Polish administration of its de facto Oder–western Neisse border and the Italy–East Europe trade-off. "That's the way most conferences go," wrote a British diplomat present at the agreement; once a major issue loosens, "the whole thing breaks free."[59]

Truman quickly departed Potsdam on August 2, convinced that the Russians were "pig-headed" and Stalin a "son-of-a-bitch," although the president boasted that the Russian probably thought the same of him. En route to America, Truman worried that the Russians would use Japan's efforts to surrender through them to raise their claims in Manchuria and to share in Japan's occupation. On August 5 Truman advised Stalin not to seek further concessions from China. When told of the Hiroshima bombing on August 6, the president exclaimed, "This is the greatest thing in history."[60]

Truman believed that the atomic bomb prompted the Soviets to enter the Pacific war on August 8, one week earlier than Stalin's Potsdam pledge (but within the Yalta timetable of ninety days after V-E Day) and without the requisite Sino-Soviet treaty. Thus, when that same day Stimson showed Truman pictures of postatomic Hiroshima, the president, who said that the destruction also imposed terrible responsibility, did not consider delay of the second atomic bomb, which fell on Nagasaki on August 9, advanced two days by the military because of impending bad weather.[61]

The Nagasaki blast, combined with Russian entry into the war, spurred Japan to propose surrender if the emperor's prerogatives were retained. Truman inclined to accept. His "horse sense" reasoning was clear, Stimson noted; it would not only save lives but the Americans would get into Japan "before the Russians could put in any claim to occupy and help rule it." Byrnes agreed but feared an angry public's "crucifixion" of the president if he modified unconditional surrender. Forrestal then urged a reply that preserved the intent of the Potsdam Declaration; Truman told Byrnes to draft the compromise, which stated that the emperor and Japan's government would be "subject to the Supreme Commander of the Allied Powers" and that the Japanese ultimately could choose their own form of government.[62]

The American proposal implied preserving the imperial dynasty. Truman and Byrnes also emphasized in cabinet meetings that an American would be the "top dog," or supreme commander; they would not be "plagued" by joint responsibility in Japan as in Germany. The president halted further use of atomic bombs—the next one would not be ready for eight or nine days—but continued conventional bombing. Truman wished to keep pressure on Japan, but atomic warfare had chastened him: it was too horrible to kill another one hundred thousand people, especially "all those kids."[63]

The surrender terms went to Japan on August 11. Debate and intrigue raged for three days. The cabinet agreed to capitulate by 13 to 3; but the "inner cabinet," or Supreme Council for the Direction of the War, deadlocked at 3 to 3, with the military demanding an absolute guarantee for the emperor. At an imperial conference on August 14, however, Emperor Hirohito insisted that they had to "bear the unbearable" and end the war immediately, lest the nation be annihilated. That evening Japan's government agreed to surrender under the Potsdam Declaration.[64] The next day Truman, having rejected Stalin's wily request to share in the choice of a supreme commander, instructed Gen. Douglas MacArthur on the surrender of Japanese forces in the Far East, and MacArthur received Japan's formal surrender September 2 on board the USS *Missouri* in Tokyo Bay. World War II had ended.[65]

The Grand Alliance was born of necessity among nations of diverse political-economic traditions united by the need to defeat Nazi Germany. After this was done and they confronted one another across war-torn Europe, great power struggles for influence were inevitable, the more so, perhaps, because of the military course of the war: the Anglo-Americans invaded and held sway in North Africa and Western Europe, and the Russians fought their Great Patriotic War in and across Eastern Europe.

So too did the Americans and Russians struggle over Germany and reparations. At Yalta, Roosevelt and Stalin shelved German dismemberment but agreed to $20 billion in reparations as a basis for discussion. On the road from Germany's surrender at Reims to negotiations at Potsdam, however, the Truman administration altered the course: it abandoned FDR's concept of "retributive justice" toward Germany and the search for détente with Russia and determined on a zonal reparations policy that augured de facto division of Germany. As one State Department official warned, zonal reparations would "split Europe down the middle economically." Truman and Byrnes may not have intended permanent division, but they were determined, with little regard for Russia's wartime devastation, to minimize its reparations claims (and influence) on western industrial Germany, which they deemed vital to American-European prosperity.[66]

Possession of the atomic bomb also infused American thinking about the end of the war in Europe and Asia. As Stimson reflected on July 30 after his return from Europe, even he had been unaware of the bomb's great psychological effect on his thinking at Potsdam. Unquestionably, the poker-playing Truman, Byrnes, and others believed that their "royal straight flush," "master card," or "ace in the hole" so strengthened their hands that they could get the Russians to accede to their terms for Germany and other nations. Truman's many reasons for delaying Potsdam included atomic ones, and he was unfazed by Stalin's "dynamite" agenda because he had his own "dynamite too which I'm not exploding now." After the July 21 reports on the magnitude of the bomb blast, Truman became "a changed man." He told the Russians "where to get on and off," was delighted at the "accelerated timetable" for the bomb's use, and had to be persuaded to give Stalin even vague notice of the weapon. Further, after putting America's tripartite ultimatum to Stalin on July 30 on German zonal reparations, the Polish-German border, and Italy–Eastern Europe, Truman expected to get his way (or quit the meeting) because he had "an ace in the hole and another one showing," knowing those aces would soon fall on Japan.[67]

The evidence confirms that by the start of the Potsdam meeting, Truman and Byrnes believed that Japan would quit the war as soon as "Manhattan" appeared over their homeland and that such a quick atomic defeat might allow the United States to "outmaneuver" the Russians in Manchuria, thus precluding their sharing in Japan's postwar occupation. Truman and Byrnes displayed little interest in exploring ways to induce Japan's surrender by proposing to retain the emperor, nor did they seek to coerce Japan by giving warning about the atomic bomb or Russian entry into the war. Only after using their unique weapon on Hiroshima and Nagasaki did they give the critical assurance about the emperor that opened the way to Japan's capitulation.

Thus the answer to the question of whether the atomic bomb was used for diplomatic or military purposes is evident: the prospect, or temptation, of diplomatic gain precluded serious thought—or "mature consideration"—not to use atomic bombs. This does not mean that Truman and Byrnes were sinners; nor were they saints. They were American politicians of limited international experience and vision suddenly thrust into positions of global leadership. Their sensibilities were undoubtedly hardened by their witnessing a global war of unparalleled devastation that included fire-bombing of cities and a Holocaust, and they felt little restraint about using the bomb against the Japanese who, Truman declared, had attacked Pearl Harbor without warning and had tortured and executed American prisoners of war.[68]

Soviet advances in Europe also appalled and frightened Truman and Byrnes. They quickly persuaded themselves that if they got "tough" with the Russians, they would become more "manageable" and accede to American principles and interests, which Truman had said were his sole priority at Potsdam. Thus it is not surprising that at the dawn of the atomic age, whose power and horrors were yet untold, American officials were tempted to use the atomic bomb not only to end World War II but to "win" the peace. Their action may not have foreordained the cold war, but it increased discord rather than unity. Accordingly, one might ponder the words of Eisenhower's naval aide, Capt. Harry C. Butcher, who wrote on May 7–8, at the time of Germany's surrender and growing American-Soviet tension, that "I've learned the hard way it is much easier to start a war than to stop one."[69]

NOTES

1. Truman to Martha Ellen and Mary Jane Truman, May 8, 1945, Harry S. Truman, *Memoirs*, 2 vols. (New York: Doubleday, 1955–1956), 1: 6; Truman broadcast, May 8, 1945, *Public Papers of the Presidents of the United States: Harry S. Truman, 1945–1953*, 8 vols. (Washington, D.C.: GPO, 1961–1966), 1: 48–49 (hereafter *PPHST*).

2. Roosevelt to Churchill, April 11, 1945, U.S. Department of State, *Foreign Relations of the United States, [FRUS], Diplomatic Papers, 1945*, 9 vols. (Washington, D.C.: GPO, 1967–1969), 2: 210; for a comprehensive record of this correspondence, see Warren F. Kimball, ed., *Churchill and Roosevelt: The Complete Correspondence*, 3 vols. (Princeton: Princeton University Press, 1984).

3. Byrnes quoted in Leo Szilard, "Reminiscences," in *The Intellectual Migration:*

Europe and America, 1930–1960, ed. Donald Fleming and Bernard Bailyn (Cambridge, Mass.: Belknap Press of Harvard University Press, 1969), 127–28; entry for July 23, 1945, Henry L. Stimson Diary, Henry L. Stimson Papers, Sterling Library, Yale University.

4. Roosevelt to Joseph P. Kennedy, October 20, 1939, in Elliott Roosevelt, ed., *F.D.R.: His Personal Letters, 1928–1945* (hereafter *FDRL*), 2 vols. (New York: Duell, Sloan and Pearce, 1947–1950), 1: 942–44; see also Arnold A. Offner, "Appeasement Revisited: The United States, Great Britain, and Germany, 1933–1940," *Journal of American History* 64 (September 1977): 373–93.

5. Lord Halifax to British Foreign Office, July 7, 1941, in Waldo Heinrichs, *Threshold of War: Franklin D. Roosevelt and American Entry into World War II* (New York: Oxford University Press, 1988), 102, and Roosevelt to Joseph E. Davies, cited in John Lewis Gaddis, *Russia, the Soviet Union, and the United States: An Interpretive History,* 2d ed. (New York: McGraw-Hill, 1990), 146–47.

6. Heinrichs, *Threshhold,* 159, 179; "horror" is found in W. Averell Harriman and Elie Abel, *Special Envoy to Churchill and Stalin, 1941–1946* (New York: Random House, 1975), 74; Eisenhower memorandum, July 17, 1942, in *The Papers of Dwight D. Eisenhower: The War Years,* ed. Alfred D. Chandler Jr. et al., 5 vols. (Baltimore: Johns Hopkins University Press, 1970), 1: 389; see also Arnold A. Offner, "Uncommon Ground: Anglo-American-Soviet Diplomacy, 1941–1942," *Soviet Union/Union Sovietique* 18 (1991): 242–44.

7. Offner, "Uncommon Ground," 244–49.

8. On the FDR–Molotov talks, see Cross memorandum and Hopkins memorandum, May 29, and Cross memoranda, May 30, June 1, 1942, *FRUS 1942,* 3: 566–71, 575–77, 578–81, and Robert E. Sherwood, *Roosevelt and Hopkins: An Intimate History* (New York: Harper, 1948), 561–77; on postponement, see Mark Stoler, *The Politics of the Second Front: American Military Planning and Diplomacy in Coalition Warfare, 1941–1943* (Westport, Conn.: Greenwood Press, 1977), 55–65, and Harriman to Roosevelt, August 13, August 14, August 15, 1942, *FRUS 1942,* 3: 618–20, 621–25.

9. Raymond O'Connor, *Diplomacy for Victory: FDR and Unconditional Surrender* (New York: Norton, 1971); on FDR's views of Germany, see Roosevelt's messages to Congress, January 7 and September 17, 1943, Samuel I. Rosenman, comp., *The Public Papers and Addresses of Franklin D. Roosevelt,* 12 vols. (New York: Macmillan, 1938–1950), 12: 33, 391, John Morton Blum, *From the Morgenthau Diaries,* 3 vols. (Boston: Houghton Mifflin, 1959–1967), 3: 341, 348–49, and Roosevelt to Hull, April 1, 1945, Roosevelt, ed., *FDRL,* 2: 1504.

10. Arnold A. Offner, "Research on American-German Relations: A Critical View," in *America and the Germans: An Assessment of a Three-Hundred Year History,* ed. Frank Trommler and Joseph McVeigh, 2 vols. (Philadelphia: University of Pennsylvania Press, 1985), 2: 175–76; see also Diane Shaver Clemens, *Yalta* (New York: Oxford University Press, 1970), 28–42, and Warren F. Kimball, *Swords or Ploughshares? The Morgenthau Plan for Defeated Nazi Germany, 1943–1946* (Philadelphia: Lippincott, 1976).

11. Clemens, *Yalta,* 137–72, 212–15; the Big Three agreed to fix the Russian-Polish border at the historic-enthnographic Curzon Line; the Americans and British

insisted on the Oder–eastern Neisse River for the Polish-German border; the Russians pressed the Oder–western Neisse.

12. Gerhard L. Weinberg, *A World at Arms: A Global History of World War II* (Cambridge: Cambridge University Press, 1994), 803, 810–14.

13. Roosevelt to Churchill, March 11, and Roosevelt to Stalin, April 1, 1945, *FRUS 1945*, 5: 509–10, 194–96.

14. The best account of the Bern episode is Bradley F. Smith and Elena Agarossi, *Operation Sunrise: The Secret Surrender* (New York: Basic Books, 1979), esp. 72–124; for diplomatic exchanges, see *FRUS 1945*, 3: 717–56, esp. the Bohlen memorandum, March 13, and Molotov to Stettinius, March 16, Roosevelt to Stalin, March 24, and March 29, Stalin to FDR, April 3, Roosevelt to Stalin, April 4, and Stalin to Roosevelt, April 7, 1945, 726–27, 731–32, 737–40, 742–43, 745–46, and 749–51.

15. On Soviet motives, see Weinberg, *World at Arms*, 818–19, Vojtech Mastny, *Russia's Road to the Cold War: Diplomacy, Warfare, and the Politics of Communism, 1941–1945* (New York: Columbia University Press, 1979), 276–78, and Lloyd G. Gardner, *Spheres of Influence: The Great Powers Partition Europe, from Munich to Yalta* (Chicago: Ivan Dee, 1993), 252–53; on FDR, see Kimball, ed., *Roosevelt-Churchill Correspondence*, 3: 586–87, 609; on the Dulles and Bern talks, see Allen Dulles, *The Secret Surrender* (New York: Harper and Row, 1966), and Peter Grose, *Gentleman Spy: The Life of Allen Dulles* (Boston: Houghton Mifflin, 1994), 221–45; on results, see Smith and Agarossi, *Operation Sunrise*, 185–92.

16. Roosevelt to Churchill, April 11, 1945, *FRUS 1945*, 5: 210, and Roosevelt to Stalin, April 12, 1945, *FRUS 1945*, 3: 756; Roosevelt reiterated to Ambassador Averell Harriman, April 12, 1945 (757), that he meant to say "minor"; Roosevelt wrote the cables on April 11 in Warm Springs, Georgia; they were sent from the White House Map Room early on April 12.

17. Truman, *Memoirs*, 1: 119–21, Truman memorandum, May 1934, President's Secretary's Files (PSF), Box 334, Harry S. Truman Papers, Harry S. Truman Library, Independence, Mo., and William Hillman, ed., *Mr. President* (New York: Farrar, Straus, and Young, 1952), 11–13, 81–85; on Yalta, see notes of Truman-Stettinius Meeting, April 21, 1945, Thomas M. Campbell and George C. Herring, eds., *The Diaries of Edward R. Stettinius, Jr., 1943–1946* (New York: New Viewpoints, 1975), 324–25, entry for May 25, 1945, Eban Ayers Diary, Box 25, Eban Ayers Papers, Truman Library, and Melvyn P. Leffler, "Adherence to Agreements: Yalta and the Experience of the Early Cold War," *International Security* 11 (summer 1986): 88–123, who calls Truman's adherence "lackluster."

18. Truman to Elizabeth ("Bess") Wallace, October 28, and November 13, 1917, and March 27, 1918, in *Dear Bess: The Letters from Harry to Bess Truman, 1910–1959*, ed. Robert H. Ferrell (New York: Norton, 1983), 233, 234, and 254; on Germany and World War I, see Truman speech, February 20, 1937, Senatorial and Vice Presidential Files (SVPF), Box 1, Truman Papers.

19. Alfred Steinberg, *The Man from Missouri: The Life and Times of Harry S. Truman* (New York: Putnam, 1962), 58, and Jonathan Daniels, *The Man of Independence* (Philadelphia: Lippincott, 1960), 100–161; "no appeaser" is from Truman speech,

March 25, 1939, SVPF, Box 1, Truman Papers; for Truman on Germany and the Soviet Union, see *New York Times,* June 24, 1941, and Truman to Bess Truman, December 30, 1941, in Ferrell, ed., *Dear Bess,* 471; see wartime views in *Appendix to the Congressional Record,* 88, part 9, A2918, and Richard S. Kirkendall, "Truman and the Cold War," *Studies in Mediaevalia and Americana: Essays in Honor of William Lyle Davis, S.J.* (Spokane: University of Washington Press, 1973), 153–54.

20. Diary entries for May 18 and April 27, 1945, John Morton Blum, ed., *The Diary of Henry A. Wallace, 1942–1946* (Boston: Houghton Mifflin, 1973), 452, 437; on loyalty, see William D. Leahy, *I Was There* (New York: Whittlesay House, 1950), 347–48, and diary entries for May 18 and June 7, 1945, Robert H. Ferrell, ed., *Off the Record: The Private Papers of Harry S. Truman* (New York: Harper and Row, 1980), 29, 44–45; on Stalin, see Margaret Truman, *Harry S. Truman* (New York: Morrow, 1972), 74–75, and Truman interview, August 30, 1949, Jonathan Daniels Notes, Box 1, Jonathan Daniels Papers, Truman Library.

21. Bohlen memorandum, April 20, 1945, *FRUS 1945,* 5: 231–34; on Truman and Molotov, see Bohlen memorandum, April 23, 1945, 256–58, Truman, *Memoirs,* 1: 79–82, and entry for April 23, 1945, Joseph E. Davies Journal, Box 16, Joseph E. Davies Papers, Manuscripts Division, Library of Congress.

22. Churchill to Truman, May 6, and Truman to Churchill, May 8, 1945, *Foreign Relations of the United States: The Conference of Berlin (The Potsdam Conference), 1945,* 2 vols. (Washington, D.C.: GPO, 1960), 1: 3–4; on the Berlin surrender, Mastny, *Russia's Road to Cold War,* 276–78, emphasizes the Czechoslovakian angle; Weinberg, *World at Arms,* 826–27, cites the need to avoid World War I ambiguity; Harry C. Butcher, *My Three Years with Eisenhower: The Personal Diary of Captain Harry C. Butcher, 1942–1945* (New York: Simon and Schuster, 1945), entry for May 10, 1945, 836–44, and Kennan to Stettinius, May 7, 1945, *FRUS 1945,* 3: 779–80, suggests Soviet desire for recognition; Stephen Ambrose, *Eisenhower: Soldier, General of the Army, President, 1890–1952* (New York: Simon and Schuster, 1983), 427–28.

23. Truman to Eleanor Roosevelt, May 10, 1945, Ferrell, ed., *Off The Record,* 20–22; transcript of Truman-Stettinius conversation, May 10, 1945, Campbell, ed., *Stettinius Diaries,* 358; Grew and Crowley memorandum for Truman, and Truman memorandum for Grew, May 11, 1945, *FRUS 1945,* 5: 999–1000; Truman, *Memoirs,* 1: 228, George C. Herring Jr., *Aid to Russia, 1941–1946: Strategy, Diplomacy, and the Origins of the Cold War* (New York: Columbia University Press, 1973), 203–6.

24. Memorandum Regarding American Policy for . . . Germany, March 23, 1945, *FRUS 1945,* 3: 471–73; Blum, *Years of War,* 400–414; Truman, *Memoirs,* 1: 236.

25. Truman, *Memoirs,* 1: 308; Bruce Kuklick, *American Policy and the Division of Germany: The Clash with Russia over Reparations* (Ithaca, N.Y.: Cornell University Press, 1972), 126–33.

26. Henry L. Stimson and McGeorge Bundy, *On Active Service in Peace and War* (New York: Harper, 1947), 571–83; Department of State, Briefing Book, Policy toward Germany (June 29, 1945), *FRUS 1945: Potsdam,* 1: 435–49.

27. Central Secretariat memorandum, July 12, 1945, *FRUS 1945: Potsdam,* 1: 500–503; and also Grew to Pauley, July 2, Briefing Book paper, June 27, and Joint

Strategic Services Survey Committee memorandum, [June 26], 1945, 519–21, 586–89, and 595–96.

28. Blum, *Years of War*, 461–73; diary entry for July 7, 1945, Ferrell, ed., *Off the Record*, 48–49; Truman to Bess Truman, July 20, 1945, Ferrell, ed., *Dear Bess*, 520; on atomic diplomacy, see diary entries for July 18 and July 30, 1945, Ferrell, ed., *Off the Record*, 53–54, 57–58, and Truman to Bess Truman, July 31, 1945, Ferrell, ed., *Dear Bess*, 522–23.

29. Martin J. Sherwin, *A World Destroyed: The Atomic Bomb and the Grand Alliance* (New York: Random House, 1977), 90–114, 121–39, and 284.

30. Robert L. Messer, *The End of an Alliance: James F. Byrnes, Roosevelt, Truman, and the Origins of the Cold War* (Chapel Hill: University of North Carolina Press, 1982), 11–70; for "horse thief," see diary entry for August 10, 1945, John M. Blum, ed., *The Price of Vision: The Diary of Henry A. Wallace* (Boston: Houghton Mifflin, 1973), 475.

31. Truman, *Memoirs*, 1: 11, 87; Byrnes cited by Szilard in "Reminiscences," in Fleming and Bailyn, eds., *Intellectual Migration*, 127–28.

32. Entries for May 14, May 15, and May 16, 1945, Stimson Diary, Stimson Papers; entry for May 21, 1945, Jospeh E. Davies Diaries, Box 17, Joseph E. Davies Papers, Manuscripts Division, Library of Congress.

33. Diary entry for May 19, 1945, Ferrell, ed., *Off the Record*, 32.

34. Grew memoranda, May 28 and May 29, 1945, *FRUS 1945*, 6: 545–49, and entry for May 29, 1945, Stimson Diary, Stimson Papers; see also Leon V. Sigal, *Fighting to a Finish: The Politics of War Termination in the United States and Japan* (Ithaca, N.Y.: Cornell University Press, 1988), 113–15.

35. Entry for May 31, 1945, Stimson Diary, Stimson Papers; Sherwin, *A World Destroyed*, 202–9, 295–304, and Messer, *Byrnes*, 87–88.

36. Entry for June 6, 1945, Stimson Diary, Stimson Papers.

37. Ibid., entry for June 19, 1945.

38. Ibid., entries for June 25 and June 26–30, 1945.

39. Ibid., entry for July 2, 1945; Stimson to Truman, July 2, 1945, *FRUS 1945: Potsdam*, 1: 888–94.

40. Entries for July 16, July 18, and July 21, 1945, Stimson Diary, Stimson Papers; diary entry for July 17, 1945, Ferrell, ed., *Off the Record*, 53–54; Truman to Martha Truman, July 18, 1945, quoted in M. Truman, *Truman*, 269.

41. Entry for July 21, 1945, Stimson Diary, Stimson Papers; entries for July 20 and July 24, 1945, Walter Brown Diary, James F. Byrnes Papers, Clemson University Library; entry for July 29, 1945, Davies Diary, Box 16, Davies Papers.

42. Entries for July 13 and July 15, 1945, Walter Millis, ed., *The Forrestal Diaries* (New York: Viking Press, 1951), 74–76; entries for July 16 and July 17, 1945, Stimson Diary, Stimson Papers; Bohlen memorandum (Truman-Stalin meeting, July 18, 1945), March 28, 1960, *FRUS 1945: Potsdam*, 2: 1587–88, and on Byrnes's instructions, Grew memorandum, July 17, 1945, 1268.

43. Diary entries July 17 and July 18, 1945, Ferrell, ed., *Off the Record*, 53–54; entries for July 22 and July 23, 1945, Stimson Diary, Stimson Papers; memorandum

of Byrnes-Churchill conversation, July 23, and Truman to Chiang Kai-shek, July 23, 1945, *FRUS 1945: Potsdam*, 2: 1216, 1241.

44. Entries for July 24, 1945, Stimson Diary, Stimson Papers, and Brown Diary, Byrnes Papers, and Truman, *Memoirs*, 1: 416; Georgi Zhukov, *The Memoirs of Georgi Zhukov* (New York: Delacorte, 1971), 674–75, and David Holloway, *Stalin and the Bomb: The Soviet Union and Atomic Energy, 1939–1956* (New Haven: Yale University Press, 1994), 116–18, reveal that Stalin was not deceived.

45. Sigal, *Fighting to a Finish*, 130; Fletcher Knebel and Charles W. Bailey, *No High Ground* (New York: Harper, 1960), 124–26; Potsdam Declaration in *FRUS 1945: Potsdam*, 2: 1474–1476.

46. Sigal, *Fighting to a Finish*, 88–145, esp. 88–89, 130, 144; entries for July 27 and July 28, 1945, Brown Diary, Byrnes Papers, and entry for July 28, 1945; Millis, ed., *Forrestal Diaries*, 78.

47. Sigal, *Fighting to a Finish*, 145–52, Stimson to Truman, July 30, 1945, *FRUS 1945: Potsdam*, 2: 1374, and facsimile of Truman message in *Whistle Stop: Harry S. Truman Library Institute Newsletter* 7 (summer 1979).

48. Diary entries for July 16 and July 30, 1945, Ferrell, ed., *Off the Record*, 50–53, 57–58, and entry for July 24, 1945, Brown Diary, Byrnes Papers.

49. First, Second, and Third Plenary Meetings, July 17, July 18, and July 19, 1945, *FRUS 1945: Potsdam*, 2: 52–63, 88–98, and 116–37; meeting of the Economic Subcommittee, July 20, 1945, ibid.,141–42, and Charles Mee, *Meeting at Potsdam* (New York: Evans, 1975), 126–27.

50. Fifth Plenary Meeting, July 21, 1945, *FRUS 1945: Potsdam*, 2: 203–21.

51. Entry for July 23, 1945, Lord Charles Moran, *Churchill: Taken from the Diaries of Lord Moran* (Boston: Houghton Mifflin, 1966), 296, and entries for July 22 and July 23, 1945, Stimson Diary, Stimson Papers.

52. Sixth and Seventh Plenary Meetings, July 22 and July 23, 1945, *FRUS 1945: Potsdam*, 2: 240–68, 290–317; also Byrnes-Molotov meeting, and Sixth Meeting of the Foreign Ministers, July 23, 1945, 274–75, 276–81; entry for July 24, 1945, Moran, ed., *Diaries*, 304–6; see also Gar Alperowitz, *Atomic Diplomacy: Hiroshima and Potsdam, the Use of the Atomic Bomb and the American Confrontation with the Soviet Union*, rev. ed. (New York: Penguin Books, 1985), esp. 205–24.

53. Diary entry for July 25, 1945, Ferrell, ed., *Off the Record*, 55–56, Truman to Bess Truman, July 29 and July 31, 1945, Ferrell, ed., *Dear Bess*, 522–23; entry for July 28, 1945, Davies Journal, Box 16, Davies Papers.

54. Ninth and Tenth Plenary Meetings, July 27 and July 28, and Soviet Reparations Proposal, July 29, 1945, *FRUS 1945: Potsdam*, 2: 436–43, 471–76, and 913–14; on Byrnes, entry for July 27, 1945, Walter Brown Notes, Byrnes Papers.

55. Truman-Molotov meeting, July 29, 1945, *FRUS 1945: Potsdam*, 2: 471–76.

56. Ibid., Byrnes-Molotov meeting, and Pauley to Byrnes, July 30, 1945, 480–83, 917.

57. Ibid., Tenth Meeting of Foreign Ministers, July 30, and Byrnes-Molotov conversation, July 31, 1945, 483–97, 510; James F. Byrnes, *Speaking Frankly* (New York: Harper, 1947), 85.

58. Truman to Bess Truman, July 31, 1945, Ferrell, ed., *Dear Bess*, 522–23; Eleventh Plenary Meeting, July 31, 1945, *FRUS 1945: Potsdam*, 2: 510–40; Kuklick, *American Policy and Division of Germany*, 128–60; Stalin on "calculation of forces" in Fourth Plenary Meeting, July 20, 1945, *FRUS 1945: Potsdam*, 2: 180.

59. Alexander Cadogan to Lady Theodosia, July 31, 1945, David Dilks, ed., *The Diaries of Sir Alexander Cadogan, O.M., 1938–1945* (New York: Putnam, 1971), 777–78.

60. Truman to Martha Ellen and Mary Truman, July 30, 1945, Truman, *Memoirs*, 1: 402, and Knebel and Bailey, *No High Ground*, 1–2; entry for August 3, 1945, Brown Diary, Byrnes Papers, Byrnes to Harriman, August 5, 1945, *FRUS 1945*, 6: 955–56, and Knebel and Bailey, *No High Ground*, 2–3.

61. Entry for August 9, 1945, Ayers Diary, Box 25, Ayers Papers; Harriman to Byrnes, August 8, 1945 (2 cables), *FRUS 1945*, 7: 958–65; Herbert Feis, *Japan Subdued: The Atomic Bomb and the End of World War II*, rev. ed. (Princeton: Princeton University Press, 1966), 126, and Mee, *Meeting at Potsdam*, 288.

62. On Japan's decision to surrender, see Robert A. Pape, "Why Japan Surrendered," *International Security* 18 (fall 1993): 154–201, who argues that Russian entry into the war was decisive for Japan's military, which now concluded that it would be impossible to defend the home islands, and Herbert Bix, "Japan's Delayed Surrender: A Reinterpretation," *Diplomatic History* 19 (spring 1995): 197–225, who says Emperor Hirohito belatedly joined the "peace camp" in June 1945 and did not move positively until August, despite overwhelming military reality and knowledge of Russia's likely entry into the war. Bix doubts that assurances of the emperor's status would have produced surrender during June-July but also says that conventional bombing and Russian entry into the war probably would have caused Japan to surrender without use of atomic bombs and before the invasion planned for November. On Truman and White House deliberations to modify surrender terms, see entries for August 10, 1945, Stimson Diary, Stimson Papers; Millis, ed., *Forrestal Diaries*, 83, and Brown Diary, Byrnes Papers.

63. Diary entries for August 10, 1945, Blum, ed., *Price of Vision*, 473–74, and Millis, ed., *Forrestal Diaries*, 84.

64. Feis, *Atomic Bomb*, 139–43, and Sigal, *Fighting to a Finish*, 224–81.

65. Harriman, *Special Envoy*, 496–501; General Order no. 1 (prepared August 11, 1945), *FRUS 1945*, 7: 635–39.

66. Kuklick, *American Policy and Division of Germany*, 162.

67. Entry for June 30, 1945, Stimson Diary, Stimson Papers.

68. Truman radio report to the American people on the Potsdam Conference, August 9, 1945, *PPHST*, 1: 203–14; for a survey of recent literature on the atomic bomb decision, see J. Samuel Walker, "The Decision to Use the Bomb: A Historiographical Update," *Diplomatic History* 14 (winter, 1990): 98–114, esp. 110–11, which notes a consensus that the bomb was used "primarily for military reasons and secondarily for diplomatic ones" but concedes that Truman and his advisers knew that the bomb was not necessary to end the war quickly without the need to invade Japan; John Roy Skates, *The Invasion of Japan: Alternative to the Bomb* (Columbia: University

of South Carolina Press, 1994), focuses on military planning and concludes that use of the bomb against "an already defeated Japan" resulted from "America's rigorous insistence on unconditional surrender and the irrational, suicidal, and hopeless nature of the Japan's last defenses" (257); Skates, however, devotes little attention to the political considerations of Truman, Byrnes, and Stimson.

69. Diary entry for July 26, 1945, Ferrell, ed., *Off the Record*, 56–57; diary entry for May 7, 1945, Butcher, *My Three Years with Eisenhower*, 836.

11. Endings and Beginnings

J. Garry Clifford

President Harry S. Truman spent his first night at the White House on Monday, May 7, 1945, the eve of his sixty-first birthday. Earlier that morning at 2:41 A.M. in Reims, France, American, British, and French officials witnessed Col. Gen. Alfred Jodl of the German High Command signing surrender documents to end the war in Europe. Truman, Winston Churchill, and Joseph Stalin would simultaneously announce the surrender at nine o'clock the next morning (Washington time). "Isn't that some birthday present?" the president wrote his aged mother on White House stationery.[1]

Millions of radio listeners heard Truman acclaim the "solemn but glorious hour" on May 8. As Americans danced and hugged from Maine to California, Universal newsreels provided same-day coverage for movie audiences, entitled *War Ends in Europe—President Proclaims V-E Day,* which showed "New York millions celebrating in the canyons of Wall Street" and "the playground of the world—Times Square."[2] New signs appeared in tobacco shops, "Yes, they're back," referring both to soldiers and to cigarettes.[3] The British ambassador in Washington described a mood of "sober triumph . . . made grave by the thought of the Pacific ordeals yet to come, of the difficulties of the path of international reconstruction, and of the devastation of Europe." Americans, he added, saw the Japanese war as "a bitter and heavy duty to be fulfilled as rapidly as possible. . . . It is as if all available emotions had been expended upon the great individual monsters like Hitler, Goebbels, Goering, Mussolini, with little feeling left . . . for the nameless mass of vermin as the Japanese are conceived to be."[4]

In San Francisco, British diplomat Alexander Cadogan listened to the speeches on the radio from the restaurant atop the Mark Hopkins Hotel. He regretted not drinking to the king's health because "the only form of celebration here . . . is the closing of all Bars for twenty-four hours, and the drink was all locked away."[5]

Winston Churchill broadcast his announcement to the British people at midafternoon (London time) from the Cabinet Room at 10 Downing Street. He paid special tribute to "our Russian comrades, whose prowess in the field has been one of the grand contributions to general victory." One of those listening to the loudspeakers in Parliament Square recorded that when Churchill proclaimed "the evil-doers . . . now lie prostrate before us," the assembled onlookers "gasped at the phrase. 'Advance Britannia!' [Churchill] shouted at the end, and there followed . . . *God Save the King* which we all sang very loud indeed."[6]

Later that afternoon Churchill hailed the crowds from a balcony over-looking Whitehall. "This is your victory," he shouted, whereupon the voices roared back, "No—it is yours."[7] Jubilant Britons cavorted from Picadilly Circus to Trafalgar Square, but no guns or sirens sounded so as not to revive painful memories—only the pealing of the bells, and the whistles of tugs on the Thames sounding the "doot, doot, dooooot of the V," and the buzzing of planes swooping over the city, dropping red and green signals toward "the blur of smiling, upturned faces."[8] That evening Princess Elizabeth and Princess Margaret were allowed to mingle with the throngs outside Buckingham Palace. "Poor darlings," their father wrote in his diary, "they have never had any fun yet."[9]

In Weimar, Germany, Iris Carpenter, a correspondent for the British Broadcasting Corporation, joined Allied soldiers drinking cognac and schnapps beneath huge battle maps marked with flags, swastikas, and numbers. She suddenly realized that the brown splotches and green splashes and blue lines no longer indicated "hills which the enemy held with perfect observation over our troops, or forests . . . to fight through, or rivers . . . to be bridged by infantry under heavy fire." They were "just woods, green and exquisite in spring, and hills, heat-hazed for a perfect May day, and rivers, sparkling in the sun."[10] In Berlin, Gen. Omar Bradley could think only of the "586,627 American soldiers" who had fallen since D day—"135,576 to rise no more. The grim figures haunted me. I could hear the cries of the wounded, smell the stench of death. I could not sleep: I closed my eyes and thanked God for victory."[11]

In Moscow, the Soviet government suspected that the Germans might still fight in the east despite the formal surrender, so the official announcement of victory was delayed until May 10. That morning George F. Kennan, the American chargé d'affaires, witnessed "a holiday mood so exuberant as to defy all normal disciplinary restraints." When hordes of marching Muscovites spotted the Stars and Stripes atop the American chancery in the center of the city, they broke into a spontaneous demonstration of "almost delirious friendship," as Kennan recalled. While more than two hundred thousand people chanted "Long live Truman!" and "Long live Roosevelt's memory!" those embassy officials who joined the celebration were "tossed enthusiastically into the air and passed on friendly hands over the heads of the crowd, to be lost, eventually, in a confused orgy of good feeling." Kennan thereupon procured a Soviet flag to hang alongside the American flag, thus eliciting further cheers from the crowd. Climbing out onto the pedestal of one of the great pillars that fronted the U.S. embassy, Kennan shouted in Russian: "Congratulations on the day of Victory! All honor to the Soviet allies." Later that evening a less buoyant Kennan told a British journalist that he felt "sad" for those Russians who "hoped for so much from victory" because "things would not be put back together again all at once; peace could scarcely be what these people dreamed of it as being." According to the reporter, in words the American diplomat later denied using, Kennan then commented, "They think the war has ended. But it is really only beginning."[12]

The termination of World War II in Europe is easily pinpointed, despite the chronological variations in official Soviet and Anglo-American proclamations. That the end of a global war was followed in short order by the beginnings of a protracted conflict known as the cold war is also indisputable. Whether the end of one war led directly and inevitably to another is less certain.

For some participants the transition seemed instantaneous. On the evening of V-E Day, for example, Churchill learned of Soviet complaints about the way Britain had protested the recent seizure and imprisonment of sixteen Polish underground leaders. "We are utterly indifferent," the prime minister replied, "to anything the Soviets may say. . . . No one here believes a single word."[13] As Churchill later wrote in his memoirs, "The Soviet menace, in my mind, had already replaced the Nazi foe."[14] Likewise, within two weeks of the Nazi capitulation, a Washington journalist confided to his editor that he was hearing "more war talk about a clash with Russia" than he had noticed in 1940 and 1941 "as to Germany."[15]

Without question, World War II had shattered the Europe-centered international system of the 1930s. Some 35 million people perished in Europe during the war, including 22 million in the USSR and 6 million in both Poland and Germany. At war's end most cities from the North Sea to the Volga lay in ruins. Ghastly numbers of human and animal carcasses littered the green fields of France and Germany, now a breeding ground for disease. Much of the Netherlands lay under water since winter 1944, its inhabitants reduced to eating tulip bulbs to fend off starvation. Throughout Europe countless cathedrals, castles, monuments, frescoes, sculptures, paintings, and other artistic masterpieces had vanished, the victims of bombs, shells, and human plunder. In only one of many wanton depredations, German armies had leveled Florence, Italy, destroyed its beautiful medieval bridges, and then mined the ruins; beneath Dante's statue in the Colonnade of the Uffizi an anonymous witness scribbled: "*In sul passo dell'Arno / I tedeschi hanno lasciato / I recordi della loro civilita* (In their passage of the Arno the Germans have left the record of their civilization).[16]

War's end also brought the liberation of the concentration camps, as the names Auschwitz, Buchenwald, and Belsen became forever synonymous with evil. Viewing the first newsreels from a movie theater in Picadilly, an American socialist-pacifist gaped at the flesh-and-bones survivors, "the sticks in black-and-white prison garb" shuffling across the screen. "It was unbearable," he recalled. "People coughed in embarrassment, and in embarrassment many laughed."[17] Few laughed when the full gory details of Nazi genocide became known—the Zyklon B gas chambers and crematoriums, diabolical medical experiments, gold fillings, human lampshades, mass sterilizations, meticulous records of deadly bureaucratic efficiency, and the unwillingness or inability of Allied governments to do more to rescue or resettle victims of the Final Solution. Of 10 million Jews in Nazi-occupied Europe in 1940, Hitler's Holocaust had claimed at least 6 million by 1945. In large measure, Jewish survivors took command of their own destiny after the war by leading the "exodus" to Palestine and creating the new nation of Israel in 1948.

A generation of young Europeans in their twenties and thirties virtually disappeared or scattered because of the war. Millions of displaced persons had become separated from their homelands. Transportation and communications networks had broken down. Factories no longer operated. Few bridges still spanned Europe's waterways. Hungry orphans, veterans, former POWs, deserters, and refugees struggled amid the rubble to reconstruct shattered nations and economies. Historian Donald Cameron Watt has described "populations on the move, walking, cycling, pushing perambulators, driving carts laden with household utensils and personal belongings, trekking less in hope than in hopelessness, searching for some point of reference where perhaps a new beginning could be made. They found little to aid them in the task."[18]

V-E Day left Europe divided between the soldiers of the United States and those of the Soviet Union, both historically non-European powers. With Germany devastated and Britain bankrupt, two British armies and one French army represented all that remained of traditional European power. The war had so enervated the British, French, and Dutch, moreover, that they could no longer hold on to their overseas empires. The British, for example, gave independence to India in 1947 and to Burma in 1948, and the Dutch relinquished Indonesia the following year. As an American diplomat had predicted during the war, any denial of self-determination to colonial peoples "would be like failing to install a safety valve and then waiting for the boiler to blow up."[19]

The contrast with prosperous America, untouched by enemy bombs and marauding armies, was stark. The United States had become a full-fledged global power for the first time in its history. The U.S. gross national product leaped from $90.5 billion in 1939 to $211.9 billion in 1945. Having produced only 5,856 military and civilian aircraft in 1939, American factories turned out more than 300,000 planes during the war, including 95,000 in 1944. At the Tehran Conference in 1943, Joseph Stalin had toasted the United States as the "country of machines."[20] Economists cheered the American "production miracle."[21] In historian Thomas McCormick's words, the United States had become "the global workshop and banker, umpire and policeman, preacher and teacher."[22] Americans, boasted one official, faced "the pleasant predicament of having to learn to live 50 percent better than they had ever lived before."[23] With troops in Asia and Europe, the world's largest navy and air force, a monopoly of nuclear weapons, and a galloping economy, Washington possessed what political scientists call "compellent" power and commanded first rank in world affairs.

In filling the power vacuum created by the retreating colonial powers and the defeated Axis, the United States quickly found itself in competition with its touchy wartime ally, the Soviet Union. Eventually a bipolar international structure emerged from the Soviet-American rivalry. The Soviets' truculent behavior, suspicious accusations, and caustic language irritated Americans. Truman complained that they negotiated "with a boorishness worthy of stable boys."[24] Soviet troops occupied several Eastern European countries and part of Germany at war's end. Although the USSR lacked a superior navy or air force and had no atomic weapons, it possessed dominant regional power by virtue of its wartime military successes. Its war scars were palpable: one-ninth of the population dead, more than thirty thousand industrial plants and forty thousand miles of railroad tracks destroyed, thousands of towns and cities leveled. Motivated by a mixture of traditional Russian nationalism and Communist ideology, seeking security against a revived Germany, and facing monumental tasks of reconstruction inside its own borders, the Kremlin intended to make the most of the limited power it possessed. Often cruel and ruthless, especially to his fellow citizens, yet cautious and realistic, Joseph Stalin vowed that his country would never again be invaded through Eastern Europe. Nonetheless, compared to the United States, as George Kennan reported from Moscow, the Soviet Union ranked as the "weaker force."[25]

The ensuing half century since V-E Day 1945, including the end of the cold war and the dissolution of the Soviet Union in 1989–1991, gives historians ample opportunity for perspective. For the past decade especially, with archival restrictions relaxed and new sources, including Soviet records, rapidly becoming available, scholars have reexamined World War II by integrating new information and asking more complex questions. What has emerged is a picture of World War II quite different from the old arguments that had previously dominated historical scholarship: conservative critics deplored Soviet control of Eastern Europe and blamed FDR and Churchill for their alleged appeasement of Stalin; defenders argued that the Anglo-Americans made the right decisions but Stalin had reneged on his agreements; and realists claimed that a pragmatic Roosevelt had to balance domestic and international priorities and win the war against Hitler before he could use American economic power, atomic power, and the United Nations to moderate postwar Soviet behavior.[26]

In addition to delineating Anglo-Soviet-American differences over military strategy and postwar goals, multiarchival studies have used social science theories to trace in detail internal (as well as interallied) disagreements within the policy-making process. Reflecting FDR's wartime remark that "I never let my right hand know what my left hand does," bureaucratic analysis suggests that the formulation and implementation of key policies, including war termination, emerged from a welter of organizational goals and routines, palace intrigues, and political trade-offs that often differed greatly from what the president had ordered or desired.[27] As for cold war culpability, "traditionalist" and "realist" scholars have argued for decades that unrelenting Soviet expansion and the cruel paranoia of Joseph Stalin precipitated the cold war and that Presidents Roosevelt and Truman only belatedly acted to save Western Europe from totalitarian conquest. Traditionalists insist that Stalin blatantly imposed Soviet rule over Eastern Europe and deliberately sabotaged the Grand Alliance because he nurtured global ambitions and cynically revived the specter of capitalist encirclement to justify his Communist totalitarian system. Revisionist historians have stressed American initiatives, especially the goal of creating a postwar international order along liberal capitalist lines, thereby securing markets and raw materials for American business and avoiding postwar depression. Revisionists claim that Washington was neither naive nor hesitant to use American power, including the nuclear monopoly, to challenge Soviet hegemony in Eastern Europe, defeat Communism in Western Europe, revive and integrate West Germany within an anti-Soviet alliance, and contain revolutionary nationalist threats in the former colonial areas.

A more recent "postrevisionist" interpretation holds that initial postwar Soviet moves *were* limited to protecting its periphery and curbing German and Japanese power and that American policy makers in 1945 actually saw the chief obstacles to a prosperous and peaceful world order in the enormous devastation wrought by the war and in power vacuums in Asia and Europe, not necessarily from machinations by the Kremlin. Before too long, however, Washington officials perceived a serious threat in Moscow's capacity to exploit postwar turmoil beyond its own borders. Thus did U.S. states-men "prudently" redefine national security to require a preponderant bal-ance of power in Eurasia, an open, prosperous, and predominantly capitalist global economy, strategic spheres of influence in Latin America and the Pacific, and the continued American monopoly over nuclear weapons. As historian Melvyn Leffler has written, "The United States wanted not a bal-ance of power but a configuration of power in the international system that was preponderantly to America's advantage."[28]

Reflecting the latest scholarship and multiarchival research, authors in the current volume ask important questions about this critical juncture in world history. How and why did World War II end as it did in Europe? Was it planned, or did it just happen? Did the circumstances of its termination make the cold war with the Soviet Union inevitable? Was it necessary for the war to end in the total defeat of German forces, amid economic privation, near famine, and ongoing genocide in the death camps? How much control did statesmen have? What were the forces operating on them that led to the choices they made (or seemed to make)? Were there viable options that might have produced better outcomes? Could leaders have made better choices? In short, how rational or logical was the course of events that culminated in V-E Day and its aftermath?

As Theodore Wilson emphasizes in chapter 1, we know much more about how wars begin than how they end. Moreover, compared to the vast and sometimes heated scholarship on the atomic bomb and the end of the war in Asia, far less scholarly attention has focused on how World War II ended in Europe. Indeed, much of the historical literature, written from twenty-twenty hindsight, evokes an aura of inevitability—a presumption that the war lurched toward a predestined and apocalyptic denouement symbolized by the blackened rubble around the Führerbunker and the mushroom clouds over Japan. Nevertheless, as Wilson persuasively demonstrates, Allied lead-ers at the time believed that the war would end differently. The tangled, pro-tracted, and bloody fight to the finish confounded expectations and adversely affected the transition to a postwar world.

Allied planners prior to D day, according to Wilson, operated under sev-eral interrelated assumptions. They believed that, once successful, the Anglo-American invasion of France would quickly induce the collapse of German resistance, probably within three months, as early as September 1944. They anticipated a swift and "rational" surrender in which Hitler and top-level Nazis would be dead or captured, with an essentially undamaged German administrative apparatus left intact. They also assumed that the Allied coali-tion would remain strong and cohesive into the postwar period, an expecta-tion confirmed by the Yalta agreements for the three-power occupation of

Germany and by the Soviet pledge to enter the war against Japan. The Allied timetable envisaged the Pacific war as primarily an American effort lasting another eighteen to twenty-four months, with postwar reconstruction scheduled to start in 1947. Interim problems of refugees and famine would be met by United Nations relief agencies, the Big Three would disarm and pacify occupied territories, and the World Bank and the International Monetary Fund would begin to operate. As it happened, the actual end of the war in Europe came eight months later than projected, followed by the sudden denouement in the Pacific war three months later. The orderly timetables turned out egregiously wrong. The eventual cost of these Allied "miscalculations," writes Wilson, proved "overwhelming to the exhausted peoples of Europe and Asia."

Aside from "wishful thinking about the intentions and tenacity" of Nazi Germany and its propensity for Wagnerian self-immolation, why did the Allies not seek alternatives to ending the war short of total victory? An early negotiated peace might have saved billions in war damages and millions of lives, including numerous victims of the Holocaust. Wilson argues that President Roosevelt's commitment to unconditional surrender sprang less from any concern for Russian sensibilities and more from his own determination to rectify Woodrow Wilson's political blunder of 1918. An advocate of "retributive justice" toward Germany who believed World War II resulted directly from the failure to make clear to Germans that they had lost once and for all, FDR wanted no one to say that the Allies had not been tough enough the second time around. Wilson even suggests that Roosevelt's refusal to modify unconditional surrender policy during summer and fall 1944 may have reflected electoral worries vis-à-vis his Republican opponent Thomas E. Dewey. Yet the very fierceness of Germany's resistance, especially during the Battle of the Bulge, militated against any serious reconsideration of peace terms. Instead of dividing his opponents as he intended, Hitler's eleventh-hour offensive and boasts about new secret weapons actually served to cement the Grand Alliance until final victory was achieved.

Nor would Germany have been likely to respond to conditional surrender terms. Those anti-Nazi leaders who plotted unsuccessfully against Hitler envisaged a peace settlement that would have left Germany as the dominant power in Europe, an outcome clearly unacceptable to the Allies. In any event, neither Churchill nor Roosevelt ever responded to overtures from the German *Widerstand*, which they assumed to be impotent in a totalitarian state.[29] Further, Hitler's own fanatical determination to fight on at any cost resonated within the Wehrmacht, which fought doggedly to the end, and within the German population, which remained blindly loyal to the Nazi regime. Even as the enfeebled führer descended into madness and mysticism in the final days, last-minute peace feelers by Foreign Minister Joachim von Ribbentrop and Heinrich Himmler did not offer viable surrender terms.

Wilson further suggests that there was no deviation from unconditional surrender in 1944–1945 because war termination does not usually result from rational actions by unitary governments. Rather, different segments of the bureaucracies in belligerent countries advocate and pursue policies that reflect their own organizational versions of the national interest. What emerges from a tangle of institutional and personal turf battles bears little resemblance to purposeful behavior. This was especially true with respect to FDR's untidy management methods, which a British diplomat once compared to "a disorderly line of beaters out shooting; they do put the rabbits out of the bracken, but they don't come out where you expect."[30] Roosevelt jerry-rigged his administrative system so that he would have the final say on all policies. But with age and ill health eroding his legendary juggling skills, his predilection for postponement often meant that bureaucratic infighting, momentum, chance, and his uninformed successor would decide in the long run. Thus did the Departments of State, War, and Treasury fight among themselves and with Allied counterparts over "soft" and "hard" postwar plans for a still unconquered and unoccupied Germany. A sprawling Anglo-American military bureaucracy made elaborate plans for disparate operations in global theaters, with planners focusing on their own military campaigns with little or no attention to the larger political aims—and without the knowledge of secret weapons that would end the war and irrevocably transform international politics. And the "unconditional surrender" formula, devised in 1943 as a public relations ploy, took on a life of its own with the unintended consequence of strengthening Germany's resolve to fight to the bitter end. In short, the coordination necessary for a swift "endgame" was conspicuously lacking.

Wilson is reluctant to embrace inevitability, however. Comparing the role of contingency in historical causation to Saturn's rings ("a stable coalition of individual elements"), he poses the "what if" question. What if Operation Market Garden had secured the Rhine bridges in September 1944? Suppose that the Bomb Plot had succeeded in July? What if Hitler had stayed in his East Prussian headquarters after November 1944 and died in battle? Such an early end to the Third Reich, as one historian has speculated, might have caused "the flooding of most of Germany by the British and the Americans, a great swirling confusion of Anglo-Saxon and German armies, the former wending their way eastward in the midst of a still largely intact German people, eventually meeting the suspicious Russians somewhere in eastern Germany."[31] For Wilson, a scenario without the Battles of Berlin and the Bulge, without thousands of corpses at Auschwitz and Dresden, and with German resistance leaders still alive might have bequeathed a less conflicted postwar world.

Conflict predominated, nevertheless. As Anna Cienciala emphasizes in chapter 2, the celebrations of V-E Day seemed less joyous in Eastern Europe because the "correlation of forces," in Stalin's infamous phrase, translated into Soviet control over the region. Disappointed that the Red Army, not western troops, had liberated their homelands, East European leaders hoped that the Allies, as stipulated under the Yalta accords, would set up representative, provisional governments, which would then hold free elections. Except for short interludes with respect to Hungary and Czechoslovakia, it did not happen.

In her detailed discussion of Poland's thwarted desire for postwar independence, Cienciala blames Stalin first and then Roosevelt, more than any intransigent, "all-or-nothing" behavior by the London Poles, for the unhappy denouement. In view of Stalin's unrelenting demand for a subservient Poland and Roosevelt's apparent nonchalance as to "whether the countries bordering on Russia became communized," Churchill's half-hearted efforts to establish a genuinely independent Polish government under Stanislas Mikołajczyk had little chance of success.[32] Indeed, given his realistic assessment that the Red Army was key to defeating Germany, FDR's chief criteria for a new government in Warsaw was that it should satisfy Stalin and Polish-Americans, not necessarily indigenous Poles.

In essence, Allied military strategy determined the political outcome. Although Cienciala suggests that Churchill's so-called Balkan strategy might have rescued an independent Poland, failure to mount an Anglo-American invasion of France in 1942–1943 (largely due to British insistence on a North Africa/Mediterranean strategy) guaranteed that the Red Army would enter Eastern Europe first; once the Russians had "liberated" adjoining countries, they were not about to open them to anyone. Nor did Churchill offer *political* (as opposed to *military*) arguments for invading the Balkans to forestall Soviet designs until after D day—after, as one recent scholar writes, "the Western Allies had designed and applied the main moves in their European strategy."[33] Indeed, the prime minister's pipedream proposal in August 1944 to send token Anglo-American forces from Italy to race the Red Army to Vienna would not have changed the fate of Poland and Germany, the key states of Eastern and Central Europe.[34] In the end, the political price for having to rely on the Red Army against the Wehrmacht was paid in Moscow's postwar domination of the region.

David Hogan's historiographical chapter on the 1945 decision to halt at the Elbe emphasizes the dangers of playing Monday-morning quarterback. If Gen. William H. Simpson's Ninth Army had been allowed to rumble into

Berlin, if the British "single thrust" strategy had prevailed over the American "broad front" approach, if Gen. Dwight D. Eisenhower had rated the political value of taking Berlin higher than the military value of reducing Hitler's mythical Alpine redoubt, if an ailing and overly sanguine Roosevelt had not already placed Berlin within the postwar Soviet zone of occupation, if Churchill had pressed Truman harder, if only the cautious Americans had been willing to expend casualties to capture Berlin, then presumably the postwar world would have turned out much more favorably.

Not so, according to Hogan. In his careful survey of the arguments and evidence, he judges the Elbe decision as basically correct because the capture of Berlin would not have advanced the Allied military goal of winning the war by destroying German armed forces. He argues that the zonal accords on Germany were a *good* bargain for the West at the time they were negotiated; the three zones (before the French were given theirs) were approximately equal in size; they left the West in control of German industry; and they offered a fair basis for future cooperation. Nor should Eisenhower have violated prior agreements to snatch Berlin for political advantages, Hogan writes, because the "Western Allies, for all their disillusionment with Stalin since Yalta, had not abandoned all hope of postwar cooperation with the Soviet Union." Besides, if the Allies had breached the accords by attempting to take Berlin, the Russians might have seized valuable territories elsewhere and not relinquished them, as they later evacuated the Danish island of Bornholm in the Baltic. As Hogan observes, most Soviet accounts have interpreted the Eisenhower/Berlin controversy as capitalist propaganda aimed at denigrating the triumphs of the Red Army, which could easily have won any race to Berlin. Recent scholarship, based on access to previously closed Russian sources, reconfirms that "having expended so much blood and energy to defeat the German Army in the field, Soviet commanders were in no mood to allow their Western allies to seize the final victory."[35]

Ronan Fanning examines in chapter 4 the end-of-the-war fortunes of Ireland, a neutral country that had fortuitously avoided invasion by either Allied or Axis armies. Notwithstanding Churchill's bitter post–V-E Day accusation that Eamon de Valera's government had "frolicked" with the Germans "to their hearts' content," Fanning notes that Eire's public display of even-handed neutrality masked a second, secret policy of cooperation with the Allies, especially in matters of intelligence and espionage. However irritating, de Valera's official expression of condolences after Hitler's death seemed a mere trifle compared to the tens of thousands of Southern Irish who served in Allied forces during the war. Righteous American anger at the punctilios of Irish neutrality conveniently overlooked the fact that until Pearl Harbor the United States, like Eire, had claimed the status of a neutral, even as it openly (and secretly) aided the victims of aggression in steps short of war. Having espoused neutrality, opposed entangling alliances, and gained advantage from Europe's distress for nearly two hundred years, Americans, despite their new superpower status, should have better understood the vulnerabilities and mixed motives of a small state on the periphery of Europe amid global war. Similarly, American diplomats who waxed furious over Dublin's refusal to state categorically that it would deny asylum to Axis war criminals did not necessarily know that their colleagues in military intelligence were launching Project Paperclip to bring German scientists and technicians, some of them war criminals, to the United States to assist in the "development of new types of weapons."[36] Finally, Fanning points to the delicious irony of U.S. minister David Gray urging the appointment of a professional foreign service officer as his successor because an "Irish American of Catholic descent is at a great disadvantage here" and then choosing as his courier none other than Jack Kennedy, "Joe's boy," later the first Irish Catholic to become president and the martyred brother of the recent U.S. ambassador to Ireland, Jean Kennedy Smith.

Hal Wert's chapter on the food crisis in Northwest Europe in 1944–1945 vividly illustrates how military vagaries adversely affected another small country. In the case of Holland, it was not military strategy dictating a political outcome, but armies and civil affairs officers not getting where they needed to go fast enough. Operating under the "collapse theory" scenario in which the Germans would evacuate the Netherlands and civil administrators would take over quickly, Allied military planners stockpiled huge stores of food in England to be ferried to Dutch ports for distribution. The failure to seize the Rhine bridges at Arnhem in September upset all timetables. Instead of withdrawing, the German army of two hundred thousand dug in to defend "Fortress Holland" through the "Hunger Winter" of 1944–1945, during which 3.7 million Dutch civilians teetered on the brink of starvation.

As Wert makes clear, catastrophe loomed because of the entrenched bureaucratic assumption that the quickest way to relieve suffering in Holland was "the rapid completion of our main operations" to defeat Germany first. Military fixations caused delays that resulted in several thousand deaths from starvation and as many as .25 million victims of hunger-edema. Only eleventh-hour appeals from Queen Wilhelmina convinced Churchill of the imminence of mass starvation, whereupon Churchill persuaded Roosevelt of the necessity for Allied intervention. The willingness of Reichskommissar Arthur Seyss-Inquart to disobey Berlin and negotiate a separate truce to permit emergency food supplies was also fortuitous. Beginning on the morning of April 28, 1945, some 253 Lancaster heavy bombers crisscrossed the Netherlands dropping thousands of "mercy bombs" in Operation Manna.

Over the next ten days some 14.5 million individual ration packages were parachuted into Holland. German forces in Holland formally surrendered on May 5, and mass starvation was narrowly averted.

Ironically, American leaders did not understand the connection between famine in Holland and graver postwar crises yet to come. Judge Samuel Rosenman's survey of conditions in Northwest Europe emphasized the appalling level of destruction and the need for long-term American aid to ensure recovery. His plea was premature. Optimistically recalling the aftermath of World War I when Europe had experienced only a year of hard times before recovery, the victorious Americans, suddenly affluent after years of depression and sacrifice, were in "no mood in the summer of 1945 to accept the burden of global responsibility that waited in the wings."

Mark Stoler also underscores the sterility of imposing cold war assumptions on the past in chapter 6 by tracing the U.S. military's assessment of wartime relations with the Soviet Union. He demonstrates that the Joint Chiefs of Staff (JCS) only belatedly viewed Moscow as a postwar adversary. Keenly aware that the Soviet Union would enjoy "assured military dominance" in Eastern Europe, the Middle East, and Northeast Asia after the war, the JCS nonetheless argued against early political confrontations because they fully appreciated the Red Army's destruction of the Wehrmacht and wanted Soviet help in the war against Japan. The War Department's decision in 1943 to limit the U.S. Army's size to ninety divisions ensured that reliance on the Red Army would continue for the remainder of the war. Despite early anti-Soviet suspicion from Navy Secretary James Forrestal and warnings from Gen. John R. Deane, head of the U.S. Military Mission to Moscow, that "we must be tougher," Secretary of War Henry L. Stimson articulated the prevailing Pentagon view on the eve of V-E Day: "In the big military matters the Soviet Government had kept their word and . . . the military authorities of the United States had come to count on it." Despite Deane's complaints about thirty-four cases of Soviet noncooperation, the Joint Chiefs rejected his recommendations to retaliate by withholding Lend-Lease supplies. As late as August 1945 the U.S. Army was still giving Moscow its highest-grade ULTRA intelligence to facilitate Soviet attacks against Japan's Kwantung Army in Manchuria and Korea.[37] Not until after Potsdam and Hiroshima did the Joint Chiefs conclude that the Soviets were bent on world domination and therefore recast their strategic plans to conform to a cold war crusade.

Just as total victory over the Axis caused seismic changes in the international system after the war, so too did the war alter internal alignments in American politics. Randall Woods captures changing congressional attitudes toward foreign affairs in 1945 through a triptych of key senators: Ohio's

Robert A. Taft ("Mr. Republican"), the voice of unrepentant isolationism; Arthur H. Vandenberg of Michigan, the former isolationist who confessed past errors and espoused conservative international goals as the Republican champion of bipartisanship; and J. William Fulbright, the Arkansas Rhodes scholar and liberal advocate for the United Nations, multilateral trade, and international federation and the eventual critic of American "arrogance of power" during the Vietnam War.

Woods suggests that, despite initial congressional disagreements over America's responsibilities in fashioning a postwar international order, the perception of a growing Soviet threat soon created a cold war consensus. Conservatives and isolationists unwilling to spend billions ("globaloney") to finance European recovery did so after 1947 when the Truman administration, heeding Vandenberg's advice to "scare hell out of the American people," depicted in lurid colors "totalitarian regimes" (i.e., Soviet Russia) that threatened freedom everywhere. So compelling did the anticommunist crusade become that even Taft, who voted against the North Atlantic Treaty Organization (NATO) and usually opposed presidential dominance of foreign policy, eventually supported the Korean War and other far-flung commitments in Europe and Asia. "For isolationists," one pacifist later quipped, "these Americans do certainly get around."[38]

Bipartisanship, which Vandenberg likened to "co-pilots in the foreign policy take-offs as well as the crash landings," actually became the perfect executive tactic for containing both the Soviet threat and congressional dissent.[39] President Roosevelt had started the policy by "eating humble pie" before Pearl Harbor and wooing conservatives who opposed the New Deal but supported anti-Axis policies.[40] During and after the war, Republicans like Vandenberg, Wendell Willkie, Warren Austin, and John Foster Dulles were consulted, invited to international conferences, indeed, were anointed as "spokesmen" for Democratic administrations. They had only slight impact on the formulation of policy, but their support in mobilizing congressional majorities became vital. A diplomat missed the point when he wrote, "I could not accept the assumption that Senators were all such idiots that they deserved admiring applause every time they could be persuaded by the State Department to do something sensible."[41] Secretary of State Dean Acheson was much more astute. "Bipartisan foreign policy is the ideal for the executive," he later explained, "because you cannot run this damn country under the Constitution any other way except by fixing the whole organization so it doesn't work the way it is supposed to work. Now the way to do that is to say politics stops at the seaboard—anyone who denies that postulate is a son of a bitch and a crook and not a true patriot. Now if people will swallow that then you're off to the races."[42]

One example of congressional bipartisanship in 1945 prefigured what was to come. Following the lead of former president Herbert Hoover, who met with Truman in late May to discuss possible surrender terms for Japan, several Republican senators pushed for clarification of the "unconditional surrender" formula.[43] They worried that Germany might "have capitulated much earlier with the savings of thousands of American lives if our Government had not insisted on such stringent terms" and feared that the complete destruction of German and Japanese power would create a vacuum for Soviet expansion to fill. The Republican National Committee thus prepared a speech for Sen. Wallace H. White of Maine, the GOP minority whip, to deliver on July 2, 1945, requesting the president to state precisely what unconditional surrender would entail.[44]

White's speech put Republicans on record as interpreting the formula *not* to mean "the destruction of the home or family life of the Japanese, interference in the religious beliefs of the people, abandonment of its agricultural activities and its other peaceful industries, and the loss thereby of the livelihood of the millions of people of the Japanese Empire."[45] So favorable was the public response to this speech that former ambassador Hugh Wilson, also working for the Republican National Committee, used his contacts in the State Department to include portions of White's speech in what soon became Truman's Potsdam Declaration.[46] Although the declaration lacked any specific reference to the Japanese emperor, as some Republicans had urged privately, it did facilitate Japan's eventual surrender, albeit *after* the atomic bombings of Hiroshima and Nagasaki, *after* Russian entry into the war on August 8, and *after* American assurances about retaining the emperor.

Republicans later claimed credit for their "constructive initiative" that helped "shorten the war and save untold lives."[47] Moreover, once the Republicans' favorite general, Douglas MacArthur, became the supreme allied commander in Japan after the war and treated Russia's representative as "a mere piece of furniture" (so Stalin complained), it meant that bipartisan support for Far Eastern policy would continue, especially when that policy changed after 1948 from "eliminating Japan as a military power for all time" to restoring "Hirohito's islands" as a "buffer state" against the Soviet Union.[48] Despite subsequent disagreements over who lost China, Cuba, and Iran, bipartisan support for global containment remained a fixture of cold war politics.

Vladimir Pozniakov, in his chapter on Soviet policies in 1945, asserts the inevitability of the cold war that followed. Using previously unavailable documents from the Stalin and Molotov Special Files in Moscow, he cites reports from high-ranking party and intelligence officials to illustrate extreme Soviet concerns about internal and external security at the end of the war.

Securing Soviet frontiers meant the suppression and liquidation of hundreds of thousands of Poles, Ukrainians, Belorussians, and Baltic nationals who had allegedly collaborated with the Germans. Lest capitalist contamination from Eastern and Central Europe infect the rest of Soviet society, the Stalinist hierarchy instructed millions of returning veterans not to discuss what they had seen, and former POWs and repatriated civilians went through a system of "filtration camps," which exiled all potential germ carriers to Siberia. What Stalin feared most, according to Pozniakov, were those millions of Soviet citizens who had done so much to win the war and who wanted a better life afterward. For Stalin, their rising expectations threatened to destroy the very political and social system he had created.

Rather than loosen government authority and seek economic and political cooperation with the west to improve living standards, however, the Soviet leadership imposed tighter controls over its people, consolidated a new empire along its periphery, rearmed the Red Army and Navy with new weapons, and justified the renewed siege mentality by initiating confrontation with former wartime allies.

Pozniakov's evidence suggests that Stalin's brutal behavior sprang not from any plan for global expansion or world conquest but from the felt need to protect himself and his system from external world realities. (In this sense, Pozniakov's analysis echoes George F. Kennan's famed "Long Telegram" of February 1946.) Although Stalin's official declaration of cold war did not come for two years, the actual process seemed well under way before V-E Day—as evidenced by harsh Soviet internal security policies, early recognition of the Lublin government in Poland, overt support for Communists in Romania and Bulgaria, military pressure on Iran and Turkey, growing penetration of western governments by Soviet espionage, and the crash program to build an atomic bomb.[49] Under such a rigid and reflexive system, according to Pozniakov, protracted conflict with the west became necessary and inevitable.

Yet any definitive judgment of Soviet responsibility for the cold war must await further archival documentation, especially those records that reveal the private assessments of Stalin, Molotov, and other leaders about western actions and motives.[50] Indeed, preliminary studies based on available Russian records suggest that "Soviet officials did not have preconceived plans to make Eastern Europe communist, to support the Chinese communists, or to wage war in Korea."[51]

Whatever Moscow's deeds and internal memorandums in 1945 might eventually reveal regarding inevitable and deliberate confrontation, historians must weigh allegations made by Soviet leaders at the time that they were responding to provocative behavior by the Allies. In particular, some historians charged that the Truman administration altered Roosevelt's policies and broke his promises. As with the revisionist interpretation, they concluded that Soviet reactions to Anglo-American initiatives precipitated the cold war. Both Warren Kimball and Arnold Offner acknowledge one aspect of this thesis—that FDR strove mightily to continue Soviet-American cooperation into the postwar era and willingly granted Moscow a sphere of interest in Eastern Europe.

Kimball juxtaposes Roosevelt's pragmatic idealism against Sen. Harry Truman's wishful recommendation in June 1941 that the United States should help Germany if the Russians were winning and help Russia if the Germans were winning. Seeing Hitler's Germany as a mortal threat, Roosevelt believed he had no such choice. With the "Arsenal of Democracy" geared to supplying Axis opponents, with the growing but still relatively small U.S. military forces deployed in scattered theaters, and with a British ally reluctant to invade Hitler's continental fortress, how else to get the Nazi monster off Europe's back? Victory over the Wehrmacht necessitated alliance with Russia; indeed, as Adm. Ernest King predicted in 1942, "Russia will do nine-tenths of the job of defeating Germany." Despite the Atlantic Charter's commitment to self-determination and his own reluctance to recognize the 1941 Soviet boundaries, FDR understood that the Red Army's victories would give Moscow dominance in Eastern Europe. Indeed, Great-Power regional hegemony remained central to the Rooseveltian postwar vision.[52] "Russia would be charged with keeping peace in Europe," he said in November 1942. "The United States would be charged with keeping peace in the Western Hemisphere."[53] It made no sense for Roosevelt to insist on perfect solutions in places where American power could not change things. "How many people in the United States . . . will be willing to go to war to free Estonia, Latvia, or Lithuania?" he asked his wife after the Yalta Conference.[54] At no time did Roosevelt or Churchill ever expect that Stalin would settle for less than a sphere of influence in Eastern Europe.

Yet geopolitical security in Eastern Europe did not necessarily mean an exclusive, closed region of Communist satellites. According to Kimball, FDR thought that "colonialism, not communism, was the –ism that most threatened postwar peace and stability," and like Woodrow Wilson, he sought middle ground between the unacceptable extremes of revolution and reaction. He hoped that Stalin's relations with Eastern Europe would follow a pattern suggested by the Soviet-Czech Treaty of December 1943, in which a restored Czechoslovakia would follow Moscow's foreign policy line but remain pluralistic in domestic affairs.[55] He even told a Catholic prelate that a decade of

Soviet dominance over Germany, Austria, and Hungary might make the Russians "less barbarian."[56]

Nor was Roosevelt alone in expecting Stalin to behave. "Poor Neville Chamberlain believed he could trust Hitler," Churchill commented after Yalta. "He was wrong. But I don't think I'm wrong about Stalin."[57] When friction did occur, especially over Poland, the president did his artful best to reconcile demands for perfectionism with pragmatic priorities, as he "evaded, avoided, and ignored" unpleasant realities, always "hoping to insulate the more important objective—long-term collaboration."[58] According to Kimball, critics of FDR's policies usually argue about what should have happened rather than what could have happened, thereby ignoring what the realistic options and likely outcomes actually were. Even if a Soviet sphere in Eastern Europe did not work out as benignly as Roosevelt had hoped, his persistent pursuit of détente, or a kind of international condominium, made more sense than a premature confrontation that could well have plunged postwar Europe into "a series of civil wars or possibly an even darker Orwellian condition of localized wars along an uncertain border."[59] Prescient or not, Roosevelt's vision offered a better alternative to early war, hot or cold, with unknown outcomes.[60]

Offner extends the comparison between Roosevelt and Truman in chapter 10 by demonstrating in detail how the new president "abandoned" the conciliatory policies of his predecessor between V-E Day and the end of the Pacific war in September 1945. Whereas Roosevelt had compromised at Yalta to accommodate differing historical traditions and security concerns, Truman thought the Russians "needed us more than we needed them" and that "we should be able to get 85 percent" in all negotiations.[61]

Harry Truman, a parochial nationalist from Missouri, began his presidency with a "straight one-two to the jaw" of Molotov, abruptly cutting off Lend-Lease aid to the Soviets after Germany's surrender and rejecting the Morgenthau Plan and FDR's "retributive justice" toward Germany. He also vowed that America should never again "pay reparations, feed the world, and get nothing for it but a nose thumbing."[62] According to Offner, Truman believed that "getting tough" would succeed because the atomic bomb, which he viewed as a "unique weapon" and "master card," would both shorten the Pacific war and guarantee diplomatic victories elsewhere. His impatient diplomacy at Potsdam rested on the facile assumption that diplomatic leverage would increase once atomic weapons had revealed America's immense new power. Like his new secretary of state, James F. Byrnes, Truman thought the bomb would make the Soviets more "manageable"—especially in Europe regarding terms for the occupation and rehabilitation of Germany and payment of reparations to Russia. Instead, Soviet-American conflict increased.

Offner offers ample evidence to support Henry Stimson's comment at Potsdam that the atomic bomb "is tying in what we are doing in all fields."[63] This pervasive concern at the highest levels of the Truman administration for what the bomb could accomplish in summer 1945 stands in contrast to FDR's more relaxed and dilatory approach. Although Roosevelt never told the Soviets about the Manhattan Project and had agreed that atomic bombs might be dropped on Japan "after mature consideration," the fragmentary record of his thinking on atomic matters suggests that he had come to no firm conclusions before his death. In early March 1945 he informed Canadian prime minister Mackenzie King that "the time had come to tell [the Soviets] how far developments had gone."[64] Although FDR's subsequent inaction could mean anything from calculated caution to forgetful indecision, he may well have concealed the bomb as a bargaining tool (or "ace" up his sleeve) to be used later. Nonetheless, only after Roosevelt's death did the conception of the bomb as diplomatic and military panacea gain momentum within the government, perhaps, as one scholar has noted, because "people grasped for something concrete to fill the sudden void of charismatic leadership and persuasiveness created by his death."[65]

The visions of atomic omnipotence that beguiled Washington in summer 1945 had only faint replicas in Moscow. Despite the wartime progress of Soviet atomic research, the recent capture of German scientists and uranium supplies, and extensive espionage penetration of the Manhattan Project, Stalin and his associates did not speed up their own atomic program. Ignorant of the science and technology involved and suspicious of their own scientists, Soviet leaders paid no heed to spy reports that the United States would test the bomb in July and, if successful, use it against Japan. As the most authoritative study puts it, "neither Stalin, Beria, nor Molotov understood the role the atomic bomb would soon play in international relations . . . they had no conception of the impact it was about to have on world politics."[66]

Even at Potsdam when Truman obliquely told Stalin about the bomb, the Soviet leader's laconic response indicates that he still did not grasp its full significance. Only after Hiroshima and Nagasaki did Soviet calculations change. Because the bomb had "altered the balance of power and would enable the United States to shape the postwar settlement to its own advantage," Stalin authorized in mid-August a crash program to catch up.[67] He reportedly told Andrey Gromyko that the Americans would try to use the atomic monopoly to impose their own plans on Europe and the world, but "No," vowed Stalin, "that's not going to happen!"[68] A nuclear arms race ensued.

Offner is careful *not* to claim that Truman dropped the bombs on Japan for primarily diplomatic motives vis-à-vis the Soviet Union, nor does he argue that American actions by themselves precipitated the cold war. Rather, he suggests that anticipations of diplomatic success to be gained from atomic weapons precluded the kind of "mature consideration" that might have provided alternatives to their use. Inexperienced and parochial, far more politicians than statesmen, Truman and Byrnes grasped at the bomb as a tempting way to end the war and "win" the peace according to American principles. Unfortunately, the way World War II ended—in Europe and in Asia—made the cold war more likely.

The chapters in this volume confirm that the way World War II ended in Europe worsened relations between the Soviet Union and its wartime Allies. From fanatical last-ditch fighting for Berlin, to bewitching allurements of nuclear capabilities, to false bravado from a new president, to unforeseen exigencies of feeding starving populations, the unexpected circumstances attending war termination exacerbated suspicions and anxieties on both sides, eventually turning allies into enemies. Given the international power vacuums created by World War II, some sort of postwar competition was inevitable. Yet the bitter, frightening pattern of cold war confrontation might not have followed inevitably, if only because neither side willed it or planned it.

Just as momentum, missed opportunities, and military miscalculation attended the end of the European war in May 1945, so too did inept diplomacy and unintended consequences contribute to the origins of the cold war. Even as Truman and Byrnes altered FDR's postwar policies on the German occupation and reparations, the two men did not anticipate that their atomic diplomacy after Potsdam would turn Stalin into a hostile adversary. Nonetheless, suspicious that the United States "wanted to use the bomb as an instrument of political pressure," the Soviet reaction emphasized toughness over accommodation.[69]

Nor did Stalin have a master plan. With respect to Germany, recent scholarship indicates that the Soviet dictator could not decide whether he preferred a unified Germany under German Communists, a demilitarized, neutral state under Allied supervision, or a Soviet-controlled East German satellite. Soviet officers wound up "bolshevizing" their zone "not because there was a plan to do so, but because that was the only way they knew how to organize society."[70] Stalin temporized on policies toward particular countries and sought to pursue "cautious expansionism" in Russia's "natural" spheres of interest without forfeiting cooperation with the United States and Britain.[71] Hoping that London and Washington would acquiesce in Soviet predominance over Eastern Europe, the Soviet dictator nonetheless ensured a hostile response by his heavy-handed tactics. New Soviet documents and memoirs depict Stalin as a blundering statesman who botched his opportunities—"impulsive, a schemer who oftentimes lost track of his own intrigues, all hidden behind a mask of calculation, planning, and patience."[72]

Thus began the cold war between the United States and the Soviet Union. The ensuing conflict reflected the different needs, ideology, style, and power of the two antagonists and drew upon a history of contentious relations. Each came to see the other, in mirror image, as a dire threat. Each charged that the other was resuming Hitler's aggressive designs. Americans likened Nazism to Communism, Hitler to Stalin, and coined the phrase "Red Fascism." Each exaggerated the intentions of the other. Each had its own ideas on how to revive Europe's power and prosperity and to maintain European security. Because the previous international system had been pounded into rubble, the task of constructing a new one engendered predictable conflict. Nevertheless, the ensuing Soviet-American confrontation need not have become an "all-embracing struggle," as Truman put it, characterized by a costly arms race, nuclear threats, military alliances, trade restrictions, military interventions, and proxy wars outside Europe. The cold war lasted nearly fifty years, cost the lives of millions, and virtually bankrupted the principal antagonists. Perhaps if it had started differently, it might have truly constituted a "long peace."

NOTES

1. Harry S. Truman, *Memoirs*, 2 vols. (Garden City, New York: Doubleday, 1955–1956), 1: 205–8.

2. As quoted in K. R. M. Short, "American Newsreels and the Collapse of Nazi Germany," in *Hitler's Fall: The Newsreel Witness*, ed. K. R. M. Short and Stephan Dolezel (London: Croon Helm, 1988), 12.

3. Quoted in Evan Thomas and Walter Isaacson, *The Wise Men* (New York: Simon and Schuster, 1988), 271.

4. Dispatch of May 13, 1945, in *Washington Dispatches, 1941–1945*, ed. H. G. Nicholas (Chicago: University of Chicago Press, 1981), 558–60.

5. David Dilks, ed., *The Diaries of Sir Alexander Cadogan, 1938–1945* (London: Cassel, 1971), 740. British admiral James Somerville wrote the following ditty in Washington: "Although no Admiral of the Fleet / Should ever take his sippers neat / You'll look VE-Day in the eyeball / With neat Rye Whiskey in your highball." See Michael Simpson, ed., *The Somerville Papers* (London: Scolar Press, 1995), 644.

6. Harold Nicolson, *The War Years: 1939–1945* (New York: Atheneum, 1967), 457.

7. Martin Gilbert, *Winston S. Churchill*, 8 vols. (Boston: Houghton Mifflin, 1966–1978), 1347.

8. Mollie Panter-Downes, "Letter from London," *New Yorker,* May 19, 1945, 43.

9. King George quoted in Angus Calder, *The People's War: Britain 1939–1945* (New York: Pantheon, 1969), 567–68.

10. Iris Carpenter, *No Woman's World* (Boston: Houghton Mifflin, 1946), 331.

11. Omar N. Bradley and Clay Blair, *A General's Life* (New York: Simon and Schuster, 1983), 436.

12. George F. Kennan, *Memoirs: 1920–1950* (Boston: Little, Brown, 1967), 240–44.

13. Quoted in Gilbert, *Churchill,* 1350.

14. Churchill, *Triumph and Tragedy,* 569.

15. Frank Hanighen to Felix Morley, May 17, 1945, Felix Morley Papers, Herbert Hoover Presidential Library, West Branch, Iowa.

16. Quoted in Donald Cameron Watt, *How War Came: The Immediate Origins of the Second World War, 1938–1939* (New York: Pantheon, 1989), 7.

17. Alfred Kazin, *Starting Out in the Thirties* (New York: Little, Brown, 1965), 166.

18. Watt, *How War Came,* 5.

19. Sumner Welles quoted in Thomas G. Paterson, *On Every Front: The Making and Unmaking of the Cold War* (New York: W. W. Norton, 1992), 31–32.

20. Quoted in W. Averell Harriman and Elie Abel, *Special Envoy to Churchill and Stalin, 1941–1946* (New York: Random House, 1975), 217.

21. Peter F. Drucker, *The Concept of the Corporation* (New York: New American Library, 1964), xi.

22. Thomas J. McCormick, *America's Half-Century* (Baltimore: Johns Hopkins University Press, 1989), 33.

23. Quoted in Eric Goldman, *The Crucial Decade—and After* (New York: Vintage, 1971), 14.

24. Truman to Eleanor Roosevelt, December 22, 1948, Box 4560, Eleanor Roosevelt Papers, Franklin D. Roosevelt Library, Hyde Park, N.Y.

25. *Foreign Relations of the United States [FRUS], 1946* (Washington, D.C.: GPO, 1969), 6: 707.

26. With respect to Roosevelt's dealings with Stalin during the war, Mark A. Stoler has enumerated at least three basic interpretations by the 1990s: "Roosevelt the realist who actually had more maneuverability than he thought and who therefore could have done better than he did to check the Soviets; Roosevelt the skillful pragmatist who unfortunately worked under a series of mistaken conceptions regarding the Soviet Union; and Roosevelt the combined 'idealist-realist' who possessed a clear and defensible vision of a reformed international order and who chose to compromise that vision because of wartime exigencies and dilemmas" ("A Half Century of Conflict: Interpretations of U.S. World War II Diplomacy," *Diplomatic History* 17 [summer 1994]: 394).

27. J. Garry Clifford, "Juggling Balls of Dynamite," *Diplomatic History* 17 (fall 1993): 633.

28. Melvyn P. Leffler, "The Interpretive Wars over the Cold War," in *American Foreign Relations Reconsidered, 1890–1993,* ed. Gordon Martel (London and New York: Routledge, 1994), 120.

29. Klemens von Klemperer, *German Resistance to Hitler: The Search for Allies Abroad, 1938–1945* (New York: Clarendon Press, 1992), chap. 4.

30. Lord Halifax to Sir John Simon, March 21, 1941, Hickleton Papers, reel 2, Churchill College Archives, Cambridge University, Cambridge, England.

31. John Lukacs, *1945: Year Zero* (Garden City, N.J.: Doubleday, 1978), 20.

32. Until early 1946, Mikołajczyk mistakenly assumed that Stalin might accept his leadership in place of the unpopular Communist Lublin regime if he guaranteed Soviet security needs. See Antony Polonsky, "Stalin and the Poles, 1941–1947," *European History Quarterly* 17 (1987): 453–92.

33. Tuvia Ben-Moshe, "Winston Churchill and the 'Second Front': A Reappraisal," *Journal of Modern History* 62 (September 1990): 533.

34. Tuvia Ben-Moshe, *Churchill: Strategy and History* (Boulder, Colo.: Westview Press, 1992), 322.

35. David M. Glantz and Jonathan House, *When Titans Clashed: How the Red Army Stopped Hitler* (Lawrence: University Press of Kansas, 1995), 256.

36. Arieh J. Kochavi, "Britain, the United States and Irish Neutrality, 1944–1945," *European History Quarterly* 25 (1995): 93–115; quoted in John Gimbel, "Project Paperclip," *Diplomatic History* 14 (summer 1990): 351.

37. See Bradley F. Smith, *Sharing Secrets with Stalin: How the Allies Traded Intelligence, 1941–1945* (Lawrence: University Press of Kansas, 1996).

38. A. J. Muste quoted in James T. Patterson, *Mr. Republican: A Biography of Robert A. Taft* (Boston: Houghton Mifflin, 1972), 482.

39. Quoted in Arthur M. Schlesinger Jr., *The Imperial Presidency* (Boston: Houghton Mifflin, 1973), 129.

40. James T. Patterson, "Eating Humble Pie: A Note on Roosevelt, Congress, and Neutrality Revision in 1939," *Historian* 31 (May 1969): 407–13.

41. Kennan, *Memoirs*, 427–28.

42. Quoted in Theodore Wilson and Richard McKinzie, "The Marshall Plan in Historical Perspective," paper.

43. See Richard Norton Smith, *An Uncommon Man: The Triumph of Herbert Hoover* (New York: Simon and Schuster, 1984), 343–46; Gar Alperovitz, *The Decision to Use the Atomic Bomb and the Architecture of an American Myth* (New York: Alfred P. Knopf, 1995), 43–45, 228, 310, 635; William R. Castle Diary, May 29, 1945, Houghton Library, Harvard University, Cambridge, Mass.

44. "Memorandum re Certain Activities of John A. Danaher While Serving as Congressional Aide for the Republican National Committee in 1945 and 1946," August 26, 1970, John A. Danaher Papers, Sterling Library, Yale University, New Haven, Conn.

45. *Congressional Record*, July 2, 1945, 7129. In White's view, unconditional surrender meant "the acceptance by the vanquished of the will of the victor. It demands the total loss of Japan's fleets, the disarmament of its other military forces, the surrender of its conquered lands, the destruction of its war productive agencies, the complete control by the United Nations of its economic capacity for war, and the punishment of Japan's war criminals."

46. "The President has with him a memorandum prepared by the State Department, with some outside help, which sets forth in amplified form the substance of what I said in the Senate" (Wallace H. White to Herbert Hoover, July 17, 1945, PPI–White, Hoover Papers).

47. Hugh R. Wilson, chief of Foreign Affairs Section, Republican National Committee, "Republicans in Foreign Affairs," mimeograph of speech before the Evanston Women's Republican Club of Illinois, November 19, 1945, in George Smith Papers, Sterling Library, Yale University.

48. Joseph Stalin quoted in D. Clayton James, *The Years of MacArthur: Triumph and Disaster, 1945–1964* (Boston: Houghton Mifflin, 1985), 26–27; George F. Kennan quoted in Michael Schaller, *Douglas MacArthur: The Far Eastern General* (New York: Oxford University Press, 1989), 144.

49. "At a time when much of Europe was in ruins, Stalin had enormous possibilities for making the Soviet Union the dominant power on a continent in which the majority of the population was at least less anti-Communist than it has ever been before or since. It was Stalin's golden moment, and he botched it" (Odd Arne Westad, "The Book, the Bomb, and Stalin," *Diplomatic History* 20 [summer 1996]: 495).

50. Memorandums by Ivan Maisky, Maxim Litvinov, and Andrey Gromyko during 1944 and 1945 indicate that the Soviet Foreign Ministry sought a sphere of influence along its borders "largely in terms of geostrategic dominance and not of Sovietization, which, as all three understood, would hardly be acceptable to the Western Allies." See Vladimir O. Pechatnov, "The Big Three After World War II: New Documents on Soviet Thinking About Postwar Relations with the United States and Great Britain," no. 13 (June 1995), *Cold War International History Project Working Paper*, Woodrow Wilson Center, Washington, D.C., 17.

51. Melvyn P. Leffler, "Inside Enemy Archives: The Cold War Reopened," *Foreign Affairs* 75 (July/August 1996): 122.

52. John Lewis Gaddis calls it FDR's strategy of "containment by integration" (*Strategies of Containment* [New York: Vintage, 1982], 3–16).

53. Quoted in John Lamberton Harper, *American Visions of Europe: Franklin D. Roosevelt, George F. Kennan, and Dean G. Acheson* (Cambridge: Cambridge University Press, 1994), 95–96.

54. Quoted in Edward M. Bennett, *Franklin D. Roosevelt and the Search for Victory* (Wilmington, Del.: Scholarly Resources, 1990), 173–74.

55. Warren F. Kimball, *The Juggler: Franklin Roosevelt as Wartime Statesman* (Princeton: Princeton University Press, 1991), 66.

56. Quoted in Robert Gannon, *The Cardinal Spellman Story* (Garden City, N.Y.: Doubleday, 1962), 222–24.

57. Quoted in Kimball, *The Juggler*, 173.

58. Ibid., 100.

59. Lloyd C. Gardner, *Spheres of Influence* (Chicago: Ivan R. Dee, 1993), xiii.

60. Roosevelt's approach served to defeat the Axis and to achieve "far more than the twenty-five years of peace he once said he hoped to ensure." See Edward M. Ben-

nett, *Franklin D. Roosevelt and the Search for Victory: American-Soviet Relations, 1939–1945* (Wilmington, Del.: Scholarly Resources, 1990), 188.

61. Quoted in John Lewis Gaddis, "Harry S. Truman and the Origins of Containment," in *Makers of American Diplomacy,* ed. Frank Merli and Theodore Wilson (New York: Scribner's, 1974), 500.

62. Quoted in Arnold A. Offner, "Harry S. Truman as Parochial Nationalist," in *The Origins of the Cold War,* ed. Thomas G. Paterson and Robert J. McMahon (Lexington, Mass.: D. C. Heath, 1991), 56.

63. Henry L. Stimson Diary, July 23, 1945, Stimson Papers, Sterling Library, Yale University, New Haven, Conn.

64. Quoted in Barton Bernstein, "Roosevelt, Truman, and the Atomic Bomb: A Reinterpretation," *Political Science Quarterly* 90 (spring 1973): 31.

65. Harper, *American Visions of Europe,* 112.

66. David Hollaway, *Stalin and the Bomb* (New Haven: Yale University Press, 1994), 129.

67. Ibid., 133.

68. Andrey Gromyko, *Memories* (London: Hutchinson, 1989), 109.

69. Holloway, *Stalin and the Bomb,* 46.

70. Norman Naimark, *The Russians in Germany: A History of the Soviet Zone of Occupation* (Cambridge: Harvard University Press, 1995), 467.

71. Vladislav Zubok and Constantine Pleshakov, *Inside the Kremlin's Cold War: From Stalin to Khrushchev* (Cambridge: Harvard University Press, 1996), 74.

72. Westad, "The Book, the Bomb, and Stalin," 495.

Contributors

Anna M. Cienciala is Professor of History and Russian and East European Studies at the University of Kansas. She earned her Ph.D. at Indiana University. Among her voluminous scholarly publications are *Poland and the Western Powers, 1938–1939: A Study in the Interdependence of Eastern and Western Europe* (1968) and *From Versailles to Locarno: Keys to Polish Foreign Policy* (1984). Cienciala is at present completing a study of the Polish question during World War II.

J. Garry Clifford is Professor of Political Science and Director of Graduate Studies at the University of Connecticut. He received his doctorate from Indiana University, where he studied with Robert H. Ferrell. Clifford's *The Citizen Soldiers: The Plattsburg Training Camp Movement, 1913–1920* (1972) won the Frederick Jackson Turner Award. He is also the author of *The First Peacetime Draft* (1986) and has coauthored *American Ascendant: American Foreign Relations Since 1939* (1995) and *American Foreign Relations: A History* (1995), now in its fourth edition. His current research centers on FDR and U.S. entry into World War II.

Ronan Fanning is Professor and Chair of the Department of Modern History, University College Dublin. He received his Ph.D. from Cambridge University. The author of such works as *The Irish Department of Finance, 1922–1958* (1978) and *Independent Ireland* (1983), he recently coedited *Religion and Rebellion* (1997) and serves as a general editor of the *Dictionary of Irish Biography*. Fanning's current research focuses on postwar Irish foreign affairs.

David Hogan is a research historian at the U.S. Army Center of Military History. He earned his Ph.D. from Duke University. Hogan has written widely on World War II and special operations. He is the author of *Raiders or Elite Infantry? The Changing Role of the U.S. Army Rangers from Dieppe to Grenada* (1992) and a study, now in press, of the United States First Army in World War II.

Warren F. Kimball is Robert Treat Professor of History, Rutgers University. Editor of the authoritative three-volume collection, *Churchill and Roosevelt: The Complete Correspondence* (1984), and coeditor of *Allies at War: The Soviet, American, and British Experience, 1939–1945* (1994), Kimball has written, among other works, *The Juggler: Franklin Roosevelt as Wartime Statesman* (1991) and *Forged in War: Roosevelt, Churchill, and the Second World War* (1997).

Arnold A. Offner is Cornelia F. Hugel Professor of History at Lafayette College. A student of Robert H. Ferrell, Offner earned his Ph.D. at Indiana University. Among his many publications are *American Appeasement: United States Foreign Policy and Germany, 1933–1938* (1969) and *Origins of the Second World War: American Foreign Policy and World Politics, 1917–1941* (1986). He is the author of a forthcoming diplomatic biography of Harry S. Truman.

Vladimir V. Pozniakov is a Senior Research Fellow in the Institute of World History, Russian Academy of Sciences, specializing in the history of Russian-American relations. He has held Fulbright and other grants for research in the United States and contributed numerous essays to scholarly publications on the era of the Great Patriotic War. Pozniakov is presently completing a study of Russian espionage activities abroad before and during World War II.

Mark A. Stoler is Professor of History at the University of Vermont, where he has taught since 1970. He received his Ph.D. from the University of Wisconsin in 1971. He is the author of *The Politics of the Second Front: American Military Planning and Diplomacy in Coalition Warfare, 1941–1943* (1977) and *George C. Marshall: Soldier-Statesman of the American Century* (1989). Stoler has held visiting appointments at the U.S. Naval War College, the University of Haifa, and the U.S. Military Academy. He has in press a book-length study of the Joint Chiefs of Staff and the Allied coalition during World War II.

Hal E. Wert is Professor of History at the Kansas City Art Institute, where he teaches U.S. diplomatic and political history. He received the Ph.D. from the University of Kansas. His research on European relief efforts and food policy during and after World War II has been supported by the Woodrow Wilson Center, the Herbert Hoover Presidential Library, and IREX. Wert is the author of numerous scholarly articles and is currently completing a book-length study on Hoover, Roosevelt, and relief aid to Europe during World War II.

Theodore A. Wilson is Professor of History at the University of Kansas, specializing in twentieth-century military and diplomatic history. He received his Ph.D. from Indiana University and was a student of Robert H. Ferrell. Wilson has held visiting appointments at the U.S. Army Command and General Staff College, the Army's Center of Military History, and universities in Britain and Ireland. Relevant publications include *Makers of Ameri-*

can Diplomacy (1975), *The First Summit: Roosevelt and Churchill at Placentia Bay 1941* (rev. ed. 1991), and *Building Warriors: The Selection and Training of American Ground Combat Forces in World War II* (forthcoming). Wilson is currently undertaking a study of the American military in the Cold War.

Randall Woods is John A. Cooper Distinguished Professor of American History at the University of Arkansas. He earned a Ph.D. in American diplomatic and political history at the University of Texas. Some of his recent books are *A Changing of the Guard: Anglo-American Relations, 1941–1946* (1990), *Dawning of the Cold War: The United States' Quest for Order* (1994), and *Fulbright: A Biography* (1995). Woods is writing a biography of Lyndon Baines Johnson.

Index